CALIFORNIA'S NAPA VALLEY

ONE HUNDRED SIXTY YEARS OF WINE MAKING

Before the Hercules gasoline pump came into popular use in the 1890s, all wine was pumped by hand from tank to tank. Too many hours at this hand-pump produced a very sore back at night.

CALIFORNIA'S NAPA VALLEY

ONE HUNDRED SIXTY YEARS OF WINE MAKING

William F. Heintz

SCOTTWALL ASSOCIATES
SAN FRANCISCO
1999

Scottwall Associates, Publishers
95 Scott Street
San Francisco, CA 94117
Telephone (415) 861-1956

Book design: Lawrence R. Peterson
Cover design: Lawrence R. Peterson
Editors: Susan Little, James Heig
Printed in Canada

First Edition: 5 4 3 2 1

Library of Congress Catalog Card Number: 98-061475
Cataloging in Publication Data:
Heintz, William F.
California's Napa Valley: One Hundred Sixty Years of Wine
Making/ William F. Heintz
Includes index.

1.Napa Valley, CA, history, 1850-1999
2. Winemaking & winemakers
3.Prohibition
4.Phylloxera vine louse infestation
ISBN 0-942087-15-1

CONTENTS

To R.E. Berner,

who asked me forty years ago what type of career I planned to pursue. A writer, I responded, never dreaming of history as well.

INTRODUCTION

California's Napa Valley is barely thirty miles long, ranging in width from a few miles at Mt. St. Helena in the north to 28 miles in the south. Yet this small valley has dominated the American wine industry for a hundred years. News stories and television documentaries about California wine always seem to focus on Napa Valley. The PBS program "Secrets of the Wine Country," shown in 1995, is one example. Newspapers, from the *Baltimore Sun* to the *Orlando Sentinel*, praise the beauties and the wines of Napa Valley, often ignoring other wine regions in the state.

ABC television's tour of California wine country in 1993, after a stop in San Francisco, moved at once to the Napa Valley. Host Charles Gibson said:

> We have come to the quintessential wine-making country in the United States. Three-quarters of all the wine produced in America is produced in California — the majority in the Napa and Sonoma Valleys just north of San Francisco.

The glaring error of this last statement — actually, only a small fraction of California's wine is produced in Napa and Sonoma — suggests the power that Napa Valley holds over visitors and wine buffs.

There has been at least one attempt recently to correct the imbalance between Napa and Sonoma Valleys. "Wine Country Experience," a CD ROM produced by Magyar Media Corporation, offers four hours of information, tours and history of the two wine regions. The authors have tried hard to be fair to both counties.

Napa began its rise to wine stardom in 1889, when Frona Eunice Wait published *Wines and Vines of California*, the first book written exclusively for the wine consumer. Wait's book reflected Napa's growing status in the wine industry, and proclaimed the triumph of

Napa wines at the Paris World's Fair that same year, when American wines were allowed, for the first time, to enter competition. Of some 42 medals awarded to American wine, brandy and champagne, more than half went to Napa Valley vintners. The publicity which followed firmly established Napa as the premier wine region in the United States.

Chapter seven of this book opens with Prohibition, which was expected to doom the wine industry. Yet many wineries operated at near full capacity during the first four years of that tragic period. "Why are most of California's wineries running full blast in these supposed days of dryness?" asked the *San Francisco Examiner* in October, 1924. Soon after the article appeared, the crackdown began. Yet there were relatively few arrests of winemakers during Prohibition. Some wineries were forced to close, but many Napa vintners managed to hang on through fourteen dry years, using their ingenuity rather than breaking the law.

Perhaps the biggest surprise I found in doing research for this book was the vital role of Ernest and Julio Gallo in reviving the Napa wine industry after World War II. For almost twenty years, beginning in 1950, they bought up everything the wine cooperatives produced, and bottled it under their own name. They may have saved the Napa wine industry from collapse. Yet today no one associates the Gallo name with Napa wines.

I have spent twenty-five years doing private research projects for people who were restoring historic Napa wineries and placing them back in full operation. Vintners now know that history sells wine. Tourists all want to see the caves dug by the Chinese, or hear stories of how wine was hidden in bogus tanks or cars or trucks during Prohibition. Beautifully restored houses and wineries draw crowds of visitors every year, and provide a proper setting for sampling fine vintages. The wine tastes better, somehow, when the taster knows something of the history of the place and the men and women who built it — where they came from, why they came to Napa, what their achievements were.

I have tried to provide in this volume a comprehensive account of the Napa Valley's history, from the earliest winemaking down to the present. It is by no means complete nor exhaustive. My only regret is that my first manuscript had to be pruned, like the old grape vines in the spring, to a manageable size.

William F. Heintz

PART
ONE

Overleaf: A view of central Napa Valley, circa 1900.

VITICULTURE AND
THE GOLD RUSH

Viticulture – a Latin-derived word meaning "the cultivation of the grape," was a subject virtually unknown to the first Americans to settle in the Napa Valley. Grapes had nothing to do with their arrival in the valley years before the great California Gold Rush of 1849. These families, from Missouri, Illinois or Kentucky, had heard about the rich farmlands of the valley and its healthful climate. Perhaps a few of them had actually picked native American grapes back home, but only for food and not, God forbid, for the making of wine.

George Yount, the first white settler in the Napa Valley, planted a very small vineyard in 1838, near what later would become Yountville, but the grapes were for eating or to provide a source of sugar. Though he was a seasoned hunter and trapper and what might be described as a "mountain man," Yount was also a product of Missouri. He had moved there as a boy with his parents and listened like everyone else to Bible-thumping preachers rail against the evils of alcohol. Yount failed to produce even one drop of wine at his Napa Valley ranch until he learned of the demand for it after the discovery of gold in California.

Very few of Yount's neighbors in those early years were trappers or hunters. They were farmers, and had brought their families

5

overland in wagon trains. Most had heard that California's climate offered a far better alternative to mid-America's harsh winters and the summer "ague," a fever which attacked many middle-American settlers. California was far different, these settlers were told. "Nappa Valley" was widely discussed long before names like San Francisco or the Sierras, where gold was first discovered, became widely known.

One man who listened intently to these stories was Enoch Cyrus of Missouri. In the spring of 1846, Cyrus heard an eyewitness account of the lands which lay along the Pacific coast and a valley inhabited by a tranquil tribe of Indians known as the "Nappas." Within weeks he organized and led a wagon train of settlers bound for California. By late fall in that same year, they had reached their destination.

Incidentally, the man Enoch Cyrus met back in Missouri, and who described Napa Valley in detail, almost certainly was a member of the 1843 expedition to the Pacific Coast and California led by Colonel John C. Fremont. Fremont directed a survey party that brought him across Carson Pass to Sutter's Fort (Sacramento) where he and his men rested for a month before proceeding south and then eastward back to St. Louis, Missouri. During the Sutter's Fort respite, Fremont and a small group of his men made exploratory trips into the countryside, one of them reaching Napa Valley. Fremont himself seems to have left no record of this visit, nor is the word "Nappa" used in his official report.

Enoch Cyrus left no written account of his transcontinental journey, but his granddaughter, who heard his stories many times, in later years recorded some of the details. Rachel Wright claims her grandfather had been told that every immigrant could purchase all the land he wanted in California from the friendly Spanish-speaking Mexicans.[1]

Unfortunately, no one told these prospective settlers that conversion to Catholicism and Mexican citizenship were generally prerequisite to land ownership. Other portions of the glowing accounts of California also turned out to be untrue, but none of this dampened the enthusiasm of Cyrus and his friends once they had arrived. The landscape they saw was worth the journey across the American West.

By a rather remarkable coincidence, a traveler already in California, Edwin Bryant, met up with Cyrus and his party shortly before they reached Napa Valley. Bryant spent one night with them on the banks of Putah Creek, west of what later became the town of Sacramento.

Bryant kept a detailed diary, and three years after the Cyrus meeting he published his account in book form, as *What I Saw in California: Its Soil, Climate, Productions and Gold Mines.**

Bryant does not mention Enoch Cyrus by name in his book, but certain aspects of his description match the details provided later by Rachel Wright. Bryant's notes for October 31, 1846 include this paragraph:

> Proceeding ten miles over a level plain, we overtook a company of emigrants bound for Nappa Valley, and encamped with them for the night on Puta[h] creek, a tributary of the Sacramento. Five of the seven or eight men belonging to the company enrolled their names as volunteers, agreeing to fight the Mexicans if they offered further resistance to American occupation of California. Earlier that summer at Sonoma, a group of Americans had declared the region free from Mexico and raised a crude flag made of white cotton cloth with a drawing of a California brown bear. The militant, well-armed "Bear Flaggers" easily overpowered the gentle Mexican residents of Sonoma—who actually outnumbered them about four to one.

Four days after the Cyrus meeting, Bryant himself rode into Napa Valley and wrote this description during the first days of November:

---

* *What I Saw in California* was one of the first books published about the land shortly to become the 33rd member of the United States. Besides being delightful reading it offers the first description of Napa Valley published outside of California.

On the morning of the fourth, we found the trail described to us by Mr. Greenwood and crossing a ridge of mountains, descended into the valley of Nappa Creek, which empties into the Bay of San Francisco just below the Straits of Carquinez. This is a most beautiful and fertile valley, and is already occupied by several American settlers.

Among the first who established themselves here is Mr. Yount, who soon erected a flouring mill and saw-mill. These have been in operation several years.

Before reaching Mr. Yount's settlement, we passed a saw-mill recently erected, by Dr. Bale. There seems to be an abundance of pine and redwood (a species of fir) in the cañadas. No lumber can be superior for building purposes than that sawed from redwood. The trees are of immense size, straight, free from knots and twists, and the wood is soft and easily cut with plane and saw.

Arriving at the residence of Dr. Bale, in Nappa Valley, we were hospitably entertained by him with a late breakfast of coffee, boiled eggs, steaks and tortillas, served up in American style.

Leaving Nappa, after traveling down it some ten or twelve miles, we crossed another range of hills or mountains and reached Sonoma after dark.

The "American style" breakfast served by Dr. Bale is the earliest recorded menu of a meal served in Napa Valley.

Bryant paid attention to small details because he was well-educated and well-traveled. His book is filled with copious notes on vineyards he discovered as he roamed the state, plus observations on California wine and brandy. He made no reference to Yount's vines, or to being served wine.

Many other travelers provided information about Napa Valley in the 1840s. In Lafayette, Indiana, in 1846, Overton Johnson and William H. Winter published their recollections of a journey made three years earlier to Oregon, southward to California and back to St. Louis. Winter described California in *Route Across The Rocky Mountains*, which mentions the raising of grapes and making of wine:

Nearly all the products of temperate climates, except Indian corn, flourish here. Oats and clover grow spontaneously in almost every part of the Province. The vine flourishes as well, perhaps in California, as in any portion of the world; its fruit is the finest, and decidedly the most delicious, that we have ever tasted. There are many large vineyards in different parts of the country, from which several thousand barrels of wine are annually made.

Winter does not mention the location of any of these vineyards or whose wine he tasted. He may have been referring to Captain John Sutter at Sutter's Fort, who had a most ambitious winemaking establishment and plenty of vines, both domestic and wild.

Had Winter arrived a few years earlier, he could have witnessed winemaking at one of the 21 missions in California. The Mexican government had ordered the missions removed from church control beginning in 1834, and most were in a sad state of decay by the time Winter arrived.

A biography of Winter, published in 1873, does claim he visited the Napa Valley sometime in 1844, very likely in early fall:

> After returning to Sutter's Fort Mr. Winter came over to Napa Valley, and visited Mr. Yount's ranch, and then passed over to Sonoma. In the latter place he fell in with Messrs. Fowler and Hargrave, and spent the Winter with them in that valley. In the following Spring, 1845, he and other parties from various portions of the State made Sutter's Fort a rendezvous, to form a party to go back across the Plains.[2]

Winter may well have tasted the grapes raised that fall at Yount's ranch or those being raised in Sonoma at the former mission, then under the control of Mariano Vallejo, who generously provided grape cuttings to any who asked for them.

With the discovery of gold in January 1848 at Coloma, due east of Sacramento, Winter's attention was again drawn to California. Within months he returned to settle at Mokelumne Hill, staking a claim on a nearby creek. Winter must have been lucky in his panning or digging for gold, because he was able to purchase 664 acres on Huichica Creek in southern Napa Valley in 1855. He added another 600 acres one year later. He planted vines almost immediately, and within two decades had the largest vineyard in all of Napa county.[3] By 1860 he was making wine, some 20 gallons, according to the federal Agricultural Census. He built a small stone winery on the banks of Huichica Creek, about 1870.

The Overton and Winter book encouraged emigration to California, and it is no wonder Winter returned to make his home here:

> It is difficult to find a people, or even an individual who has not some good trait of character; and even these Californians, with all their faults, are hospitable at their houses.
>
> If a stranger goes into one of their houses, he is made welcome to whatever it affords, and as comfortable as their limited means will allow; he must however, furnish his own bed. It is always expected that a traveler in California will carry that article with him. [Winter meant bedding, not a bed per se. Fleas were a terrible problem in the state; a friendly host did not want his bedding infested.]
>
> When he departs, nothing is demanded, and nothing will be received by them, as compensation; the almost universal and beautiful reply is, when payment is offered: 'No! God will pay'.

By the mid 1840s Napa Valley was nearly overrun with new immigrants and visitors. Sonoma Valley pioneer Nicholas Carriger left a memoir with historian Hubert Howe Bancroft many years later describing a visit to Yount's flour mill and farm in the same year Edwin Bryant stopped there. Carriger did not mention grapes or wine.

Major Stephen Cooper's autobiography, published in 1883 in Missouri, contains a most flattering recollection about Yount:

> We struck the Sacramento Valley on the 5th of October, 1846. That winter I stopped at Yount's ranche in Napa Valley—a man who, in my opinion, did more for the early immigrants of California than all the Sutters did. . . On the

4th of July, 1847, George Yount and myself gave the first public 4th of July dinner ever given in California. We had a large turnout, and everything passed off pleasantly.[4]

Cooper's recollections are not quite accurate, since Jacob Leese hosted California's first Fourth of July celebration in 1836 in Yerba Buena, which later became San Francisco. The Cooper-Yount dinner is still noteworthy in that it was probably the first social event held in Napa Valley by Americans. Cooper fails to mention whether Yount served Napa Valley wine at the dinner; perhaps that detail was overlooked.

Anyone who lived in the Mississippi or Missouri Valleys would have looked with favor on Napa Valley's freedom from the sickness known as ague, a malarial fever characterized by regular and recurring paroxysms. John Bidwell, who later settled at Chico, California, told of meeting a California traveler named Roubideaux, in Platte county, Missouri, in the fall of 1840:

> Generally the first question which a Missourian asked about a country was whether there was any fever or ague. I remember his answer distinctly. He said there was but one man in California that had ever had a chill there, and it was a matter of such wonderment to the people of Monterey that they went eighteen miles into the country to see him shake. Nothing could have been more satisfactory on the score of health.[5]

Missourians took this health matter most seriously, and if Roubideaux had told the story somewhat tongue-in-cheek, Bidwell missed the humor entirely.

GEORGE YOUNT

Missourians would have felt quite at home in Napa Valley, for the first person they would have met was ex-Missourian George Yount. After living in the valley for a half dozen years with only Indian companions, he would have joyfully welcomed them all. Yount was born in North Carolina in 1794. When he was ten, his family moved to a farm in southern Missouri. After a rudimentary education he enlisted in the army during the War of

1812. He quickly became an expert marksman with the rifle, and later participated in several Indian battles.

Yount married 15-year-old Eliza Wells in 1818, when he was 24. They had two daughters, Frances and Elizabeth. But Yount was not cut out for family life; he was unwilling to change his life style of roaming the American West. In 1826 he sold all his goods, gave the money to his wife, and took employment with a pack train of mules going to Santa Fe. Eliza also bore him a son, Robert, after his departure from Missouri, but Yount did not learn of this until fifteen years later.

That Yount and his wife did not get along well seems a safe conclusion, since he never returned to Missouri after his trip to Santa Fe. In 1830 he headed west to California, where he became expert at hunting sea-otters. He reached San Francisco Bay in 1833 and spent the winter in Mariano Vallejo's adobe at Petaluma.

Padre Jose L. Quijas, in charge of the nearby Sonoma mission, welcomed Yount because his skill as a carpenter was badly needed. Yount also knew something about the art of blacksmithing and was handy with an axe; he split wood to make shingles. For the latter task he was supposedly paid $25 a day by the mission priest, though he seems not to have been paid in cash.[6] The poor padre certainly would have had no funds. In the years before the Gold Rush in California, the barter system worked very well.

The huge land grant of 11,814 acres given to Yount in 1836 was in partial payment for the work he did for the Sonoma mission and for Vallejo. Mexican authorities usually gave such grants to outsiders only if they married into Mexican families and converted to Catholicism. Yount was baptized by Padre Quijas and given the name Jorge Concepcion, but he never followed the Catholic faith. He could not marry a Mexican woman, having a wife already.

Yount's Caymus Rancho was in the heart of the neighboring valley to the east, inhabited by the Nappa Indians, far from his friends in Sonoma. Mariano Vallejo, who proposed the grant, wanted an experienced Indian fighter as a buffer against hostile

GEORGE YOUNT

tribes to the north. Interviewed late in life, Yount claimed that ✓
he had very friendly relationships with the local Indians.

Yount selected a home site near a hot spring, beside a small
stream and near a large knoll. He built a Kentucky-style block-
house first, and then later the traditional California adobe. He
took several Sonoma Indians with him to help him build his
block-house. The first floor was one large room, 18 feet square,
and the second was 22 feet square with port-holes through which ✓
a rifle could be fired at unwelcome visitors.

The Wappo Indians who lived in Napa Valley (of which the
Nappas were but one small band) were far different from the
Indians of the central plains or mountains of western United
States. These Indians did not have horses, which made them
rather less of a threat to white settlers. There are no reliable figures on the number of Indians living in the valley in the 1840s;
travelers like Edwin Bryant make no reference to them. Estimates
vary from as low as one thousand to as high as three thousand

Indians, clustered in small family units or tribelets, widely scattered. There was no need for a chief or head man; with abundant wild game in the valley, food was plentiful, and the tribelets lived peacably.

There were reports of some resistance to the white settlers by local Indians north of San Francisco Bay, but much of this may have been hot-headed talk. With Yount's assistance Vallejo "prevented" an Indian attack shortly after Christmas 1840 by settling a quarrel at Soscol, just south of today's Napa City. In a story published in San Francisco in 1859 in *Hesperian* magazine, Yount claimed local Nappa Indians once attacked his Kentucky blockhouse:

> At one time the Indians of Sonoma made a great feast and dance. The Indians of Mr. Yount's place took it into their heads to go to the feast; so a young Indian came forward and asked Mr. Yount if he might go; at the same time signifying that five or six more of the tribe would also like to attend.
>
> Mr. Yount readily gave his consent; but the young Indian became depressed in spirit, seemed moody and sad and finally declared he would not go to the dance . .
>
> The air was still and calm, and the night wore quietly away until just before day-break, when suddenly arose upon the air the fearful warhoop! Louder and louder it sounded, as if the very fiends incarnate had been set loose.

The flowery language of the *Hesperian* writer hints strongly at some excess in describing the fight, in which Yount and a Frenchman fired rifle volleys down upon Indians armed with bows and arrows. The outcome of this fierce confrontation was not difficult to imagine, but the author, a Mrs. F. H. Day, never explained on whose side the troubled young Indian fought, or if he survived. Within a decade or two, most of the Indians were dead, killed by such diseases as smallpox, syphilis or cholera, brought by white settlers.

When Yount planted his first small vineyard, his Indian workers, brought from Sonoma, probably did all of the actual digging and planting of grape vine cuttings. Vallejo no doubt offered advice, since he was the only one with any viticultural knowledge.

NAPA VALLEY'S FIRST VINEYARD

George Yount must have looked upon the pursuit of agriculture with some horror, or at least with downright apathy. He was not a farmer. He had roamed the American West, hunting and following his instincts at whim. His Caymus Rancho was overrun with California brown bear, deer, elk and other wild game including ducks and geese. For a man who liked to hunt, it was paradise.

All of which may explain why there are only two known references in print to statements by him concerning his vineyard. These two recollections survive because of visits by a Committee of the State Agricultural Society, charged in the early 1850s with encouraging agriculture in California. The committee awarded prizes for Best Farm, or Most Improved Farm, and the like. Newspapers covered these visits, and the society published its own accounts of what it discovered.

The first visit came in the fall of 1855. At Yount's home they observed his flour mill in operation, and noted that Yount had grown wheat "for eighteen years in succession," or since 1837.

Yount did not mention the age of his vineyards; there seemed to be a young one and another of some years in age. He rectified this oversight when the Committee visited him again the following year. In the *Official Report of the California State Agricultural Society For 1856*, the traveling farmers suggest 1838 as the year Yount first planted vines. Yount told them he had been a "twenty year resident of the valley," and they added:

> Mr. Yount's Farm comprises about 13,000 acres of land, 8,000 of which lies in the valley, all first class land; 800 acres of it enclosed, containing a good variety of fruit trees; an old Orchard and Vineyard, planted eighteen years ago, was attractive for the great growth and healthy appearance of the trees and vines.

About this same time, a local minister, Reverend Orange Clark, began jotting down Yount's recollections, especially as they referred to his hunting exploits in California. Yount was

15

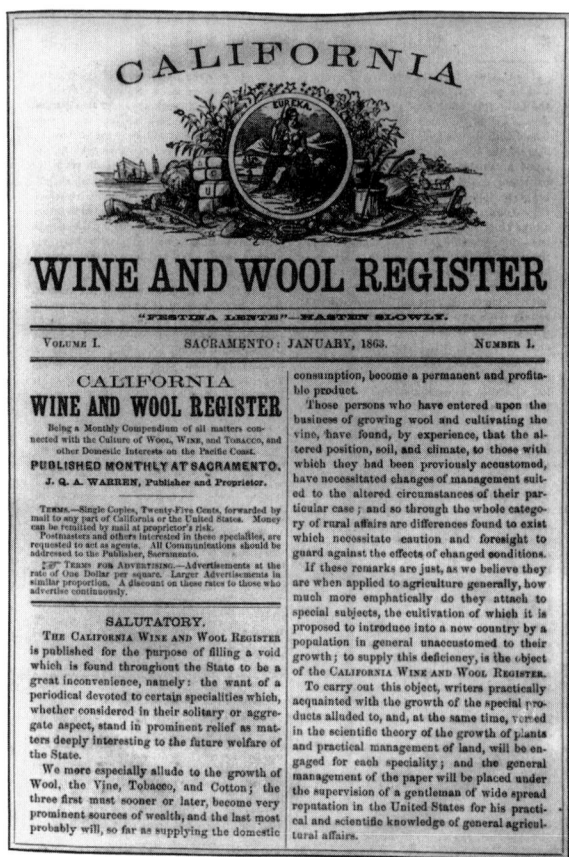

look @

California's first wine publication, the Wine and Wool Register, survived only two years, but is a rich source for the early history of grapes and wine in the state. Napa Valley's early history is documented in several stories, like this one in 1863.

rather blunt in what he said, and much later his second wife went through the manuscript and removed many pages that contained remarks unflattering to local people.[8]

Farming or ranching before the influx of white settlers was unhurried, and usually required little expenditure of energy. There was no business to conduct. Each rancho was large enough to be self-sufficient. If the rancho were near enough to the bay, hides and tallow might be traded for goods from merchant ships. When the California sun warmed the long summer days and the coastal breezes stilled, all activity ceased anyway. William Winter claimed that the "principal business of all classes, is attending to animals; there are some, however, who cultivate small patches of ground."

Early settlers in Napa Valley included Englishman Dr. Edward T. Bale, who married a Mexican woman, converted to Catholicism and gained thereby a large land grant a dozen miles north of Yount. Others who followed Yount to Napa Valley included Nicolas Higuera, Salvador Vallejo and Cayetano Juarez. Higuera was granted his Napa rancho the same year as Yount; his land included all of the present city of Napa. Salvador Vallejo, brother of General Mariano Vallejo, received his Napa Rancho deed in 1838; and the Tulocay Rancho went to Juarez in 1841.

Dr. Edward Bale was as colorful and eccentric as Yount. He, too, built himself a mill, which for years afterward served as a landmark for travelers in the valley. Called simply "Bale Mill," it is today the oldest structure in Napa County, and is California State Landmark #359.

Bale was granted the curiously named Rancho Carne Humana in 1841 and moved there three years later. His quick temper made it difficult for many—especially his relatives—to get along with him. One story was told that he challenged his wife's uncle, Salvador Vallejo, to a duel because Bale suspected some sort of romantic involvement between uncle and niece. This would have been only a minor scandal in those days. Eligible lovers were not easy to find. The younger and stronger Vallejo easily defeated Bale in a clash of swords, and he may have used his sword to flay Bale's backside. Disgraced, Bale then attempted to shoot his opponent, but failed. Since this was "all in the family," Bale escaped incarceration, but the fracas did his health no good. He died at age 41, in 1849.

If Bale ever cultivated grapes he probably did so only out of necessity. He had no interest in agriculture, except in what it might produce for his table, and he left all the labor to the local

Indians. But the planting of grapes might well have been the second order of business, ranking only below the construction of a house and barn. It was too far to travel frequently to Sonoma for whatever meager supplies might be had for barter. Since grapes grew easily and abundantly and provided a quick source of sugar, they were a high priority. Left on the vine until very late, grapes attain a high level of sweetness.

Bale deserves some small place in the annals of Napa Valley's history for entertaining the writer-traveler Edwin Bryant on November 4, 1846. Bryant thought enough of his meal to record the menu: "Coffee, boiled eggs, steak and tortillas, served up in American style."

Many Americans, from Missouri and other points eastward, and several Europeans, moved into the valley in the early 1840s. E. Barnett stayed briefly with Yount before bravely going to Pope Valley, where Yount must have told him he had fought an Indian skirmish or two. William Pope obtained ownership of the valley named in his honor in 1841 and had already settled there with his family.

Other early settlers included William Fowler and his sons Henry and William, who reached the valley in 1844. William Hargrave and Harrison Pierce arrived the same year. Colonel J.B. Chiles returned the following year, on his second visit to the valley, and purchased what later would be called Chiles Valley.

After that, the list grew rapidly: the Clyman family, Enoch Cyrus, the Coombs, York, the two Hudsons (David and William), Elliot, the Grigsbys (who would help raise the Bear Flag in nearby Sonoma in June, 1846), Baldridge, Kilburn, Hopper, Boggs, Tucker, Keseberg, Ritchie, Jesse, Nash and Harbin. All of these settlers arrived before the discovery of gold in California.

Neither gold or grapes had anything to do with attracting the earliest newcomers to Napa Valley. This surprising fact is acknowledged in a story in the *San Francisco Alta California* newspaper of August 30, 1866:

PIONEERS — No one part of the State can boast of so many pioneers among its inhabitants as Napa. In the Upper Valley, most all of the settlers are of long standing, and belong to the little army of hardy adventurers that penetrated these Western shores long before the discovery of gold. It is an interesting sight to see, here and there, over the valley, the log cabins that sheltered the pioneers of a State still young, but mighty in growth. [None of the log cabins have survived.]

Some of these newcomers apparently suffered memory lapses when viticulture did become popular decades later. John York, for example, who settled in 1845 in what later became Calistoga, claimed for himself the honor of planting the first vineyard in Napa county of "any commercial consequence." The St. Helena Star published his bold assertion on several occasions without anyone refuting his claim.[9] York's statement suggests that Yount did not have a large vineyard or produce wine until after the Gold Rush. But York's neighbors, such as William Nash or F. E. Kellogg, could have challenged him.

Kellogg and Nash were among the "seventy or eighty" Americans (according to the California Star, San Francisco's first newspaper) living in the valley by late 1847. Both men purchased land near Bale Mill and set out orchards and vines between 1845 and 1847. They sold their grapes in San Francisco.

The Star in January 1848 carried a story entitled "A Trip Across the Bay," with Sonoma and Napa Valley being the focus. The background for the story was clearly gathered the previous fall:

We arrived at Farmer Y[ount] in the evening, ate and pushed on to Dr. B[ale]. George Yount arrived in the valley in the summer of 1832 and shortly settled there.

The valley of which we speak presents over its surface, scarce a rise of ground deserving the name of hill . . . . The soil is of richest quality and yields, as we shall in a little time show, immensely and with comparative slight labor. Delicious water may be found within ten or twelve feet of the surface in any part of the valley . . . .of white residents, the valley contains seventy or eighty souls.

The next day, however, we were led through the cultivated lands of the aged pioneer, and first farmer of the valley — Mr. Yount. Within his vineyard, the young vines bending with the luscious fruit, perfectly ripe, in great purple clusters, over which the dew of the passed night seemed delighted to linger.

There is no reference to wine being made or even offered. Yount's vineyard, the first planted in all of Napa county, was almost certainly located on what is now Yount Mill Road, about two miles northeast of what later would become Yountville. A California State Landmark sign marks the location of Yount's first Kentucky-style blockhouse.

Yount had at least three different vineyards in his lifetime. A second now lies under the waters of Rector Dam. A third was located at the north end of what is now State Lane, in Yountville, Yount's last homesite. Yount never stated in precise terms where he planted his first vines. His comments to the State Agricultural Society suggest that the vineyard was near his mill, on Napa Creek. In a legal suit in 1861, Henry Fowler testified that he and his father spent the summer of 1845 with Yount, and provided details of the Yount farm as it existed at that time.[10]

Of the small communities which had sprung up near the great bay of San Francisco before the Gold Rush, Napa Valley was second only to San Francisco in population. Napa City wasn't much of a town, just an embarcadero for small ships; the residents were widely scattered. Still there were more white settlers per square mile in Napa Valley than in any other region except the village of Yerba Buena (San Francisco).

It is difficult now to comprehend what the Napa Valley must have been like just prior to the discovery of gold in California. Many of the Indians had already died or were pushed back into the hills, and they posed no serious threat to the newer settlers. Besides, there was plenty of space for both Indians and farmers to coexist peacefully.

The valley was overrun by wild animals, particularly bear. These were a greater threat in the early years than were hostile Indians. The chronicles of George Yount describe his bear hunts in detail; they had become legendary by the time the pioneer died. Elk, in herds numbering in the hundreds, grazed the wetlands of the lower portion of the valley. Deer were so numerous and tame that they could easily be killed, especially when the summer drought drove them to invade new crops of wheat or oats. Food, in the form of fresh wild game, was certainly no problem for the seventy or eighty settlers in Napa Valley by 1848.

The near-wilderness aspect of the valley changed dramatically within months after the discovery of gold. At first mainly local residents left San Francisco and headed for the gold fields. Then hundreds of sailors and thousands of passengers left the high-masted trading vessels which had brought them to the Pacific coast and swarmed up to the Sierra foothills.

Any Napa farmer with an extra horse for sale quickly had a dozen callers at the front door. Sometimes the horse was stolen from the back corral while negotiations were in progress. Napa Valley was a little off the main trail to the Sierras, but that did not matter— food, shelter, and supplies were available, as well as accurate directions from farmers who were familiar with the mountains.

By 1850, a full two years after gold was discovered, the valley's population had tripled. The official census gave the region 405 residents, 159 of them living in the thriving village of "Nappa City." The census also provided personal information about the citizens. At the age of 56, Yount was perhaps the oldest resident; he gave North Carolina as his previous residence. His real estate was valued at $150,000, easily making him the richest local farmer. Sharing his wealth that year were his grandsons, Jesse Yount and John Yount. There were six new residents from England, Wales and Ireland, and one from Switzerland. But the majority listed "Missouri" as their last previous address. Anyone with a Spanish surname simply called himself "Californian."

This federal census included a special section for "Agriculture" with fifty-two farmers being tallied. Pigs, horses, cows, barley, and "Irish" potatoes were counted; Yount's storehouses were overflowing. There was simply no category for "Grapevines" although "Wine, gallons of" was listed. Nothing was recorded under Yount's name.

Brun & Chaix used "Nouveau Medoc" — reflecting their French origins — as a brand name for their wine, produced at Oakville and Howell Mountain in the late 19th century.

George Yount's bounty quickly became exhausted as the months passed and hundreds of men stayed on permanently in the valley. The California legislature ordered a new census in 1852; Napa County's population mushroomed to 2,116 — five times the previous figure. Only 252 women were listed.

Local residents developed an early taste for celebrating the Fourth of July in grand style. With Yount's 1847 party as a precedent, a much larger event was held in Napa City in 1850. A traveling English journalist, Frank Marryat, described the affair, in which the explosion of a cannon nearly killed two men, in his book *Mountains and Molehills*:

On approaching Napa . . . we entered a very beautiful valley about three miles in breadth, studded with oak trees, and bounded on either side by mountains that rose abruptly from the plain, and whose summits were crested with heavy masses of the redwood tree and white pine.

As yet there was no sign of cultivation or enclosure, nor did we see a dwelling-house until the village of Napa appeared in sight; but the whole of this rich and fertile valley was shortly to be made productive, and it was to supply the wants of the many settlers, who were now on the eve of improving this wild tract, that the little bunch of houses called 'Napa City' had sprung into existence.

We had to cross a small stream in a ferry-boat to enter Napa, and we found the little place in a lively state. Music was playing, the stars and stripes were waving from each house, whilst the street was thronged with people.

The outside settlers had come in to celebrate their Fourth of July, it was now the fifth, and they were in the thick of it and there was to be a 'ball' in the evening.

At twelve o'clock they prepared to fire a salute from three old honey-combed cannons that had probably been fished up out of the river; whether or not, a serious accident immediately occurred — the first gun exploded like a shell, blowing off the arm of one man and destroying the sight of another, besides peppering the spectators more or less seriously.

This damped temporarily the pleasure of the afternoon, but the public dinner, which took place under an enormous booth, seemed to restore cheerfulness.

The settlers were nearly all 'Western people', small farmers from Missouri, and other Western states, who emigrated with a wife and a half-dozen children to California in search of good land; on this they squat until the land-claims are decided, and with their thrifty habits made money, not only more surely and comfortably, but faster than the miners, whose wants they supply.

With so many new residents arriving daily and weekly, a better system of local government had to be organized quickly. Someone had to hire a sheriff and deputies, and this required a county council. On February 8, 1850, the county of Napa was formally created — seven months before the United States

Congress approved a bill admitting California as a state. Napa County was one of the original 27 counties forming the new state. (There are now 58 counties.)

The more than two thousand people who called the valley their home created an enormous demand for food, much more than could be supplied by Yount and the few farmers who were established before the Gold Rush. The immediate need, almost an emergency, was for someone who could supply seeds, young fruit trees, and grapevines. As a consequence, one of the first nurseries in California was founded at Soscol (originally Suscol), fives miles south of Napa City, in 1852.

The man who stepped in to fill this need was Simpson Thompson, from Bucks County, Pennsylvania. Thompson was nearly fifty years old when he left Pennsylvania to come to California. His original plan was to set up a gas plant in the young city of San Francisco and light the streets. He even brought with him some of the fixtures and equipment needed for the project. But San Francisco was too wild and chaotic for such civilized ideas, and Thompson quickly abandoned them. Within weeks he located in Napa City and obtained from Mariano Vallejo the land he needed for a nursery.

Thompson first had to construct ditches and dikes to control the Napa River and drain the precise location he wanted for his orchard. His first young trees came from New York and New Jersey. By some accounts, he picked ripe peaches within sixteen months of planting his first seedling; given the richness of the soil and a mild winter, he may actually have done so.

Thompson had similar success with grapevines, for that Visiting Committee of the State Agricultural Society in the sum-mer of 1856 found a vineyard of 8,000 vines, "comprising thirty varieties of native and foreign grapes." [11] Simpson Thompson was soon joined by his two sons, James and Thomas. The nursery quickly established a precedent in California by not irrigating its trees, shrubs and vines. Irrigation was assumed to be an absolute necessity by eastern Americans who had moved here, for they could not fathom how any plant survived all summer without water. (There is usually little or no rainfall in California from May to October.)

The State's first agricultural newspaper, the *California Farmer*, praised the Thompson nursery in 1857: "Among the Nurseries that stand prominent for reliability and fairness in dealing, we are most happy to name Thompson's Suscol Nurseries . . . Trees in these Nurseries are raised without irrigation and in great perfection."

Sixteen years later, in a biography of Thompson in his *Historical and Descriptive Sketch Book*, C.A. Menefee wrote:

> This gentleman is well known all over the Pacific Coast as the proprietor of the celebrated Soscol Orchards, and is entitled to the honor of having introduced the system of fruit culture in California without irrigation.[12]

Simpson deserves a special honor for winning the first prize ever given in Napa Valley for a local wine — unfortunately not a grape wine. The State Agricultural Society in 1859 awarded a "Special First Premium" of $15 to Thompson for his white "currant wine, one year old." He picked up an additional "First Premium" for the "greatest number of good native varieties [of grapes], and best grown specimens, three bunches each." Yount exhibited four bottles of native wine at the same fair, but won no award. Whether this was the very first exhibit of Napa Valley grape wine at a fair is uncertain.

Another man who advanced viticulture in the valley in the 1850s was John Osborne. In 1856, his farm won the First Prize for Best Farm given by the State Agricultural Society. That award drew considerable attention to Napa Valley's agricultural resources. Osborne may have been the first person to use fine Napa sandstone for the construction of farm buildings. By 1856 he had a stone granary capable of holding eleven thousand bushels of wheat, and a stone building for his fresh milk, butter and cheese. Osborne's vineyard was then second only to Thompson's in size, with 6,000 vines, of which half were foreign varieties. There was no standard spacing of vines; if he planted

680 to the acre (rather common), he would have had about ten acres in all.

Among the "foreign" or not-so-foreign vines Osborne culti-vated was a grape he called the Zinfandel, which had been grown in New England hothouses for years before being introduced in California. Osborne, a native of Massachusetts, and other New Englanders, including Frederick W. Macondray of San Mateo, were ardent experimenters with grape varieties, exchanging information and cuttings. It could be that Colonel Agaston Haraszthy in Sonoma actually obtained his Zinfandel cuttings from Osborne, rather than — as the famous story has it — from Haraszthy's native Hungary. The Zinfandel was available in the San Francisco Bay area for some years before Agoston Haraszthy settled in Sonoma.

At least one person claimed to have firsthand knowledge of how Haraszthy acquired the Zinfandel from Osborne's farm. William M. Boggs, Haraszthy's closest neighbor in Sonoma for several years, wrote a letter in June 1885 to the *St. Helena Star*:

> About the year 1859 we organized the Sonoma Horticultural and Viticultural Gardens, of which Col. Haraszthy was President, and the writer one of the two Directors, as these gardens were owned by joint stock by members of the ass-ociation.
>
> Col. Haraszthy, in company with Judge Tott, and several of his friends who were assisting him, paid a visit to J.W. Osborne, the former owner of the Oak Knoll ranch, Napa County, and Mr. Osborne showed these gentlemen his grafted vines and the success of his experiment in grafting foreign cut-tings on the Mission vine. The crop of cutting was large and thrifty.
>
> Col. Haraszthy reported the fact to the Board of Directors and recommended the purchase of the entire lot of trimmings from these grafted vines, which Mr. Osborne's gardener had kept carefully labeled . . . Many thousand were planted from them the same season in the nurseries of the Horticultural gar-den under my supervision. Among them were the Zinfandel.

Arpad Haraszthy, the son of Agoston, apparently chose to ignore Boggs's letter. He championed unconditionally his father's

SIMPSON THOMPSON

contributions to California viticulture. The elder Haraszthy died in 1869. Whether Boggs had correctly identified the Zinfandel poses still another unsettling question. And in any case, the Zinfandel currently in use may be only a close cousin of the original.

Rapid advances in agriculture in the Napa Valley led to formation of the Napa County Agricultural Society — the first in California — on March 23, 1854, with John W. Hamilton elected president.

> On motion it was agreed that every member exert his influence to extend the circulation of the farmers own journal, published by Messrs. Warren & Son, San Francisco, and called the 'California Farmer'.

The corresponding secretary was then directed to transmit to the journal all news of the society. The complete text of the motion, plus a story on the formation of the new group, were carried in the *California Farmer* for April 13, 1854. Thereafter, the *Farmer* published every scrap of news about Napa Valley, and editor James Warren made frequent visits to see for himself what was transpiring. This very early public relations maneuver did as much to establish Napa Valley as the premier farming region in California as did the Best Farm First Prize won by John Osborne for the work at Thompson's fruit nursery.

An eyewitness to all of this was John Russell Bartlett, a member of the U.S.-Mexican Boundary Commission, whose travels in the early 1850s covered much more than the boundary region. He galloped up and down the length of California, viewing the landscape, including the mysterious geysers northwest of Mount St. Helena. On March 10, 1852, he rode into Napa Valley for the first time and wrote:

> Here we entered Napa Valley. The hills on both sides as well as the valley were covered with a luxurious growth of wild oats, and immense herds of cattle were roaming about feasting on them.
>
> Wild flowers of varied hues were thickly scattered around, and everything showed that the heavy and continued rains had given new life to vegetation. Our course was now a northerly one, directly up the valley . . .
>
> The valley soon became perfectly level, without a hill or depression. In many places ploughmen were at work turning up the soil, which was of the richest description. Barley appeared to be the principal grain sowed, this being in more general use for horses than oats, and found to give a better yield.

Bartlett spent several days as a guest of Osborne, noting in his diary: "Mr. Osborne's place was the most beautiful and picturesque I had seen in the valley. If fact, it was the only house where there was any attempt at taste and comfort."

His observation that "A road has just been laid out through the [valley's] centre" suggests that by 1852 there was some type of road or trail the entire length of the valley.

Barlett's diary, eventually published as *Personal Narrative of Explorations and Incidents in California* and various portions of other states, offers some of the best descriptions of Napa Valley Indian villages from this early period. He also stopped at Yount's farm, observing: "he has cultivated very little of it, but has used it like the other great land-holders of the country, for a cattle range."

THE FIRST NAPA VALLEY WINE

Since George Yount planted the valley's first vineyards, it seems only natural that he should have built the valley's first winery, but there is no evidence that he did so. Of the many visitors to take advantage of his generous hospitality, none mentions being served wine. There is an explanation, of sorts, for Napa being so "dry" in those early years: many of the residents came from Missouri, bringing with them their strong religious beliefs. They thought the use of alcohol was a sin, worse than breaking any of the Ten Commandments.

It does not quite follow that Yount would have adhered strictly to this code. He had forsaken his Missouri homeland, as well as his own wife and children, to travel west. Yet there is no record of Yount ever drinking to excess, even at the dinner table — unusual for a rough and tough Indian fighter and bear hunter. Most Mountain Men were famous for carousing.

The earliest record of Yount's winemaking is a brief story carried in San Francisco's *Alta California* newspaper of February 2, 1854:

> NAPA WINE — We are indebted to Mr. Geo. C. Yount for some wine from his ranch in the upper portion of Napa Valley. The wine is evidently new. It is clear, bright red, and bears a good deal of resemblance to the Bordeaux wines, but is better than most of the claret offered in the San Francisco market, and probably, with more age, and, perhaps, a little better management, would equal the best French wines.

That same day, Yount apparently walked down the street to the offices of the *California Farmer* to give the editor some of his wine. In its March 16 issue this brief item appeared:

> CALIFORNIA WINE — We have received, by the polite attention of George Yount, Esq. of Napa City, two bottles of wine made from his vineyard, from the Los Angeles grape.

> The wine has a good flavor, like the 'Bordeaux claret'; has a
> fine body and [is] free from the objectionable taste usually
> found in domestic wines. Mr. Yount manufactures about one
> thousand gallons.

These two references are the earliest documentation of winemaking in Napa Valley. A number of references to Vallejo's wine
at nearby Sonoma date back to the 1830s. Each rancho almost
certainly made wine for use by the Catholic priests when they
visited and said Mass. Higuera probably raised grapes and made
wine before Yount did, although he may have simply bartered for
wine with Vallejo.

But why did the Visiting Committee of the State Agricultural
Society not see wine in storage at Yount's farm in 1855 or 1856?
In the latter year especially, the society's annual report discusses
wine production statewide. Yount probably would not have made
the wine himself. Diverse as his talents were, he was unlikely to
oversee the fermentation of grapes. He may have hired someone
to do it. But he apparently sold the wine, and he sought out news
coverage of his achievement in San Francisco newspapers.

Yount had no building set aside for making wine; although
the Agricultural Society commmittee saw no winery, they must
have been permitted to look inside all of his buildings. The
report of the Society for 1855 documents a half dozen winemaking operations elsewhere in the state.

When the editor of the *Farmer* visited Yount in September
1856 he reported to his readers (in the issue of October 3) that
he had been "refreshed with new wine from the new-pressed
grapes." He evidently did not see a room filled with wine, or even
witness a modest crusher in operation. It was probably made outdoors by Indian labor, with the wine stored in leather bags strung
between the trees. Charles Krug witnessed this method of wine
storage when he first arrived in the valley a few years later.

NAPA VALLEY'S FIRST WINERY

If George Yount has the distinction of being the valley's earliest winemaker, another man vies with him for the title of "First

Vintner" — an immigrant from England named John Patchett. Patchett did not begin wine production until three or four years after Yount, but he shipped wine regularly from 1857 on, and won far more publicity for the valley's wine than Yount did. Moreover, Patchett built the valley's first bona fide winery, a native stone structure measuring 50 by 33 feet, in 1859, two years before Charles Krug fashioned a small winery at St. Helena out of an excavation dug into a hillside.

Patchett is easily the most obscure figure in the long and fascinating history of Napa Valley wine. His name is not often found in accounts of Napa's viticultural past, probably because he died with no children to remind later generations of their father's contribution. Born in Lincolnshire, England, in 1797, he emigrated in 1817 to the United States, settling in Pennsylvania. Two decades later he began moving west, never remaining in one place for long. A brew-master by trade, he had difficulty finding work, and finally took up farming.

By the time of the Gold Rush, Patchett was an old man (for that time and place) of some 50-plus years. He left his Iowa farm and headed west. In the fall of 1850 he was panning for gold near Placerville. Eventually he saved enough gold to invest in his own farm. After a journey to Napa Valley to see what all the agricultural excitement was about, he purchased his first vineyard. In May 1852 he bought from James W. Brackett a hundred-acre parcel near the junction of the Napa River and Napa creek, now the very heart of Napa city, for $3,000. Patchett added eighty more acres to the south two years later.

"The first one to plant a vineyard of any consequence — one for any other purpose than for grapes for table use — was J.M. Patchett" claimed C.A. Menefee in his *Historical and Descriptive Sketch Book*. Menefee noted that as early as 1850 a small vineyard had been planted on the site, and that Patchett immediately added vines and a small orchard.

Patchett's role as vintner was mentioned by others as well. William A. Trubody, who arrived in the valley in 1847, later wrote in his memoir: "Yount had a small vineyard — an acre or two. The first to have large vineyards was Paget [sic], Krug and

Dr. Crane." [13] Frank Leach, who came to Napa City as a youth in the 1850s, wrote many years later: "The first vineyard for wine-making purposes was planted in the latter part of the '50s by John Patchett on a piece of land about a mile northwesterly from the court house in the town of Napa. Here the first wine on any scale was made." [14]

The Patchett vineyards and orchard may have been located, in part, on the site now occupied by Fuller Park, directly west of the courthouse. Old-timers like Mrs. Frank Noyes, who was born in Napa in 1900, recall playing in the "Patchett Grove," now Fuller Park. Patchett's winery, the 50 by 33-foot stone structure, may have been in the same park or a few blocks further west, just across Jefferson street in the Patchett Addition to the city of Napa.

Another source for Patchett's historic winemaking is none other than Charles Krug himself, the man considered the father of Napa viticulture. He mentioned Patchett in a long account of the history of winemaking in Napa Valley, published in the *Star*, December 19, 1890:

> In October, 1858, I made the first lot of wine ever made in Napa county, at the place of John Patchett, Napa city. As a cellar used an old pioneer adobe house built on the banks of Napa creek and close to the lot where at present stands Napa College [Calistoga Avenue at Seminary Street].

Krug quickly clarified his recollection by stating that his was the first lot of wine made other than by the old Spanish process of foot-stomping the grapes in a leather bag.

Menefee's *Sketch Book* adds some further details:

> In 1859, having become convinced that the business of raising grapes and winemaking could be made remunerative, [Patchett] erected a stone cellar 33 x 50 feet. He had made 600 gallons the year previous, selling it at $2 per gallon. The stone for his cellar was quarried out of the hills back of the residence of Cayetano Juarez. The cellar is still standing and is as good as ever [1873].

Menefee credits Patchett with shipping wine out of Napa Valley as early as 1857 — six casks and 600 bottles of wine, probably all sent to San Francisco.[15] Where Patchett would have found six hundred bottles is a mystery. They may have been gallon jugs, but nearly all wine then was retailed out of casks. Menefee may be mistaken.

Patchett decided not to keep his wine success a secret. This story ran in the March 18, 1859, issue of *California Farmer*:

> We have always believed that California would make her mark as a wine growing country; for years we have urged attention to this all-important subject, and most heartily rejoice to see our citizens turning their attention to it.
>
> We were pleased to receive a call from one of our subscribers at Napa, John Patchett, Esq., and to learn that he had been very successful the past year in growing the vine and making wine. He kindly informs us that he has now about twenty-six acres of vines, and they are doing well. They are principally the Mission grape, although he has some ten varieties of foreign grapes, all doing well.
>
> The wine brought to us by Mr. Patchett was a fine White Wine, of very superior character in flavor, much resembling the Hock wine. Most earnestly do we commend the enterprise to every man having land.

One year later the editor traveled to Patchett's vineyard and winery to see the improvements. He now had about 55 acres in grapes, the largest vineyard in the county. One wine vat could hold 1,600 gallons, and his white wine was described as "light, clear and brilliant, and very superior, indeed; his red wine excellent; we saw superior brandy, also." [16]

Unfortunately, Patchett's age caught up with him. Nearing his 70th birthday he was reportedly suffering from "cancers." The federal census of 1860 credited him with making 4,000 gallons; there is no record of wine production after 1865. In 1873 Patchett created the "Patchett Addition" to the city of Napa and began selling off most of the land he owned surrounding his home.

In January 1878, a freak thunderstorm over Napa sent a bolt of lightning into the Patchett winery. The roof caved in; the walls cracked open in several places.[17] Patchett did not have to endure the pain of seeing his winery rent asunder by Mother

Nature, for he had died on August 13, 1876. The obituary notice in the *Napa Reporter* noted he had "been a sufferer from cancers for a long time" and that death came in the "family residence," with no address.

His wife's death in 1904 helped to clarify the location and possible site of the valley's first bona fide wine cellar. The *Reporter* of August 30th stated Martha Patchett died "at the family home on West Second street, near Jefferson . . . . She came to California and Napa in 1861, forty-three years ago, and has been a resident of this city ever since. Mr. Patchett came to California about 1850 and purchased in 1852 the place in Napa where both he and his wife lived and passed away."

Patchett certainly deserves great honor for his pioneering work; he was there first, and he built the valley's first wine cellar. But the contributions of Charles Krug, who survived Patchett by nearly two decades, make Patchett's historic efforts pale by comparison. Some sort of private feud seems to have existed between the two men. Neither gave credit to the other for participating in their sometimes joint efforts. For example, Krug's memoir in the *Star* of December 1890 states: "In October 1858, I made the first lot of wine ever made in Napa county, at the place of John Patchett, Napa city."

What about Patchett's 1857 wine? Krug meant, of course, wine made other than by Indian labor stomping the grapes. He also failed to mention Patchett's significant production thereafter.

For his part, Patchett never credited Krug with helping him in 1858. He had ample opportunity to do so in his long biography and background to winemaking published in Menefee's 1873 *Sketch Book*.

VITICULTURE AS A CALIFORNIA OCCUPATION

When John Patchett began purchasing land for planting grapes, viticulture was a prospect held out to potential California farmers as a new and tantalizing pursuit. Only a handful of the thousands of young men attracted by the Gold Rush had ever

CHARLES KRUG

worked in a vineyard, and most of those who had were Europeans. The cultivation of the grape, and even more so the making of wine, were a mysterious occupation — but a very timely one for California.

By the mid-1850s, newspapers in Northern California began a campaign to stimulate the growth of agriculture. The motive is not difficult to discern. The 1856 Vigilante movement in San Francisco offered a fearful demonstration of what can happen when strong young men are idle for long periods of time. Crime and violence became commonplace; the death of a person under mysterious circumstances barely rated mention in the newspapers.

The *Monterey Sentinel* in April 1856 offered this suggestion for those seeking a new direction in life:

> From the first settlement of the country to our time, nothing has given continental Europeans, who have visited California, more admiration and surprise than the extra- ordinary facility with which different species of the grape have succeeded in our mellow and fertile soil.

The editor claimed everyone from traveling Frenchmen to Germans and Italians expressed the observation that California soil and climate equaled that of their homeland and that wine and brandy of the finest quality could be produced here. The newspaper also pointed out that the valleys of the Sierras had already demonstrated the adaptability to grapes, which had been grown there since 1848.

The editor of *California Farmer*, James Warren, began beating the drum vigorously for viticulture before most other publications. In July 1857 Warren devoted two and half columns to "The Commerce of the Vine, Olive and Mediterranean Fruits." He described how easy it was to grow such products in a climate comparable to that of Italy and Greece, an idea which may not have occurred to most transplanted eastern Americans.

There were more grapes grown in Santa Clara county in the early 1850s than in any other location except Los Angeles. Although most growers were French immigrants, L.A. Gould was singled out for special attention in an early wine story on the county:

> We are constantly reminded of the excellent quality of wines in California. We tasted some of the wines made by L.A. Gould of Santa Clara, some two weeks since, that would vie with the best hock wines of Germany. Mr. G. has been very successful in making wine, although in small quantities. He has a vineyard of the Isabella and Catawba that promise wonderful things.[18]

German-born Charles Krug and Hungarian Agoston Haraszthy were among the first to seriously heed the advice of the editors. Both men had lived for some years in the eastern United States, but Haraszthy had caught California fever first. Preferring to be called "Count Haraszthy," he was an entrepreneur quite suited to the times in San Francisco.

Haraszthy would invest in almost any venture. He had planted vines first in San Diego, then moved them to San Francisco. Alarmed by the cool, foggy climate, he uprooted the well-traveled grapes and hauled them south to San Mateo County. Among his many jobs was working as supervisor of the U.S. Mint in San Francisco.

San Francisco's leading daily newspaper then was the *Alta California*, followed by the *Bulletin*. The *Alta* had carried brief items on vine planting at Sonoma, but the first major story describing a wine boom in the Sonoma Valley was published December 6, 1858:

> Sonoma Valley is going into the vines business extensively. The vine was introduced there by the Missionary priests about thirty years ago, and it has thriven admirably.
>
> "*The wine of Sonoma is different from that of the southern portion of the State, being lighter and more like the French wines.* The red wine of Col. Haraszthy has taken some of the highest premiums at our late fairs. The fitness of the soil and climate of Sonoma for the production of excellent grapes and wine has incited the people there to plant vines extensively, and they are now in the beginning of the wine fever." *

This story listed thirteen growers who were planting new vineyards, among them being Charles Krug, who had 15,000 vines. Nearly 200,000 vines had been planted that year alone, more than had previously existed in the entire valley.

Haraszthy and Krug deserve some of the credit for this "wine fever." Many new German vine growers were undoubtedly friends of Krug. The fever had taken hold earlier, however, for the Sonoma County assessor reported a 656% increase in vine planting in 1856 and 1857. Haraszthy settled in Sonoma Valley in 1857. This fever had spread to nearby Napa Valley as well, but on a smaller scale. Patchett was influenced by it, though he had already begun expanding his vineyard some years earlier. John Osborne, too, north of Napa City, had planted vines. At Soscol,

---

* Italics have been added here for emphasis. This observation seems to be the earliest recognition that wine quality differed between Los Angeles and San Francisco.

the Thompsons had thirty varieties of grape vines for sale by 1856. Even Yount seems to have begun expanding his vineyards about this same time.

The first St. Helena resident, or resident-to-be, to catch the wine fever was Dr. George Crane, who left this memoir:

> My first visit to Napa was in May, 1858, thirty-two years ago, when I was surprised by the muddy roads contrasting so broadly with Santa Clara valley, where the plows had been mainly idle for years for want of rain. My attention was then drawn to the fact that while the prevailing Summer winds in San Jose, where I lived, were from the North, they were on the same days and hours there blowing toward the North.
>
> This apparent anomaly I found was explained by the Sierra Nevada mountains. They arrest the atmospheric current which comes landward through the Coast range at the Golden Gate, when in obedience to hydrostatic law it divides and like water, takes the course of least resistance. This brings a portion of that air, fresh from the ocean, ladened with its evaporation, up through this valley.[19]

The winter following Crane's first visit, he purchased 335 acres of land at St. Helena and shortly began planting his first vines. Within a few years he turned to winemaking, sharing with Krug the honor of being the first St. Helena vintner.

An amusing aspect of this vine-planting saga is Charles Krug's sudden decision to leave Sonoma and settle in the Napa Valley. His friends, including Haraszthy, must have shaken their heads in bewilderment. In 1858 Krug borrowed an apple press and hauled it to Napa City to crush the grapes of John Patchett and make wine. The next year he made wine for the Bale family at St. Helena. In 1860, when he was helping Yount with his crush, he inserted the following advertisement in the *California Farmer*:

> NOTICE — Vineyard For Sale. The Undersigned offers for sale his Beautifully located VINEYARD 'MONTEBELLO', consisting of 16,000 to 17,000 VINES (some of them foreign). One-fourth of the Vines will bear next year. A Young ORCHARD of 125 choice FRUIT TREES, together with Two small Dwelling Houses and a Stable. The place, 35? acres, with several living springs

upon it. The soil is eminently adapted for Vines, and adjoins the well-known Vineyards of Col. Haraszthy, Gen. Williams and Mr. Dresel.

Having in mind to commence a more extensive plantation, this place will be sold cheap, the owner not being able to carry on both. Terms easy. Apply by letter, or personally, to CHS. KRUG, Sonoma.

Krug's little farm was right in the heart of what soon became the vine capital of California, Sonoma. Why give all this up and move to Napa Valley? Apparently he had fallen in love with Caroline Bale, daughter of the late Dr. Edward Bale. They had met when he made wine for the family. As one of the heirs to the Carne Humana Rancho land grant, Caroline was due to inherit a good portion of that land when she married. Krug may have been as interested in his wife's dowry as in the ability of Napa Valley's soil to produce fine grapes. In any case, Caroline and Charles were married December 26, 1860.

Krug, loquacious as he was, never left a hint in subsequent letters or writings on local history as to his reason for moving to St. Helena. Thirty-two years later, in 1890, he described for the *Star* the status of grape growing and winemaking in the valley as he first witnessed it in the late 1850s:

> When I first visited Napa county I found less than a dozen small vineyards of the so-called Mission vines, about six or ten years old, all planted for the purpose of enjoying the sweet juicy fruit and partly to sell the grapes at splendid, paying prices. The old pioneer, Capt. George Yount, near the present Yountville, had several acres. On Dr. Bale's rancho was about one acre of vines in a flourishing condition.
>
> David Hudson and John York, near St. Helena, were proud owners of about an acre of vineyard each. C.C. Griffith, now of Vineland, had furnished both gentlemen the cuttings for planting from the above mentioned Buena Vista vineyard, 1849.
>
> There were a few acres of vineyard near Dr. Bale's flour mill, at present the property of W.W. Lyman, about an acre at George Tucker's place, the vines having been planted by Colonel Ritchie, a few vines planted by Mr. Owsley on

Lincoln's farm, and about one acre of vines near Calistoga
at the place then belonging to Henry Fowler. Most of these
vines, as a matter of course, all Mission, are not any more in
existence.

Although Krug had penned some of these recollections in
1878, by 1890 his health was not good; he seems to have forgotten the three largest vineyards in the county: John Patchett's,
John Osborne's, and the Thompson nursery near Soscol. The
two references to Bale vineyards are to the home, south of St.
Helena, and of course, to the vines at Bale Mill.

Horace Greeley came to California in 1859 to see for himself
why he might want to urge young men to "go west." Famous as
editor of the *New York Tribune*, his comments on the potential
for growing grapes in California only served to fire the boom
already in progress:

> Of grapes, it is hardly yet time to speak so sanguinely as many
> do; for years will be required to render certain their exemption
> to diseases and the devastators known to other lands of the
> vine. But it is certain that some kinds of Grapes have been
> grown around the old Jesuit Missions for generations, with lit-
> tle care and much success.
>
> That [California] is destined soon to become largely and
> profitably engaged in the manufacture and exportation of
> wine, is a current belief here, which I am at once unable and
> disinclined to controvert. [20]

Cautious tone and old-fashioned rhetoric aside, Greeley's
words had a powerful effect. Just the acknowledgment by so
famous a journalist and traveler as Greeley meant that for the
first time thousands of eastern readers of the *Tribune* learned of
California's viticulture potential. Since Greeley's comments
were carried in the *Farmer*, they were widely read in Napa Valley,
as well.

Viticulture obviously was not an all-consuming passion for
Napa Valley farmers. Cereal grains and cattle were the mainstays
of every farm, with the horse racing possibly requiring more
hours of both idle and serious time than any other endeavor. A

DR. GEORGE B. CRANE

Jockey Club was formed at Napa City in 1858; its members did nothing but argue the merits of horseflesh and exchange gold dust in private bets. A favorite Sunday occupation on many farms was the coming together of neighbors, who raced their best horses down a dusty stretch of valley roadway.

It was also common to lay a very generous table of food after the races, with beverages to slacken the thirst. Some farmers, or most especially their wives, frowned on the drinking of spirits on the Lord's Day — or any day, for that matter. With each new acre of grapes planted, some portion of the crop could not find a ready market, or the farmer could not afford to ship them to San Francisco. These excess grapes were made into wine. By the end of the 1850s, Napa Valley wines must have been available at most of the Sunday horse races. Very little of this local wine could have been of very high quality; early winemaking was strictly amateur. Still, grapes, if left a long time on the vine in the fall, developed a high sugar content and fermented easily.

Since wild game such as bear, deer, elk or wild duck were sta-
ples of the big Sunday dinners, a good hearty red wine would
have been the perfect complement to the strong flavors inherent
in such meats. Fish were abundant in the Napa River in that
period, the water table remaining high year-round. Salmon could
be caught by the dozens, far upstream. Served fried or baked, fish
must have complemented the early homemade Napa Valley
Rieslings.

THE BIRTH OF THE
WINE INDUSTRY

In April, 1860, San Francisco's *Hesperian* magazine published a long piece called "Notes on Napa Valley." No general circulation magazine in California had done anything similar on the small farming region, and why should they? There was nothing in Napa Valley to compare with neighboring Sonoma's topography. Sonoma had beautiful mountains and a valley of ominous geysers and fumaroles, called the "Geysers," which was already a popular tourist attraction. Napa County couldn't boast of gold strikes such as those which made the Sierra foothill counties famous.

But freelance journalist John Hittell decided to do a travel piece on Napa, and *Hesperian's* editor, Mrs. F. H. Day, already had an interest in the area. She had written a vivid biography of George Yount which the magazine had published barely a year earlier.

Judging from the opening lines of Hittell's story, he believed most of his readers had never heard of the region:

> North of San Pablo Bay and opening upon it, are three valleys side by side and parallel with each other and with the coast, their general direction being N.N.W. and S.S.E. Each is drained by a creek bearing its own name, and bounded by a steep range of Mountains on both sides; and each is rich in wealth different from that of the others. Petaluma has the

dairies, Sonoma has the wine and Napa has wheat. . . The latter, of which I propose now more particularly to speak, makes a better appearance than either of the other two.

Hittell's observation that ". . . Napa has wheat," reflected the generally accepted view of what constituted agriculture in these three valleys north of San Francisco. Agoston Haraszthy's speeches and published writings had produced some measure of recognition regarding wine in the Sonoma Valley, but he had no counterpart in Napa.

The journalist pointed out that Napa Valley, "in proportion to its size, [is] the richest and most productive grain district in the State." Indeed, Salvador Vallejo alone had one field which measured 2200 acres in size. His grain fields were being tilled by an Italian named "Basciano" — possibly the first Italian immigrant to settle in Napa Valley.

"Notes on Napa Valley" expanded the history on George Yount and documented the fact that the valley was a pre-Gold Rush destination of many settlers:

> About 1842 the Fowlers, father and son, and Mr. Kilburn settled in Napa, and in 1844 Mr. Bartlett Vines [son-in-law of Yount]. In the fall of 1846 a number of Americans arrived in California from Missouri by way of the plains.

It was a wonderful article, but vineyardists like Patchett, Krug and John Osborne must have despaired of Hittell's failure to pay more attention to grapes and winemaking. Hittell did observe that "more vineyards have been planted since my visit to the valley."

It may be that the time of year of Hittell's visit kept him from seeing the growing number of vineyards in the area. Vines are dormant in January and would have been barely visible among the early winter greenery.

The San Francisco writer probably made the trip to Napa City in just over four and a half hours on the small steamer "Paul Pry," that is, if the tide was not out, necessitating a stop at Soscol to change to horse and wagon. An account of such a trip made in August 1860 speaks eloquently of the sights along the way:

The steamer stops at Vallejo and Soscol, giving a view of Mare
Island, the Navy-Yard, Vallejo and all the inland views on the
creek up to Napa, which are really beautiful, showing the wide
expanse to the hillsides, with grain-fields and orchards, and
proving the great fertility and productiveness of this section.
The very circuitous winding of the creek affords interest to the
passenger, and takes away much of the monotony of such trips.[1]

Eight days after the first transcontinental telegraph was completed, connecting California to the East Coast, a party of U.S.
government surveyors arrived in Napa Valley, camping at Soscol.

The man in charge of the survey party was William H. Brewer,
32, a Yale graduate in agriculture. Brewer kept a diary of his nearly two weeks in the valley which was published many years later
as *Up and Down California In 1860-1864*.[2]

Brewer records drinking Napa Valley apple cider, and one
wonders whether he tasted the local wine as well:

I lounged down to the Tavern to read the news. While there,
a rough but intelligent-looking man entered into conversation
and invited me to his house a few rods distant for a 'glass of
good cider'. I went, got the cider, the best I have tasted in this
state, and went into his house.

I found him an intelligent man, quite a botanist, and even
found that he had some rare and expensive illustrated botani-
cal works, such as Silva Americana . . . He does not own the
ranch, is merely a hired man, having charge! There is an
orchard of ten or twelve thousand trees and a vineyard —
he makes wine and cider and sells fruit.

Brewer described watching the tule burn along the marshes of
the Napa River, which went on for several nights of fascinating
viewing:

The swamps bordering all the rivers, bay, or lakes, are covered
with a tall rush, ten or twelve feet high, called 'tule' (tu-lee),
which dries up when it joins the arable land.

On the plain below camp, fire was in the tules and in the
stubble grounds at several places every night, and in the night
air the sight was most grand—great sheets of flame, extending

over acres, now a broad lurid sheet, then a line of fire, reflected from the pillar of smoke which rose from each spot — a pillar of fire it seemed — was magnificent.

There was wild game in abundance in the marshes for the surveyors, especially geese, and the flavor was exceedingly fine, according to Brewer. After a long visit at George Yount's ranch Brewer and an associate climbed the hills east of Napa Valley where he recorded what he saw lying below:

> The view from the top is finer than any we have had since crossing the bay, more extensive and more grand. San Pablo Bay gleams in the distance; the lovely Napa Valley lies beneath us, with its pretty farms, its majestic trees, its vineyards and orchards and farmhouses. Its villages, of which three or four were in sight, the most picturesque of which is St. Helena, are nestled among the trees at the head of the valley, a bold broken country around us.

After Brewer returned east in 1864, he taught at Yale University for many years.

In May, 1864, the *Atlantic Monthly* published an article titled "California as a Vineland." The story does not actually mention Napa Valley by name, but certainly establishes the importance of California wines and viticulture:

> It has been reserved for California, from the plenitude of her capacities, to give us a truly great boon in her light and delicate wines.
>
> Our Pacific sister, from whose generous hand has flowed an uninterrupted stream of golden gifts, has announced the fact that henceforth we are to be a wine-growing people. From the sparkling juices of her luscious grapes, rich with the breath of an unrivaled climate, is to come in future the drink of our people . . . We are to make wine as common an article of consumption in America as upon the Rhine.

There were in California more than ten and a half million vines, the writer claimed, mostly young and not yet bearing, and three-quarters of a million gallons of wine made annually, compared to one and a half million gallons made in all the other states combined.

California soon had a reputation for boasting that everything grew bigger and better along the shores of the Pacific, and it is conceivable this worked very much against the sale of wine from the state. Certainly, eastern Americans during much of the nineteenth century exhibited a snobbery against "native wine" that made it almost impossible to sell California wine. The wine from eastern states with its "foxy" flavor of the native New York or Ohio grapes fared even less well. Almost any French label was vastly preferred.

The 1860 U.S. Census reports a population of 4,872 in Napa County, compared with 405 residents a decade earlier. In the special Agricultural Census of that same year, 640 Napa residents listed their occupation as farmers, but only nine of those also categorized themselves as vintners.

The nine pioneer winemakers of Napa Valley were: Lolita Bruck, 400 gallons; Reason P. Tucker, 200 gallons; Samuel Tully, 65 gallons; A. Chamilla, 80 gallons; Thomas Knight, 1000 gallons (all of St. Helena); William H. Winters, 20 gallons; John Patchett, 4,000 gallons; G.C. Genno (the illegible handwriting makes the spelling here uncertain), 1,500 gallons; and Joseph B. Chiles, 280 gallons. There is no listing for Yount, but a story in the *California Farmer* in the summer of 1860 states Yount would make 2,000 gallons, the same amount as the previous year.[3]

Wheat was the principal interest of farmers in Napa County and the Census confirms this fact. Only San Joaquin County produced more wheat than Napa, with 685,000 bushels. Napa farmlands yielded 591,375 bushels. And although cattle raising was of diminishing importance to the economy by this time, Napa still had about 22,000 range cattle.

It is easy to understand why wheat and cattle still had such a strong role in the economy when the size of the average farm is considered. Of the 640 farmers in the county, nearly four hundred cultivated farms of five hundred acres or less. This diversified ownership of the arable lands of Napa County was one of the strengths of the region, for it attracted farmers with interests in all areas of agriculture, who could shift crops readily depending on rainfall, or as market prices dictated.

Dr. George B. Crane of St. Helena may have initiated Napa's enthusiasm for grape growing, although his early experiences were enough to discourage all but the most avid growers. An unknown writer in the 1881 publication *History of Napa And Lake Counties* credits Crane with beginning the local boom in viticulture:

> So he came into Napa Valley and purchased the place he now owns near the town of St. Helena. Here he planted the pioneer vineyard of the great St. Helena district for wine purposes. What a grand pride must swell the heart of the hardy old pioneer in wine vineyards when he now looks forth upon the broad acres of the lovely valley all covered with thrifty, bearing vines, saying to himself in the meanwhile, 'I set that movement on foot which has accomplished all this!' And did he not? He broke the path, and what followed was in his footsteps. (page 203)

The author may have had clippings from the San Francisco *Alta California* to support his beliefs. In the issue for March 11, 1866, a brief article datelined "St. Helena" reads:

> In this vicinity, there is quite a furor about grapevine plantings. The soil for several miles around, both valley and hills, being well adapted to its growth, almost every land owner is putting in more or less the present season.
> Dr Crane — just across the Sulphur Creek from this village — besides owning what is considered the number one place for such purposes, is a sort of leader in the enterprise, having a vineyard of considerable size, planted five years ago [1861] and, of course, now in full bearing. He had made some very good wine, both red and white, from a variety of grapes.

The *St. Helena Star* of August 25, 1876, honored Crane's viticultural work as well, but limited his sphere of influence slightly: "Fourteen years ago [1862] Dr. Crane inaugurated the wine business in St. Helena by making two pipes — about 300 gallons. To-day three quarters of a million gallons are made."

Many years later Crane admitted knowing next to nothing about viticulture when he purchased his first five to six thousand cuttings ("all I could find for sale within 100 miles"), and stuck them two feet into the ground. He admitted that neither a plow nor spade had turned over any of the soil beforehand, but he did not say how many cuttings survived.

> I made what proved to be the costliest blunder of all in shipping [my wines] East before I had learned that there swindling was the rule and honesty the exception," wrote Crane. "Had I knocked in the heads of all my pipes at home, and spilled the wine, as it turned out I would have been $20,000 better off in 1870; but I have prepared the way to success for later shippers of California wine and I have survived my own misfortunes.[5]

George Belden Crane was born in 1806 in Dutchess County, New York, where he took up the profession of school teacher after his graduation from high school. At the age of twenty he enrolled in the State University of New York majoring in medicine. For nearly twenty years he served as a country doctor before the lure of adventure and the California Gold Rush caused him to head west.

Many of Crane's friends were in the Temperance movement and he was faced with the delicate problem of justifying to them his new interest in viticulture and winemaking. He was present at a religious meeting led by a preacher who asked in his prayers that "God would blight the vineyard business now being commenced in the valley." Crane quickly rose to his feet and in a voice clearly heard by everyone present told the preacher, "That prayer won't go six feet high." Much later, Crane took pride in noting that in his lifetime, no blight had visited local vineyards.

By the time the Napa County Fair was held in 1864, many proud new vineyardists came forward to exhibit grapes, including W.S. Jacks, H.N. Amesbury, S. Wing, R.S. Thompson, J.S.

Trubody and Henry Boggs. There weren't many bottles in the wine exhibit, not surprising given the youth of the business, but Wing had six bottles, there were nine from Krug, nine from R. H. Sterling, and a half dozen from T. Vann. Napa Valley could now count about two dozen men patiently planting, pruning and eagerly picking the clusters of grapes in the fall.

About twelve months earlier, German-born Jacob Schram climbed the rugged hillsides between St. Helena and Calistoga and began burning off the chaparral and trees for a small vineyard. Historian Titus Fey Cronise cites that year for Schram's first planting.

In his 1868 book, *The Natural Wealth Of California*, Cronise cited Schram as a perfect example of an immigrant who had a day job (Schram was a barber) and planted vines by moonlight:

> The career of the proprietor of one of the Calistoga vineyards, affords such an excellent illustration of what a 'poor man' with no other capital than intelligence and industry, may accomplish in California, that we give some particulars about Schram, and his vineyard, as an example worthy of imitation.
>
> Schram is German by birth, and a barber by profession. When he arrived in the state, less than seven years ago, he had neither money nor friends, and could scarcely speak our language; but he had tact and courage. Believing that the hillsides around this valley would produce a superior quality of grapes, he procured a tract of land for a trifle — being covered with timber and underbrush, it was not considered to be worth anything.
>
> By dint of hard labor, he cleared a few acres and planted them with vines, acting as a barber at the springs on Saturday and Sunday . . . He now has, at the end of five years, 15,000 vines growing, about one-half of which bear fruit, from which he has made sufficient wine to pay for considerable improvements.(page 181)

There is no evidence as to precisely what year Schram had his first crush. If his vines were planted in late 1863, the first possible crop could not have come before 1865 or 1866. Schram's crush of 1866 is documented in the Alta California of April 28,

JACOB SCHRAM

1867: "His cellar, cut into the rock, has scarcely room for three to stand in, and he has only one barrel of wine, all the rest being in kegs." By this time, his vineyards held 14,000 vines.

Schram may have been responsible for Gottlieb Groezinger's first taste of Napa Valley wine. Groezinger was impressed, and shortly began buying bulk Napa wines, blending them to his taste, and selling them at his wine store in San Francisco. He also purchased Napa grapes and had them crushed at his store, controlling the winemaking process to improve wine quality.

The quality of California wine disturbed Groezinger. He was not particularly concerned with how the grape grew or how the soil was cultivated. But he was concerned with what his customers said about the taste. He was very successful as a retail wine merchant: one publication crediting him with having "the best 'Home Trade' in wine, of any house in this city." "Home Trade" meant California, or "native" wine.

Groezinger soon decided to buy vineyard land in the Napa Valley and build his own winery. His brick winery, enlarged many times after construction in 1870, still stands in the center of Yountville. He became the first in the young Napa Valley industry to place the emphasis on the taste of the wine. No one who wished to be competitive could any longer settle for a simply palatable product.

As soon as it became obvious that Europe's finest grapes could be grown in many places in California, the state's winemakers saw Groezinger's point. They wanted to match the highest quality wine Europe could producer. Any competent farmer could grow excellent grapes given the rich, youthful soils of California and its temperate climate. But the chemistry was another issue altogether. Californians were filled with enthusiasm but short on experience, observed its wine critics. But those critics may have overlooked the fact that most of the winemakers were sons of old European winemaking families.

The debate over California wine quality hit the newspapers after the largest wine firm in the state, Kohler & Frohling, began regular shipments to New York. Kohler & Frohling had begun shipping wine to Boston in 1858 and established its own New York agency two years later. The K&F wines sent were all vintages of the years 1857 and 1858 and included California brandy. The only other California wine firm shipping to the East Coast was Sansevain Brothers of Los Angeles.

On November 16, 1860, the *California Farmer* carried a story on its front page regarding the controversy:

> It is perhaps, for the interest of persons engaged here in importing and dealing in foreign Wines, to throw discredit upon our California production, and thus prevent it from supplanting the foreign. And this may account for the articles which have lately appeared in several papers, endeavoring to cry down our Native Wines, and to make it appear that our whole production is of inferior quality.

A story with this orientation had recently been published in New York's *Mercantile Gazette* after news was carried in the daily newspapers of shipments of California wine to New York. The story was reprinted in San Francisco's *Daily Bulletin*. In it, the crux of the East Coast argument seemed to be that since California wine sold for only seventy-five cents a gallon, it could not possibly be any good.

The *Atlantic Monthly* article agreed there was national hope for California wine. The story concludes: "It only remains for the vintners to keep their wines pure, and always up to the highest standard, and to take such measures as shall insure their delivery in a like condition to the consumers, to build up business which shall eclipse that of any of the great houses of Europe."

Two months after that article the editor of the *California Farmer* picked up the "wine quality" theme when he wrote:

> California wine, like every other 'good thing' in this world, will be more or less spoiled. California Wine can be made to bear a good name and only a good name, if the true friends of our State will exert themselves to this end; but in this State and abroad there is to be found so much vile stuff, bearing the name of 'California Wine' that we are not surprised it holds as yet a second place, when it should be first.[6]

The publication noted that Gottlieb Groezinger seemed to be doing the best trade in local wines, largely because his wine, in their opinion, rivaled "much that is sold for Rhine wine — it has all the 'bouquet' of the best Hock, imported." The same compliments were given to John Patchett's wine.

Although wine quality may have been of some concern to Charles Krug when he settled in Napa Valley, he seems to have made no special attempt to improve on what he found. A San Francisco reporter thought his wines "rather strong," a none-too-flattering comment, although admitting at the same time that he may have "tasted a little too much."[6]

His first wine cellar was really primitive, not that it took much of a facility to make one hundred gallons of wine. *The Napa Reporter* for January 3, 1873, carried this description:

> The pioneer wine cellar of the valley now stands near the new one on the premises, and is quite a curiosity. Mr. K. intends keeping it to mark the difference between then and now. It is 14 x 20 feet, sunk two feet into the ground and raised some

five feet above, covered first with straw, then with earth, and over all with lumber and shakes that had served their time on the pioneer saw mill of the valley, after it had exhausted the stocks of redwood in the vicinity, and had become useless property.*

Gordon Backus, reminiscing twenty years after he arrived in St. Helena, wrote: "When I arrived in St. Helena in 1870, Krug had a cellar (a hole in the ground), Mr. Pellet one above ground."[7]

Other Napa farmers carefully watched Krug, with his boundless energy, Crane, a highly educated and intelligent man, and Patchett, whose early success was amazing. They saw three very different men in a new industry that obviously had a lot of potential. One by one, they began to change their crops. Two hundred and fifty thousand vines were planted in Napa Valley between 1860 and 1863. An even greater number were spaded into the soil before the decade was half over. In 1866, the County Assessor reported 700,210 vines and a production of 50,000 gallons of wine.

"Probably at no past period in the annals of Napa City and county has property changed hands and been held at such high figures as at the present time," claimed the *Napa Daily Reporter* in early December of that year. The newspaper story added that San Francisco seemed to be overflowing with investment money, much of it coming from the bonanza of silver being dug out of the Comstock Lode in the hills of western Nevada.

The spread of vineyards in the valley was so rapid that some old-timers objected to all the changes taking place. One or two had complained in the public press that vines were destroying the pastoral beauty of the valley. A resident of St. Helena promptly responded in an April, 1867, issue of the *Alta California:*

---

* The writer's use of the phrase "pioneer wine cellar of the valley" is curious. Patchett's stone cellar, though closed, was built before Krug's. "Pioneer saw mill" referred no doubt to Bale's saw mill, which also was not the first; Yount built the earliest such facility.

> The charge that we are converting grain producing land into vineyards, though untrue, suggests the consideration of a most important politico-economic question. By far the largest portion of the cultivated lands of this State cannot be made to yield a remunerative return to the farmer, and very large portions are comparatively or entirely valueless for pasture.
>
> Shall this extensive territory remain forevermore a sterile waste — a disgrace to our country? or, shall we profit by the proof already obtained of its capabilities when used as nature evidently designed, and make it, by viniculture, a source of individual and public wealth, exceeding in value all other agricultural productions combined?

Wheat was an important staple to the economy of Napa County and, once harvested, could be handled much more easily than grapes or wine. It was sacked and transported by teamsters. Most of it ended up in Europe, particularly England.

Wheat was the inspiration for the settling of Napa County's Berryessa Valley in the mid-1860s. A town site, to be called Monticello, was surveyed "two miles from the upper and last crossing of the Putah Creek." The work on a wagon road to the valley was begun in 1867, and eventually would wind a total of 24 miles over hillsides and through Wooden and Capell valleys directly to the warehouses and flour mills of Napa City.

"There will be over 100,000 sacks of grain produced in Berryessa Valley alone, this season," observed the *Reporter* that spring. The financial returns to Napa City, it seems, would be considerable.

Still, the weather in Napa Valley often seemed at cross-purposes with agriculture. The valley experienced severe droughts and frosts, and occasional flooding. It was almost enough to send people back to the Sierra foothills to pan for gold. The first drought came in the winter of 1862-63, following a previous winter which saw flooding in the valley. By summer, moisture was so short that range cattle, mostly left over from the early Mexican settlements, had to be sold because there was neither grass on the hillsides nor alfalfa in storage for food.

Bale Mill, north of St. Helena, was only about four decades old when this photo was taken. It has been rebuilt as California State landmark #359 and is believed to be the oldest man-made structure in Napa Valley.

The following two winters were again moderately wet, which prompted someone at the *Reporter* in November, 1866, to offer this report:

> Old settlers in the mines generally predict that this will be a dry winter, and the prediction is based upon their experience for many years in this climate. We have now had two winters in succession in which larger quantities of rain and snow have fallen . . . Experience has proven that every third season, or fourth, in California, is a dry one.

Settlers also believed that unusually wet winters usually announce themselves by mid-November with big storms. But in this case, the old settlers' weather forecasting was wrong. The heavy rains started December 19th, and by the 21st water was coursing down Napa's Main Street. Water reached the second story of Captain Phillip's grain warehouse. Bridges disappeared and a portion of the railroad embankment southwest of town gave way. Thankfully, no lives were lost. The high water mark was the same as in the floods of '61-'62.

Frost was severe in the valley in the spring of 1866 and widespread over much of northern California. William Nash and Frank Kellogg, whose property was located between St. Helena and Calistoga, suffered the greatest losses. The oldest vines, some as much as sixteen years old, were hurt far less than the young vines, something no one could explain. "The frost appears to act according to some law not well understood. In some neighborhoods, it attacked some vineyards and missed others, without any apparent reason. Generally, those on high ground escaped with little injury," reported a local vineyardist.[8]

But weather wasn't the only focus of attention in the Napa Valley. In the fall of 1862 the first commercial photographer arrived on the scene. Many residents had never seen an "ambrotype" likeness of friends or relatives, and the novelty was an amazement to everyone. W.A. Maxwell, an itinerant photographer, advised potential clients he would be in town "but a short time."

There was also the murder of John W. Osborne, and the hanging of his murderer in Napa City. Unknown men passing through Napa had been found shot or stabbed to death, but no one really paid much attention. Osborne's death in April, 1863, was far different. He had done much to assist in agricultural development and publicity for the county and was a respected citizen. Everyone in the county was outraged.

Osborne had employed a young man named Charles Britton. When the two men began to have personal difficulties, Britton was discharged. He was paid for his last days of labor with a check drawn on a San Francisco bank and sent on his way. When the young man attempted to cash his check, the bank advised him that his former employer had insufficient funds. Assuming he had been cheated, Britton acquired a revolver and took the steamer back to Napa and the Osborne ranch. There was an argument, and Osborne was felled with a volley of three shots. Britton did not attempt to flee and was very shortly arrested. His trial was short, and his hanging was the first in Napa County carried out under sentence of law. On April 8, 1863, the *Reporter* printed a one-paragraph story of this sad affair:

EXECUTION OF BRITTON — This individual was hung by the neck, and suffered the 'extreme penalty of the law' about 4 o'clock yesterday afternoon, for the murder of J.W. Osborne, of Oak Knoll. He was hung in the jail yard, in the presence of some fifteen or twenty of our citizens. The culprit was attended by his spiritual advisers, but no impression could be made upon him by their kind and Christian admonitions. He met his fate with the most stoical indifference — requesting the sheriff to bury him as 'a gentleman, for he had always lived like one.

A little over a year later another death of a pioneer viticulturist saddened valley residents. George C. Yount died October 5, 1865, in his 71st year. By the standards of the time, he had lived to be an old man, but he did not live long enough to the see the name of the village he established changed from "Sebastopol" to "Yountville." That took place formally on May 14, 1867. He had been honored in so many ways already that naming the village after him might have seemed incidental. Mrs. F. H. Day's interview with Yount published in the *Hesperian* some years previously, had elevated the long-time resident to "grand old man of the valley." Yount's death was not covered in the press, but such an oversight is understandable. Grapes and wine were rapidly growing in importance in the valley's economy, but two or three dozen vineyardists out of a total of 640 farmers didn't draw much attention.

Also, there were recurrent rumors of possible gold and silver discoveries in the county. In the winter of 1860 a vein of silver was supposedly discovered in King's Canyon, north of Calistoga. Miners by the hundreds flocked to the site, staking out claims on land that gave no hint whatsoever of any precious metal. A miner who did witness silver dug from mines later in the nineteenth century, said of the first mining excitement:

Many small holes were dug and sham assayers and silver sharps reaped a small harvest. At that time our American citizens had not learned anything of the nature, appearance or localities of the precious white metal and they had everything tested from blue mud up to the volcanic rocks, with varied and most generally unsatisfactory results.[9]

A valuable material of much greater quantity was discovered in February 1860 in the Geysers region of Sonoma and Napa counties. But no one knew anything about cinnabar mining and the means of extracting quicksilver. The red cinnabar would lie undisturbed for many years.

Of course it would have been difficult to transport mined products on Napa roads: they were awful. The sad plight of the valley's wagon trails was reported by the *Alta California* in the spring of 1866: "Napa county certainly needs one good public thoroughfare, for a large portion of her roads are impassable."

Napa's travel routes were often submerged under water or mud, for swamps covered great areas of the valley. Traveling by horse and buggy to St. Helena meant constantly taking detours around the "wet spots."

The first road the length of the valley was laid out in 1852, as reported by John Russell Bartlett in his *Personal Narrative of Exploration*. The phrase "laid out" meant exactly that, for improvement of the road bed was not completed until the summer of 1860.[10]

Road improvement usually meant that the road bed was raised above the surrounding land so that it did not flood easily and was made passable with coarse gravel. But these improvements didn't make it easy to transport heavy pipes or puncheons of wine by horse and wagon. The route went from Calistoga or St. Helena to Napa City, for eventual water shipment to San Francisco.

It must have been with a great sigh of relief that up-valley winemakers heard the news that a San Francisco company was formed in December 1863 to build a Napa Valley railroad. Although that company never met its goals, in March 1864, Assemblyman Chancellor Hartson introduced a bill in the State Legislature providing for the issuance of county bonds in the amount of $225,000 to aid in building such a railroad. A county tax on property would help to pay for the project. The rail line builder would receive $10,000 per mile for the first five miles (starting at Soscol in heavy marshes) and $5,000 per mile for the remaining thirty-five miles to Calistoga.

Napa county citizens donated most of the rights-of-way for the railbed, and a public subscription raised another $60,000 within a few weeks. The contributors' names would shortly become a Who's Who of the wine industry, perhaps because most of them stood to benefit so much. A relative newcomer to Calistoga was credited with the largest individual donation: Sam Brannan gave $5,000. He had more than shipping wine on his mind, as the public soon discovered.

The ground was broken for the railroad November 21, 1864. The builders were grateful for an only moderately wet winter, and within the record time of fifty-two days, the first five miles from Soscol to Napa City were completed. The total cost came to only $32,000.[11]

Then, all of a sudden, the financing plan changed for the remaining 25 miles to Calistoga. Instead of the agreed-upon $5,000 per mile, it was proposed that different miles would require different payment. Assemblyman Hartson succeeded in having himself named president of the railroad company overseeing the construction. He also introduced a new legislative bill calling for $15,000 per mile. It passed.

Delays ensued. Some growers complained that the east side of the valley was being ignored. It was. A railroad on the east side would have found itself swamped, literally, since the elevations there were considerably lower than on the western side. Anyway, more farmers lived on the western side. Finally, in the spring of 1867 survey work was completed for the rail line to run almost parallel to the county road. Grading of the roadbed began immediately, but construction seemed to move at a much slower pace: the line eventually reached Calistoga in October.

With the railroad came another change in the valley, this time in the ethnic makeup of the population. Chinese laborers were not unknown in the county, since several ranches employed Chinese cooks, and some businesses in Napa City hired Chinese as general laborers. But the railroad employed dozens of Chinese for the preparation of the remaining dirt-and-gravel roadbed. The Chinese laborers became the center of much curiosity in

Napa Valley, and many farmers and their families drove for miles to watch them work and listen to their peculiar language.

Napa Valley's railroad was completed in October 1868, only seven months before the Golden Spike ceremony at Promontory Point, Utah, which joined the two sections of the first transcontinental railroad, the western portion of which was also built by mainly Chinese laborers.

Napa, St. Helena and Yountville were the first three towns to be established in the valley. Previous to the coming of the railroad to the upper end of the Napa Valley, there had not been enough buildings to justify calling Calistoga a village. John York purchased land in 1845 near what later came to be Calistoga and planted a small vineyard. But when the following summer brought the Bear Flag Revolt and unrest throughout the countryside, he temporarily abandoned his farm and vines. Captain John Ritchie held the title to the future town site in 1859, when wealthy San Franciscan Sam Brannan arrived and virtually showered him with gold pieces. This marked the beginning of the town.

Brannan was best known for being a major figure in the founding of the city of San Francisco. He arrived in the then village of Yerba Buena in 1846, with a ship loaded with fellow Mormons, nearly half of whom were women and children. He brought along a printing press on which to print San Francisco's first newspaper, the *California Star*.

Brannan was at Sutter's Fort one day in May 1848 when John Sutter could not keep the discovery of gold to himself. Brannan took the secret back to San Francisco and told everyone. He did not dig for gold himself but instead invested in property and built mercantile stores. Every invested dollar returned the proverbial hundredfold, and he was soon very rich.

A decade after the gold rush had begun, Brannan decided that wealthy San Franciscans needed a playground. He acquired John Ritchie's land in upper Napa Valley with its numerous warm springs. Then Brannan built cabins and bath houses around the hot bubbling waters and waited for the guests to arrive. But even when San Francisco was covered with cold summer fog, few guests came to enjoy Napa's warm evenings.

Brannan realized the problem was the lack of adequate transportation, including a good all-weather road, to his health spa. This problem could be solved by having visitors take a ferry from San Francisco to Vallejo and a train from there to Calistoga. Brannan soon became the close friend of Assemblyman Chancellor Hartson.

Six months before construction began on the second stage of the Napa Valley railroad, the first store was built in Calistoga. Henry Gettleson and Morris Friedberg, a Jew, put up the 26 x 36-foot wooden building at Brannan's invitation. (Robert Louis Stevenson changed Friedberg's name to Kelmar in his book, *The Silverado Squatters*.)

Other commercial structures soon followed in Calistoga, and by the time the first train pulled into the station, the town was ready for San Francisco's elite. Brannan knew his spa would need publicity, so he provided stories about Calistoga to all the newspapers and invited reporters to sample his hospitality. Yount had done the same thing with his wine in 1854; so had John Patchett later in the decade. Brannan scored immediately with a front page story in the *Alta California* for May 7, 1866. "Trip to Napa Valley and Calistoga" took up an entire long column and was signed "Pioneer":

> CALISTOGA — I found a number already of the beauty and fashion, and 'chivalry' of San Francisco, and other portions of the State, promenading through the delightful grounds, which are embellished with a profusion of aromatic shrubbery and the fairest flowers. Feeling somewhat tired, I seated myself beneath the whispering foliage of a locust, and looked upon the magnificent amphitheater of hills, while a living fragrance filled the air.

Story after story followed in all of the San Francisco newspapers — so many in fact that it was clear Brannan had created a tourist attraction to rival the nearby Sonoma Geysers. He had, incidentally, created the town's name by linking "California" and "Saratoga," New York's famous spa.

In spite of all that Brannan did for Calistoga and Napa Valley he was not well-liked. In fact, there was an attempt to murder him in April, 1868. Brannan and two men named McDowell and Snyder had a disagreement over the operation of a mill Brannan owned. On their way to the mill, McDowell suddenly stopped, leaving Brannan to proceed on with another companion.

When Brannan reached within fifty feet of the mill, Snyder, who was already inside, ordered Brannan to halt. They argued, Snyder fired a gun and Brannan fell to the ground along with his companion.

That Brannan survived this attempt on his life is truly remarkable. According to one account of the dispute, his body took eight shots, although whether they were separate bullets or shotgun pellets is not clear. He was hit in the right arm, the hip and near his spine, and a projectile passed through his neck near the trachea and esophagus.

Believing that Brannan was about to die, the *Napa Register* carried this editorial:

> Mr. Brannan has done more, perhaps, than any one or two other men for Napa County — has expended his means freely and extensively in developing the resources of the valley, and should his death follow from his wounds, his place would not be filled. It is only now, when death seems about to rob us of him, that his good qualities are recognized and appreciated according to their real merits.[12]

By the summer of 1869, visitors to Calistoga required only six hours to travel by ferry from San Francisco to Vallejo, then by train the length of Napa Valley. The trip could begin at 7 a.m. or 4 p.m. "No one who has resided in San Francisco for any length of time can fail to find here any day at least one familiar face," wrote one reporter. Vacations were taken not to get away from one's friends, obviously, but to leave behind the cold winds and fog that blew all summer long in the city by the bay.

Brannan planted his first vineyard in Calistoga the same year that Charles Krug founded his winery, 1861. According to at least one source, Brannan had 330,000 vines, which should have made him the largest grower in Napa Valley.[13] But historian Titus Fey Cronise, who often visited the valley during this period, recorded a somewhat more modest vine count for Brannan in his book *The Natural Wealth of California*, published in 1868. The book listed 28 growers, with Brannan topping the list at 100,000 vines.

Cronise devoted much space to a description of Napa Valley in general, adding:

> Fruits of all kinds, and the vine in all its varieties are also very productive. The lower hills are covered for miles with vineyards, and the area of this cultivation is rapidly expanding . . . The vines on these hill-sides are never irrigated — they produce a wine essentially different from that made from grapes grown on the low lands, or where watered.

Cronise also pointed out that "there appears to be considerable difference in the quality of the wine made from grapes grown in different localities." This supported the vintners' belief that soil and climate made a huge difference in quality and taste of grapes.

Nowhere in the text of *The Natural Wealth of California* was any mention of how much wine had been or was being produced. Most of the vines were young, of course, and few grapes are harvested until the third, fourth or fifth year. But the Pacific Coast Business Directory for 1867, published in San Francisco, printed wine production statistics for the entire state and showed Napa County seventh with 50,000 gallons.

One of the people contributing significantly to Napa's growing stature in the wine business was Swiss-born Henry A. Pellet. He left Switzerland in 1848, after being involved in the revolution against the King of Bavaria, who wanted to hold on to Switzerland. Pellet emigrated to the United States and took up watch repairing in St. Louis. In the spring of 1850 he joined a wagon train for the Pacific coast. Eight years later he was in Napa County. He leased John Patchett's vineyards for two

HENRY A. PELLET

years, made wine for the Englishman and himself, and bought some land of his own.

In the mid-1860s St. Helena banker D.B. Carver invited Pellet to join him in a winemaking venture. Pellet was already interested in St. Helena's wine quality. Soon after the two men opened Pellet & Carver Winery, their wine earned a notable reputation.

In 1860, John J. Sigrist and his brother Theodore set out a vineyard northwest of Napa City, near the entrance to what soon would be called Brown's Valley. Cronise credited the Sigrist brothers with having the second largest vineyard in the county. By the end of the decade their winery was capable of handling 100,000 gallons of wine.

Henry W. Crabb was living in southern Alameda County in 1868 when his former neighbor, John Lewelling, stopped by to tell him about the Garden of Eden he had discovered at St. Helena. Both men had grown up in eastern states which had native grapes and a developing wine industry. When gold was

JOHN LEWELLING

After the completion of the transcontinental railroad in 1869, Chinese workers flocked to Napa Valley. These two were house servants for John Lewelling, only one being identified in this old photograph as "Tan."

discovered in California, they came west but quickly returned to their roots in agriculture. Lewelling purchased land first in the lower part of Napa Valley, then sold abruptly and moved to St. Helena. Crabb soon moved north as well, although he took a chance on a more central valley location, soon to become Oakville. Although grapes were the major interest to both, each also planted an orchard.

As native-born Americans, Crabb and Lewelling were in the minority in the wine industry. "The greater part of the wine making of Napa Valley is conducted by persons of foreign birth," observed a writer in *Illustrations of Napa County, California*, published in 1878, "and generally by those who have had experience in the business elsewhere. They are from Switzerland, Germany, France and Italy."

Like Pellet, Frank Salmina, who purchased land on the east side of the Valley, was from Switzerland. John Weinberger came from Germany via Indianapolis, Indiana in 1869. He selected a vineyard site near what later would become known as Tychson Hill, a very modest rise of ground two miles north of St. Helena. This put him close to Krug and Schram, and to the location where the Beringer brothers would shortly settle.

From Italy in 1866 came that nation's first Napa Valley grape grower and winemaker, Giacomo Migliavacca. Like most nineteenth century Italian immigrants, he did not have the funds necessary to go into viticulture, so he opened a store on Main Street in Napa City. Migliavacca's first advertisement in the *Reporter* of November 15th, 1866, features "Family Groceries and Provisions" and "Fresh Fish received by every boat." The back of the store was quickly converted to the making of Italian-style wine from local grapes, and his reputation grew rapidly. He began planning to build his own winery along the Napa River, stoutly constructed of brick.

Two American Civil War generals found their way to Napa Valley late in the decade and turned to winemaking. General Erasmus D. Keyes founded Edge Hill vineyards at the mouth of Sulphur Springs canyon. He barely had time to bring his 12,000

JOHN WEINBERGER

vines into production before selling to an old compatriot, General R. W. Heath. Heath constructed the first winery on the property in 1872. The old winery has recently been the home of Louis Martini and his wife, Elizabeth.

Three years into the decade of the 1870s, some Napa residents were still upset about having a railroad in their county. But editor C.A. Menefee, in his *Sketch Book of Napa and Sonoma*, had a different perspective.

> Looking at the facts thus far presented, it would seem that the County has made a very bad bargain. But in fact, the County has been evidently a great gainer. An impetus has been given to every branch of business, and both County and City have awakened as if from a long slumber. The value of land in the upper half of the valley has been enhanced from 100 to 300 per cent, and this advance alone would repay the [railroad] subsidy four-fold. The railroad, by giving us the means of rapid communication with San Francisco, and all parts of the State,

and the East, has called attention to our town and valley, and caused a heavy immigration of the best class of citizens.

If the railroad were to be removed, a million dollars would not cover the loss. It is not here intended to defend or apologize for the management, or heavy rates of fare and freight charged on this road, but merely to state the general proposition, that nothing yet has done so much to call forth the latent resources of the County, and increase her wealth and population, as the railroad.[14]

Napa was the first county in the state to have a rail line traverse its entire length. Neighboring Sonoma County's first rail construction project began in 1869 and did not reach Cloverdale until three years later. There were earlier rail lines in portions of other counties. Transporting wine easily and relatively inexpensively by rail played a crucial role in the development of the local wine industry, and wine production began growing at an ever faster pace.

What was transpiring as the decade ended would not have been possible without pioneers like John Patchett, Dr. George Belden Crane and Sam Brannan. Krug was there too, and his accomplishments would make his name a household word.

Napa Valley has an abundance of fine building stone. The wine cellar pictured on the right is much more typical of wineries in the last century than, say Inglenook. If the wine cellar survives today, its name or location is unknown.

WHEAT, CATTLE,
QUICKSILVER AND GRAPES

The spring of the year 1870, when the ground had dried from winter rains, Gottlieb Groezinger stood in the middle of Yountville and carefully selected the site for his winery. A half dozen workmen stood around him, watching as he paced off the dimensions: 150 footsteps to the west and 80 footsteps to the north. This building would take some time to construct, they all agreed, especially since it was to be two stories high. There would also be a wing, 84 footsteps long and 60 wide, with a full basement.

When the foreman of the construction party had noted these dimensions, the walking began again. There had to be a fermenting room, as Gottlieb called it, of 185 footsteps by 30. Gottlieb also identified the site for a brick oven. Even though there was plenty of inexpensive native stone available, brick had been used universally in Gottlieb's home country, Germany, and he wanted his winery constructed of brick, made right on the property. Gottlieb's would be the first brick winery in the valley and would dwarf every competitor.

By the end of that day, everyone in Yountville knew about the scope of Groezinger's new winery, and within a few days everyone in the Valley knew. Growers were excited that they would have a new, wealthy buyer for their grapes. Many began thinking of expanding their vineyards.

But Groezinger was not really wealthy, especially compared to those who had made their fortunes in Nevada silver. Still, he had done very well, providing his customers with fresh fish, fresh vegetables and well-made local wines. When he had to borrow, he stayed away from banks and went to his close friends.

In Germany Gottlieb had apprenticed in hotel management and baking; he had picked up winemaking along the way. He immigrated to the United States in 1848, arriving in San Francisco shortly after Sam Brannan told the world about the discovery of gold. One biography of Groezinger claims he returned to his homeland to collect "several thousand grape cuttings of the best varieties. In 1858 he turned his attention to the manufacture of wine in San Francisco, buying his first grapes of Colonel Haraszthy, and paying him for the same three cents per pound."[1]

Groezinger might have shared some of the cuttings he brought from Germany with Haraszthy. The Hungarian avidly sought new grape varieties for his Sonoma vineyards. In 1861, months before he undertook his own celebrated vine-gathering tour of Europe, Haraszthy advertised in the *Sonoma County Democrat* that he had 186 foreign vines.

Groezinger became a major purchaser of Napa Valley grapes and wines in the mid-1860s; he believed the grape had reached its peak of perfection. In the latter part of the decade he purchased his first land in the valley, and constructed his winery in 1870. A short description of the winery and its operation was published in *Menefee's Sketch Book*:

> The roof of the fermenting room is nearly level, and comes up within six feet of the eaves of the main cellar. This roof is very strongly built, and is on a level with the upper story of the cellar. On this is all the grape crushing done, in the open air, skylights being fitted in directly over large fermenting vats below, in which falls the juice from the crushers.

Behind the winery, 150,000 vines were planted on roughly two hundred acres of land, spreading toward the west and north. Only one-sixth of these vines were the heavily bearing Mission grape, which Groezinger had planted sparingly, as he believed they produced an inferior wine.

The Changing
Napa Valley Population

Napa County began the decade of the 1870s with 7,163 residents, a gain in population of 2,291 people, including 446 from Missouri and 401 from New York. Foreign-born citizens constituted nearly a quarter of Napa's residents.

More and more small farms were being created from formerly large parcels. The 1870 census noted 746 farms, many growing grapes. Ten years previously, there were 640.[2] The Transactions of the California Agricultural Society for 1870 reports 2,172,900 vines in Napa; at an average of 700 to the acre, there would be 3,104 acres in viticulture. This vine and wine boom was going on in many parts of California. Bancroft's 1871 *Tourist Guide* reported: "The number of vines now in cultivation is about four million, and Sonoma stands first among the wine producing counties of the state." Los Angeles County no longer held first place.

Oddly enough, the Civil War, fought thousands of miles away, had a strong effect on the wine industry. Because of the interruptions in shipping many goods manufactured in the east were unable to reach California and other western destinations; thriving home industries began to meet just about every consumer need. French wines, which had a strong foothold in San Francisco restaurants, became unavailable, and California vintners were delighted with the new demand for "native wines." Especially on Dupont Street, the French Quarter of San Francisco (renamed Grant Street to honor the great general), native wines had been scorned.

Publicity during the '60s had helped too. In June, 1867, the *New York Sun* carried its first California wine story, although it ignored Napa and Sonoma valley wines:

> The whole southern part of the State is noted for its adaptability to grape culture. At that time the native grapes of Los Angeles arrived in San Francisco almost by the ship load, and in such profusion that during the season this fruit formed almost the common staple of food.

The *Home Journal* of St. Louis, Missouri was very enthusiastic about the new California wine country in 1866:

> The opening of the California Wine region is most opportune. There, in the virgin soil and blander atmosphere of the sunny slopes of the Pacific, the vine flourishes in all its pristine health and vigor. It grows almost without human care, spreading its branches over the earth and bearing its rich loads of fruit every year, scarcely failing once in a century. California is unmistakably one of nature's most carefully prepared Wine Gardens.[3]

No single published source accomplished so much for California wines in the east as did Titus Fey Cronise's book, *The Natural Wealth of California* (1868). The book gave for the first time a comprehensive overview of the young industry, even listing principal vineyardists in counties like Napa and Sonoma. Cronise divided the state into three grape growing regions. Cronise's section on "Viticulture" begins:

> If there be any one vegetable growth which more than any other finds a congenial home over hill and dale and high mountain ranges in California, and which nearly everyone plants, it is the grape vine. So general is the distribution that it is not easy to number the vines now growing. But there cannot be less than twenty-five million of vines; and men of good judgement say at least thirty millions.
> First, the southern, or Los Angeles, making Port and other sweet wines, and white wines of much spirit and little aroma; second the Coast Range, including Sonoma, Napa, etc,

making white and red acid wines — Hock, Sauterne, Claret, etc. [Claret was the name given by the English to the red wines of the Bordeaux region of France]; third, the foot-hills of the Sierra Nevada, in the gold mining range, including Folsom, Sonora, El Dorado, etc.

Cronise's geographical distinctions were soon generally accepted, and were responsible, in part, for the growing interest in Sonoma and Napa counties as excellent areas for grapes. Cronise also noted that the preference in the East for California wines was almost exclusively for those in the sweet wine category. He claimed 150,000 gallons of Port and 80,000 gallons of Angelica were shipped from Los Angeles to New York in 1867. Claret, produced in Napa, was a good wine, "but not yet sufficiently tested in the Eastern markets."

A publishing milestone back in 1863 may have been the original source for much of the background and statistics used by Cronise and later copied by eastern newspapers. In January of that year J.Q.A. Warren issued the first copy of the *California Wine and Wool Register*. This was the first wine publication on the west coast. The first two issues were published in Sacramento, the rest in San Francisco.

The transcontinental railroad was bound to affect California's expanding wine industry. California, which had sat serene and alone on the Pacific shores during the Civil War, was no longer separated from other states. With the east now only a week's ride away, family and friends from both coasts could be reunited quickly. Products before rarely seen on one side of the country or the other were now common everywhere. Even though large bulk shipments could be spoiled by high summertime temperatures, many wines headed east on rails.

In the winter and spring of 1873, a local journalist, probably Charles A. Menefee, owner of the *Napa Reporter*, spent time traversing the Napa Valley and wrote about what he saw. His first column, titled "Ramble Among the Vineyards of Napa," appeared on January 4, 1874. Most of the column was reprinted word for word later that year in Menefee's *Historical and Descriptive Sketch Book.*

Menefee hitched up his horse and buggy and followed one of the trails out of Napa City. He recorded each farm and wrote a few sentences about the products being raised, especially grapes. It was pretty obvious that Menefee was enamored of the wine industry. His first column opens with a visit to Charles Krug. The new Krug winery, completed only the year before, was 90 x 104 feet, built of concrete liberally mixed with rock, with a two-story central area. The bottom floor had small rooms surrounding a main central room, keeping the temperature uniform and cool. The top floor absorbed much of the sun's heat on very hot days. This two-story winery design was an architectural innovation which may have originated with Krug.

"The very old wine...will always be found in the pioneer cellar" wrote the reporter, referring to a 14 x 20-foot sunken area of wood with a straw roof, dating to 1861. Krug had made only 58,000 gallons of wine because of a shortage of grapes caused by spring frosts. He had sixty-eight acres of vines, nearly half of which were foreign.

Dr. Crane had just built himself a new cellar as well. "The first cellar was built in 1862," wrote Menefee. "It was of small dimensions, built of wood. The present cellar was built in 1870-1, of concrete, and is partly underground. It is 44 by 75 feet and, including underground portions, is two stories in height." Crane produced 24,400 gallons yearly.

Just south of Crane, a third new cellar had been constructed by the Giaque brothers. It, too, was of concrete, 100 feet long by only 26 feet wide. The brothers made 24,000 gallons the previous year, a small production possibly due to a lack of cooperage.

Down the road another half mile, Gordon Backus had just completed his cellar, 80 feet in length by 30 feet, and had crushed only 5,000 gallons. The cellar offered another example of architectural innovation: he enclosed his concrete walls with wood, both inside and out. "The temperature is stated to be remarkably uniform," wrote Menefee.

To the north of St. Helena, the new owners of the old Bale Mill had just completed their concrete wine cellar nearby. W.W. Lyman, son of Reverend Theodore B. Lyman, rector of Trinity Episcopal Church in San Francisco, had invested some of his mother's funds in his new business venture and hoped fervently for a bright future.[4] Built in 1871, the 50 x 30-foot, two-story building could handle production of about 12,000 gallons yearly.

Three miles south of Yountville, the new Vine Cliff winery celebrated its second crush. Owned by George Burrage and George Tucker, it was tucked into the side of a hill like a giant swallow's nest. In the *Reporter* column of January 25, 1873, Vine Cliff is described as follows:

> One of the most romantic spots of Napa Valley is the same Vine Cliff Vineyard. A semi-circle of inaccessible rocky side hills, in the canyon in which nestle the buildings, has, by the energy of many, been turned into a useful and picturesque piece of property. Hundreds of tons of rock have been patiently gathered off the hill-sides, which now teem with grape vines, and hauled away. Truly does it look to one who saw it years agone (and not many at that) as though the finger of enchantment had been pointed at its frowning, rocky surface and changed into a thing of beauty.
>
> The wine cellar is four stories high, the lower story of masonary, in the construction of which seventy barrels of cement were used. The stories above are built of lumber, 50,000 feet having been used in their construction.

Mention is made of grapes being crushed the previous two years, which dates the winery to 1871.

An intriguing experiment was going on in the cellar. A redwood cask of 2,100 gallons had been built and filled with Claret wine. "If the wine tastes of the redwood...then goodbye redwood for wine casks — an adieu we will be sorry to extend to it, as it certainly is the cheapest material that can be gotten for that purpose."

At Oakville, Menefee met Henry W. Crabb, more or less the founder of the new village. Crabb retained title to the land on which the community store was located, as well as a warehouse and new depot. He owned one of the largest vineyards in the valley: seventy acres of Zinfandel, Muscat, Malvoisie, Rose of Peru, Golden Chasselas, Grey Riesling, Muscadelle, White Malaga, Black Hamburg and Black Frontignan.

Referring to vineyard size in acres was new. Vine statistics had previously been given in actual number of vines, a figure that would sound more impressive. But Crabb had so many vines that he was proud to refer only to his total vineyard acreage. The Robert Mondavi winery and vineyards now take up most of the original Crabb ranch.

Two days were required to visit and write an account of the new vineyards and orchards in Brown's Valley, west of Napa City. Theodore Sigrist and his brother John had been making wine there for just about a decade. In his 1868 book Cronise had listed the Sigrist brothers as owning the second largest vineyard in the valley.

The Carneros region of the county, the last area visited by Menefee during his vineyard travels of '73, had as much frantic vineyard activity as any of the other areas in Napa County. Taking the old Sonoma road out of Napa City, Menefee's first stop was at the farm of Bennett James. Here he found 18,000 vines, three-fourths of the Mission variety, the others foreign. Most of the vines dated to the year 1861, the same age as Scotsman Donald McDonald's vineyard nearby.

> The road to Sonoma is dry, but in a terrible condition and shows signs of having been in a very bad state during our late rains. At noon reached Carneros Creek, where at its one hotel were welcomed by the genial proprietor, A. R. Walden. Below the hotel is the shop of our old friend, Mont. Rose, the inventor of the celebrated 'Mont. Rose' Vineyard Plow.

Five miles further was William Winter's ranch, where grapes had been planted in the late 1850s. Winter probably built his stone winery in the early years of the 1870s, though the only documentation is a mention in the *Sketch Book* of winemaking taking place there in 1873. The 1860 U.S. Census for "Manufacturing" credits Winter with producing twenty gallons of wine. The stone ruins of the Winter's winery may still be found on Carneros creek on land leased for vineyards by the Mumm winery.

One of Menefee's columns documents the fact that Napa Valley wine was shipped in carload lots to the East as early as 1873, via the new transcontinental railroad. In a visit to the Pellet & Carver winery in St. Helena, Menefee was told that Pellet and Krug had pooled resources and sent a carload of wine to Detroit, Michigan. This may have been the first large-scale shipping of wine from the valley to the eastern states.[5]

Six months after Menefee's wanderings among the vineyards of Napa, he combined data contained in his columns with a good deal more information and published his *Historical and Descriptive Sketch Book of Napa, Sonoma, Lake and Mendocino.* The book is subtitled: "Comprising Sketches of their Topography, Productions, History, Scenery, and Peculiar Attractions."

In 350 pages Menefee packed in statistics on the economy of the four counties; portraits of leading businessmen, vineyardists and winemakers; and even a few brief biographies. His work deserved an award, if for no other reason than that he had preserved so many of the rich details of the early Napa Valley wine industry. Two-thirds of the Menefee book is about Napa County, and in a brief final chapter he speculates on the future of his home county:

> The pleasant climate in Napa Valley, and the facilities for travel, have already attracted many from the city [San Francisco], and we find the valley gradually being divided up into small tracts for homesteads, and elegant improvements being made. The wealth and culture of the city is in great numbers looking to this valley for a county seat, for a pleasant home where the substantial comforts of rural life may be enjoyed, and still the facilities of a rapid transit place them at the doors of the metropolis.

Menefee's book provided writers in the eastern United States with a ready reference source for the history of viticulture in

Lost in the trees and underbrush just across the Napa-Sonoma County line on Highway 116 is this remnant of the William Winter winery — the old Talcoa Winery — built about 1872. It is described in George Husmann's 1883 book, *American Grape Growing and Wine Making.*

Northern California, even though he might have exaggerated a little when he gave the impression that Napa Valley would quickly become the focal pont of the state's wine industry. There was nothing similar to the *Sketch Book* for other wine regions in the state. J.J. Owen published his *Santa Clara Valley* in the same year. His fifty pages of text present a very clear word picture of that valley, but viticulture is treated in the most general of terms, with no statistics or names of the winemakers.

There was very little rivalry at this early date between Napa and Sonoma winemakers. The Grape Grower's Association of Sonoma, Napa and Solano Counties had been formed in the fall of 1871, and the fact that Sonoma's name came first didn't really ruffle any Napa feathers.

The Grape Growers' meetings allowed a free exchange of information and opinion on diverse subjects, including methods of cultivating the soil, and field or bench grafting of vines. One subject on which everyone agreed was the need for laws on the fencing of cattle and other farm animals. Too many cattle, horses and sheep roamed free, doing a good deal of destruction to the vines.

In early April 1873 a heavy frost spread over most of the vineyards in Napa and Sonoma. Discussion at subsequent Growers meetings centered on pruning or not pruning the injured vines. Dr. George Crane argued that pruning had no positive effect. John Sigrist went further, arguing that the cane or spur which was cut to remove the injured growth would leave "a sore, bleeding spot, and injure the dormant bud." He added that "one of his neighbors had burned brush freely, with a view to influencing the temperature of the air [to combat frost], but the result was nil."[6]

A large group from the Association traveled in September to Sacramento to attend the California Vine Growers and Wine Brandy Manufacturers Association. Major J.R. Snyder of Sonoma made a rather startling announcement at the meeting:

> The phylloxera, which made its appearance in Europe, has also been discovered in California. This may be owing to atmospheric influences, probably the large amount of magnetism which has been thrown out through the solar system by the sun for the last two years past and this may have something to do with generating a particular class of insects. Accounts from France do not say so much about the phylloxera as they do about frost.[7]

In December 1875 the St. Helena Vinicultural Club was formed by Henry Pellet, Charles Krug, and a newcomer named Seneca Ewer. (For some time after the naming of the club, the *Star* used "Vinicultural" and "Viticultural" interchangeably.) Krug was chosen the first president; within a short time a hundred names were added to the membership. Meetings were held twice a month. By 1880 the club had its own Vinicultural Hall, a two-story building in downtown St. Helena.

Krug was asked some years later to summarize some of the accomplishments of the club:

> The vast amount of good the St. Helena Viticultural [sic] Association has done during the few years of its existence cannot be doubted. It has, by publication of its minutes and deliberations, spread a great amount of information among the grape-growers and wine men of this county and State. It has drawn the attention of many persons looking for vineyard land to this section, caused them to buy and settle among us, and to assist the building up of our county.
>
> It has started an organization to keep the pernicious phylloxera from our beautiful vineyards, and you are well aware one man alone can do nothing in this line — only united action by all can ward off the dreaded calamity.[8]

One other goal of the St. Helena club was the "collecting and publishing of valuable statistics showing the superiority of our climate, and the great fertility of our soil." The members were convinced that the Napa Valley was God's chosen spot for viticulture.

The cost of hiring vineyard workers became a major concern in the mid-1870s after the depression of 1873 had caused wine sales to drop. In order to cut the cost of producing wine, Napa Valley wine men began to consider the use of Chinese laborers. Chinese were available in large numbers, whenever needed. That kind of fluid labor force was the answer to a grape grower's prayer. A letter to a Chinese contractor in San Francisco would bring as many workers as needed on the next day's passenger train. The Chinese willingly worked for one dollar a day and provided their own food and cooking. Most of them also brought their own bedrolls. Caucasian laborers expected food and some sort of sleeping or living quarters to be provided, in addition to the daily wage, which was twenty-five cents higher.

Charles Krug's winery was destroyed by fire in August, 1874, just weeks before the crush would have begun. His 90 x 104-foot, two-story wooden cellar had been completed only two years earlier. He was not even able to save the 300,000 gallons of wine inside.

Krug barely gave the fire's embers time to cool before he ordered lumber to rebuild. He must have hired a small army of

Between 1868 and 1900, Chinese laborers picked most of the grapes and tended the vines in Napa Valley. After passage of the Chinese Exclusion Act in the 1880s, their numbers diminished.

workers, for he completed his annual crush right on schedule. He moved his distilling plant to a separate building the following year, and when the machinery arrived from the East Coast, the *Star* described it as "immense" and called his crusher "the largest thing of the kind on the Coast."[9]

By 1877 the United States Congress passed a bill which helped Napa Valley vintners considerably, as well as those throughout the state. The bill permitted the establishment of bonded warehouses for the storage of brandy without prepayment of federal taxes. Many vintners made brandy from excess stocks of wine.

Newspapers and Books Describe the Valley

Three years before the Bonded Warehouse Act was passed, another event had occurred in Napa Valley which, in the long run, was to have even greater impact on local viticulture. This was the establishment of a weekly newspaper in St. Helena, the

Star. From the very first issue, the paper was a leading proponent of winemaking and viticulture.

The *Star* was founded by DeWitt C. Lawrence, who printed his first issue on September 25, 1874, and sold the first copy for a twenty-dollar gold piece to one A. Clock, Esq. No one is sure how Lawrence came to St. Helena, but more than likely he was simply an itinerant printer, like many others who roamed the American West in the gold and silver mining era.

Less than eighteen months later the newspaper was purchased by Charles Gardner, who quickly became one of the chief spokesmen for local vintners. Gardner was born in Illinois in 1843, which made him 33 years old when he settled in St. Helena. He had been trained in the practice of law, being admitted to the California bar in Los Angeles in 1870. Gardner never mentioned in his newspaper how or why he came to the Napa Valley, except that he worked briefly for the *Napa Register.* Very soon after he moved to Napa, he planted his own vineyard.

Energetic almost to a fault sometimes, Gardner attended the meetings of the viticultural organizations and then wrote and published lengthy accounts of what transpired. He regularly visited wineries and asked opinions on the future of the industry. By the end of the decade major newspapers in San Francisco were reprinting accounts from the *Star* on many wine subjects. Some copied liberally without crediting their source, which irritated Gardner considerably.

Every year for almost 25 years, the *Star* published a column listing all Napa Valley wineries and the amount each produced in the fall crush. The column was widely reprinted in other news journals and brought a vast amount of publicity to Napa's wine industry.

When the book *Illustrations of Napa County* was published in 1878, the publishers acknowledged borrowing heavily from the columns of the *Star.* Three years later, when the publishers of the *San Francisco Call* compiled a guide to the state, *California As It Is,* Gardner wrote the chapter on Napa County. His bias toward wine was undisguised:

PRODUCTIONS — The great product of the county — and almost the only increasing one — is wine. A brief review of the others will tend to a consideration of this. The latest county statistics are the Assessor's of 1877, and the grain yield showed therein is probably as large as it has been since, or ever will be.

There were 3,360 acres devoted to grapes, claimed Gardner. The final paragraphs of Gardner's chapter deal almost exclusively with grapes and wine. He left the impression that Napa Valley was the premier area for viticulture.

Publications like *California As It Is*, printed in a handy size, with an eye-catching full color cover, had wide circulation throughout the eastern U.S. and possibly even in Europe. There was still a hunger for information about California, left over from the gold rush. The county summaries in *As It Is* are not listed alphabetically but seem to be arranged in a ranking by economic development. Napa County follows Sonoma about one-third of the way into the 178-page book..

Clarence Smith and Wallace Elliott's *Illustrations of Napa County* brought to the outside world for the first time lithograph illustrations, by C.J. Dyer, of many of the major vineyards and wineries of Napa County. Charles Krug was given (or paid for) a two-page spread showing the winery and neat rows of wine barrels. It would have been easy to believe in the dominance of viticulture and winemaking in the county by looking at the Smith and Elliott book. There are fifteen lithographs showing farms which included vineyards or wine cellars. Less than half a dozen illustrations depict the growing or harvesting of wheat, and most of these are in the Berryessa region.

Shortly before the artists for Smith and Elliott began tramping about the valley for the best views, Miss Hannah Millard of San Jose visited the region to "faithfully" reproduce in watercolors some of the local grape clusters and leaves. She had been selected by the State Viticulture Society to undertake watercolor studies for a book to be published by the Society. H.W. Crabb was one of three committee members to oversee the project.

Krug was in charge of negotiating the details and cost of the publication. The Society originally planned to publish 500 copies of the book. A hundred years later, in 1978, with only a half dozen copies of the original known to exist, the book was re-published. The auction price of an original copy is estimated at $25,000.*

Charles Gardner appears to be the author of 48 pages on "Viticulture in Napa County" in the *History of Napa and Lake Counties, California,* published in San Francisco by Slocum, Bowen & Co. in 1881, with over 900 pages: Lyman L. Palmer is credited in the preface as the historian; Gardner's contribution is acknowledged but not defined.

In addition to a lengthy background study of grapes and wine-making in California since 1769, when the Catholic missions were founded, there are pages of statistics and long lists of vine-yardists — just the kind of material Gardner liked to collect and publish in his newspaper. No other single individual had such an excellent overview of the county's developing wine industry. Even Charles Krug could not keep up with Gardner's travels.

One of the subjects Gardner carefully avoided, however, was the use of Chinese laborers in Napa vineyards. He did not avoid the subject in the columns of the *Star*, but had to tread carefully when the prospect arose of attracting the sandlot rioters of San Francisco to Napa Valley. Unemployed Caucasian workers in San Francisco began congregating daily in the open sandlots south of Market street to listen to fiery anti-Chinese oratory. Out of this evolved the Workingmen's Party of California, which by 1878-79 was strong enough to elect city mayors and state legislators, and even rewrite the state constitution. Several of their changes, as they applied to Chinese, were shortly declared illegal by the courts.

Chinese workers began to be hired into the vineyards and wine cellars of Napa Valley in large numbers by late 1870, partially because they worked for lower wages, but principally

---

* See *Grapes and Grape Vines of California,* San Francisco, Ca. Edward Bosqui & Co., 1877.

because they were more reliable. C.A. Menefee put the problem in perspective in his *Sketch Book*:

> One of the most important questions presented to the agriculturist is that of labor. The farmers frequently find it impossible to get laborers to perform their work. A great portion of the labor employed during the vintage in picking and shipping grapes is Chinese. People are not favorably disposed to these Asiatics, but often find themselves reduced to the necessities of accepting these or none.
>
> There is no State in the Union where the laborer has so easy a time as in California, but this very fact has an injurious effect upon the laborer. It is harder here to find good and trustworthy laborers than elsewhere. Few think farther than the best means of shirking responsible labor, of getting the largest sum and make the least return therefor. Many, after the week's work is over, stroll away to dens of vice, and crime, to come away, by no means benefited.

Menefee was not alone in this opinion. The same kind of strong anti-labor statements can be found in the columns of many weekly newspapers of the time. One of the worst labor problems of the 1870s arose whenever news of a new gold or silver strike spread through the countryside. The white workers would abandon hoe and spade in the middle of a vineyard and take off for the mountains. Employed Chinese rarely joined their white counterparts in this search for riches.

Napa Valley newspapers often carried advertisements for the Chinese labor exchanges, like this one in the *Star* of July 27, 1877:

> CHINESE HELP FURNISHED — San Sing, at Ginger's China Store, St. Helena, will furnish all kinds of help, for cooking, railroad work, chopping wood, etc., at Yountville, Oakville, Rutherford, St. Helena, Calistoga, Pine Flat, or any of the surrounding country. Good [work] at cheap prices.

In San Francisco, Crosett's & Co. also provided workers, although their advertisements in Napa Valley publications left out the word "Chinese." Since their address was 623 Clay Street, right in the heart of Chinatown, the race of workers provided was clearly understood.

Quong Goon Loong, dealer in "China goods" in St. Helena's large Chinatown, "across the bridge," was another clearinghouse for vineyard labor. If Quong was typical of his time, all wages were paid directly to him, then after deducting his fee and advances for food, he paid his fellow Chinese whatever remained.

The Chinese pursued a wide variety of tasks in the Napa Valley beside vineyard work. When the first road between Calistoga and Pope Valley's quicksilver mines was opened in late 1873, the *Napa Reporter* could record that "twenty-seven Chinamen and three white men" were doing all the work. John Lewelling used Chinese to build fences around his vineyards and fields. He lost a large pile of fence posts when Chinese workers burning grass inadvertently set fire to them. Simpson Thompson at Soscol reduced the wages he paid to his regular workers, who then left. He had no difficulty finding Chinese replacements.[10]

The Chinese dug tunnels into the rock hillsides for C. Lemme when he built his winery west of St. Helena in 1877. The *Star* reported June 8th: "A Chinaman was killed at Mr. Lemme's place near town, by the caving in of a bank where they were cutting into the hillside for a cellar."

Chinese were also hired for the construction of the huge Occidental winery in 1878 for Terrill Grigsby. Grigsby used Chinese almost exclusively on his ranch for cutting hay, harvesting grain and other tasks. He paid a high price, however, for that decision. Not long after the winery was completed, his barn was burned down by someone who left a note warning of further fires if he did not discharge his Chinese workers.[11] For several years fires broke out mysteriously in wheat fields of other farmers who hired Chinese laborers.

Another aspect of Napa County's economic development, was burgeoning too in the 1870s. This was the mining and reduction of cinnabar ore into quicksilver. No appreciable amounts of gold or silver had been mined in the county until this date, but quicksilver gave the local residents a reason to brag about Napa's mineral wealth. Profits of hundreds of thousands of dollars were made in the county's quicksilver mines, but there is no record of any one person becoming rich from them.

The first cinnabar discoveries came in the 1850s, with new ledges periodically uncovered into the 1870s. There would be great excitement for a few weeks or months, then disappointment. When a major discovery of the ore was made at the Geysers in nearby Sonoma County in the summer of 1873, the fever spread into Napa and beyond. Wealthy San Franciscans by the score wanted to invest in this newest bonanza, or what they hoped would be a sure source of wealth.

Pope Valley was the major location for most of the Napa mines, although others were opened at widely scattered locations. The Phoenix mine opened in 1861 in Pope Valley and was operated without much success until the early 1870s. As many as 45 men were employed at one time at the mine, many of them woodcutters who supplied the furnaces to produce the high heat needed to force the quicksilver to run free from the red cinnabar. Up to 75,000 pounds of quicksilver were produced annually, returning an income of around $50,000.

It was expensive to operate a quicksilver mine. Most were located high in the hills, far from nearby towns or railroads which could bring in the necessary furnaces, boilers, condensers, hoses, lumber and other necessities. Few mines survived longer than a half dozen years, the price of quicksilver always fluctuating dramatically and the cinnabar ledges rarely very extensive. One typical example was the Summit Mine, located in the Mayacamas mountains west of Yountville. It was discovered by the Whitton brothers, Green and John. The Whittons sold their rights to the mine for $45,000 in the early 1870s to J. Pershbaker, though it is doubtful the Whittons were paid the full amount before the mine closed down. This was the pattern in many similar transactions.

The mining excitement pushed news of winemaking off the front page of the *Star* on October 29, 1874:

> CINNABAR AND SILVER EXCITEMENT — Well, it has come to pass. They have it; we have it; everybody had it — the fever we mean — not that of the aches and shakes, but of the cinnabar, silver and gold.
>
> It is raging, the acme, the tip-toe of an old fashioned '49 excitement is reached. We look for depopulation and population. By depopulation we refer to the amount of stampeders from town, to the mountains three miles East and West of us and by population to THE RUSH, that is just commencing from other parts. During the past week the excitement has been so furious as to start prospectors out with lamps, and the cold drenching rain had no effect in quenching the fire of the thirst for the almighty rock that produces THE ALMIGHTY DOLLAR.

DECIDING ON THE BEST GRAPE VARIETIES

Meanwhile, there was an almost constant debate in the Napa Valley over what varieties of grapes to plant for winemaking, table use or raisin production. The wishful thinking seemed to be that one variety could fill all purposes. Many vine growers sympathized with the farmer near Rutherford who admitted planting forty different types, then spent years trying to select the best, never satisfied with any of his choices.[14]

One vineyardist wrote to the *Star* in November 1875 that he found the Black Malvasia to be the best grape:

> We have tried to get all the points possible, on the subject, pro and con — and we would advise all vine growers to put in the Black Malvaisia [sic]. Our reasons are these. It will make No. 1 Red wine and it has proved by our young wine maker, Mr. Richard Heath, to make a No. 1 White wine — Now if the wine market calls for a white wine, you can make it from your Malvaisia, and on the other hand, if Red wine is the salable article, you can make a first class article from the same grape.

Judging from the number of vines planted to that grape, most people agreed with the writer. Just a year earlier, someone using the nom-de-plume "Vitis" (there was one in nearly every weekly newspaper) agreed, and recommended as well the Zinfandel, Burger, Muscat and Chasselas, plus the Rieslings.[13]

The Mission continued to be the most popular grape among all growers, in every county of the state. Other frequently planted varieties included White Muscat of Alexandria, Flame Tokay, Black Malaga, Black Hamburg, Rose of Peru, Royal Muscadine, White Malaga, Red Frontignac and several varieties of Chasselas. Some of these grapes doubled as table grapes or were used for raisins.

This was an era of much experimentation, especially since so few knowledgeable people were available to give expert advice. Frank Schleiter of Napa decided to try making champagne in the fall of 1874. Press reports called the end product remarkably like the champagne being made in France. Whether this qualifies as the first real champagne made in the Napa Valley is uncertain, especially since he used the Muscat grape, a fine table grape, but one usually with too much sugar for good quality champagne.[14]

"Dr. Crane is just now engaged in an enterprise that is new to this part of the country," reported the *Star* in early January 1877. He is "building a house especially for the manufacture of sherry wine." Sherry was one of the most popular wines in California, as well as in the eastern states. The newspaper erred in crediting Crane with being the pioneer sherry maker in the valley, for this honor went to Portuguese immigrants John Ramos and Joseph Mathews. The process was not the true solera-oven method followed in Xeres, Spain, where sherry originated. (Xeres has been Anglicized to Sherry.)

The first sherry-type wine was produced in Napa Valley at William Woodward's ranch northeast of Napa City. The *Napa County Reporter* described the process (similar to Crane's) in November, 1872:

We next crossed the road, entered a house containing 7,500 gallons of that never to be forgotten sherry. One end of this building is a bake oven, 17 x 30 feet, which was filled with pipes of new-made-sherry, and in which it has to be baked for six months, a fire being kept under it, day and night.

John opened the oven door for us, and we saw the casks inside with the 'green' oozing out of their seams. This 'green' is just like the grease one can find on the hubs of a buggy wheel, and it is the purging of this stuff from the Sherry by its six months 'heated term', that makes it not only so palatable, but frees it from that horrible adjunct to so many vintner's vintages, the headache.

The "John" referred to here was John Ramos, but another worker present was Joseph Mathews, who later produced sherry in the basement of his stone and brick home in Napa City. In 1882 he constructed the Mathews, or Lisbon, Winery on Brown street and added a sherry-baking oven.

Charles Wetmore, writing in an 1891 treatise on the production of wine, observed that the sherry produced in the sherry houses above described did not even approximate real Spanish sherries, and he seemed to loathe comparisons of the two.

THE BOUNDARIES OF NAPA VALLEY

At this time there was so much public confusion as to the precise boundaries of Napa Valley that Gardner at last felt duty-bound to explain it in some detail. This peculiar story appeared in the *Star* on January 16, 1883:

WHAT IS THE NAPA VALLEY? — 'Inquirer,' San Francisco, writes, 'To solve a question, please kindly state in your valuable paper what portion of Napa county is known as Napa Valley, and which are its boundaries?'

ANSWER — Napa Valley is that portion of Napa county which is included in the Valley of that name. It heads above Calistoga, about Mt. St. Helena, (at the Northern boundary of the county), and runs in a Southwesterly direction, almost to the Southern line of the county, below the City of Napa. It is about 35 miles long, by one to 5 miles wide, and contains about 87 square miles. The area of the whole county being about 800 square miles, it will be readily seen what proportion the one bears to the other in this respect.

Viticulture was pursued in all of the satellite valleys to Napa from the 1870s onward. M. Kaltenbach was the first to grow vines in Conn Valley, at the start of the decade. He was also the first winemaker, although by mid-decade Everett Musgrave was producing about ten times as much wine as Kaltenbach's annual five hundred gallons.[15] Fred Metzner and Louis Corthay soon joined their neighbors in wine production.

Chiles Valley, like Conn, is located in the folds of the hills on the eastern side of Napa Valley. The principal entrance then was a road just east of Rutherford which wound its way gradually to the higher elevation of Chiles. The low and irregular hills which separated Chiles and Conn, and Pope, for that matter, made it rather difficult to ascertain exactly when the traveler had left one valley and entered another.

There was a small vineyard in Chiles Valley by 1877 which had likely had been there for some time. Alfred Boothe, a local resident, provided this brief description in June, 1877:

> The whole valley is about eight miles long, by an average width of half a mile, and contains 20 or more families, with two schools. The well known Chiles mills are situated about the center, and makes a market for all the wheat raised in the vicinity. These mills are among the oldest in the State, built in 1848.

The remnants of the mill are now a State Landmark.

Pope Valley was the best known of Napa's neighboring valleys because of the quicksilver mines which began operating there about the time of the American Civil War. Many San Franciscans had traded in Pope Valley mining stocks without even being too sure of how one traveled to the mines. The valley lies east and northeast of St. Helena and could be reached by two roads. The first road went up and over Howell Mountain, one of the steepest in California's coastal region. A second road could be taken from Calistoga to the valley.

Pope Valley has a higher elevation than in Napa Valley, receives slightly less rainfall and was home for many centuries to hundreds of Indians. George Yount told in the *Hesperian* magazine of his difficulties with the Pope Valley Indians, having to engage them directly in an armed fight on at least one occasion. William Pope obtained a land grant for the area in 1841 from the Mexican government, but it was Col. Joseph Chiles who planted the first vines in 1851.[16]

William Haug built the first modest winery in the valley in 1880, producing 1,000 gallons. Considering the numbers of men employed by the quicksilver mines and still living in the area, there may have been a serious demand for wine.

The *San Francisco Call* in January 1884 carried a brief description of Pope Valley, with special emphasis on its vine-growing potential:

> The hillsides are well adapted to the growth of the vine, but viticulture, which has become one of the chief industries in other portions of Napa county, is as yet in its infancy in Pope Valley. It is, however, enjoying the attention of some who have been and are preparing to plant vineyards of considerable extent, among the number being the farm of the late Dr. Maxwell...T. H. Ink is preparing to plant a hundred acres . . . The nearest railroad at present is at St. Helena, eighteen miles distant, where grain and all kinds of farm produce are hauled.

There were few vineyards planted as yet on Howell Mountain, although Edwin Angwin was being urged to open a resort so others could enjoy the natural beauty of his farm:

"We all agree that Mr. Angwin has a beautiful place situated in a little valley on the top of the mountains, the land is very rich, an abundance of water, mountain springs, running streams and the healthiest place in the county. Mr. Angwin should make of it a resort for health and pleasure for others and profit to himself."[17]

CONNOLLY CONN

Berryessa Valley was totally devoid of vines in this period; most of the land was farmed and devoted to wheat. Berryessa had a much more serious problem than Pope Valley when it came to its semi-remote location. A local correspondent named simply "Mallie" once described the travel situation for anyone who called Berryessa home:

> The export and import business troubles us not a little. Along those drowned plains in the lower vallies, our neighbors wishing to visit San Francisco or go back East, can step aboard a train without any disagreeable prelude to their journey.
>
> It is very different with us; we have 'to wait for the wagon' or about the same thing, the rumbling stage-coach, which is worse, and then be driven and jolted and mutilated over a road of thirty miles that just begs description. Webster hasn't coined the word descriptive of the condition of the Napa grade during the long and rainy winter. As as for the Winters' road, its condition has been impassable and the Berryessa people are perfectly disgusted with it . . .

> During the long rainy season we live here 'hermetically sealed', even the schools are closed, but with the appearance of spring, two schools have opened in the valley, and another soon to commence.[18]

Calistoga, like the outlying valleys of the county, was often overlooked in all the viticultural excitement around St. Helena, and between there and Napa City. The oversight could be traced in part to the lack of an aggressive newspaper, like the *Star*, to publicize the town.

A weekly newspaper was founded in Calistoga in 1871 and ran rather fitfully for years. A second journal was established in 1874, only to close after a few months. In 1876 *The Calistogian* appeared, but the owner, J. H. Upton, carted off the presses to Hollister within the year. J. L. Multer finally remedied this unhappy situation with *The Independent Calistogian*, which debuted the day after Christmas in 1877. Multer more closely shared Gardner's enthusiasm for local events than any of his predecessors.

Despite the fact that winemaking and viticulture were scattered across the length and breadth of Napa County in the 1870s, the center of the industry was clearly the town of St. Helena. No other portion of the county gave itself so completely to the grape. Editor Gardner in the *Star* put it precisely in an editorial called "Our Chief Interest," in the issue of March 11, 1876:

> The chief interest of St. Helena is the vine. Her soil and climate are especially to it, years of labor and enormous sums of money have been expended in the pursuit of its culture and attendant industries. It is our great preponderating interest — so much so that to take it out of the calculation we have little else to sell and bring an income.

Gardner and friends undertook a private census of the vineyards located in the "upper valley," that region lying north of Oakville and including the "small vallies adjacent to Napa Valley." There were 2,054,000 vines, planted about 700 to the

George Risley, who obviously had a green thumb, owned this small house in St. Helena in the 1880s. His wife stands on the front steps, and his daughter, in mid-garden, is ready to help him mow the lawn. The railing on the porch is a fine piece of Victorian whimsy. Atop the roof is the iron cresting common in houses of the period.

acre, or 3,000 acres of grapes. It was not just the acreage in vines that was increasing rapidly: Gardner discovered to his surpise the next year that the number of wineries had doubled between Calistoga and Oakville. Where there had been fifteen cellars, now thirty or more could be counted. Over the succeeding weeks Gardner took his readers on a tour of these wine cellars, beginning with the dean of all local vintners, Charles Krug.[23]

Most valley vintners realized that something had to be done to increase the sale of wine outside California. The Napa Valley

Wine Company was one result of their concern, formed early in the decade by Krug, Jacob Beringer and M.G. Ritchie. These three men may have taken action as the direct result of a story carried some months previously in the *Curtis Quarterly Wine Circular* of San Francisco. In a study of the distribution of wine during the year 1872, The Curtis investigators found that only about one-tenth of the state's annual wine production was being sold outside California.[24]

Much of the credit for the expansion of the wine market belongs to Charles Krug. He was a man of unlimited energy, traveling to Washington, D.C. when it became necessary to oppose or gain support for a law which affected the making of wine. He rarely missed a meeting of winemakers, whether on the local, regional or state-wide level. He was Napa's ambassador of wine and conviviality.

The wine boom of the mid-1870s saw the establishment of several wineries to rival Krug and Groezinger. Jacob Beringer's winery was one of these, although it would take him some years to complete the winery buildings and tunnels, as well as a mansion for comfortable living. Beringer did not have quite the colorful background of Charles Krug, although he may have been a better vintner; when Beringer arrived in Napa Valley in 1870, Krug hired him to be his winemaker.

Beringer had apprenticed at the age of fifteen in the Berlin, Germany, wine firm of Tim & Kloske. After several years with a winery at Mainz, he emigrated to the United States, arriving in 1868. He opened his own shop in New York City, probably with the help of an older brother, Frederick, who already lived in in New York.

Jacob Beringer never explained why he suddenly put everything aside after only two years and headed directly for the Napa Valley. If he did reminisce to friends or to descendants, the story was never recorded, and the details have been lost. It is quite possible that Beringer and Krug met in New York when Krug was selling some of his wine. He may have liked what he tasted and wanted to become a vintner. He may also have preferred country life to city life, making wine rather than selling it.

Three days before Christmas in 1876, Beringer and a crew of workmen began excavations for the first Beringer winery. Jacob and his brother had purchased their land just north of St. Helena from William Daegner. The cornerstone was laid the following March, the year Jacob reached his thirtieth birthday.

The Beringer winery was the object of considerable public interest even before it had produced its first crush. Jacob had bought himself one of the most beautiful stone hillsides in the valley. On closer inspection, it was obvious the rock was ideally suited to the building of wine storage tunnels which would rival those of Buena Vista in Sonoma.

"Through the back wall is pierced one archway, pointing straight into the hillside, and already extending 16 feet in. At the end of this archway work has begun, and is to be pushed forward until a depth of 50 feet, by 17 wide is reached," began a detailed description in the *Star* in March 1878. In another twelve months, the tunnel reached a depth of 100 feet through the fine continuity of the stone. Two more tunnels were then dug, of equal length and width. The three tunnels were connected at the rear with a cross tunnel. All of this took several years to complete and must have drawn scores of on-lookers. It was a remarkable feat of engineering.Five years after the wine caves were completed, the Beringers began construction of a magnificent house at the winery. The architect was A. Schröpfer, a German immigrant from San Francisco who moved to St. Helena in the 1880s. The Beringer house, begun in 1883, was at least two years under construction. Its soaring rooflines, beautiful interior woodwork, and stained glass windows immediately made it a showplace, reminiscent of great 19th century houses in the Rhineland. Today, beautifully preserved, it is one of the most popular sites for visitors to the valley. Schröpfer also designed other imposing houses in the area, including the Tiburcio Parrott house, now known as Falcon Crest, and the Thomann house,

Over a century of tree growth has obscured this view of the Beringer winery, shown not long after its opening in the late 1870s. The central building survives, but several of the adjacent structures are gone.

now the site of Sutter Home winery. He is buried in the St. Helena cemetery.

Most wineries built thereafter in the valley were built into a cutaway hillside. Grapes would be hauled by horse and wagon to the top floor for crushing. Wine pumps were thus rendered unnecessary, as gravity brought the juice to the fermenters and finally to the bottom floor for aging. At best, pumping, done by hand, was a slow process.

When a winery was on the valley floor, an artificial hill was sometimes created against one side, or a loading device was needed to bring the lugs of grapes to the top story. A full lug weighed from 20 to 40 pounds.

One mile north of the Beringers, John C. Weinberger built a very modest stone structure for his winery in 1876, 42 x 62 feet, of two stories. A wooden third floor gave him the customary space for crushing grapes with a hillside created on the north end for bringing wagonloads of grapes to the crushers. Three years later Weinberger added another 28 x 50-foot structure alongside the first and slightly offset. The two units could handle 180,000 gallons of wine. The two-foot-thick walls of red lava rock were quarried on the property. The heavy interior timbers were meant to give the cellar a long, long life. The winery was converted to a private home by William Gonser and his wife Alice in the 1940s. The building has stood the test of time very well.

Almost directly across the road, Jean Laurent built a new winery in the same month and year as Weinberger added his second addition. By the time it was finished he could store almost as much wine as his neighbor.

Giovanni Bustelli, superintendent of the Uncle Sam Winery in Napa City, warned that unless local grape growers made some plans to expand their acreage, Uncle Sam would plant its own vines and possibly ignore the local grower.

> The farmers of the vicinity of Napa, says Mr. Bustelli, are planting no new vineyards and do not even take creditable care of what they have. This is a discouraging fact for wine-

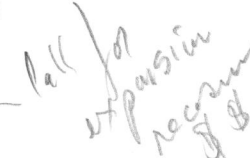

makers there, for it gives poor promise of a supply of grapes to work on.[21]

Henry W. Crabb of Oakville operated a large, most unusual winery capable of holding 300,000 gallons. The first portion, built in 1872, was of wood, 56 x 110 feet. Seven years later, Crabb completed a second section, almost identical. Then he built another section, 58 x 124 feet, plus a fermenting cellar and a huge distillery. The complex looked like an eastern factory or mill. He used no stone.

But Crabb was much more interested in the vine than in wine, or so it would seem. In 1876 the *Star* reported he had 183 separate varieties of grapes. Two years later, in the *Illustrations of Napa County*, that count had climbed to 250. He may have been trying to match the accomplishments of Agoston Haraszthy.

Crabb's growing reputation attracted the attention of George Husmann of Missouri, who had edited or written most of the book *American Grape Growing and Wine Making*. The second edition, published in 1883, carried a section on Napa Valley viticulture written by Crabb. Crabb reviewed the decade of the seventies, ending with a very positive future outlook:

In 1876 the business dragged heavily, nearly bankrupting numbers. Wines were in large stock, and had to be sold to distillers and vinegar factories, at ten to fifteen cents per gallon.

> There was no market for our wines. They were in bad repute, due mainly to adulterating processes which were carried on to a great extent in the interest of importers, and for the purpose of crushing the wine and brandy industry here. But since that time business has greatly increased. The report of the Surveyor General of the State for the year 1876 gave 35,000 acres of vineyards; the next year 41,000; the next 77,000; and this year may be estimated at from 85,000 to 90,000 acres, making an average increase of about 35 per cent for the last four years.

Other wine men, notably Charles Wetmore, would shortly dispute these figures, but not the grape planting boom then getting underway. Crabb believed the reason for the boom was the phylloxera devastation then taking place in France's vineyards. If the reports of the phylloxera in France were true, Crabb could foresee a very rosy future for California:

> If the industry be not stifled by Congressional legislation, whoever lives a half century hence, will find the grapes of California in every city in the Union; her raisins supplying the Western Hemisphere; her wines in every mart of the globe, and then, with her golden shores, her sunny clime, her vine-clad hills and plains, will California, indeed, be the Vineland of the World.

PHYLLOXERA AND THE
WILD VITICULTURAL BOOM

O ne week before Christmas in 1880, Professor Eugene Hilgard of Berkeley, California, boarded the San Francisco to Vallejo ferry for a quiet trip to St. Helena. From Vallejo he traveled by railroad, enjoying the journey with several friends and colleagues. Hilgard was the first faculty member of the University of California assigned to the teaching of viticulture, and was to be a special guest that afternoon at the local Vinicultural Club. Eugene Hilgard's remarks later that day were to seal the destiny of Napa Valley and help precipitate a wine boom that would not be matched for many, many decades.

Distinguished men of Hilgard's stature did not often visit the small town of St. Helena, and this occasion quickly became a major event. Even the wives of Vinicultural Club members came to hear what he had to say. Possibly the only person with an interest in grapes who did not attend was Charles Krug, who was unable to leave his sickbed. Krug was the perennial host of most notable visitors — he must have been seriously indisposed to miss this one.

The *Star* devoted more than half of its front page the following week to covering Hilgard's reception and remarks. This was an historic occasion, wrote editor Gardner. Hilgard's remarks, which required about two hours to deliver, were the result of an act of the State Legislature, which created the new Board of State Viticultural Commissioners. One point made by the learned professor stood out like no other:

> The turning point of the tide [in California] was at the time when the havoc carried by the phylloxera into the European vineyards created a panic as to future supplies; so that those who had thus far turned up their noses at the nameless and fameless American wines, were led to reflect and at least try what could be made out of the promiscuous material, in case there could be no other available source.

Napa's young wine industry needed just this sort of bolstering by a distinguished man of letters. "Try the local wines, you might like them," he announced. But in any case, get used to them, for the phylloxera vine disease was about to destroy or seriously injure the wine industry of France. What had been rumor was now reality, in part because Hilgard said so.

A new fever spread across the California landscape, not caused by gold or silver, but brought about by the Vitis Vinifera grape of Europe, which had found such a hospitable home in California. Charles Wetmore, the chief executive officer of the Board of Viticultural Commissioners, attempted to convey what was happening when he wrote in his Second Annual Report: "About one hundred thousand acres of grapes have been planted in the past four years."[1] Wetmore expected 30,000 new acres the following year of 1884. He estimated that the entire state had no more than 50,000 planted acres prior to the start of the boom. Napa Valley itself had barely 3500 acres of grapes when the 1880s began. Within two years there were nearly 12,000 acres in vines.[2]

A story in the *Napa Reporter* in early 1873 claimed that phylloxera had been first discovered near the city of Avignon, in France. Within a decade it had cut in half the production in many districts. "It is certain" stated the *Reporter*, "that if the insect plague continues and increases at the same rate for the

next five years, as it has for the last five, California grape growers will have nothing to complain of on account of cheap French
wines." By the late 1870s, the insect was crawling about France's
vineyards with wild abandon.

Scientific American reported in February 1876 that one M.
Dumas had discovered that a compound of sulpho-carbonates
was a certain remedy for the new disease. Others came forward
with blends of chemicals, but like Dumas' concoction, none
proved to be effective. By the late 1870s American envoys were
reporting that the French had generally accepted that American
vines were resistant to the phylloxera. Eastern America, where
the vine and the dreaded insect lived in harmony, was pinpointed as the source of the disease.

American vines were tougher than their European counterparts and seemed to secrete a substance which surrounded and
isolated the phylloxera. The solution seemed to be obvious,
although by no means universally accepted: graft the fine noble
grapes of France, Germany and Italy onto American rootstock.
In reporting on the failure of the grape crop in Germany, the *San
Francisco Chronicle* editorialized:

> The important bearing of these circumstances upon the wel-
> fare of California is obvious. Here the vintage is plentiful, the
> wines are always good and pure, the future is full of promise.
> Already the consumption of California wines in the East and
> Europe has reached respectable proportions.
> California has every right to become the leading wine-pro-
> ducing country of the world. Let our fashionable and wealthy
> families set the example of using none but native wines.[3]

The *San Francisco Post* castigated the wealthy local investor
for not putting his money into grapes, particularly in the Napa
Valley: "Now that the destruction of the French vineyards is a
fixed fact . . . The eyes of the world will be turned to our valleys
in tremulous hope and anticipation of good wine."[4]

Still, within a year or two other concerns arose. In January
1882 Arpad Haraszthy, president of the Board of Viticultural
Commissioners, issued a warning that vine planting was moving

Many of the early photographs in this book were taken by
Harvey J. Lewelling, who took hundreds of pictures of Napa
Valley between 1885 and 1920. His pioneering work in pho-
tography was carefully preserved by his descendants.

ahead much too rapidly. Reports reaching him suggested that
"200,000,000" grapevines (surely a typographical error — the
actual number was probably 20,000,000 grapevines — 1000
vines to an acre, 20,000 acres) were readied for planting
statewide. He warned that the high prices paid for grapes in
recent years could not continue.[5]

But not everyone agreed with Haraszthy. The *Healdsburg Enterprise* hinted that "Possibly Mr. Haraszthy looks upon the matter from a dealer's standpoint, and thus his fears of over-production of wine and low prices for grapes are groundless."[6]

Others were optimistic as well, as shown in this article published in the *New York Grocer*:

> The barriers of prejudice against California wines and brandies seem broken down at last in the Atlantic States, and not only have prices appreciated here, but the demand is greater than the local dealers can supply . . . The future for California winemakers and distillers seems to be a bright and lasting one.[7]

In Napa Valley, the area stretching from Yountville to St. Helena, known as the "St. Helena district," contained by far the most vines, nearly 7,000 acres. Napa City and the surrounding area had 3,300 acres, the upper valley around Calistoga, 1,100 acres of vines. A fairly thorough canvassing of the production of wine for 1880 for Napa County, arrived at a figure of 2,857,000 gallons. There were 52 wineries in the county as this new decade opened, a number which would quickly rise. Only nine of these wine cellars could handle over 100,000 gallons.

The Board of State Viticultural Commissioners had been created in the spring of 1880 by the California state legislature, in recognition of the fact that viticulture was becoming a major industry and required its own governing board. The recently-discovered phylloxera vine disease in California certainly helped to justify the Board's formation. How the phylloxera traveled to California is uncertain. Eastern grapes such as the Catawba were here by the 1860s; perhaps the pest came with those grapes. More than likely, though, it came on imported bench-grafted French vines. Krug and other winemakers knew some systematic approach would soon be needed to combat the vine louse, and that state authority was essential to force growers to follow the decisions of the Board regarding eradication of the pest.

Arpad Haraszthy, named the first president of the board, declared in his report at the end of his first year:

One of the most important labors accomplished by the Board has been the discovery of the phylloxera in Napa, Solano, Yolo, El Dorado and Placer [counties], whereas, before the board began its labors, this fatal pest to the vine was considered to have existed only in the County of Sonoma.[8]

Haraszthy's disclosure must have upset many Napa grape growers and land speculators, who had been hoping the disease might not invade the valley, but would confine itself to the neighboring valley to the west, Sonoma, where it was first discovered. Three years earlier the *Star* had carried an angry denial of any phylloxera in Napa County after the *San Francisco Chronicle* made such a claim.[9] But the phylloxera did attack Napa Valley grapes, probably as early as 1880.

Despite what Arpad Haraszthy said, no one in Napa was really alarmed about the root louse. Even if it were present in a few isolated pockets, it had progressed very slowly in Sonoma Valley, taking fifteen years to infect widely scattered vineyards. Surely a cure would be found before it could do any real damage in Napa.

There was clear evidence of that optimism: "The land boom still continues, and property is changing hands" wrote the Rutherford correspondent to the *Star* in January 1881. O.S. Sargent had just purchased fifty acres from the Ross family east of town, and twenty acres were being planted to grapes. The Harris ranch had just sold, and 75 acres were being set aside for grapes. Precisely one year later, the weekly newspaper listed 597 property transactions that had occurred in Napa County in the previous twelve months.

Charles Wetmore, the chief executive officer of the Board of Viticultural Commissioners, said in 1884 that the value of a vineyard depended on access to a railroad, a town with a labor supply and one's neighbors. "For instance, to be a neighbor of Mr. Krug of St. Helena, or such men elsewhere in the vine growing communities, would add at least $100 to the value of land."[10]

Wetmore's kind remarks about Krug would not have escaped the notice of San Francisco investors. Alaska fur dealer Gustave Niebaum had already made up his mind to spend a portion of his

fortune on vines and a new winery in the valley, but Wetmore's statements were the kind of assurance he needed to go forward vigorously.

Niebaum was unknown to most local residents when the *Star* published this brief item in late November 1880:

> A big land sale has been made at Rutherford, the particulars of which we are not accurately informed of; but understand that a member of the Alaska Commercial Company has bought Mrs. Ruhlwig's farm and the Nook Farm property of Judge Hastings for $48,000.

Niebaum's name was linked to the sale in subsequent issues, and the newspaper let it be known he was a millionaire. He quickly became the "man of the hour," someone of substance who would attract other wealthy San Franciscans to Napa Valley. Niebaum would later build one of the best reputations for quality wine in California.

Niebaum (spelled Nybom in his native Finland) was born in Helsinki on August 30, 1842. His father was an official with the local police and earned a sufficient income to educate his son well, although this did not include attendance at a university. Language study may have been a required part of the curriculum at the Finland Nautical Institute, where Niebaum earned his master's papers and the right to command a cargo vessel. Niebaum claimed to speak five languages fluently: Russian, German, French, English and his own, Finnish.

By the age of nineteen he was on the high seas, headed toward Alaska's waterways. His ship traded in furs, especially the seal, so highly prized in Europe. After Alaska was sold to the United States in 1867, Niebaum sailed to San Francisco, looking for an opportunity to link his experience with a new American commercial enterprise.

There were three men in San Francisco just waiting for a man with Neibaum's background: Louis Sloss, Lewis Gerstle and John F. Miller. They had formed the Alaska Commercial Company. In January 1868 Niebaum joined the company and played a vital role in the its growing domination of both the fur and fishing industry in Alaska. Niebaum saw little of San Francisco for the next decade: he was in charge of Alaskan operations and was the chief fur salesman. He made trips to Europe to sell furs, especially to London and St. Petersburg. His proficiency in Russian and French was indispensable. The company prospered and so did Niebaum, far beyond what he had ever imagined.

By the late 1870s, Niebaum's counsel was needed at the San Francisco headquarters of his company. Niebaum was happy for the change: his travels had taken him away far too often from his wife. In 1873, at the age of thirty-one, Niebaum had married Louise Shingleberger, a next-door neighbor of the Sloss and Gerstle families, who had played Cupid for the sea captain.

Though Niebaum's youth was spent in modest surroundings, he did not let that influence him when he began building his Napa Valley estate. Perhaps he had acquired a strong competitive instinct in his personal as well as in his business life and wanted a showcase in the valley to match the grand San Francisco homes of his business partners. Niebaum hired a large workforce to plant new vineyards, construct barns, houses, waterways: projects were so numerous that local newspaper reporters could not keep up with all the changes.

The name "Inglenook" had been applied to the ranch for some years before Neibaum arrived. W.C. Watson planted vines there as early as 1871, and it was he who named the ranch. In 1878, lithographs of Watson's "Inglenook" were published in *Illustrations of Napa County*.[11] Judge Clinton Hastings called his small Rutherford vineyard "Nook Farm." In later years, the founding date of the Inglenook Winery would be debated. Advertisements in the *Merchant* in the 1880s always read: "Inglenook Vineyard — Established 1880." But the *Star* verifies winemaking at Nook Farm in 1879 — 76,000 gallons made by Charles Krug and E.B. Smith.

Gustave and Louise Niebaum may have spent their first Christmas in the Napa Valley in 1880, for the year had not ended before he was overseeing the clearing of sixty acres for

S. CLINTON HASTINGS

vineyard. In the first week of the following February, Sauvignon cuttings (probably Sauvignon Blanc) arrived from San Jose. Within weeks a new distillery was under construction, and then a stable for his horses.

Judge Hasting's modest wine cellar, which Niebaum also purchased, was next dismantled and a new winery constructed of the old materials, increasing it to 55 x 120 feet.[12] Cooperage for 100,000 gallons was installed. The *Star* soon carried an item stating another wooden cellar of the same size would be built right beside the first. Clearly, Niebaum was not concerned about the growing anti-Chinese movement, for the same newspaper recorded that seventeen white men and eight Chinese were doing his construction work.[13] In early November, 1881, the *Star* reported Niebaum's first crush, barely 6,000 gallons.

Niebaum brought some innovations to his crushing procedures which may have seemed a little peculiar to his neighbors. In his '82 crush, he hired men to stand alongside a conveyer belt carrying grapes inside the winery, and snatch away any grapes that appeared unripe. They also removed leaves, stems, etc. "This is something of an experiment as yet, but it seems reasonable that the quality of the wine should be improved by it, and we hope that Mr. Niebaum may so find his very commendable care rewarded" observed the St. Helena newspaper.

> Besides these points, the proprietor is paying particular attention to grape varieties — not only those which are esteemed the best here, but which most nearly answer the demands of consumers and will thus make the wines of Napa Valley acceptable to those before whom they must come for a market. It is gratifying to thus see not only money but brains put into the business.[14]

The following summer Niebaum invited his ranch foreman, Hamden W. McIntyre, to discuss over lunch the new winery he wanted at Inglenook. This was to be no ordinary winery, no wine cellar of long wooden sheds. Rather, Niebaum had in mind a castle (or two) he had seen along the Rhine river in Germany: he wanted the same thing for Napa Valley. McIntyre was to draw up the general plans, incorporating a number of innovations. Why McIntyre? Because there were no winery architects. Also, he trusted and liked McIntyre, who had a knowledge of drafting. He could draw up plans following Niebaum's directions and offer valuable advice.

McIntyre was born in Vermont in 1834 and was trained in civil engineering and mechanical drafting. He and Niebaum had met more than a dozen years earlier, when McIntyre went to work for the Alaska Commercial Company on St. Paul's Island, Alaska. Niebaum convinced McIntyre to move to Napa Valley.

The new winery would boast a singular innovation: there were to be distinct compartments within the winery for the storage of each variety of wine. Most wine cellars had one large room with puncheons filled with Zinfandel stored right beside a white variety like the Burger. Most wineries, which were no more than ten to twenty thousand gallons in size, often blended everything into just two wine types – red and white. The average wine consumer *démi Johns*

Europe

purchased wine in bulk for home consumption and in pitchers of red or white in restaurants.

Niebaum planned to bottle all of his wine, which was unheard of, partially because it was terribly expensive. He would offer the varieties pretty much standard in England at that time: Claret, Burgundy, Sauterne, Chablis, etc. The wine stored in the new Inglenook wine vaults would rest in twenty one-thousand gallon "ovals," or ten five-hundred gallon barrels. There would be four wine vaults in the first portion of the new winery, in a building approximately 70 x 40 feet with a flat roof. A second story would be added later.

Work on the first building was begun in June 1883 and was completed in time for the fall crush. Niebaum did not see much of the vintage; he was taken ill in September at Lake Tahoe with what was described as "congestive lungs." Nothing more was done to this modern portion of Inglenook for nearly two years. Niebaum's health may have been part of the reason, but he also left in early 1884 on a long trip to Europe. While in St. Petersburg selling furs, especially fur hats, he was made a vice president of the Alaska Commercial Company.

In July 1885 workmen began excavation for the foundation for a second portion of Inglenook. They had to excavate down to hardpan, a solid rock-like layer, and here McIntyre and his laborers found a surprise: hardpan under the winery ran at least twelve feet deep below the surface when it could be found. For this and other reasons, construction was halted.

A neighbor at Rutherford had heard of McIntyre's talents and asked him to design a winery. It would be more modest, 100 x 126 feet, two stories, and built of stone taken from Howell Mountain. The building eventually became the center of Ewer Vineyards.

One morning McIntyre was invited to meet railroad magnate Leland Stanford on Stanford's special railroad car which had been parked at a rail siding at Rutherford. Stanford and Niebaum were friends and would have frequented the same clubs. Niebaum may have arranged the meeting between his friend and

The historic Inglenook winery was built in stages. The ground
floor south wing, at left, was finished in 1883; two years later a
matching north wing was built. Then the second floors were

added, and finally the central tower. The whole building (shown here in its modern state) was finished in 1887. Today it is owned by Francis Ford Coppola.

the engineer over drinks with Stanford in San Francisco. Stanford wanted a winery design for his new Vina vineyards site in Tehama County. It would be built of brick and wood, a massive structure stretching 300 feet by 60 feet.

It is possible there was another guest at that meeting between Stanford and McIntyre, a wealthy San Franciscan named John Benson. He owned a large producing vineyard at Oakville and needed a modest three-story winery, too. Benson had made wine on a modest scale at his country ranch, but now wanted something more imposing for a small hillock a mile north of his home. Everyone would be able to see it while passing on the main valley road. McIntyre drew up plans for an all-stone cellar with conspicuous cupolas on the roof, almost a scaled down version of Niebaum's concept. McIntyre stayed up nights thereafter drawing plans for wineries all over northern California. There was no one with his expertise in the state; indeed he seems to have become the first winery architect in the entire country.

By the spring of 1886 Niebaum was ready to resume construction on his own magnificent plan. A trained San Francisco architect named William Mooser came up to offer his assistance; this suggests some serious problems again had been encountered. Certainly the grand central core of the winery designed by McIntyre had to have very solid footing, or the vast weight of three stories of stone rising to 90 feet, with tower, might sink into the earth.

The arched ceilings in the ground floor wine vaults also may have caused some of the delay. The ceiling was to be composed entirely of concrete, a type of construction so new that much experimentation was required. Iron pillars were needed for additional support. The cement itself was in the process of development and not always available.

By that fall, Inglenook, which had begun to take shape three years earlier, consisted of a three-story central core and a one-story southern wing. It would take another full year to finish the grand structure. The formal sampling room, which set Inglenook apart from every other winery in the state, was probably not finished before 1890. The *San Francisco Merchant and Viticulturist* offered this description in a January issue:

> The sampling room, on the right as the building is entered, undoubtedly represents a small fortune in its cost. The walls and every piece of furniture are of solid oak — the chairs, tables, side-boards all being made to order in Germany. The walls are adorned with costly pictures and plaques of bronze and porcelain. Near the ceiling, shelves project from the wall and these are lined with unique vari-colored bottles, glasses, vases and ewers, held in place by a railing.

There really was nothing like this room anywhere in the wine industry in California. Niebaum intended to entertain in the grand style, to impress his visitors and perhaps the press. With Inglenook, Napa Valley winemaking advanced a giant step toward producing and marketing the highest quality wine.

Two people who are rarely given credit for playing an important part in the creation of Niebaum's winery are his wife, Louise, and Ferdinand Haber. Niebaum was a sea-faring man before he moved to Napa, and even as a corporate leader he probably would not have taken the time to collect the artifacts and bric-a-brac that adorned his new winery. Louise Niebaum undoubtedly deserves credit for the beauty of the winery interiors, including the painted frescoes on the tasting room ceiling.

But if Niebaum knew little about interior decorating, he knew nothing about the promotion of wine. The genius behind the wine image Inglenook was fast acquiring belonged to Ferdinand Haber. Haber worked for Alfred Greenbaum & Company, a San Francisco company which distributed Inglenook wine. His knowledge of wine advertising put Inglenook into private clubs on the east coast and obtained plenty of press.

San Francisco news journals were already reporting on the growing interest in Napa Valley wine before Niebaum arrived. A woman journalist — there were few at the time — was one of the first to describe the burgeoning wine industry. Her name was

Sallie R. Heath, and she worked for the *Californian*. Heath became interested in the unjust treatment of valley Indians, most of whom had been driven out by white settlers. This was a subject to which few writers paid attention. The *Californian* of September 1880 carried a story in which Heath described six different tribes and their locations. The story also talked about wine:

> Let us turn to the interest at present paramount — grape cul-
> ture. This is a subject of more than passing interest to the
> world at large, for the day is not distant when California will
> claim her right to stand upon equal footing with the European
> wine States. She will undoubtedly rival, in maturity, those
> with whom she now, in infancy, competes.

Heath points out that some of the Napa wine cellars were of considerable architectural beauty, especially those constructed of stone. These cellars were beginning to attract tourists, especially young men on spirited horses, who sometimes tried to visit all forty in one weekend.

The wine industry received additional national attention through a story published in Frank Leslie's widely read *Illustrated Newspaper of New York*, in the Christmas issue, 1880. The story "Our National Industries: The Vineyards of Sonoma Valley, California" placed Napa in second place, but the opening para-graph was highly complimentary:

> General as has become the use of California wines, not only
> in this country, but in England, France, China, Japan,
> Australia and the Sandwich Islands [Hawaii], to which places
> regular consignments are now shipped, it is believed that the
> industry of viniculture has not yet passed out of the experi-
> mental stage. The gifts of nature are so vast in that section of
> our country, and the energy of man so tireless, that the possi-
> bilities of the future are scarcely comprehended.

The following spring, the San Francisco *Chronicle* editorial-ized that the Napa Valley would soon be one big vineyard. Tourists publications such as *California and the West* were going out of their way to include descriptions of the valley. When the

History of Napa and Lake Counties was published in 1881, readers were astonished to find that the history of a rural county could fill six hundred pages. But the chapter on viticulture and wine-making required almost fifty pages alone, and biographies of leading wine men took several times that number. Charles Gardner, editor of the *Star*, no doubt wrote the viticulture history for the book.

Many ensuing publications about Napa Valley liberally copied from the book, often without acknowledging the source. The county itself did some of that in *Resources of Napa County*, which devoted much space, including the first photographs, to Inglenook. F.L. Jackson borrowed statistics for his *Napa County and Its Many Great Resources*, as did K.F. Kettewell for the *Napa County Land Registers*. A San Francisco publication called *Resources of California* borrowed liberally from all these sources for its frequent stories on Napa Valley in the 1880s. George Husmann, who had recently settled in the Napa Valley at the Simonton "Talcoa Ranch" in the Carneros, hurriedly put together a new edition of his book, *American Grape Growing and Wine Making*. H.W. Crabb of Oakville contributed the chapter on Napa Valley. Crabb didn't manage to capture the excitement of the industry with his writing style, but it was important to Napa grape growers and winery owners to be included in what was then the most popular viticulture book available in the country. The new edition, incidentally, was inscribed: "Talcoa Vineyards, Napa, Cal.; Nov. 9, 1883." It would soon be a collector's item.

The effect of all this publicity on the valley can be measured by the industry's growth. At the beginning of the decade, there were 49 wineries. By 1886, there were 175. Charles Gardner announced in his newspapers that he would no longer be able to survey each winery for the annual crush: the list was just too long. Wine production increased greatly in the same span of six years, from 2,910,700 gallons to 4,800,000. And somewhere

Julius Fulscher built this winery in Calistoga in the late 1870s, but Louis Kortum acquired the cellar in 1880 and made rather famous wines thereafter. As late as 1884 Kortum was still the only winemaker in Calistoga, despite Samuel Brannan's efforts to promote the town.

around 1884, Napa Valley took over as the leading producer of dry wines in California.

Many of the new wine cellars were being built by long-time residents such as Chris Adamson, whose vineyard had been planted almost a decade before the wine business really took off. Built in 1880, his Rutherford cellar could hold a half million gallons.

It seemed that nearly everyone built new homes with basements that could be used as wine cellars. Frank Sciaroni built a two-story home in St. Helena, 30 x 35 feet, over the stone base-ment which was his first winery. Frank Kraft did the same thing, crushing and fermenting outside and storing 8,000 gallons below the house. A gentleman named Croft followed suit, but the Baretta brothers were satisfied with a small 46 x 26-foot wooden cellar near the John York ranch north of town.

In Calistoga a relative newcomer named Louis Kortum kept the town's wine tradition alive by reviving its only winery, built by Julius Fulscher. Kortum soon acquired a significant reputation for high quality wine.

Two miles east of Oakville, at his Mt. Eden ranch just taking shape, George S. Meyers of Oakland completed his winery in 1883. His premier crush was at first listed in local newspapers as 2,500 gallons, corrected the following week to 22,500 gallons.

About the same time, Henry Hagen caught a ferryboat from San Francisco and moved to Napa Valley. He gave up his posi-tion with the state's oldest wine firm, Kohler and Frohling, and bought the ranch and winery known affectionately as "Bill Woodward's Whiskey Ranch." The ranch sat in the hills north-east of Napa and included a long winding entrance lined with cedar trees. Hagen promptly renamed it "Cedar Knolls Vineyards." He would make that wine brand famous by the end of the decade.

Alton L. Williams left his position with the railroad in Vallejo and followed Gustave Niebaum to Rutherford. He named his new place "Inglewood" and never explained the similarity of that name to Niebaum's Inglenook. His cellar was only 14 x 60 feet, but his Victorian house rivaled Niebaum's mansion. Probably he was interested in gracious living, with wine as a hobby. (Williams' Inglewood winery has long since been dismantled, but the house was faithfully restored by new owners William and Lilia Jaeger in 1965.)

In 1886, brothers James and George Goodman, of a pioneer Napa banking family, founded the Eshcol winery with an assist from architect Hamden W. McIntyre. The brothers had settled in the valley in the mid-1850s, turning to banking for their

HENRY HAGEN

livelihood. George also served as county treasurer for several years. The stability of the bank may have had something to do with that county job, since county funds were deposited in the Goodman's bank. George's main interest was in viticulture and winemaking, while James spent more and more of his time in San Francisco tending to investments. George was also a member of the Napa County Immigration Association which helped attract new settlers with publications like *Napa County and Its Many and Great Resources*.

The name given the property, "Eshcol," pronounced "Esh-ol," was a mighty peculiar choice. It had been suggested by a family friend, Napa Judge Henry C. Gesford. The word is Hebrew and is translated "valley of the grape." But neither the Goodmans nor Gesford were of the Jewish faith.

Anyone passing under the large wooden entrance sign of Eshcol would have marveled at the symmetry of the various vine plots. Each variety was laid out in long narrow blocks of 1,160 vines each and separated by avenues sixteen feet wide. At the corner of each block, white posts were driven into the ground with the name of each variety of grape. Eshcol almost looked more like a huge nursery than a vineyard.

The winery was built entirely of wood, a departure from most of the others that McIntyre designed. It was also one of McIntyre's most innovative buildings. He constructed it like an ice house, utilizing every technique to keep the interior cool no matter what the outside temperature. Some of his ideas were absolutely revolutionary.

In July, 1886, the Goodmans accepted the bid of J.L. Robinson to build a cellar 125 feet x 60 feet. He was to receive $1,500 for his efforts, all lumber supplied by the Goodmans. The winery was to be three stories in height in the central portion, with two wings. It bore a slight resemblance to Inglenook. Even the cupolas on the roof matched what McIntyre had drawn for Niebaum.

"The building will be constructed of wood and heavy tar paper, the latter being used for lining and diaphragm between the studding, to form dead air compartments in the walls, to insure a suitable and even temperature. Thorough ventilation and drainage is secured. Capacity of the winery, about 175,000 gallons," claimed the *Napa Register* of July 16.

McIntyre was attempting something quite new to the wine industry: he hoped sufficient insulation would be created between the double-sided, heavy-timbered walls, and, with the help of dead air space, control the temperature inside the winery. The timbers used for the framing were so heavy a small railroad engine could have traveled over the second-story flooring with no visible sagging. "The best features of the other cellars have been incorporated into it," noted the *Register*. The building was entirely successful. Although the winery suffered through many years of fitful operations by different owners, in 1968 the Trefethen family, including son John and his wife Janet, restored the cellar to its former grandeur.

A year before McIntyre began work on Eshcol, he was creating plans for the Ewer winery at Rutherford, and a few miles to the south at Oakville, demonstrating to John Benson what he could do for his Far Niente winery. The actual construction of Far Niente began in March 1885, according to the *Register*. Morris Estee's new stone cellar, Hedgeside, began in April. Stonemasons at the Ewer vineyard began in May. McIntyre was definitely busy. It seems he put more of his original ideas into Far Niente than into the others. The new winery roof design had to be McIntyre's single most important contribution; the problem of dripping winery ceilings may have been his inspiration.

For some time, insurance companies had required metal roofs whenever possible. Most often, corrugated iron was used. On wineries, a light wooden understructure was built, with large sheets of corrugated iron laid on top. In fall and winter, moisture condensed on the underside of the roof and dripped on everything below. In summer, the heat penetrated to make the rooms below uncomfortably hot.

McIntyre pondered the situation carefully and came up with an easy solution:

> To avoid this, it occurs to me that change might be made without any material addition to the cost. It has been customary heretofore in the use of iron plates, to place the rafters quite a distance apart, say eight feet and across these to lay horizontally purlins [wood cross beams], on which the iron should be laid — the purlins to be set three feet six inches or three feet four inches between the centers, or nearer if required.
>
> Abandoning this construction, I laid a roof with timbers, as for shingles, with about two feet and half to three foot between centers of the rafters, and then covered with boards, laying them close together, edge to edge, and on this covering laid the corrugated iron. I laid the iron the full width of the sheet. . .
>
> To my great delight, not altogether surprise, I found that this obviated the difficulties named. Since the roof has been constructed, there has been no condensation or moisture shown.[15]

McIntyre made these remarks at the sixth annual Viticultural Convention in San Francisco in March 1888. He also pointed out that the space created between the solid wooden underlining and the iron provided for the free and rapid movement of air from the edge of the roof upwards (hot air rises), and this kept the iron from sweating. The solution was so comparatively simple that it is a wonder no one had thought of this before.

McIntyre argued successfully at the convention for the concept of building multi-storied wine cellars. He appears to have been the first to use concrete in the construction of the floor of the winery. Previously, it had been common to leave that floor dirt. McIntyre incorporated all these concepts into the building of the Far Niente winery at Oakville.

All crushing was carried out on the top floor of the winery. The movement of a large volume of wine within the winery was a serious problem made simple by allowing gravity to do its job.

There was another aspect of winery design which had been taken for granted. Whenever possible, a winery was located abutting a hillside. A large hole was excavated into the hillside for the first floor and the second and third stories sat firmly against the hill. A road was built from the valley floor along the hillside to the top floor for direct access to the crushing equipment. Sometimes, artificial hills were created where natural ones did not exist.

John Benson, who hired McIntyre to design his new winery, was a wealthy San Franciscan who invested lavishly in the Napa Valley but never called it home. Benson was born in 1824 in Boston. By April 1, 1849, he was in California. He never admitted to having found gold in the Sierras, but on his return to San Francisco from the mines he immediately began buying and selling city lots. He seems to have made his first small fortune fairly soon. City directories often listed him as a broker of real estate, or, as many wealthy men then preferred to be called, "capitalist."

When the transcontinental railroad was completed in 1869, Benson took long trips to New York and occasionally sailed to

Europe for the summer. His personal fortune accumulated sufficiently by 1871 to allow him to invest in 306 acres of George Yount's Mexican land grant, Rancho Caymus. He set forty acres to the Muscat of Alexandria grape, primarily a raisin grape. (Most grapes grown at that time were used for several different purposes.)

Benson's country home and ranch was about one and a half miles south of the knoll where he would build his winery. He had a small wooden winery in place near his home by 1881 or '82, but he did not call it Far Niente. The 60 x 100 foot winery of native stone was to be built by San Francisco stonemasons Ranson and Hill. Only a small portion was completed when a dispute erupted between the stonemasons and Benson. Benson fired both men but was still able to produce 20,000 gallons of wine during the next crush.

St. Helenans J. Delucchi and Mixon and Son were given the job of completing the winery the following spring, with the central portion being raised to three stories. Capacity would now be 175,000 gallons. The total cost was $8,000. Three years later a local newspaper reported: "He does not sell in quantities but bottles and disposes of [his wine] to clubs. Makes wine only of the first quality."[16]

If anyone asked Thomas Williams, the foreman for the ranch and winery, what the formal name meant, "In Dolce Far Niente," he would have been hard pressed to answer. It was an Italian phrase which had become popular with English poets like Lord Byron, who vacationed frequently in Italy, and even with America's premier poet, Henry Wadsworth Longfellow. The latter poet once wrote to a friend:

> Your letter was just what I wanted. That is, it was a letter which gave me a graphic picture of yourself and your situation. I could see you at your study window, enjoying Narragansett and Mount Hope a delightful (certainly a very faint) reminiscence of Naples and Vesuvius. It is there Tasso and Ariosto sound sweetest to the ear, that the *dolce far niente* of a summer evening is most heavenly.[17]

Ah, John Benson, the wily old capitalist, must have been a dreamer at heart, for the English translation of this phrase means "sweet doing nothing" or simply "sweet nothing."

CHINESE LABOR

With over one hundred new wineries and 12,000 acres of grapes planted in Napa in just the first three years of the 1880s, a very serious labor shortage was created. The Chinese were the most dependable workers and easily available overnight from San Francisco or St. Helena agents. But growing numbers of vintners feared the consequences of hiring these laborers.

Still, it took four years before the anti-Chinese forces in St. Helena organized to remove the local Chinatown. The *Star* covered the event:

> Four o'clock Tuesday was signalized by the tooting of whistles and ringing of bells, and a large crowd soon congregated at the Town Hall. W. T. Simmons took charge of the company and formed them in line. He told them before starting that the demonstration was expected to be quiet and orderly, and that one man should do the talking. If anyone could not submit to this he had better stay behind.
>
> The company then marched to Chinatown to the sound of the drum, beaten by W.D. Ayers. Arriving there, not a Chinaman was to be seen; the doors to their shanties closed and bolted, shutters were up at the windows and the town seemed deserted.

St. Helena's Chinatown was just across the first stone bridge heading south.

Police officers Allison, Spurr and Fee had arrived before the marchers and stood their ground on the warm day in February 1886. Several Chinese shop owners were finally induced to come out and listen to the complaints. Then everyone retreated into the gathering twilight, perhaps because the man who owned most of the shanties was John Gillam, who would not stand still for any outrageous behavior.

Gillam explained in a long letter to the local newspaper that the first Chinese in St. Helena arrived about 1868 when the railroad was under construction. Housing was needed and Gillam supplied it, supposedly on a temporary basis. At that time St. Helena residents had found the Chinese interesting and enjoyed watching them work; they also hired them to undertake all sorts of tasks. If the community now wanted the Chinese to leave Gillam said he was willing to ask them to do so if someone would buy his houses or replace the expected loss of revenue. He had no takers.

In March 1889 Edward Roberts wrote an article published in *Harper's Weekly*, estimating that California employed 30,000 to 40,000 men in the production of wine. He mentioned the use of Chinese laborers in the vineyards:

> Grape varieties in California, with the exception of a few foreign varieties, are pruned very low, the stem being only about a foot and a half high . . . Gathering the grapes is laborious work, the picker being obliged either literally to kneel or to bend his back to a painful angle . . . Chinamen are generally employed as pickers.

Napa Valley residents did not really object to differences in skin color or religion, but they didn't like the fact that so many 'foreigners' were coming into the county. When a train arrived at Rutherford or St. Helena and a hundred or so Chinese disembarked amid considerable noise and confusion, they were whisked away quickly to nearby vineyards by their labor contractor. But the intrusion on local culture was inescapable.

VIOLENCE IN THE VALLEY

For many Napa residents, the booming 1880s was not to their liking for other reasons. With more than 14,000 residents, and dozens of new arrivals each day, the serenity of the Napa Valley was seriously threatened. And it was not just the Chinese who were unwelcome. Other laborers found the locals hostile and uncaring. When young white males traveled to the vineyards for field work, they demanded roofs over their heads at night and prepared meals. What they found instead were often flea-infested barns or haystacks and marginal food.

But there were other, much more serious conflicts. One was the murder of winemaker John C. Weinberger. No man had been more active in the local wine industry than Weinberger. He was the first to state publicly that he believed the phylloxera had invaded Napa Valley and was in his vineyards. He imported equipment to make grape syrup when there was an excess of wine. His winery was one of the most attractive in the valley.

Weinberger was shot three times at the Barro (Lodi) train station in March 1882 by a 29-year-old former employee named William Gau. Gau hailed from Germany, as did Weinberger. He had fallen in love with Weinberger's daughter, but Weinberger opposed the relationship. Weinberger died within minutes of the shooting, which occurred at noon. The coroner's jury, assembled the following day to bring a verdict on the cause of death, was a list of the Who's Who in Napa Valley: Charles Krug, Jacob Beringer, C.T. McEachran, John Thomann, William Castner, Ed Heyman and others. The jury voted to try Gau for murder, but he committed suicide before he could be brought to trial.

Sometimes high drama visited the small, supposedly quiet winemaking town of St. Helena. As the *Star* editorialized May 12, 1888: "The lynching of an eighteen year old boy by the citizens of St. Helena last Saturday night will forever remain a blot on that town." The deed was carried out under a bridge crossing a creek near the Beringer winery. The youth's name was John Wright.

According to eyewitness testimony given at the coroner's inquest, a local resident named Budd Vann had become intoxicated before deciding to visit a local house of ill repute. He was denied entry at the door by Wright, who was the brother of a woman inside. Vann, whose courage was considerably enhanced by his condition, forced his way inside where he was shot and killed by Wright.

Wright was brought to trial so quickly he did not have time to obtain a lawyer. When he refused to testify and offer an explanation of his impulsive action, Vann's many friends were outraged at Wright's arrogance. They felt their friend's condition should have been taken into consideration and that Wright had acted without just cause. If Wright had explained himself, tempers might have cooled. But as it was, the crowd got out of control and lynched him. No charges were ever brought against anyone for the lynching.

Yet, in general, this was an era of fine living by country gentlemen and their ladies in a lovely pastoral place. The grape and wine boom of the 1880s was mainly responsible for the wealth and comfort of those people. Many local men were earning handsome incomes, building large, expensive homes and spending hours at viticultural meetings. St. Helena grape growers were especially active: no city in the state sent larger contingents to wine conventions or district meetings sponsored by the Board of State Viticultural Commissioners.

This explains why Santa Clara vine grower J. B. Portal told a meeting of his county vine club that St. Helenans were "one of the most unified and best organized associations of this kind on this coast."[18] Santa Clara would do well to pattern itself after their aggressive neighbors to the north, he suggested.

Even residents of the city of Napa realized that St. Helena had something very special going for itself: "Why should St. Helena, an obscure village of the valley, enjoy greater thrift, according to its population, than Napa City, the shire town of the county, the Oxford of the Pacific, the most favorably situated place in California?" asked the *Register*.[19]

As the decade of the 1880s progressed, more and more time was spent arguing about the phylloxera. Everyone held a strong opinion on the subject: that the disease was not going to be serious in Napa Valley; that it could be overcome with good animal fertilizing, mercury treatment, electric shocks, or defeated with a resistant vine.

The Zinfandel grape was also a subject of debate. Everyone grew the grape because it produced so well and earned growers a lot of money. Yet many reputable wine men denounced the Zinfandel. Krug said at a Napa District Viticultural convention in 1883:

> Among the claret grapes we have an abundance of Zinfandel, and we commit a great blunder in planting Zinfandel as we have done. Instead of planting the Zinfandel on the hills, where their proper home is, in warm, loose soil where they make a splendid A No.1 noble wine, we have committed the blunder of planting in rich, adobe soil. I myself confess to have committed that blunder.

But Napa vineyardists paid absolutely no attention to Krug's remarks on the Zinfandel. Four years after his comments, the Annual Report of the State Viticultural Commissioners showed that the Zinfandel far overshadowed every other grape in the valley, even surpassing in acreage many other varieties combined. Nearly 6,000 acres were planted to the Zinfandel.[20]

In June 1885 William Boggs, who was on the Board of Directors of the Sonoma Horticultural Club, published a long letter in the Star describing his early years at Sonoma when Agoston Haraszthy, president of the Club, had been his neighbor. Boggs remembered being told that John Osborne of Oak Knoll ranch, north of Napa City, had cuttings available for a number of unusual grape varieties. He recalled that in 1859:

> Many thousand [vines] were planted from [the cuttings] the same season in the nurseries of the Horticultural garden under my supervision. Among them were the Zinfandel. Prior to that time there were no foreign vines introduced into Sonoma.[21]

Boggs's letter also is noteworthy because he included the "Catawba" grape among those being grown in Sonoma before the American Civil War. Catawba is, of course, a major eastern grape variety which could easily carry on its roots the phylloxera vine louse. Unless only cuttings, which would not have carried the phylloxera, were shipped west, it is possible that the disease could have been imported to California by 1860.

Had there been more French immigrant winemakers in the valley, grapes like the Zinfandel would not have been so popular. San Jose was the center of the French viticultural colony in California, but more French were moving to the Napa Valley. The first French immigrant may have been one L. Roux, who established his "French Restaurant" on Napa's Main Street in 1862. One could eat three solid meals a day, seven days a week, for $6, about thirty cents a serving. French-operated schools were always popular in small towns in California, and Napa had the Paccaud School on old Sonoma Road in the early 1870s. It advertised: "English, French, Music, Board and Washing . . . $30.00."

Henry Pellet, who began making wine in 1859 for John Patchett, was referred to as the first French vintner in Napa Valley, but he was born in Switzerland of French ancestry. Bordeaux native Jean Laurent, who began making wine in 1874 opposite the Weinberger winery, was arguably the second Frenchman to own a cellar in Napa Valley. Laurent was born in 1837 and by age fifteen was panning for gold near Tuolumne in the Sierras. Apparently, he didn't do very well, but he was able to open a small vegetable farming business near Napa a few weeks after the Civil War ended. In the early 1870s he purchased land between Krug and Weinberger.

In 1879 Laurent hired some of his fellow countrymen to help build a two-story stone cellar, 60 x 100 feet. He probably direct-ed the construction himself, for the cellar had none of the dis-tinctive qualities that McIntyre introduced later into valley win-ery design. Still, it was highly functional and could hold 200,000 gallons.[22]

About the time Laurent was scurrying about St. Helena plan-ning his new enterprise, two French brothers named Giaque began modest winemaking two miles south of town. Charles Menefee claimed the brothers had built a winery in 1871. This cellar burned a few months after the crush, and they rebuilt the following year.

The most famous French names in the valley were Jean Brun and Jean Chaix, who after their first wine was made in 1877 were referred to as Brun and Chaix. Jean Chaix was one of the first to advocate planting grapes on Howell Mountain. He liked the intense red volcanic soil and suspected the grape might rise to new heights of perfection when stressed by the hillside gravels and intense sunshine. In early 1880 the first of twenty acres were planted. William Woodward had set a half acre in vines nearly five years earlier, and a neighbor, Higginson, also had an experimental patch of 200 vines, but Chaix's planting was the first commercial vineyard on the mountain. Other growers in Napa County watched the Brun and Chaix vineyard carefully after a severe frost in 1882 left the mountain virtually untouched.

The two Frenchmen had started their winemaking in a tiny 20 x 34-foot wooden winery south and east of Oakville. That August (1877) construction began on a 160 x 34-foot winery next to the town's railroad, making it possible to produce more than one hundred thousand gallons per year. They imported nine grape varieties from the Medoc region of France, preferring not to rely on local rootstocks. No record remains as to the grape varieties, but they could have been Bourdeaux varieties like Cabernet Sauvignon. The brothers would have followed French tradition and blended everything, paying no heed to varietal wines.

Brun and Chaix quickly realized they had a problem communicating between their Howell Mountain vineyards and the Oakville winery. It took too much time to send a horse and rider back and forth, up and down the mountain. They ordered construction of a 50-foot-high water tank with an inside stairway to the roof, which was surrounded by a high railing.

> But the principal point of the item is that their mountain vineyard about 10 miles to the north, on Howell Mountain, is within range of vision, and they first propose to establish a

system of signals which will be seen by the aid of telescopes, to communicate whatever is desirable from cellar to vineyard and the reverse.[23]

To the top of this structure they added a fifteen-foot-high windmill with a twelve-foot wheel which made the entire edifice a prominent feature of the landscape. A well supplied water for a 10,000-gallon tank whenever the wind was strong enough to turn the huge wheel. The fifty-foot signal tower next to the Brun and Chaix Oakville winery caught the imagination of everyone for miles around. Six years later, Brun and Chaix constructed an elaborate three-storied, 60 x 60 stone wine cellar on Howell Mountain.

French immigrant Charles Carpy had arrived in Napa City shortly after the Civil War and worked in the Uncle Sam Cellar. A year after Brun and Chaix founded their winery, he and a French partner, C. Anduran, purchased the Uncle Sam Winery. They quickly expanded it to 146 x 120 feet with a capacity of nearly half a million gallons. Carpy soon became a major figure in the Napa Viticultural Association and involved himself in anything having to do with wine in the valley or San Francisco.

Emil Bressard and Louis Debanne built a small wine cellar at Oakville the year after Brun and Chaix. August Jeanmonod (or Jeanmond) began crushing grapes the same year at Oakville. (St. Helena seemed to attract mostly German immigrants, like Krug and Beringer, while Oakville appealed more to the French.)

R. Chabot completed a stone cellar a decade later near Crystal Springs with the name "Villaremi" cut into the stone. Vincent Courtois made wine in several cellars, including Larkmead, in the 1880s. There was a Franco-Swiss winery in Conn Valley owned by G. Crochat, C. Volpers and Fred Metzner.

Despite their collective years of experience, the French immigrants tended to exert less influence than other nationalities for one reason: few spoke English well enough to converse in technical terms. The typical French immigrant was not interested in dropping his native tongue in favor of English. Some meetings of the Board of Viticultural Commissioners and wine conventions were conducted in French during the mid 1880s; in May 1885 a wine meeting in San Jose held an evening session in French.

QUESTIONS OF DENSITY AND HEIGHT

In France, where the soil had nurtured grapes for centuries, it was common to plant as many as 2,000 vines to the acre. But in California the common spacing was no more than half that amount, and often considerably less. Henry Crabb, in his chapter on viticulture in Husmann's book *American Grape Growing*, advocated 1,000 vines to the acre. Krug wrote in 1884 that the "most common system of planting adopted in California is that of squares with the vines planted at seven feet apart."[24] This plan would result in 889 vines to the acre. In 1876, the *Star* reported that 666 vines were planted to the acre.

When the St. Helena Vinicultural club put aside the subject of vine spacing they took up the questions of best height for the vine trunk and whether or not to stake. Agoston Haraszthy liked to keep his vines close to the ground. The daily *Alta California* reported on October 1, 1859: "Col. Haraszthy does not train his vine in a strong trunk three feet high, as was the old Spanish custom, but he cuts off the stock about ten inches from the ground."

Husmann's *American Grape Growing* confirmed that this was still the case in the 1880s. Gustaf Eisen wrote that in the Fresno area: "The trunk of our vines is generally kept to 2 feet," and Julius Dresel of Sonoma added in the same book, "the vine stem is commonly 18 inches to 2 feet high."

Charles Krug changed all this. In July 1886 Krug discussed his practice of training vines to grow higher along wire supports strung through the vineyard. He claimed he got longer canes from vines whose trunks were trained to a "head" about waist high. With the vines higher off the ground in spring, frost damage was reduced. In the summer heat, the grapes suffered if too close to the hot ground. (In Haraszthy's native Hungary, cold fall weather required vines be trained close to the ground in order to ripen.)

Krug was one of the first in the valley to purchase a new machine built by John L. Heald. Heald's steam-powered crushers, built in Vallejo, could empty lugs of grapes directly into one end, then move the grapes into the crusher on a conveyor device. The Beringers ordered one, Henry Crabb purchased two, and Isaac DeTurck in Santa Rosa purchased one. Heald was in business.

ADULTERERS AND FRAUDS

Napa winemakers were concerned about the practice of diluting or adulterating California wines, particularly on the east coast. They also did not like the fact that some California wines ended up being sold under foreign labels. After a wine-selling trip to the east in the fall of 1888, Gottlieb Groezinger angrily announced that it was "next to impossible to obtain a good glass of [California] wine anywhere in the East."

Jacob Schram had earlier told the *Napa Register* the same thing after an eastern trip in 1886. He had discovered that most California wine being sold in New York, St. Louis or Boston, was sold with a foreign label: "Competition compels us to sell California wines under foreign labels," claimed eastern dealers, for they felt the consumer was not educated as yet to drinking wine from America's west coast.

The *New York Post* actually broke this news in the spring of 1883: "The trade journals are again directing attention to the fact that a large portion of wine sold in this country as foreign wine [French] is produced in California and sold in bottles labeled with imitation foreign labels."[25]

California wine could be purchased at a far lower cost than French and then retailed at a higher price with a bogus French label. Unfortunately, many bottlers also "cut" their wine by adding fruit juice. The *Post* reported that blame was not entirely to be placed outside California:

> Even in San Francisco, where some local pride might be expected to help the sale of native wines, they are bottled and sold largely with French labels, some being imitations of labels

of celebrated houses, and others being more innocent of deception because they do not steal trademarks.

Newspaper publicity such as this encouraged the California Legislature to pass the Pure Wine Law in the spring of 1887. The law declared in Section 2: "In the fermentation, preservation, and fortification of pure wine, it shall be specifically understood that no materials shall be used intended for substitutes for grapes, or any part of grapes; no coloring matter shall be added which are not the pure product of grapes."

This was the first time in California, and probably in the United States, that a law had been enacted which guaranteed the purity of wine. Wine and, indeed, most alcoholic beverages had been tampered with since colonial times.

Not everyone was pleased with the new law, as it seemed to put the burden of proof of purity on the winemaker, not the dealer. There was really only one solution, and it would be costly: all wine would have to be bottled at the winery. Wine bottles were hand blown, and far too expensive for general use. Most wine was sold directly from barrels in stores, saloons or hotel cellars: customers brought their own containers.

Gustave Niebaum was one of the first to circumvent wine adulteration by bottling all of his wine at his winery. He could afford the cost of glass bottles and believed his customers could pay the higher cost as well. The *Star* of August 31, 1888, claimed Niebaum allowed "no wine to leave his cellar under two years old, and then only in bottles." But even Niebaum was forced to abandon bottling eventually. The cost was too high. That would change shortly.

Bottling costs, foreign labels, the phylloxera or even frequent spring frosts could not deter the continued investment in Napa Valley vineyards by wealthy San Franciscans. When Morris M. Estee purchased land north and east of Napa City and announced plans to build a large winery, designed by none other than Hamden W. McIntyre, the entire valley rejoiced. He was the most prominent Californian to recognize the valley's wine future, more important even than Niebaum or Samuel Brannan.

MORRIS ESTEE

Estee had come to California at the age of twenty in 1853; he grabbed a gold pan and shovel and headed for El Dorado County. He had been a school teacher in Pennsylvania and returned to that profession to earn a living when gold proved too elusive. Because he had a gift for oratory, a friend suggested he study law, and by 1859 he was admitted to practice in Sacramento. Three years later he was elected to the State Assembly, and his successful political career was launched.

Estee had moved to San Francisco by the time he became secretary of the state Republican Party and then Speaker of the Assembly at Sacramento. He was nominated twice by his party to run for United States senator, but Republicans were out of favor. In 1882, a year after purchasing land in Napa Valley, his party nominated him for governor of California.

He had already been elected president of the newly formed Napa Viticultural Association a year earlier. Would it now be possible that the next governor of California would be a Napa

Harvey Lewelling was born in this handsome, symmetrical house, just south of St. Helena. The bare oak trees confirm the date in his album: February 28, 1885. He did not identify the man and child on the porch, nor the man on the balcony.

Valley resident? The concept was so exciting that "Estee Clubs" were formed in most towns. But Estee made a tactical error which contributed to his defeat at the polls that November. He began passing himself off as a gentleman farmer. Estee knew that the Grange could deliver a large block of votes, so he appeared at a state Grange meeting in work clothes, trying to look like one of the boys. It didn't work.

The California press quickly took note of his several wardrobes, as evidenced by this notice in the September 30 issue of the *Healdsburg Enterprise*: "When he addresses his San Francisco and Oakland audiences he assumes the dress of a fastidious man of fashion. Perhaps he occasionally takes a harlequin character for political purposes."

A letter printed in the *Napa Reporter* charged Estee with spending too much time with Krug, Pellet and the Beringers rather than with American-born residents like Lewelling, Crabb, Ewer and William Bourn. Some people even criticized the man for traveling with his Jewish friend from San Francisco, Emanuel Goldstein. Jewish wine merchants were not well-liked. For whatever combination of reasons, Estee lost the election with 67,175 votes to George Stoneman's 90,694.

At the Republican National Convention in Chicago in 1888, Estee was elected chairman and helped guide the name of Benjamin Harrison through the nominating process. He ran for governor of California again in 1894 and lost by a slim margin.

Hamden McIntyre's plans for the Estee winery on Atlas Peak Road were drawn in 1885. The winery would be 125 x 60 feet, with two stories of stone and one of wood. Stone tunnels carved into a solid wall of rock would provide the most attractive wine tunnels in all of the state.

The stone came from a quarry "not a mile away, and is easily worked and splendidly adapted to building purposes. It can be cut and molded into any shape with an axe when first taken out, but hardens with age," noted the *Register* in April, 1885. The winery is still in nearly perfect condition but has been used only occasionally, for storage. Dale and Delores Buller purchased the property in 1954 and live in the elegant house next door.

In 1882, Alfred A. Tubbs, a founder of the Tubbs Cordage Company in San Francisco, rode the same train as Estee, but he didn't get off until the final stop, Calistoga. He purchased the John Hoover farm of 200 acres and the J.M. Wright farm of 122 acres. His mansion was built immediately; the winery could wait. His home reportedly cost $40,000 to build, much more than most wealthy newcomers spent on their wineries.

Tubbs' interest up valley stemmed from his friendship with the men who had founded the Napa Valley Wine Company in the '70s: Krug, the Beringers and M.G. Ritchie. Tubbs was named president of the wine organization the year after he arrived in the valley even though he was not yet making any wine and had no grapes for sale.

Naturally, Tubbs would have to have the best winery architect in California. He went to Rutherford in July 1886 to see McIntyre. Work began one month later, but the plans abruptly changed: "The excavation made for the Tubbs wine cellar is not satisfactory, as the rock at each side slacks and falls to the floor. This will be overcome, however, by constructing a wall of stone or brick against the crumbling rock," explained the *Star* of August 20.

The carpenters worked overtime to have Tubbs' wooden winery ready a month later for the first crush. It was not until two years later that the Tubbs stone wine cellar was completed. He called his winery "Hillcrest." It was described as "castleated," built like a castle with turrets and battlements.

It was not unusual for two wealthy men to combine resources for the construction of a winery; this is what Seneca Ewer and J.B. Atkinson did in Rutherford. Both men arrived in California in '49, Ewer going to Butte county where he ranched, practiced law and served occasionally in the State Assembly. Atkinson went to San Francisco where he operated a very successful wholesale business. Ewer was in the valley by 1870. He helped found three banks, served as president of the Bank of St. Helena, and gave the city its first water system.

No one knows how the men met and formed their partnership, but during one of the lulls in the construction of Inglenook, they talked McIntyre into designing an all-stone structure near Ewer's 100 acres of grapes in Rutherford. Enough stone was quarried on Howell Mountain for a 60 x 125 foot winery of two stories. The *Star* described its operations a year after it was built:

> The grapes are carried direct from the wagon to the crusher, some 40 feet above, by means of an improved elevator, which takes back the empty boxes at the same time. The juice and pomace are carried from the crusher by means of long shutes running the whole length of the cellar, from which they are distributed to the various tanks by heavy galvanized iron spouts. The arrangement seems to us to be as near perfection as any we have seen.

In 1923 Georges de Latour moved his Beaulieu wine operation into the Ewer and Atkinson winery. Because of additions built afterward, the facade is largely hidden from view, making it impossible to compare it to Far Niente or other wineries which McIntyre designed.

In the *Star's* Christmas edition of 1885 is a list of construction projects for the previous year. Among the twelve parties who either built a new wine cellar or added to one is Fritz Rosenbaum.

Rosenbaum had just settled north of the Beringers, in the German neighborhood where he could speak his native tongue. Very successful at importing and selling plate and window glass in San Francisco, he began making wine in his basement in 1879. His home was a large Victorian with a commanding view. In 1962 Michael Robbins restored the house and began making Spring Mountain wines in the basement. Thirteen years later, William and Alexandria Casey of San Francisco purchased the home and built an addition, where they made their St. Clement brand.

Not more than a mile or so south of Rosenbaum, William Bourn selected a site for what soon would become the largest winery in California. Something about the land just north of St. Helena caught the eye of many investors; it was close to the winery of Charles Krug, who ranked among the top winemakers in the state. Bourn had struck it rich in gold and silver and could afford to buy or build anywhere. He had an idea for a semi-cooperative winery which might change the way the entire valley functioned thereafter. The least he could do was make a profit.

Henry Pellet understood what Bourn was trying to do. As president of the St. Helena Vinicultural Club, Pellet brought the issue before the membership:

> This meeting has been called for the purpose of hearing the proposition Mr. Bourn has to offer, and the opinions of those present on the matter. The object of his cellar is to lift the wine industry out of the slough it is now in and to get out of the clutches of the San Francisco wine dealers who have us by the throat. We should erect this cellar so as to be able to hold our wines and not sell at the prices offered to us.[26]

Viewers of the television series "Falcon Crest" may recognize this mansion, which became a signature of the program. The photograph was taken in 1885, only a year after it was built for San Francisco banker Tiburcio Parrott.

What Bourn and his partner, Everett Wise, proposed was to build a one-million-gallon winery on the following terms: 1. they would produce wine from anyone's grapes, on shares, and store the wine separately under the owner's name; 2. the wine would be held until a buyer could be found and then the grower would be paid; 3. or the grower could sell his grapes directly to the winery. "No Malvoisie, Mission, inferior grapes or grapes in bad condition will be received for winemaking."

Bourn and Wise would build an inventory of well-aged, quality-controlled, superior Napa Valley wines. They would sell the wines for prices far above those offered by the great San Francisco wine emporiums, which paid little or no attention to varieties. To them, all wine was "California."

145

The site chosen for the new winery was a relatively steep hillside until a cut was made into the side, providing a level spot for construction. The soil removed was carefully spread down to the main road and then terraced: a year later the change in the hillside was hardly noticeable.

Hamden W. McIntyre came up from Rutherford to offer his advice, though he was not the architect: this project was much larger than the small wine cellars he designed. San Francisco architects Percy and Hamilton drew up the plans for a building 400 feet long by 70 feet wide with a front center section, 50 feet wide, jutting out 20 feet. The cost was staggering: a quarter of a million dollars.

The walls of native stone came from a nearby quarry, and mortar was mixed with newly available Portland cement. Portland cement was poured over iron bars to provide additional strength on the first and second floors. Columns were reinforced with iron. Traditional heavy wood timbers were used for third floor construction. All three floors would be used for aging and storage; the crushing took place in the attic.

"Greystone," as the winery soon came to be called, was the first winery in California to be operated by electricity and lighted by electric bulbs. (Charles Krug had gas lighting in his wine cellar.) The boiler and engine to produce this new kind of power were located under the 20 x 50 foot wing projecting from the central portion.

NAPA WINES GO TO PARIS

By 1889, Napa wines were suddenly the topic of conversation all over the country. They were going to the World's Fair in Paris. *Harper's* of March 9 carried a three-and-a-half page article providing a rare, intimate look at California wines: there was no way to buy that kind of advertising.

Author Edward Roberts raved about the Napa Valley: "The two best known valleys — those having soil and climate adapted for the production of the choicest grapes from the Medoc, Bordeaux, and Rhine Valley districts — are Sonoma and Napa . . . I cannot imagine a more sheltered, pretty nook than the upper Napa Valley . . . It is a little world in itself . . . Several of the Napa growers own estates that have no counterpart in America." He mentioned particularly Inglenook, Beringer, Krug, Tiburcio Parrott and Estee.

Napa Valley had given Roberts very special treatment: he was wined and dined and carriaged from one end of the valley to the other. Roberts was candid enough to admit in print:

> There is little to choose between Sonoma and Napa valleys. Both are picturesque, shut in by low hills, and in either are many vineyards where one may initiate himself into the mysteries of wine-making. In selecting Napa Valley we were influenced to some extent by the introductory letters given us in San Francisco. Having them, we knew that the largest vineyards would be open to our inspection.

The Napa Valley united as never before to send wine to the World's Fair. France had never allowed American wines to compete in one of its international competitions, although it had given a few certificates to American wine. The French may have felt the need to be more friendly to their American cousins, since American rootstock which was resistant to the phylloxera had just proven the salvation of their great winescape.

George Husmann accepted the responsibility of gathering the California wine to be sent to Paris. In a letter to the *Register* of October 25 he described the difficulties of his task:

> I was treated more like a beggar asking alms, than the agent of a Department [U.S. Dept. of Agriculture] trying its best to advance the interest of the wine growers of the State.
>
> From Sonoma County, which is so fond of calling itself the cradle of the wine industry of the State, I could get but five or six exhibits, and not one from the southern part of the State, although I spent several weeks there trying to wake them up. Nearly all of the exhibits came from Napa county, and a few from the dealers in San Francisco.

Varieties of Grapes Planted
Annual Report of State Viticultural Commissioners.

Post Office	Acerage 1881	Acerage 1887	All Riesling	Chasselas Font., Palomino, and Burger	Sauternes, incl. Sauv. Vert	Cab. Sauv., Fr. Merlot, Malbec	All Reds, except Zin., Miss., & Malv.: all Pimots, Ch.Noir Alicaute, Petit, etc.	Zinfandel	Mostly Miss. and Malv.	Table and Raisin	Tons of Grapes 1886	Gallons of Wine made 1886	Gallons of Brandy made 1886	Resistant Vines, Acres 1887
Conn Valley	233	657	32	112	3	5	60	390	53	1	1,390	150,000	-	-
Spring Mountain	55	355	11	58	5	10	20	216	32	3	400	21,000	-	-
Pope Valley	20	165	2	29	-	1	1	36	85	4	156	4,000	-	-
Beryessa	18	33	-	5	-	-	-	12	16	-	150	-	-	-
Childs Valley	13	129	15	16	8	5	10	55	20	-	196	6,000	-	10
Howell Mountain	100	690	85	110	20	65	150	215	45	-	40,000	-	-	20
Calistoga	250	1,710	254	243	25	119	160	522	275	12	2,600	646,000	-	72
St. Helena	1,611	5,246	963	797	83	255	551	1,831	694	17	14,387	1,777,000	-	49
Rutherford	721	1,527	260	213	55	45	191	452	94	-	4,611	464,000	-	20
Oakville	429	1,085	317	144	33	54	89	433	99	11	4,302	800,000	-	30
Yountville	585	1,674	264	339	43	28	117	582	195	12	3,960	212,000	-	25
Napa	1,260	3,340	433	531	137	192	259	1,000	423	50	7,303	348,000	-	425
	5,285	16,611	2,636	2,597	412	779	1,608	5,744	2,031	109	39,595	4,468,000	102,322	651

Still, he managed to put together some fine entries, and at the Paris World's Fair that year, more wine medals were won by Napa entries than those from any other region in California or any other state. Charles Krug's insistence on quality over quantity was paying off at last.

Of thirty-four awards won by California wine, brandy and champagne, Napa Valley collected twenty. Migliavacca in Napa City won the only Gold for the valley; Wetmore and Adrian Chauche of Livermore each won Golds. Silvers went to Beringers, Greenbaum & Co., which represented Inglenook, Henry Hagen, Napa Valley Wine Co., and the Weinberger winery. Bronze awards went to Chris Adamson, Brun & Chaix, Krug, John Matthews, and V. Courtois. There was a long list of Honorable Mention awards for Napa winemakers as well, and eight awards for California brandies, most of which went to Napa producers. It could be said that Napa won this contest by default, because so many winemakers did not bother to enter. But that sounds a lot like sour grapes.

It took most of the following winter for valley residents to calm down after the Paris wine competition. Everyone wanted to believe what the *San Francisco Merchant and Viticulturist* claimed on October 22:

> In fair competition with the whole world, the wines of California have carried off twenty-seven medals [for wines only], of which four were gold, eleven were silver and twelve bronze, besides honorable mention in seven cases . . . It means that France, our greatest rival, has declared to the world that the products of California's vintages rank with those of her own in point of excellence.

Facing page: The chart shows what grape varieties were growing in the Napa Valley a century ago. It is easy to determine from this chart which were the most popular. Published in 1887 by the State Viticultural Commissioners it shows Zinfandel was the favorite grape with 5,744 acres. Cabernet Sauvignon was lumped together with several other red varieties and only accounted for 779 acres

The *San Francisco Chronicle* was more than willing to give credit where credit was due. On October 6th it carried a long story on Napa Valley, calling the lower portion the "California Medoc," and announced that a major shift had taken place:

> Napa vineyards are well known on the Pacific coast, but until within the past few years the district nomenclature of wines were comparatively unknown to Eastern people, the generic term of 'California wine' being the title under which the productions of the State, no matter from what county they originated, were introduced.
>
> To-day Napa wines stand high in public favor. Vineyardists such as Morris M. Estee, Jacob Schram, Captain G. Niebaum, H.W. Crabb, and others have in many ways attracted attention to the superior productions of the valley.

When Frona Eunice Wait, San Francisco's first woman journalist, published her *Wines and Vines of California* that fall, there was a lengthy chapter on Napa, entitled "The Banner Wine-Making County." Everyone was acknowledging Napa's honors.

Letters soon arrived from eastern publications asking what time of year was best to visit the Napa Valley. Another letter came from Charles Oldham of London, England. He was a member of the wine importing firm of Grierson, Oldham & Co., and wanted to know about accommodations. When news leaked out about Oldham's trip, the *Merchant* put the story on the front page. At last the English were coming to get a look at the California wine industry. Oldham spent months sampling wines and brandies and being treated like a king. When he went back to England, he took wine from Inglenook and other wineries.

The year 1889 saw Napa Valley wines elevated to the front rank in California and across the nation. The Valley did brilliantly in Paris and had done just as well at the Sixth Annual Viticultural Convention held in San Francisco in March 1888. Napa won 22 medals in the table wine category, more than any other county. The Goodman Brothers received a first place ribbon for a 1886 Cabernet Sauvignon produced at Eshcol. It appears this was the first award ever given in California, and likely the entire country, for a Cabernet Sauvignon.

Cabernet Sauvignon was the darling of France's Bordeaux wines, and Wetmore and Krug championed the variety in many viticultural meetings. It had been imported and planted by French immigrants in Santa Clara County in the early 1850s, but none would then consider using the name of the grape on the wine they produced. That would have been an unheard-of departure from centuries of European tradition of blending wine.

It almost certainly was a retired English army captain who introduced the concept that wine made almost exclusively of the Cabernet Sauvignon grape could be sold under its own name. He was James Drummond.

Drummond, descendant of a Scottish banking family, settled in nearby Glen Ellen, Sonoma Valley, in 1878. He knew fine wine from having had it served in the household where he grew up and from travels through France's wine region. Drummond planted the grape immediately, along with several hundred varieties. He offered it for tasting in 1884 at the State Viticultural Convention. Wetmore said of that event: "It is only experimentally known here at present. The sample of wine made by Mr. Drummond in 1882 was more admired than any other on exhibition — notwithstanding its youth."[27]

It may be that Drummond's curiosity and willingness to break with tradition (he married a divorced woman and was ostracized by his family, which may be why he moved to California) led to the first varietal wine of the Cabernet Sauvignon. This helped trigger the movement in the 1880s to experiment with the production of other wines without following the tried and true standards of France where blending was the only correct procedure.

WOMEN AND WINE

All the publicity over Napa Valley's wine triumphs at Paris and in San Francisco, and even the emergence of a varietal Cabernet Sauvignon, were overshadowed by another astonishing change in the industry. Women vintners were taking home some of those coveted wine medals and emerging as a major force within the industry.

There were hints of this change for some years previously, but the men who dominated the craft of winemaking preferred to ignore it. Not surprisingly, it was a Frenchwoman who led the way. The Duchesse de Fitz-James was born in Sweden, went to Paris with her diplomat father, and married into the Fitz-James family of St. Benezet. She was among the first to see the benefit of using American root stock to save the French wine industry from phylloxera. At the International Phylloxera Congress at Bordeaux, France, in 1881, the Duchesse described her success with the new root stock, and sharply criticized her French neighbors' reluctance to try the method. She managed to win over the majority of delegates, and the story was quickly carried back to America.

In the 1880s in California, women in the wine industry were just beginning to emerge from kitchens, where they might sip wine very discreetly, but never in public. When Josephine Tychson's husband took his own life very unexpectedly, she proceeded with their plans to build a winery just north of St. Helena, not far from Weinberger and Krug. The Tychson Winery was barely completed in the fall of 1886 when it was time for the crush. The *Star* first reported the construction August 27, and a week later noted that winemaking had begun. Nels Larsen was in charge of the new facility, which had a capacity of 30,000 gallons.

The Tychson winery lacked artistic elements such as McIntyre used in his buildings down valley. It was 50 x 50 feet square, entirely of wood, two stories high, and built into a hillside excavation. The winery was demolished in 1899 and replaced with Freemark Abbey, built of stone. In 1967, after years of neglect, partners Charles Carpy, William Jaeger and Frank Wood resumed wine production.

Josephine had a carriage and spirited horses, and loved to drive her rig as fast as her team could pull. When she drove her carriage into town for supplies she frequently picked up her clos-est neighbor, Mrs. John Weinberger, who would beg her to rein in the horses. (Mrs. Weinberger was also a widow; her husband had been murdered.) When Josephine's three children accompa-nied her, they were given a brief directive to hold on, and off the four of them went, chickens flying, dust swirling and the Chinese watching with amusement.

Josephine did not send her wine to the World's Fair in Paris in 1889. As a matter of fact, there is no record of Tychson wine being entered in any wine competition, though records for entrants do not exist for most wine events. But Mrs. Weinberger won a Silver medal in Paris and considerable praise as the only California woman in the famous competition to be so honored.

Hannah Weinberger took over a much larger winery than Josephine's after her husband's death, and was much more active in the actual winemaking process. When *Resources of California* for June 1885 carried a story on the Napa Valley, Hannah came in for special praise:

> We next come to Weinberger's Winery, Mrs. J.C. Weinberger, proprietor. The vineyard consists of 100 acres, eighty acres of which are yielding handsome returns. The cellars are well arranged and supplied with all the wine-making apparatus necessary for a first-class winery. During 1884, there were 90,000 gallons of all kinds of wines made here. The residence is located, like the cellar, on the slope of the hill, thus com-manding a fine view of St. Helena and the valley.

When Frona Eunice Wait visited the valley in early 1889, gathering material for her book published that same year, she almost completely overlooked women. In *Wines and Vines of California*, Hannah name is mentioned only once. *Wines and Vines of California* was the first book written for the wine consumer, and it surprised some that the book was the work of a woman. Wait's book was so successful that William Randolph Hearst asked her to oversee the special section on California wine that was carried in the San Francisco *Examiner* in April, 1890.

Kate Field accomplished even more for California wine than Wait. Born in St. Louis, Missouri, to parents who traveled the country acting in stage dramas, Field took to the stage quite naturally. She did not pursue acting, but turned to public lecturing, which was a widely popular form of entertainment. In June 1888 the California Board of Viticultural Commissioners, which included Charles Krug, hired Field to undertake a national lecture tour on the subject of wine.

The Viticultural Commissioners realized some action had to be taken to counter the effectiveness of Temperance lecturers like Carrie Nation, who drew huge crowds with fire-and-brimstone speeches. Many gospel preachers built their reputations on sermons dealing with the evils of alcohol. It was a hot, timely topic.

Marie Austin of Fresno was another successful and respected woman in grape farming. She was independent and opinionated. She pointedly hired Chinese laborers to pack her huge supply of raisins for shipping all over the United States. She also had a lot of technical expertise. In an interview in the *San Francisco Merchant and Viticulturist* in March 1884, she argued that "with natural moisture at eight feet below the surface," excessive watering or irrigating would be injurious to grapes in San Joaquin valley. Austin pointed out that the "saccharine" or sugar content of the grape was directly affected by water at the wrong moment in the growing cycle. For a woman to discuss grape growing in such technical terms was almost unheard of.

In central Sonoma Valley Kate Warfield, Eliza Hood and Ellen Stuart all continued to make wine after their husbands died and won medals in many county and state competitions. At an 1883 competition at the state level, brandy made by Warfield won the Gold Medal, much to the chagrin of many male entrants. The losers forced the judges to repeat the blind tasting and Warfield repeated her honors. This event earned her widespread publicity.

Women also were making a major contribution to the wine industry through advertising. Wealthy men had rushed in to plant vast vineyards and build huge and beautiful wine cellars with sweeping views. But for some peculiar reason many did not understand the need to invest as much in selling their product. It may have been that they understood that direct sales were crucial but couldn't recognize the value of promotion such as Kate Field undertook, or the good accomplished by Wait's book.

But now Napa Valley's winemakers were the leading producers of dry table wines, and they realized that the attention which had been focused on growth and development, testing grape varieties, new wine equipment and unpredictable labor supplies wasn't going to sell wine.

Few who entered the wine industry had considered whether there was a market for the product. Most vintners weren't aware that most eastern wine drinkers weren't interested in California wines, which they considered inferior to French and other European wines. But when they finally realized the problems, they went looking for solutions.

Women made a major contribution in marketing and the production of varietals; by and large they were non-traditionalists who carried few long-held beliefs about wine production because, being women, few had been passed on to them by fathers or husbands. They were absent from most wine meetings and convention and were very, very rarely among the speakers. They concentrated on business.

It would take everyone's help to overcome what lay ahead when the phylloxera would so devastate the valley. For women, it offered an unprecedented opportunity to become equals in the industry. As Carrie Nation and other feminists emerged to fight alcohol, women in the wine industry were just beginning to take their rightful places as vintners.

Despite years of searching, it was not until 1998 that this bottle of Far Niente wine was discovered with an original label intact. Winslow Homer designed it, making the label worth far more than the hundred-year-old wine inside.

PHYLLOXERA DESTROYS
THE VINEYARDS

E arly in the spring of 1891, officials in the White House in Washington, D.C., announced a train tour of the western United States for President Benjamin Harrison. This was not to be a whistle-stop tour to win votes; Harrison was only in his third year in office. Rather, the President wanted to see the country, its people and what it produced, from manufactured goods to agricultural products. That included wine, of course. Or did it?

In California the Presidential train ride was to begin in San Diego and traverse the entire length of the state. The vast array of activities packed into each day suggested how starved Americans on the West Coast were for national attention. The President was venerated here as if he were royalty. Napa Valley residents had high hopes that the President might spend some time in their lovely countryside. After all, Morris Estee had nominated Harrison for President at the Republican convention. Surely the President would return the favor by staying a night at Hedgeside, Estee's home and winery on the outskirts of Napa City.

The grand highlight of the President's visit to San Francisco was to be a banquet in the magnificent Garden Court of the Palace Hotel. Several hundred could be seated for dinner, but this would not begin to accommodate all who felt they deserved an invitation. It quickly became apparent that a great many reputations were going to be tarnished by being left off the guest list. This was the case with many of the Presidential luncheons and sightseeing tours. Even California's governor, Henry Markham, felt slighted and returned to Sacramento in a huff.

What the banquet committee did to California and Napa Valley wine was at least equally insulting. An elaborately printed dinner card for the evening, with enough courses to produce indigestion, did not include one locally produced wine. The wines and champagne to be served to the President of the United States during his visit to the California wine country were all from France.

Charles Wetmore was so furious that had dueling still been in practice he might have challenged General W.H.L. Barnes to a duel. Barnes was the Presidential aide who oversaw the details of various parties and banquets, including the wines used. Wetmore had served as chief executive officer of the Viticultural Commissioners and still acted as spokesman for the entire wine industry. This slight hurt Wetmore's pride for another reason, as well. The *Examiner* had asked him to write a story on viticulture for a special edition for April 26, 1891. The entire top half of page 14 carried the industry's proudest statistics: "Twenty Million Gallons of Wine Produced Annually. One Hundred Twenty Thousand Acres Cultivated In Raisin and Table Grapes. Fifty Thousand People Engaged Directly in the Rural Work."

"Pure wines, good enough for the President, are prominent features in the wonderful development of American industry on the Pacific coast," wrote Wetmore in his highly informative, modestly biased report. He added:

> It will probably occur to the President at the coming banquet to have his glass filled with a California wine, when he responds to California's welcome. Try it, Mr. President. We assure you that you will survive the ordeal and that you will say you have tasted worse things than California wine.

Wetmore could have left out the last line; Ferdinand Haber or Kate Field should have been asked for their advice.

When Wetmore discovered Barnes's "oversight" several days before the arrival of the President, he quickly collected a case of the best wines available, including his own, and sent them to General Barnes. Not one word of the controversial matter had leaked out to the press or public. Barnes refused to open even one bottle and returned the case, at Wetmore's expense. He may have done this on the advice of other committee members, some with suspiciously sounding French names like Alfred Bouvier and Marcus D. Boruck. The story was finally picked up by the *Examiner* the day Harrison reached San Francisco. Within 24 hours many of the other dailies, the *Alta, Call, Bulletin* and *Chronicle*, also carried the story. Harrison, only mildly disturbed by the incident, asked Barnes to have a new menu printed and to include, of course, some of the local vintages.

The new dinner card added insult to injury in a way only a piqued Presidential aide might engineer. The original card had been handsomely engraved, the type of keepsake people put into attic trunks and pass on to grandchildren. The second card had the appearance of being printed by a beginning calligrapher; none survive except in newspaper reproductions.

The banquet lived up to all that was expected of the marvelous Garden Court of the Palace, the finest hotel on the West Coast. The first course was served promptly at 9 p.m., "Eastern Oysters on Half Shell," followed by consommé. Hors d'oeuvres included stuffed olives, caviar, and anchovy salad. The accompanying wines were listed simply as "Hock — California" (a sweet Riesling) and "Sherry — California." There had to be some grumbling that no brands were mentioned, but at least it was California wine. "Sauterne — California" was served with Sacramento salmon.

Four meat courses were offered next: Chicken a la Louis, Filet of Beef a la Richeleau, Lamb Chops, and Tripe with Truffles. "Claret — California" was the accompanying wine.

How there could be room for another meat course is hard to imagine, but Roast Young Turkey followed, with the only beverage which might help the sated dinner guests, champagne. At this point any California vintner present should have stalked out of the Garden Court. All five of the champagnes were from France, and they were listed by maker. Champagne was also used to accompany the California Asparagus, served before the selection of four desserts and fresh fruit, cheese and coffee.

Most San Francisco newspapers the following day were kind enough to list all of the California wine brands served. Five of the nine were from Napa Valley: Hock from the Napa Valley Wine Co.; Riesling from Inglenook; Jacob Schram's best white wine, called "Schramsberger"; Estee's best Sauterne from Hedgeside; and the finest Claret (Cabernet Sauvignon) of the Napa Valley Wine Co.

Alameda County contributed three wines: Wetmore's Haut Sauterne and his Margaux Souvenir Claret, plus Julius P. Smith's "Olivina" Sauterne. John Doyle's "Las Palmas" Claret, from Cupertino, Santa Clara County, was served, and finally Arpad Haraszthy's "Eclipse" Champagne.

General Barnes's refusal to list the California wine brands could only be taken as a personal affront. A reporter for the Associated Press found the incident so intriguing that he sent the details out over the national news wire. As a result, the presidential banquet turned into a priceless publicity bonanza for California wine. As it turned out, Harrison did not visit the Napa Valley on his trip, and the votes he lost because of this oversight didn't help his re-election campaign. He lost the next election to Grover Cleveland.

Actually, President Harrison's re-election difficulties could be traced, at least in part, to the growing Prohibition movement in the United States. The Prohibition Party was stirring up emotions with growing success. In June 1892, General John Bidwell of California was nominated for President at the Party's convention. Bidwell received only 264,133 votes compared to over five million for Cleveland.

This winery, photographed by Harvey Lewelling, was built in 1885 by Captain William Peterson. It later became the Napa Valley Cooperative Winery, and today is Golden States Wine Co. This important building deserves landmark status.

San Francisco's *Pacific Wine and Spirit Review* claimed in June 1893 that even "Napa City has voted for the Prohibitionists and gone dry," but the story was not accurate. The Prohibitionists had succeeded in getting a ballot measure in Napa outlawing the sale of alcoholic beverages and came very close to winning. In one eastern voting district of the city, those opposed won by only 30 votes, 496 to 466.

The hiring of Kate Field some six years previously by the Viticultural Commissioners of California was partially in response to the threat posed by the Prohibition movement. Someone had to counter the rapidly-growing press coverage of the Anti-Saloon League and the Prohibition Party by pointing out that alcoholism was due not to the presence of such stimulants but to the economic plight of so many working men and their families.

161

For those who dig into the origin of such campaigns, the birth of the Prohibition movement in the United States can be traced to the founding of the women's suffrage movement by Elizabeth Stanton and Lucretia Mott in 1869 in Seneca Falls, New York. Voting rights and improved conditions for women in the home were linked to curbing the abuse of alcohol. The Prohibition Party actually came into existence the same year, partly as an after-effect of the Civil War. Garrit Smith, who ran twice as the Abolition Party candidate for President, needed a new cause once slavery was ended. He saw it in alcoholism.

> Our involuntary slaves are set free, but our millions of voluntary slaves still cling to their chains. The lot of the literal slave, of him whom others have enslaved, is indeed a hard one; nevertheless it is a paradise compared with the lot of him who has enslaved himself — especially of him who has enslaved himself to alcohol.[1]

It was a young woman Prohibitionist from Kansas named Carrie Nation, however, who caught the attention of the press. She and several other brave female companions walked into local saloons carrying axes and destroyed whatever they could. Glass flew in all directions, and so did the male inhabitants, once they realized how serious Nation and her cohorts were. The Women's Christian Temperance Union (WCTU) was founded in the same years, as well as the highly political Anti-Saloon League.

One indication of the strength of the movement is seen clearly in the General Assembly of the Presbyterian Church in 1887. Meeting in Philadelphia, the members voted to adopt unfermented grape juice for use in the Holy Sacrament of Communion.

A PRESIDENTIAL VISIT

Benjamin Harrison finally made it to Napa six months after he lost the election to Grover Cleveland. He was attracted by hunting, not wine, but Napa locals were still happy to have a visit by so distinguished a gentleman. The *Napa Daily Journal* of March 27, 1894, gave this report:

> No less than fifteen hundred people were at the depot Monday morning to witness the arrival of Gen. Benjamin Harrison . . . The public schools were dismissed, the College, likewise, and even the children of Shurtleff district, out near the Asylum, were excused from their lessons and, headed by their teacher, tramped into town to catch a glimpse of the only living ex-president.

There were no reports of Harrison visiting the Hedgeside manor of Morris Estee, but he did spend three days at Napa Soda Springs, and journeyed to the marshes of Suisun for a day of hunting geese. He may also have paid a visit to J.P. Jackson. According to Jackson's obituary in the September 27, 1900, issue of the *Journal,* he and Harrison had been law partners at one time.

The visit turned out to be so uneventful that it did not become part of local history, even as a footnote. Certainly, some local winemakers must have assumed Harrison would mend his political fences after the Palace Hotel incident, but this was not the style of the taciturn Harrison, who had probably forgotten the whole thing anyway.

Disappointment in the ex-president contributed to a deepening mood of uncertainty in the valley. There was far too much wine in storage. All the excitement engendered by the Paris World's Fair had abated, although magazine writers were still sending inquiries about Napa wines and seeking suggestions on whom to visit and where to stay.

CHARLES KRUG'S LEGACY

Then, to have the father of Napa Valley viticulture die suddenly, though perhaps not unexpectedly, was a further serious blow. Charles Krug died on Monday morning, November 1, 1892. He was 67. "Mr. Krug has lived to see the ups and downs of the wine industry and of life generally," reported the *Star* four days later. "His pathway has not always been strewn with flowers, but has oft times been rugged and covered with thorns. Adverses in business frequently visited him, but were met bravely and battled manfully. He had always taken an active part in the furtherance of the wine industry."

Krug's obituary covered two full columns. His attendance at the University of Marburg was noted, as well as his participation in the "Free Thinker's School" in Philadelphia in 1847. This school was the reason he first came to America. After a brief return to Germany to help with an attempt to set up a German Republic, he sailed for San Francisco, arriving in 1852. He never again set foot on his native soil.

It seems unlikely that Krug would have chosen to move to Napa Valley and begin working in viticulture had he never met Hungarian Agoston Haraszthy. He worked as editor of a German language newspaper in San Francisco for some time, then met Haraszthy when the two worked in the U.S. Mint in San Francisco. All Haraszthy ever talked about was grapes and wine.

When Haraszthy moved to Sonoma, convinced he had found the Garden of Eden for grape growing, Krug followed. He planted a vineyard, but he was very short of money. When he heard that Napa Valley had several large vineyards where he might find employment, he borrowed an apple press and went to work crushing grapes.

He was not used to this type of difficult physical work. But Lady Luck apparently felt sorry for him and stepped in to help. At the Bale Mill just north of St. Helena, he put his cider press to work for Louis Bruck. One of the people who came to watch the crush was Caroline Bale, a daughter of the late Dr. Edward T. Bale, who had died in 1849. Their attraction blossomed into love, and the day after Christmas, 1861, the 31-year old Krug married Caroline. They settled on a generous portion of land inherited from her father.

Krug promptly sold his Sonoma vineyard and thereafter rarely mentioned that he had once lived in Sonoma. He even seems to have wiped his slate clean of Haraszthy, for he left not even a

Winemaking at the Charles Krug Winery, circa 1900. Grapes were crushed and fermented on the second floor, after being elevated in the conveyor shown here. The building at right, built in 1881 and still in use, is the oldest structure dating back to Krug's lifetime. The winery is owned today by the Peter Mondavi family.

brief recollection of him in his writings. Krug accomplished far more for California viticulture than Haraszthy, although the latter's achievements were embellished and enhanced over time, primarily because Haraszthy's son, Arpad, treated historical fact regarding his father with much artistic license. Krug was one of the architects of the Board of State Viticultural Commissioners, and the principal organizer of the St. Helena Vinicultural Association. He translated many German documents into English for use by his neighbors. He was on the committee which saw to the publication in 1877 of *Grapes and Grape Vines of California*. He also attended every viticulture meeting or convention held in the state.

Perhaps the highest tribute to Krug was paid by Charles Wetmore, who once stated that to be a neighbor of Krug automatically increased the value of one's vineyard by $100 an acre.

Krug also dealt with some hard times. In June 1885, the *Star* surprised many readers by carrying a story on Krug's financial failure. It required almost a full column to list all his creditors. Probably during this time he borrowed heavily from the Moffitt family in San Francisco to pay his debts.

During the summer before his death, Krug had been in ill health and frequently went to the German hospital in San Francisco. In September, he suddenly suffered a partial paralysis, which included the loss of use of his tongue. Two months later, his wife Caroline died. His world was unraveling: he must have welcomed death twelve months later. Krug's funeral was the largest ever held in Napa. He had made many friends: "He was exceedingly hospitable, the latchstring on his door always drawn to receive and entertain friends and his lovely home near town has been the scene of many happy gatherings," observed the local newspaper. His creative hospitality had really set Krug apart from many of his contemporaries. Krug was survived by four of the five children born to him and his wife Caroline: Linda, Anita, Lolita and Karl. Charles, Jr. died in infancy.

A SURPLUS OF WINE

"The planting of grapes for winemaking purposes has practically ceased," claimed one authority some months before Krug's death.[2] The emphasis in California was shifting dramatically to raisin grapes, with most of these being planted in the San Joaquin Valley. Statewide wine production had leveled off at about 15 million gallons annually, and there had been little growth in the past five years. Sales had not increased either.

Discouraged, some growers began planting fruit trees between the rows of grapes. The prune was the new favorite. Clarence Wetmore, brother of Charles, explained why: "It may take one or two years to clean up the surplus wine that has accumulated during the past three years." The situation was so bad that it might take even longer.

"Something is the matter with the wine industry of this State," warned the *Chronicle*. "Our annual production of wine is very little, if any greater than it was six or seven years ago. . . It is not on account of any defect in the quality of our wine. . . There is not a more unprofitable calling in the State today than vintaging and winegrowing."[3]

One solution proposed for the market slump was to build brand identification. Napa Valley winemakers were pioneering this field for the entire state, especially Gustave Niebaum and his right-hand man, Ferdinand Haber. They knew Napa's reputation was growing and that the area's wines were premium.

Very few wineries marketed their wine under their own brand name. Some years earlier, Isaac de Turck of Santa Rosa had candidly told an interviewer for historian Hubert Howe Bancroft: "No, I have no brand for my wines. All wines produced in Sonoma County are known as Sonoma wines." But Niebaum and Haber felt the time had come to change emphasis. It would now be "Inglenook" rather than "California," and the goal would be higher quality and more expensive wine. To control quality, Inglenook wines would only be sold in glass bottles.

The *Chronicle* had offered the recent observation that until a few years ago, the "district nomenclatures of wines were comparatively unknown to Eastern people." Now that was all changing, very rapidly. In an article entitled "Establish More Brands," the *Wine and Spirit Review* applauded this new direction in selling wine. "The tendency of the principal producers and merchants during the past three or four years has been toward the establishment of distinct brands. We have encouraged it by every means possible."[4]

It took a long time to build a reputation, unless one had sufficient funds to spend on promotion. Niebaum sent Haber east to meet with wine buyers of private clubs and restaurants, and the press. Rumors of his success and the growing reputation of Inglenook quickly caused others to emulate, at least in a small way, what was happening at Rutherford. Growers, who wanted a greater share of the profits in winemaking, decided to open their own wineries. After all, the real money would be made in wine.

Fortune Chevalier of San Francisco, a dealer in imported French wines and also in the so-called "native" or California wines, had acted on this wisdom for a long time. In the spring of 1891 he began construction of a winery high on the side of Spring Mountain, west of St. Helena. Chevalier may have had an ulterior motive for building a winery. For some years he had faced a declining supply of French wines, brandies and champagne for his San Francisco store because of the phylloxera in Europe. The supplies he did receive were not up to the old quality. One solution was to make wine himself.

The success of wineries founded by French immigrants contradicts in part the concerns about the overproduction of wine in the 1890s. Chevalier sold every barrel of wine he produced. The quality was excellent, no doubt, and he had his retail outlets in San Francisco. He also had plenty of French-born wine consumers. Krug had maintained all along that there was no surplus of fine wine, only of mediocre or poor quality wine.

Other men of wealth were still willing to gamble on Napa's wine future. George Schoenwald, manager of the elegant new Hotel del Monte in Monterey, had owned vineyards in western St. Helena for years. He had built a stone wine cellar in 1885, but had made wine in the structure only one year. He spent little time in St. Helena until 1890, when he built his elegant mansion, which he called "Esmeralda," on Hudson Street. He built a full basement under the house for winemaking, which he resumed in 1891. A later owner named the place "Spottswoode." The old house was renovated in the late 1970s by Mary Webber Novak. A Spottswoode wine label was introduced in 1982.

Schoenwald knew Napa's wines first hand — the hotel featured Estee's and Schram's wines on the dinner menu. The dapper hotel manager attracted special attention to his viticultural work when he imported from France vines which were all bench grafted to the Rupestris St. George root stock. Some of his neighbors may have laughed behind his back, because that grapevine was not the first choice for being phylloxera resistant. But which vine had really proven it could handle that terrible insect? No one had an answer.

Lillie Hitchcock Coit, a San Francisco socialite with a somewhat eccentric reputation, had a small winery built in 1892. Her father, Dr. C.M. Hitchcock, had settled in the hills behind Bale Mill more than a decade earlier for his health, so Coit was no stranger to the area. She sent a collection of dried grapes to the Paris Fair so that she actually could share in some of the great honors bestowed on the valley in 1889.

Lillie gave the name "Larkmead" to her home. The Southern Pacific railroad later named a nearby train stop Larkmead. The area was filled with larks which awakened even the heaviest sleeper on spring mornings. Coit had the financial means to indulge her whims and fancies; she did so by going to places shunned by proper ladies. She had ideas about feminine decorum far ahead of her time and would have made a good suffragette, except that she had no interest in social causes.

Not far away, St. Helena cooper S.P. Connors had erected a small wooden winery nearly a decade earlier which he generally referred to by the name "Larkmead". It was perhaps the *Star* which first formally called Connor's wine cellar by the name during its second year of operation. In September, 1885, the journal noted: "The Larkmead cellar presents a very busy appearance," and a few weeks later: "The Larkmead Cellar of S.P. Connor is worked to its utmost."

Larkmead went through a series of successive ownerships and operators. It was rather small, built of wood and not very attractive. Kohler & Van Bergen, the San Francisco wine house, leased it one year; so did V. Courtois. Finally, in 1893, a Swiss family named Salmina fell in love with the location and settled in. They did not have the funds to buy the winery, but they were willing to bide their time. At least two of the many Salmina cousins had been in the valley for thirty years before leasing Larkmead. Frank Salmina had begun making wine shortly after the Civil War on a ranch just south of Horace Chase's Stag's

Leap. He was already producing wine when Chase dug into the hillside for his first wine tunnels.

Cousin Battista Salmina had wanted to lease or buy a major vineyard and winery. He waited for an opportunity to invest when prices were low. In the mid-1890s he knew the time was right, and convinced a nephew to join him in going counter to the trend of abandoning the vineyard business. That was a wise tactic, especially if one still believed wine had a future in America.

Antone Nichelini, another Swiss immigrant, may have sat in on some of Battista's economic lectures at the William Tell Hotel, which Battista owned. There were only a few Swiss natives in the entire valley, and they loved to gather to converse in their native language, make music, dance, enjoy food and beer and sometimes wine, and to share news of Switzerland.

Nichelini had a vineyard on the steep slopes of Sage Canyon, east of Rutherford. He did not make wine commercially, but he knew the potential for good wine was there; he had been making it for some time in his basement. Finally, he decided to launch a commercial enterprise. The Nichelini winery took shape in the spring of 1896. It was of modest proportions, of stone for the first level and wood for an upper floor. It clung to the side of a canyon wall almost as if glued in place. Antone must have felt right at home.

Nichelini knew that the success of small wineries in Napa Valley depended on finding a specialized market for their wine. He had only to transport his puncheons of wine seven or eight miles in order to sell it to dozens of magnesite miners (mostly Italian) who had an unslakable thirst.

"The Chiles Valley magnesite mines have undergone more than the usual amount of annual development during the past year," recorded the *Star* of December 28, 1894. "These are the only lodes of this material now being worked on this coast." Magnesite was a hard form of carbon of magnesia; "So hard is it, that a sharp edge will cut glass," added the writer.

The Founding of Stag's Leap

Horace Blanchard Chase was the son of a wealthy Chicago businessman. He dabbled in several investments, including vineyards. He had a home in San Francisco and, like most of his friends, traveled frequently to Europe, particularly Italy. He wanted to make wine as a hobby and purchased land on the east side of the valley, where he built a summer home he named "Stag's Leap."

The first mention of Stag's Leap in a valley newspaper came in a story in the *Register* of May 19, 1893:

> The person who leaves the train at Yountville and inquires the way to 'Stag's Leap', has no trouble in gaining the desired information. The road rises gradually to the eastward, leaving the Napa Valley behind. Here are vineyards and cozy homes, and here 2 miles from the station is 'Stag's Leap', the delightful summer residence of Mr. and Mrs. Horace Chase. . . Rising sharply behind the house are towering hills from which the inspiration 'Stag's Leap' was derived. They stand in majestic grandeur and as sentinels seem to give the place a certain individuality.

Following were several paragraphs of florid description of the gardens and grounds.

Still, to credit Horace Chase with the first use of the Stag's Leap name might be incorrect. Just down the road lived one W. K. Stagg. He had lived in the area for some years, an ambitious farmer with hundreds of fruit trees, acres of corn, vegetables, berries, and thirty acres of grain, but no vines.

Chase's list of priorities at Stag's Leap began with his elegant, two-story stone house with an imposing tower, which was built four years before the winery. The house was finished inside with polished woods, and the grand staircase and floor-to-ceiling fireplace impressed first-time visitors. Chase started the winery in 1893: "Mr. Chase has just completed a tunnel 150 feet long, which will be utilized as a wine cellar, and 40,000 gallons can be stored therein," stated the *Register* of May 5 of that year. The tunnel length was slightly exaggerated. A more complete stone cellar in front of the tunnel was completed the following year.

Winemakers of Scottish origin were a rarity in Napa Valley. Scotlanders did not even show up in the count made of nationalities in the city of Napa in 1892. An inquiring reporter for the Christmas edition of the *Register* counted nearly 400 German immigrants, 276 Irish, 149 Swiss, 128 English, 89 Italian, and 43 French. But there were two Scottish brothers named Rennie in St. Helena. The two may have wished they had not chosen the valley for their home; bad luck seemed to plague them. Both were well-educated and had university degrees. William had emigrated to Australia, and was on his way home to Scotland for a visit when his brother James talked him into taking a look at the wine potential of Napa Valley.[5] The year was 1887, and William eventually decided to postpone his trip home and pool his savings with James's to invest in the Martin Furstenfeld ranch. The location was good, just north of Inglenook. The closeness to Niebaum's lovely estate must have been of some influence.

There was a producing vineyard on the ranch, which enabled the brothers to make wine the following year in an outbuilding. Two years later, in August 1890, their three-story stone wine cellar was completed just in time for the fall crush. For several years they managed to produce 50,000 gallons annually. They claimed to have introduced the first gasoline engine used to run a hydraulic press. James liked to boast that he extracted more free juice from pressing the pomace than any other winery in the valley.[6]

Although the Rennie brothers had room for at least 80,000 gallons of wine, the winery was half empty when E.C. Priber rode up in his buckboard, seeking phylloxera damage information. One-third of their vines were infested, they told Priber, some of which could produce only one more year. From sixty acres they harvested only eighty tons. The infection was likely already established when they purchased from Furstenfeld. Had he advised them about the vine louse? They were innocents from abroad who perhaps should not even have built the winery. In November 1900 the interior was entirely gutted by fire. There was no winemaking from 1900 until 1979, when the Komes family refurbished the building, calling their new wine Flora Springs.

PHYLLOXERA PLAGUE

It is truly remarkable that any winery was established in Napa Valley during the early years of the 1890s, and especially after 1893. A growing restlessness with the national economy had sown seeds of deep discontent with banking institutions and stock market investments. In early May, a sell-off began on the stock market which turned into a panic. Over 15,000 businesses failed that year, and 642 banks had to close their doors.

Not one of Napa Valley's banks suffered such a fate, which testifies to the stability of the economy in spite of the phylloxera and the tricky wine market. But in San Francisco the Pacific Bank, the leader in agricultural loans, did fail. A large loan to the California Fruit and Raisin Growers Association, which had defaulted, was given as the reason for the failure.[7]

It is no surprise then that many Napa growers reacted with anger whenever the subject of the spread of the phylloxera was mentioned in the newspapers. That kind of publicity was certain to hurt land values and the price of vineyards. And there were already too many problems for the grower — the producer got all the credit, the vineyardist little or none. Certainly some growers hid their phylloxera damage from public scrutiny.

When Priber's report on phylloxera damage was published, Napa grape growers were so furious that many were ready to do hand-to-hand battle. (A. Warren Robinson collected most of the information, it turns out, although Priber may have written the work.) Priber's report showed a decline of from 18,229 to 16,651 acres of grapes in only two years. Of 577 vineyards in the county, 244, or nearly half, had marked evidence of the disease. The Board of Viticultural Commissioners was supposed to support the

growers, but publishing these damaging statistics was hardly sup-
portive. Several growers said so in a long article in the *Register* of
January 24.

George Husmann agreed with Priber's figures in a letter to the
Register on January 27: "I venture to predict that there will be but
little left of all the vines in Napa Valley, except those on resistant root, within two years." The disease was within three miles
north of St. Helena.[8]

Henry W. Crabb had his own theories about the future of the
valley if the disease was not stopped. He, too, foresaw that the
only surviving vineyards would be those on resistant rootstock,
but he was just as concerned about damaging overproduction.
"Vines cannot, for any great length of time, remain healthy and
vigorous with the annual overproduction of from six to twelve
tons of fruit per acre."[9]

There was one more bit of salt to rub into California viticulture's open wound. The report to the governor of California by
the Viticultural Commissioners, released in 1894, estimated
France's wine production at "thirteen hundred million gallons."
This was double the figure of just a few years previously. Through
careful management of vineyards and the widespread introduction of resistant rootstock, France's vineyards were rebounding.

For the Italian immigrant families flocking to the valley and
replacing the Chinese laborers, all of this was a blessing in disguise. Many vineyard owners abandoned their farms, or leased or
sold them to the Italian farmhands, and returned to San
Francisco. By doing all of the work themselves, an Italian family
could cut production costs and survive on a meager income.
Many began planting European vines on their own roots
between rows of dying vines.

Italian immigrants began showing up in small numbers in the
Napa Valley in the early 1880s. "A large number of Italians find
employment in the vineyards in town and vicinity" noted the St.
Helena newspaper in April 1880. The newspapers in the small
communities in California generally ignored the names of the

new immigrants, somewhat as they had done with the Chinese. No one could spell or pronounce the names anyway. In the *History of Napa and Lake Counties*, published in 1881, twelve pages were devoted to a listing of every vine grower in the county: there was not one Italian name. The Baretta Brothers, Sciaroni and Salmina were Swiss-Italian. There were about 4,600 Italian immigrants in all of California at the beginning of the decade, most being residents of the Gold Rush counties. In Napa, Italian woodcutters sometimes advertised to sell wood which was left over from that shipped to market in San Francisco.

THE CHINESE CONTRIBUTION

With the growing number of Italians came a corresponding decrease in the number of Chinese employed in the valley. By the turn of the century, most had disappeared from the vineyards and certainly from any wine cellar activities. Those who remained were mostly household employees.

The Chinese contributed to their own displacement by finally demanding higher wages, just as the Italians arrived. Most Chinese were not aware of this new influx of workers. They knew that because of the Chinese Exclusion Act (and the extension of 1892, authored by Santa Rosan Thomas Geary) their numbers were dwindling. They thought the law of supply and demand would result in higher salaries. The *Star* recorded in the late 1880s that the strike of Chinese for more pay had "led to the employment of more white labor than usual," and the *Calistogian* added that they wanted $20 a month salary, up $5 from the usual fee.

By the fall grape harvest of 1889 the situation was crystallizing. "There seems to be a growing disposition to substitute white labor for Chinese. . . Although early in the season to estimate, we think there will be quite a decrease in the number of Chinese employed in this section this year," added the St. Helena editor.[10] The growing violence against the Chinese throughout California and the American West was the final and most compelling reason for them to abandon Napa Valley. They were simply too vulnerable as isolated farm workers. There was at least some safety in numbers, especially in the large cities.

The Italian immigrants who rapidly replaced the Chinese in the vineyards did so for an unexpected reason. It had to do with the previously-mentioned change in grape vine height. This was a Krug contribution to Napa Valley viticulture. He had noticed that vines on taller-than-usual trunks did not suffer so much from frost or summer heat. He advocated trunks with heads about waist level. As Edward Roberts wrote in *Harper's* of March 9, 1889: "Gathering the grapes is laborious work, the picker being obliged either literally to kneel or to bend his back to a painful angle." White workers had refused such stoop labor, or had complained so much that vineyard owners would not hire them. But when the Board of Viticultural Commissioners advocated the change in height, most replanting to phylloxera-resistant vines was carried out following this advice, and taller pickers could be employed.

The Chinese were missed by most valley residents who had come to depend on them for household help, gardening and even child care. Many children grew up not with a nanny or a mammy, but with a stern Chinese male who complained constantly that his employer's sons and daughters were poorly disciplined. For more than thirty years, since the building of the railroads, Chinese people had been a familiar part of rural and small-town California life. They certainly made life easier for the average family, freeing them of most domestic chores. The Chinese also hauled tons of rocks out of vineyards and piled them neatly along the roadsides, creating miles of picturesque stone fences. No one knows how many stone wineries were actually built by the Chinese, but there is photographic evidence that in the 1880s, when most of the valley's stone cellars were constructed, the Italian stone masons cut the soft stone from hillside quarries with the help of Chinese laborers. The slow, arduous task of creating tunnels out of solid rock was almost invariably the work of Chinese laborers. This was done with hammer and chisel, a million tiny cuts into the stone, requiring infinite patience and diligence.

The most significant contribution of the Chinese was actually their willingness to share their culture, which enriched the quality of life in Napa. No Napa resident would think of missing the opportunity to attend a Chinese funeral, especially if the funeral was for a wealthy person. When Lea Hau, a man of wealth and stature in the Chinese community, was killed by a falling tree on the Niebaum farm in January 1894, his extraordinary funeral was attended by many non-Chinese St. Helenans:

> After a long performance in Chinatown, in which mourners and members of the Chinese Masonic order took part, the body was conveyed to the cemetery in due form. First came the express wagon filled with roast pig, roast chicken, rice, burning punk, etc., then the hearse, flanked by six Chinamen on each side. The hearse was followed by some fifty Chinamen, all wearing a band of red and white.
>
> A Chinese band was the next feature, making a hideous noise. Judging by the sound, we were made to believe they were playing 'The Lost Chord'. There were about ten vehicles, another Chinese band making up the end of the procession.[11]

When the rituals were completed, the food was carted back to Chinatown, where the invited guests enjoyed a feast.

Unfortunately, the Chinese contribution to the wine industry was ignored or quickly forgotten. The following quote from a booklet published by the California Wine Association later in the decade, includes a perfect example of this common oversight:

> Grape growing in the Napa Valley dates from the earlier sixties, while Livermore Valley and Santa Clara County, the last of the principal producing sections, were not brought into prominence until much later. The story of the growth of the industry in nearly all of these districts is much alike. In all there was a hardy mixed population — American, French, Germans, Italians; in all every attainable variety of wine was tested.

No mention of the Chinese, while the Italians were accorded attention, in part because so many were moving into winery ownership. Still, the booklet would hardly win any prizes for accuracy. The statement on Santa Clara County was completely wrong; Santa Clara's viticulture and wine making industries were far earlier than those in Napa.

THE CALIFORNIA WINE ASSOCIATION

It was not long before the initials "C.W.A." were included in many conversations in Napa Valley. Many believed the California Wine Association offered real hope for stabilizing wine prices and quality. Others thought the C.W.A. was a terrible idea. Four Napa Valley wineries were part of the original C.W.A., formally inaugurated in August 1894: The Greystone winery, owned by Charles Carpy, the Uncle Sam Winery, C. Carpy & Sons — Napa, and the Napa Valley Wine Company. In San Francisco, the large wine warehouses of Kohler and Van Bergen, Kohler and Frohling, B. Dreyfus & Co., S. Lachman & Co., and Arpad Haraszthy added the real muscle behind the association. (Haraszthy withdrew in less than a year's time.)

An Englishman named Percy T. Morgan was the most energetic person behind the project, although it was the money of bankers Issias Hellman and Benjamin Dreyfus that guaranteed its operation. Henry Lachman was given complete authority in the buying of grapes and blending the wine. Young Almond R. Morrow, who after Prohibition became the first president of the San Francisco Wine Institute, was also a part of the organization.

There was no question that the C.W.A. viewed Napa Valley as the centerpiece of its quality table wine promotion, as described in the booklet they published:

> Whoever visits the Napa Valley and reaches the town of St. Helena in the heart of the Napa Valley Wine District, must inevitably have his attention called to 'Greystone', our magnificent stone cellar which is a landmark for miles around, and which, for centuries to come, will be an enduring monument

to its builders and owners. After the first classification at 'Greystone', the wines not retained in the lower vaults are removed every year to the City of Napa.

In San Francisco, the C.W.A. had wine warehouses holding two million gallons, and at Second and Folsom, the organization's headquarters, there was room for an additional three million gallons. San Francisco's natural summer air conditioning created good weather for long-term wine storage.

This control of the wine production of the state still did not suit the higher vision of Morgan and others. They began buying or leasing wineries; as fast as the ink would dry on a contract they would begin negotiating another. It was rumored they would soon purchase Brun & Chaix, lease the Chevalier winery and expand to every wine region in the state.

The editor of the *Star* saw nothing wrong in all of this activity. An editorial on June 29 asserted: "It seems the height of folly to oppose a scheme which comes to us offering such terms at this opportune time and our producers should, we believe, stand in and make the formation of the syndicate possible."

By September the wine industry was facing serious dissension. Charles Wetmore abandoned the C.W.A. concept, claiming the growers were being cheated by their rating system of "inferior, ordinary, superior and fine." Judge Stanly was vehemently opposed to the C.W.A., as were Jean Chaix, R.W. Lemme, John Swett and Pietro Rossi (the latter with Italian Swiss Colony).

The result was a new group called the "California Winemakers Corporation" which offered fifteen cents a gallon for all wine then available. That was a five cent increase over the C.W.A. offer. If a battle map had been drawn in any district, it would have been a mess: even close neighbors could not agree. It was a sad and disgraceful situation after the long history of cooperation which had always prevailed among Napa Valley vintners. A few people blamed the Viticultural Commission, since the syndicate concept had evolved from the June meeting of the Commission's board. But the C.W.A.'s emphasis on Napa Valley had hurt the pride of many wine producers elsewhere in the state, and that was no one's fault but their own. Yet there really was no way to contain Napa's growing, and deserved, reputation. Soon, judges from Dublin, Chicago, San Francisco and Atlanta agreed that Napa's wines were of extraordinarily high quality.

Competing for Medals

In August 1892 Dublin hosted a Distillers' and Brewers' Exhibition, inviting makers of all such beverages plus wines from all over the world. Fifteen awards were made to California, with Napa taking half, including Henry Crabb, Jacob Schram, Beringers, Inglenook, Migliavacca and the Napa Valley Wine Company. San Joaquin Valley vintners took four medals.

The *San Francisco Chronicle* reported the awards and quoted Judge H. E. Hudson as saying he believed California had attained world class rank with its wines, many of which surprised him with their exceptional quality. The judges could not believe an 1882 brandy sent by George West & Sons of Stockton was really from California; it bore a striking resemblance to French cognacs.

Next came Chicago. This was to be the big test for California, an American world's fair with international judges. Chicago was a special wine market as well, growing and expanding with a large immigrant population. Several Napa Valley vintners had major distribution offices there. The World's Columbian Exposition opened May 1, 1893 to much fanfare. This was to be the first time California wines competed in an open American judging.

Napa had its detractors, of course, and they would be waiting to have the last laugh if Napa Valley did not repeat the Paris awards of six years previously, or those at Dublin. French wine snobs in the United States were still convinced that the native wines did not rate on an equal basis with Bordeaux's finest.

The sense that all was not well in Chicago began with the furor over the method of judging. The Fair Board appointed John Boyd Thatcher to oversee the competition. He found this new prestige so heady he proved extremely difficult to work with, even for the jurors themselves. There were other problems as well. A. E. Dubois of Florida later described the unusual circumstances he and other jurors faced:

> Owing to the late date the jurors were summoned to Chicago, the lack of a suitable place for the storage of California wines, and also, to all appearances, as shown by the dryness of the cork, to the bottles being kept standing too long, many samples were found out of condition, especially white wines and Burgundies.[12]

John T. Doyle, president of the Viticultural Commissioners of California, later wrote: "Whatever result of good may have attended these efforts in other departments, it is certain that so far as viticulture is concerned, they were a dismal failure."[13]

California wines were to be made available at the restaurants at the fair, but the caterer refused to carry more than a few brands. It seemed nothing would be able to change the situation. Then Doyle discovered that Thatcher had appointed only one wine juror for each classification of wine. He also had placed all American entries into one group, with no comparisons possible with the French entries. It was enough to make a grown man cry.

The Viticultural Commissioners of California hastily arranged for Charles F. Oldham, of the London wine firm of Grierson, Oldham & Co., to sample and report on all the California entries. The views of one of the most prestigious wine firms in England would be some compensation for not having a clear-cut international competition. Oldham's observations were widely quoted thereafter in the press and reproduced in detail in the Viticultural Commission's Treatise on Wine Production, published in 1894.

Oldham may have had some difficulty standing up after his marathon sampling of 370 wines. He knew the international wine community was looking over his shoulder, and he wanted to do his job perfectly. He covered wine purity, proper classification, and proper use of a wine bottle (Claret in Bordeaux style bottles). The findings of a judge this fastidious would be hard to criticize. The tastings were all done blind; labels were removed or covered, and the wine was poured into glasses by Oldham's wife, or by Dr. H.W. Wiley of the U.S. Department of Agriculture.

Once back in England, Oldham summed up his California wine experience for *Ridley's Wine & Spirit Trade Circular* in the issue of February 12, 1894:

> That California, with its manifold advantages in all these respects, is rapidly taking its place as one of the principal wine-producing countries of the world, is undoubted, and it is not surprising to those who know the facts of the case. The sooner these facts become more widely known the more quickly will California wines attain, more especially in this country, the high place in public estimation to which their excellent qualities assuredly entitle them.

Because of the changes in awards categories, it is difficult to ascertain how many medals Napa won, but 24 seems pretty accurate, about twice those won by any other wine county in California or the United States. Among the winners in Chicago were Brun & Chaix, C. Carpy & Co., Crabb, Ewer & Atkinson, Beringer, Estee, Louis Zierngibl, Napa Valley Wine Co., Otto Norman, Migliavacca, Parrott and Schram. There was very little time for self-congratulation before all of those producers, and many more, were scurrying about their cellars for wine to submit to the San Francisco Midwinter Fair. Since this was a California event, the mistakes made in Chicago would surely be avoided. The aim of this exposition was to demonstrate to Easterners how lovely were the winter months on the western shores of the United States. The Fair opened January 27, 1894, in Golden Gate Park.

A strikingly beautiful Viticultural Palace, a building 75 x 50 feet in size with a dome over its center, was still under construction and wouldn't be finished until April 7th. Visitors would have only a couple of months to get to know California wines before the fair closed. The Viticultural Palace was only one problem for the wine industry. The Executive Committee included such Napa names as Parrott, Repsold, Priber, Carpy and Frederick Beringer. Napa had more representatives than any other county. Of 216 wine entries, in all categories and representing all of California, only 39 awards were made. The jury was most parsimonious in granting recognition for wine quality. For example, only five awards were given in the Sweet Wine category, which attracted 36 entries.

There was no overwhelming victory for Napa Valley wines either. Napa vintners did win the most medals, nine, which went to Brun & Chaix, Schram, Beringer, Crabb, Parrott, Ewer & Atkinson, and several new names, including A. Grimm, Henry Hagen and Kortum & Fuelscher.

Enthusiasm in the valley for fairs and expositions cooled a little, especially by those passed over again. Judge Stanly was not a winner, nor were George Schoenwald, Inglenook, Chevalier, and Edge Hill. But there was still the Atlanta Exposition coming up in 1895.

Atlanta wanted to awaken America to its existence too, for, like Chicago, it was the trading hub of a vast territory. About two dozen California wineries entered the wine competition, nine from Napa Valley. Fourteen of the entrants came away with medals, some of them significant. Henry Crabb and Tiburcio Parrott each won the Diploma of Honor and Gold Medal. Inglenook picked up a Silver medal, and Parrott a second medal, Bronze. But in general, the Napa showing this time was disappointing.

The Bordeaux, France, exposition took place at the same time. This time, French officials were not so excited about American wine entries; apparently the judges came prepared to dislike foreign (American) wine. They even admitted to such prejudice in the journal *Le Nouvelliste*:

> All of us had been spoiled, as it were, by the wines of our own countries, and having palates accustomed to these, attended this tasting with disagreeable impressions on our minds and such feelings were certainly unfavorable to foreign wines.
>
> Nevertheless, in the long series of red and white wines, of different proprietors and years, and of different vintages, which were shown us, we found many wines which resembled our best hill products of the wines of Burgundy.[14]

This emblem was used by the Winegrower's Union. Below the litho cut ran the slogan; "In Union There is Strength."

The French publication warned that California wine was likely to become a "formidable rival" although pointing out that "incontestably, Bordeaux wines are better than those of California." Of course.

There were no top awards accorded California or American wines at Bordeaux. Silver medals went to the Cupertino Wine Company and for Inglenook Brandy. Bronze awards were picked up by Charles Carpy and Henry Crabb. Honorable Mentions went to Beringer, Crabb and the Napa Valley Wine Company.

Bordeaux left the Napa wine industry a little more down to earth, but happy that the valley could still boast of more wine awards in the 1890s than anyone else. Anyway, what happened or did not happen in Bordeaux was of little consequence, since there was very little press coverage of the event.

Meanwhile, the problems caused by the creation of the California Wine Association refused to go away. In mid-decade, the St. Helena Winegrowers' Union finally gave full vent to its collective anger by passing a resolution urging the abolition of the Board of State Viticultural Commissioners. This was horrifying to those who had long associated with the Board and knew what good it had accomplished. Charles Krug probably turned over in his grave.

But St. Helena held fast, and Governor James H. Budd signed the legislative bill disbanding the Board in the spring of 1895. San Francisco's *Wine and Spirit Review*, captioned its obituary of the Board: "A Case of Prohibition Rejoicing." The journal had long supported the Board. The *Wine and Spirit Review* was also after the Viticulture department at the University of California, Berkeley, and its head, Eugene Hilgard. When the wine journal discovered that two women were enrolled in classes, even though only on a part-time basis, it wanted the entire department abolished. Women studying diseases of the grape vine?

ROBERT LOUIS STEVENSON

The general bad mood which seemed to have invaded the valley may have contributed to the unsympathetic treatment of the death of Robert Louis Stevenson. Stevenson, who was born in Scotland, died on December 8, 1894, at his home in Samoa. Fourteen years before his death, he had lived in almost total obscurity on the side of Mt. St. Helena where he wrote his first book with a Napa Valley theme, *The Silverado Squatters*. Stevenson began his narrative in a quiet tone, which he would never have suspected might later give offense:

> The scene of this little book is on a high mountain. There are, indeed, many higher, there are many of nobler outline. It is no place of pilgrimage for the summary globe trotter; but to one who lives upon its sides, Mount Saint Helena becomes a centre of interest.

Silverado Squatters was first serialized in *Century Illustrated* in November and December of 1883. When the book was published a month later in Boston, not one word about it was noted in the *Calistogian*, the *Star*, the *Journal* or the *Register*. Disregarding the fact that Stevenson was an unknown writer at the time, a book on Napa Valley should have excited some local interest. But the book was unflattering to Napa County.

If Stevenson was anonymous in those days, he certainly wasn't after the publication of *Treasure Island* and *The Strange Case of Dr. Jekyll and Mr. Hyde*. His death was reported in the St. Helena newspaper on December 21:

> Robert Louis Stevenson, the novelist died at his home in Apia, Samoa, December 8th of apoplexy. In 1880 he came to Napa County for his health and lived for several months on Mt. St. Helena where he wrote 'Silverado Squatters' founding the story on the old Silverado mines in that locality.

No other newspaper mentioned his death.

Stevenson's wonderful adventure story, *Treasure Island*, had also had its genesis during the summer Stevenson spent on Mt. St. Helena with his wife, Fanny, and her young son, Lloyd. The abandoned mine shafts, piles of slag, old lanterns, boots, rattlesnakes and the ghosts of departed miners all provided inspiration. *Treasure Island* was actually published before Stevenson's book on Napa Valley, in the summer of 1883. In Chapter Four of *Silverado Squatters*, Stevenson indicates he was aware of the phylloxera invasion in France's vinelands:

> And at the same time, we look timidly forward, with a spark of hope, to where the new lands, already weary of producing gold, begin to green with vineyards. A nice point in human history falls to be decided by Californian and Australian wine.

But it seems Stevenson did not find California wine particularly to his liking: "Meanwhile the wine is merely good wine; the best that I have tasted better than Beaujolais, and not unlike."

There is much else in *Squatters* that is unflattering to the wine country. His introduction to the city of Vallejo and a night spent in a run-down inn is filled with not-so-subtle criticism. He also seemed to look at the valley residents as country bumpkins, full of self importance. When he writes about reaching Calistoga, he says: " . . . here probably, is the office of the local newspaper (for the place has a paper — they all have papers)." Perhaps Stevenson was stung by the fact that California newspapers did not buy or publish his writings. The editor of the *Calistogian* had every right to take offense at the writer's snootiness.

Stevenson's main characters in the book are even less flattering. The Hansons, who lived in the old Silverado Hotel, are depicted as moronic, as are the boarders, including the school teacher. A Jewish shop owner who hauled him up to the abandoned mine near the Toll House was described in extremely derogatory phrases. He called his Jewish merchant "Kilmer," but the character was very likely modeled after Morris Friedberg.

Robert Louis Stevenson was quite ill during his 1880 summer sojourn on Mt. St. Helena, and his financial situation was critical until his father sent him a cable granting him an annual stipend. Perhaps his remarks about Napa Valley reflect his own problems. Or maybe it was simply a case of literary style. In that era, no one could match the English for intellectual snobbery. Still, to the residents of the small valley north of San Francisco, Stevenson was not a favorite. To the wine industry, however, Stevenson will be remembered for the often quoted phrase "wine is bottled poetry."

HENRY W. CRABB

Henry W. Crabb's death on March 2, 1899, was as critical a loss to the valley as Krug's demise. He had picked up where Agoston Haraszthy left off in vine experimentation, planting far more varieties in carefully-controlled plots than did Haraszthy. Then he shared his knowledge willingly with any vine grower who was interested.

Frona Eunice Wait, in her book, *Wines and Vines of California*, gave an entire page to Crabb's fine wine, adding: "As a successful

DIRECTORY

OF THE

GRAPE GROWERS, WINE MAKERS AND DISTILLERS

OF

CALIFORNIA,

AND OF THE

PRINCIPAL GRAPE GROWERS AND WINE MAKERS OF
THE EASTERN STATES.

PUBLISHED BY THE

BOARD OF STATE VITICULTURAL COMMISSIONERS OF CALIFORNIA.

SACRAMENTO:
STATE OFFICE, : : : : : A. J. JOHNSTON, SUP'T. STATE PRINTING.
1891.

This directory, published in 1891 by the California Viticultural Commission, documents the wine boom in Napa County: more than 500 grape growers are listed, with 18,229 acres in grapes, and 166 wine cellars.

wine-maker Mr. Crabb is without peer in the State." The previous year he had won seven First Place awards at the sixth annual Viticultural Convention.

Crabb and Krug had something else in common: major financial mistakes which resulted in a loss of their wineries and vineyards. For some unknown reason, Crabb had borrowed $41,000 from the Goodman Bank in Napa only months before his death. Three months after his death, To-Kalon, one of the finest wine brands in Napa Valley, was sold at public auction to E.S. Churchill.

Six years later a twenty-acre plot of To-Kalon was deeded to the University of California for an experimental vineyard site. Crabb's work would go on, a fitting memorial to this wine pioneer. His original winery burned in a fierce blaze on the morning of May 28, 1939. It was never rebuilt. In 1965, Robert Mondavi purchased much of the former To-Kalon estate, built his winery and planted his vineyards in the same soil.

The near crisis state of the wine industry at times during the 1890s never seemed to affect Napa City as much as other localities. One reason was the diversity in agriculture, especially in the lower end of the Napa Valley. This diversity was fueled by pressure from local Prohibitionists.

Beginning June 7, 1895, the *Register* ran a summer-long weekly column called "Visit to the Farms," in which it was made clear that crops other than grapes were being grown in Napa County. Still, the column also showed how pervasive viticulture was, noting that winemaking was done even on small farms.

"Southwest of Town," was the heading for the second week's column, about the Carneros district. It reported that James Duhig had four acres of vines (on which phylloxera was first identified); his neighbor, U.H. Anderson, had a "small family vineyard." The Priber report of only two years earlier credited Duhig with forty acres in vines. Further down the column, Charles Robinson is credited with "35 or 40 acres" of vines, but Priber had recorded him as growing 60 acres in vines. At this rate, viticulture in the Carneros could soon die out entirely.

WILD HORSE VALLEY

One area completely ignored by the *Register's* "Visit to the Farms" column was Wild Horse Valley. But it is understandable: the principal road into Wild Horse Valley was so rugged and had so many switchbacks that even horse and buggy travel was difficult. Wild Horse Valley lay high in the hills directly east of Napa

City, a good portion of it in Solano County. Its name could be traced back to the 1860s, when an escaped stallion found a mate of similar wild instincts and they founded an obstreperous herd that angered the local populace by jumping over farm fences. Joseph Vorbe and his brother Ephrem loved the story about the wild horses and purchased a good chunk of the valley about 1880. Within a year the area had its first vineyard. Ephrem was cashier for the Swiss-American Bank of San Francisco.

One late arrival in Wild Horse Valley who had a strong interest in wine medals (Vorbe apparently did not), was Constance Malandrino. The Swiss immigrant was superintendent of the large Uncle Sam winery for Charles Carpy (and subsequently the C.W.A.). Malandrino purchased the Behrens ranch in October 1897 and immediately began expanding the vineyards. There were fine grass-covered hillsides on which to plant vines, although some were steep. He did not build a winery because he could crush all of his grapes at no expense at the Uncle Sam winery.

Wild Horse Valley remained one of the least-known regions in all of Napa County until a drought in the 1890s turned the attention of the city of Vallejo to its lack of water storage facilities. Vallejo, a dozen miles south of Napa City and built along the shoreline of the San Francisco Bay, had prospered in recent years from the establishment of drydocks for the United States Navy. When the town wells began to go dry, city officials feared the Navy might close up shop and move its ship repair facilities. The city launched a frantic search for a dam site to catch and hold water from the heavy winter rains.

City supervisors learned that the hills above Wild Horse Valley received unusually heavy rain in winter. Since the land was largely in Solano County, they knew their collective prayers had been answered. In 1894 a dam creating Lake Frey, named after a former city supervisor, was completed, and the water crisis was over for some years to come. All of this frantic activity was recorded carefully in Napa newspapers; Wild Horse Valley would never again be ignored in geographic descriptions of the county.

SPRING MOUNTAIN

Spring Mountain, west of St. Helena, was another part of Napa county with difficult access; roads to the area usually were closed in winter. No wonder Priber missed these growers too in the 1893 phylloxera study. "It is a long, steep grade that leads upward, at least one who travels it for the first time will think so," observed the *Star* in a story on Spring Mountain in the December 5, 1890 issue:

> On the way we pass the extensive and well kept vineyard of the Beringer Bros., cared for by tenants who reside in one of two houses located on the hillside. [Now the site of the Streblow winery at 2849 Spring Mountain Road.] Then on and on till the beautiful home of W. R. Lemme is reached away on the summit. Nature has done much here, and the hand of man has assisted in making this one of the many ideal mountain homes to be found among the hills bordering Napa Valley . . . Yes, there is a vineyard near at hand, and a wine cellar of goodly dimensions.

Lemme's other neighbors, except for Tiburcio Parrott, were barely mentioned in the story, possibly because so few were major winemakers or grape growers.

Lemme's wine cellar had been built in 1876, making it the third oldest on the west side of the valley. Until Lemme finally built his own road across the face of the high hills, he had to drive down to St. Helena and then take the long Spring Mountain Road back to visit his neighbors. His winery, called La Perla, ceased operations with Prohibition.

A third Spring Mountain winery was mentioned briefly in the 1890 story, that of Otto Hirchler. He owned land straddling the Sonoma/Napa County boundary and appropriately called his cellar the Summit Winery. It was built of stone, 64 x 64 feet, and three stories high.

Carl Conradi of Oakland never told a newspaper reporter why he chose Spring Mountain for a vineyard site in 1890. His location, like Lemme's, required the building of a road to reach it. He was in the cigar and tobacco business, and since it was popular then for many businessmen to smoke cigars, his was a very profitable enterprise. There is no record of when Conradi's first vines were planted or whether he used resistant stock. He must have used the new Rupestris St. George, for his production was so good by 1904 that stone was cut from a nearby hillside for a winery. The name "Conradi" was cut into the stone over the door of his winery but, contrary to custom, no date was included.

FROST, WORMS AND PHYLLOXERA

The subjects of mountain-planted vineyards and frost damage came up all too often during the 1890s. There were three major frosts, some of the cold so severe it wiped out the entire grape crop in portions of the valley. The first of these frosts came on March 31, 1892. At a meeting of the Winegrowers Union eight days later in St. Helena, George Husmann was one of the few to report "his vineyard in Chiles Valley had escaped with but little damage." [15]

1892

In April 1895 the frost was so widespread that it was described as the worst cold weather for the vine in northern California since 1880. The newspapers called it a "calamitous frost." The following spring was no better, with Sonoma County growers around Geyserville finally adopting a technique used for a decade or more in Napa Valley:

> Claus Meyer, a well-known vineyards of Geyserville, has experimented upon means of averting frost until he had found something which has proven most efficacious. During the cold nights recently, between the hours of 3 and 7, he built large straw fires and wherever the smoke hovered the frost failed to appear and he has, thereby, saved his whole crop of grapes. Other growers should follow his example. [16]

This method of preventing frost damage by using smoke had been practiced in Europe for centuries. In 1882, when frost damage was widespread in California, the *Star* had reported, "that smoke does actually protect the vines against frost, was demonstrated during its recent visitation, when on one occasion, the temperature fell to 28 degrees, and those who smoked thoroughly suffered but slightly."[17] The same report noted that for several mornings, "the valley was completely smudged." Why the message took so long to reach Geyserville is not clear.

Jacob Beringer boasted in 1881 that he had discovered that frost barely nipped his vines where he had trained them to grow high on the stake (low-growing vines were the common practice). Arguments over high and low staking seemed to go on endlessly among vintners and growers, as with so many aspects of the industry. Manuring of vineyards drew nearly as much heated discussion. In Europe, it was absolutely necessary to rejuvenate the age-old vineyards with fertilizer. Many believed it was not needed in California.

Jacob Schram complained of insects boring into his wooden casks, deeply enough for the casks to leak. A solution proposed was to soak the barrels in hot water liberally diluted with alum, then apply linseed oil as a coating when the casks were dry. Farmers also discovered that the worms that collected in huge numbers on the native oaks were voracious consumers of grape leaves. The only remedy for this problem seemed to be frequent cultivation of the soil to kill the worm in the chrysalis stage.

But none of these problems were so threatening in the mid-1890s as that microscopic devil, the "phylloxera vastatrix." As one so-called resistant vine after another failed, calamity seemed unavoidable. Vine culture was just about doomed in Napa Valley.

One of the last publications of the Viticultural Commissioners, its report for 1893-94, devoted half of its space to the most advanced view on phylloxera, a translated text by French scientist Valery Mayet. Mayet's report began:

> To write on a subject after so many other authors, and to summarize and recapitulate the mountains of books, treatises, memoirs and pamphlets concerning it, offers many difficulties. Such is the situation, however, of whomever desires to-day to write upon the phylloxera. . . With the phylloxera, the abundance of material becomes almost an obstacle. It is true that

some researches were made in the past decade; but during this short period what floods of ink, what outbursts of impracticable ideas, what foolish plans have been devoted to securing the prize of 30,000 francs offered for a remedy.

Mayet wrote that Dr. Henry Schimer of Philadelphia identified in 1867 both the wingless and winged form of the insect. Schimer did not know it had been able to live comfortably on the roots of Eastern American grape vines, which somehow tolerated the pest. It was supposed that the American phylloxera had traveled to Europe sometime in the 1860s, first to England.

Back in the Napa Valley, the concept of replanting with American resistant rootstock gained widespread acceptance. Charles Krug was one of the first growers in Napa Valley to begin wholesale replanting of his vineyards. He initiated the "avenue system." In the first row, he had his field workers plant a Riparia root between each dying vine. He skipped the second row, letting it continue to produce. He repeated his "avenue" system in the third, fifth, and subsequent odd rows. The diseased rows were removed as the vines died.

The Riparia vine was the favorite of German immigrant Julius Dresel of Sonoma, who may have been one of the first in California to plant so-called resistant root stock, beginning in 1878. The vine he used originated in the woods of Missouri, Iowa, Kansas and portions of Texas. But the Riparia was unquestionably a river-bank grape, not accustomed to drier climates.

John Stanly in the Carneros, Husmann at the Simonton farm, and Henry Hagen were early advocates of the Riparia root. Husmann later switched to the Lenoir and never ceased talking about it. The Lenoir did graft well. But when the University of California at Berkeley began researching resistant vines, Professor Arthur Hayne found problems with the Lenoir. It did not adapt well to California's climate unless the year was unusually wet. If planted where sub-surface moisture was abundant, it did well.[18]

In his report to the Viticultural Commissioners, Priber demonstrated clearly that the Lenoir vine was not going to work in California. A year later, Charles Wetmore reported, "The Riparia is still the favorite variety, and in fact, hardly any other is planted, simply for the reason that our knowledge of the other resistant varieties is limited."[19]

In another twelve months, phylloxera had been confirmed in Contra Costa County and then was also discovered in Livermore. In the *Healdsburg Tribune*, a writer using the pseudonym "Vitis" wrote somewhat sarcastically of the fear no one wished to utter:

> A report has been going the rounds of the press, that the Riparia vines in Napa county are dying out on hillside locations. Local growers here have been much exercised over the statement, fearing that resistant vines were not doing all that is claimed of them."

The University of California and Professor Hayne, much to their discredit, found a high, strong fence and straddled it. Hayne wrote to the *Star* on January 3, 1896, agreeing with George Husmann's explanation that cuttings were often mishandled, and that vineyard plows did not always reach deeply enough. He also had to answer Husmann's charge that Hayne had not yet been born when Husmann was tromping the vineyards of America. Hayne suggested that Husmann's Missourian perspective appeared shortsighted.

Much of the proof that the Rupestris was best for California came from a single Napa Valley grower. George Schoenwald had opened a winery in the stone basement of his grand home on the western outskirts of St. Helena. He first planted Riparia, but by mid-point in the decade had lost most of his vines, and switched to Rupestris. His story is best told by a neighbor, Henry Tucker, whose interview was published on February 16, 1900, in the *Star*:

> He [Tucker] thinks Mr. Schoenwald is entitled to great credit for expending large sums of money in importing Rupestris St. George cuttings from France and experimenting with them as he established beyond doubt, the fact of the adaptability to the soil and climate of Napa Valley."

Schoenwald had his first Rupestris St. George roots in the ground in the spring of 1898. The grafted vines grew so rapidly that his field crew had to cut them back severely after only the second year. That kind of news made headlines. By the early spring of 1901, the local newspaper could report:

> There is greater activity in vine planting this season than for many years. Rupestris St. George is undoubtedly the favorite variety and vineyardists are basing great hopes of success on the French stock which is doing so well wherever tried. The young vineyards of George Schoenwald and Beringer Brothers in and near St. Helena are pointed to as offering sufficient encouragement for renewed efforts and not only in Napa County but in other dry wine sections . . . "[20]

A French immigrant, Georges de Latour, who settled not far from Inglenook in 1900, quickly arranged for millions of bench-grafted Rupestris St. George to be shipped to him.

It's not surprising that there was such ready acceptance of the Rupestris rootstock. Napa Valley's wine industry was nearly wiped out by the year 1900. In August 1908 the *Star* pinpointed the worst years of phylloxera damage as 1896-1898:

> The acreage in bearing vines in Napa County this year is larger than at any time since the phylloxera wrought such havoc in this valley, ten or twelve years ago.

ALTERNATIVES TO THE GRAPE

While the vines were succumbing to disease, olives and olive oil were another way to earn money. Olive orchards spread rapidly through the valley during this period. Adolphe Flamant had done much pioneering work with olives on his portion of the Simonton ranch in the Carneros, even publishing a booklet on how to grow them. The major influx of Italian immigrants during the decade of the 1890s helps account for the new trend.

At a Farmer's Institute meeting held in Napa City in November 1896, young professor Arthur Hayne came up from

Berkeley to impart his knowledge of olive cultivation. He told growers that olive trees will fruit within two years "but never twice on the same spot of the tree." He also claimed that olives were improperly processed in California, resulting in poor profits. Ripe olives were first soaked in a weak solution of lye and two percent potash. Four to six hours later, this was drained and the olives washed in fresh water to remove the bitter taste. Insufficient washing was one of the problems, said Hayne.

Tourism was a growing part of the economy by the end of the 1890s. San Francisco had added fifty thousand new residents and considerable wealth. Sonoma County's hot springs were a favorite choice for city vacationers. Aetna Springs in Pope Valley was a bit far to travel except for those who planned to stay several weeks. Calistoga's hot springs were making a strong comeback, as were White Sulphur Springs at St. Helena, Napa Soda Springs near Napa City, and Samuels Springs in Berryessa Valley.

Local mineral waters were very much the fad. Each resort advertised the mineral content of their water in San Francisco newspapers or booklets free for the asking. It was simply amazing how many minerals could be found in such waters by a good chemist. The founding in March 1897 of *American Wine and Mineral Water News*, in New York, offers additional evidence of the popularity of this young industry.

All those tinkling bottles of Napa mineral water had an effect not anticipated by valley winemakers. The thousands of tourists who tasted the waters also tasted an occasional glass of wine, maybe for the first time. Wine sales began to pick up. But that wasn't the only explanation for the increasing sales of wines. Large numbers of Italian immigrants throughout the state helped, though many of these families preferred to buy grapes and make their own wine. Still, that helped the grape farmer.

Then too, the national economy was booming. American wheat farmers were selling wheat for $1.09 a bushel to European countries where the crop had suffered from adverse weather conditions. The discovery of gold in the Yukon excited investors in stocks; everyone seemed to agree that this Gold Rush was the "big one."

The *San Francisco Call* sent a reporter to the valley to do a feature story which barely mentioned wine, and focused instead on the natural beauty of the valley.[21] Hundreds of small farmers discovered they could renovate a small outbuilding and rent it by the week or month to vacationers. If they provided meals, that was more income. Many farm families moved out of their main home during the summer and rented it.

America's conflict with Spain over Cuba, and the eventual declaration of war on April 25, 1899, threw the country's economy into a wartime boom. With a large army, unemployment practically disappeared, and wages increased substantially. The *Wine and Spirit Review* for October announced in a lead story that the "Wave of Prosperity is Here": "The situation in the wine business has not had such satisfactory features in many years." By "features," editor Winfield Scott meant good prices. Wine was selling for 20¢ to 35¢ a gallon, depending on its age, and grapes were going for $25 to $30 a ton. Grapes were abundant, but not in Napa Valley. Northern Sonoma had hardly been touched by phylloxera, but the pest had virtually eliminated Napa grapes.

Books about wine were becoming popular too. Frona E. Wait's *Wines and Vines of California* was clearly written for the new wine consumer. Daniel O'Connell's *The Inner Man* aimed higher; it was about fine food and fine wine. Ben Truman's *See How It Sparkles* filled a large void in educating the public about champagne.

Champagne production really came of age in California during this period. Arpad Haraszthy had mastered the secrets of champagne with little competition. Now Paul Masson in the Santa Clara Valley joined him, as did Charles Wetmore in Livermore, Italian Swiss Colony, the Korbels and others. Champagne had been known as the beverage of royalty and the wealthy class. Now working men wanted to bring it home for anniversaries, spurred on by a popular dance hall tune called

"Champagne Charlie." It was easy to remember: "Champagne Charlie is my name/ Good for any game at night, my boys/ Who'll join me in a spree?" No one in Napa Valley was producing champagne, but that would soon change.

Other changes were taking place. The Charles Krug winery was now the property of James Moffitt. Alfred Tubbs did not live to see the wonders of the new century; he died in his Palace Hotel apartment in late December 1896. Judge Stanly, too, died just before the new century began.

It had been a busy and fascinating decade, during which Napa Valley had grown and matured into its middle age. This aging was none too graceful at times, especially considering the debacles of the California Wine Association and the demise of the Board of State Viticultural Commissioners. But the result was extraordinary. The Napa Valley stood alone, above every other wine-growing region, or so thought one prescient Sacramento journalist:

> Valleys and mountains comprise the topography of Napa county, expressed in general terms. To be more explicit: a range of the Mayacamas Mountains forms the western boundary line of the county, at the base of which, and extending the whole length of the county, lies Napa valley, the queen of all the valleys in the county, as well as in the whole state.[22]

Fire had not seriously damaged the interior of Fritz Beringer's new home in St. Helena when Harvey Lewelling took this photograph about 1885. Construction had begun in 1883; the fire occurred two years later. Still standing, the house on the grounds of the Beringer winery is one of Napa Valley's most beautiful structures – inside and out.

RUPESTRIS ST. GEORGE,
RECOVERY AND PROHIBITION

The French immigrant influence in Napa Valley winemaking increased dramatically with the arrival of Georges de Latour. Like many of his predecessors, de Latour had difficulty with the English language, but he had no difficulty whatever in seeing that California wine could one day match that of his native land. He might need a half century to prove his point, but he wasn't going anywhere. Any return to France would be only for a visit, and — much later — to share his vast wealth with his former neighbors.

What de Latour accomplished can only be compared to the work of Charles Krug, the father of the Napa Valley wine industry. De Latour nursed it back to health with imported phylloxera-resistant vines, and made quality wine his primary goal. Niebaum, Stanly and Krug would have toasted his endeavors had they been his contemporaries.

De Latour's road to success in the wine industry was rocky at best. His wallet was often so empty that he was sued frequently for back wages or failure to pay his bills. Local newspapers covered these stories, but they were buried in the back pages: his work with resistant vines and Cabernet Sauvignon wine made the front pages.

De Latour was a native of the Bordeaux region of France. That in itself was enough to qualify him as a wine expert. He had been trained as a chemist in a Catholic university, which gave him a status in California few other winemakers possessed. Most of his peers were men who had grown up in winemaking families but had little formal technical training.

For fifteen years after de Latour arrived in California he gathered unwanted and unused argols, a crusted deposit scraped from inside wine tanks. He processed this material at San Jose, Healdsburg and finally Rutherford, into cream of tartar for home baking. He was well known to Napa vintners by the time he purchased four acres of land with a house and barn in May 1900 from Charles P. Thompson at Rutherford.

There were many more French immigrants living in San Jose and between Healdsburg and Cloverdale than in the entire county of Napa. San Jose could have been the unofficial French capital of California in the nineteenth century. So why would de Latour settle in Napa Valley? There are several possible answers to this question. Napa's reputation is one. The opportunity to be near the Inglenook winery is another. Or de Latour may have believed that the soil of Rutherford provided what he wanted for his future wine production. He knew the Zinfandel and Mission grape would grow anywhere, but the Cabernet Sauvignon was more finicky.

Meanwhile, he had to pay his bills. He soon discovered that he could make both an income and a positive impact on the valley by importing bench-grafted phylloxera-resistant vines of the finest European varieties of grapes. He did so not in the tens of thousands but in the millions. Between 1900 and 1920 de Latour helped replant and rebuild the grape industry of much of California.

Napa County had less than 5,000 acres of wine grapes when de Latour arrived. A train ride up the west side of the valley and a wagon ride back down the east side gave him a chance to see how sick the vines really were. Many growers had tried so-called resistant roots, only to find they were not adaptive to California's climate and soil.

George Schoenwald got rave press notices for his work with the Rupestris St. George, but he didn't seem interested in providing his neighbors with the St. George root, which came from France. On the other hand, de Latour had friends there who could provide the bench-grafted vines. A letter or two was all it took to make the arrangements. By 1907 de Latour was receiving shipments of millions of the vines. He had agents in many counties selling for him. The October *Wine and Spirit Review* was pleased to publish this recommendation:

> Since the destruction by phylloxera of the vineyards in California, the farmers have been looking for a vine with which to restore their vineyards permanently. Many experiments have been made, but few have been successful.
> The *Wine and Spirit Review*, having at heart the interest of the public, has constantly watched the progress made in California, and now is in a position to conscientiously recommend to vineyardists the vines imported from France by G. de Latour, of Rutherford.

De Latour's personal experimentation with the Rupestris St. George had started in April, 1901. The *Star* reported in March 1909 that de Latour had 450,000 vines ready for planting. By 1915, the *Wine and Spirit Review* referred to de Latour's vineyards as "famous" and could not honor him enough for his work.

De Latour began buying bulk wine in the valley in 1900 and may have regarded this as the founding year of Beaulieu. In 1901 he leased the Harris winery for storage, and in 1904 rented the Thomann cellar for his first crush. De Latour made his first wine in 1904 in this rented cellar. The first Beaulieu winery did not come into existence for another three years.

The bulk wine he purchased in 1900 may have been sold for altar wine, which is a story in itself. Early in that year the San Francisco *Examiner* carried a story regarding a St. Helena priest, Father Blake, who recommended certain local wines to other

Catholic churches. It was implied that he or the church received some sort of kickback. (The *Examiner* delighted in digging up dirt on sacrosanct institutions like the Catholic church.) The *Star* printed Father Blake's explanation that he did live, after all, in the heart of fine wine country, and inquiry letters from fellow priests did arrive in his mailbox. He vehemently denied any wrongdoing and declared he would henceforth make no such recommendations.

De Latour must have been pleased that the good father was out of business. Eventually, he obtained letters from the San Francisco archdiocese stating he produced wine according to strict canonical law. In those early years, his profit from church wine was small, but when Prohibition began this segment of his wine business expanded phenomenally.

Since ready cash was always a major problem, de Latour contracted to sell all of his grapes, as soon as they came into production, to the California Wine Association, to be crushed at the Greystone winery. This crop came from the vines he planted as well as from vines on 125 acres he purchased in 1903 from Joseph A. Donohue.

Beaulieu Winery was finally built on de Latour's Rutherford farm in 1907. An Italian immigrant, Joseph Ponti, confirmed the date many years later; he started to work for de Latour on the morning of February 4, 1907:

> He came down to the vineyard, and we talked. I talk French, still do, as much as I do my own language. . . He says, 'You look like an intelligent boy, I want you to learn the business. Would you care to do that?" At that time here was no winery, it was just the beginning. They had an old barn there, it was two story, up above they used to keep the hay, and down

Overleaf: Unusually square in design, the old Larkmead winery in St. Helena is unique in other ways as well. The ground floor is of cement, five feet thick; the second floor timbers are so massive they could support a steam locomotive. Built for Battista Salmina in 1906, the winery was later sold to Hanns Kornell.

below the horses. So he had made some partitions there, and he had about, oh I would say two dozen barrels of wine. That's all he had.[1]

The renewal of Napa County's vineyards, helped so much by de Latour, brought a resurgence of winery construction during the early years of the century. The Salminas at Larkmead hired builder Wilbur Harrison of St. Helena to erect a new all-stone wine cellar, 33 feet in height and 66 feet square, with flooring so massive it could hold a railroad engine. Actual work on the winery began in March 1906 with the pouring of a five-foot-thick concrete floor, designed to hold sixteen tanks of 160,000 gallons capacity each. Huge redwood beams were used for the second floor to support fifty tanks of 1,250 gallons each, plus all the fermenting equipment.

Larkmead was a monument to the man who drew the plans and oversaw the construction. Like Hamden W. McIntyre, who drew so many designs after Inglenook, Wilbur Harrison soon became the local expert on winery construction. Harrison's father had built Victorian row-houses and commercial buildings in Oakland and Berkeley. Before he began building wineries, young Harrison built bungalows and fruit dryers. He had so many projects going at one time that he could visit each only briefly, barking out orders, then galloping off to the next site.

Some of the men who hired Harrison were not easy to please. Battista Salmina was one of those who might have given Harrison an ulcer.

Battista did not want to interrupt his winemaking in the original Larkmead winery. So he told Harrison to build the stone walls of the new winery around the old cellar. Winery workers would come and go, dodging the men building the stone walls or putting the redwood beams in place. Salmina insisted on climbing up a ladder and pouring a bottle of champagne over the location for the front door. When the stone walls were in place and the roof completed over the new Larkmead winery, the walls of the still-intact original winery were removed, piece by piece. Not a drop of wine was spilled, and not a minute of work-time was lost.

Up on Spring Mountain Road, the Hart family asked Harrison to build a stone bridge 75 feet long between the main road and the hillside, spanning an often dry creek. Halfway into the project the winter rains arrived, and a torrential rainstorm took out the half-finished bridge. Harrison replaced all the materials at his own expense and began again, building the bridge so solidly that nothing could dislodge it. Today the bridge is the main entrance to Chateau Chevalier Winery.[2]

In the same year as the new Larkmead winery was built, but six miles closer to St. Helena, Anton Forni completed his stone winery. He even copied the Salminas by insisting the wooden wine cellar inside and its contents not be disturbed. When the stone walls were finished, the redwood wine cellar inside was dismantled.

Forni, like Salmina, had been a hotel owner in St. Helena. He entered the wine business when grapes became scarce because of phylloxera. Forni first leased the Tychson winery from a nearly bankrupt Josephine Tychson in 1895, after phylloxera had decimated her vines. Shortly after the purchase Forni ordered the construction of the new stone wine cellar. It took seven years to complete. The stonemasons must have been confused, but they had to be happy for the work. First Forni ordered stone walls to be built around the 50 x 50 foot wooden Tychson winery. The stone walls would be two stories, 50 x 73 feet. Then he had a stone addition built on the St. Helena side. Next he ordered a stone addition to run 143 feet on each side and 92 feet front and back. The front of the new wine cellar would reach almost to the St. Helena-Calistoga highway.

When the building was finally completed in 1906, Forni had workmen install bronze plaques on either side of the front door, facing the highway, reading "1895" and "1906." These would confuse visitors for decades afterward, everyone assuming the first winery on the site dated to 1895. Since Josephine Tychson had made wine in the first cellar nine years earlier (1886), that should have been acknowledged as the real founding date.

Anton called his new cellar Lombarda. He had a wild scheme for selling his wine: not a drop locally. Forni had Italian cousins working in the marble quarries of Vermont. While on a visit there, he had discovered that hundreds of Italian immigrant laborers had no ready source of good red wine. For years Lombarda wines went monthly by the rail carload to Barre, Vermont. Anton died in August, 1908, just as the fall crush was getting under way.[3]

Ironically, not far from those Vermont quarries, a death occurred one year after Forni's which should have been noted with considerable solemnity in Napa Valley. Instead, not one word of the passing of Hamden W. McIntyre was carried in the local newspapers. McIntyre was a native of Randolph, Vermont. When a brother died, he felt a family obligation to return home and run the family business, which included the small town's telephone exchange. At the time he was called back to Vermont, he was employed by Leland Stanford in Tehama County. McIntyre's obituary, covering a full column in his hometown newspaper, mentions his work at Inglenook and for Stanford but there is not one word on all of the architectural plans he drew for so many wineries in Napa, Sonoma, Livermore, Tehama and other locations.

Had he returned to live in California, McIntyre might not have recognized the local wine industry by 1909, so much had changed. Electricity had come to the valley, with the capability to turn night into day, almost, a dream come true during the late-night work of the crushing season.

ELECTRICITY COMES TO NAPA VALLEY

Some Napa residents first saw the glow of an electric light bulb in a circus. In September 1880 the *Petaluma Courier* report-ed that the Cole Circus had exhibited the "first introduction of

Josephine Tychson was far better known in Napa Valley for how fast she drove or rode her horses than for the fact that she was the first woman to open a winery. Founded in 1886, Freemark Abbey was directly across the highway from her modest house, shown here with two adults and four children in the front yard. Josephine is riding side-saddle, probably a rarity for her.

the wonderful electric light." In those days electricity was produced by a gasoline engine of thirty horsepower. (Similar generators were used in local vineyards to shock grapevines with noise and vibration, hoping to kill the phylloxera, but that concept also failed.)

The Napa Gas and Electric Company provided Napa City with electric street lights for some years before electricity generated from mountain streams became available in 1900. The generators often ran erratically, illuminating the town brightly some nights, hardly at all on others. In St. Helena, water-powered electricity arrived in June 1909. Two years later the *Star* was able to report: "A great step forward in cellar equipment has been taken during the past year by the installation of electric motors and electric lights." The electric motor meant that wine could be pumped more rapidly from tank to tank, saving the cost of a half dozen laborers who used hand pumps.

The first winery in the valley to be electrically lighted was probably Greystone. A gasoline generator was installed at Greystone in April 1888 to provide electric power. In 1903 John Benson had a water-driven generator installed at Far Niente, but whether he had water year-round for power is questionable.

Electric pumps were crucial in the experiments to cool freshly crushed grape must so that it would ferment at temperatures considerably below those outside. "Stuck" wine was a constant and discouraging problem, particularly when hot weather settled in for a protracted stay. Wine does not ferment well, or sometimes at all, if the must temperature is too high. Leaving grapes to sit overnight to cool them sometimes helped.

By encircling wine fermenters with copper tubes and pumping cold water through the pipes, the fermentation temperature could be lowered substantially and controlled. The University of California at Berkeley described how to make such a cooling device in its Bulletin No. 174, issued in April 1906, but few vintners could afford the cost.

Glass Bottles and Yeast

High cost was also the reason so few winery owners bottled their wine. Hand blown bottles were expensive, and even Gustave Niebaum abandoned his advertised intention to "Bottle Only In Glass" as too costly. The railroads also discouraged glass case shipments by charging a rate three times that charged for bulk. But wine quality simply could not be maintained as long as wine left its place of origin in barrels.

In 1903 a scientist named Michael J. Owens partially solved the problem by inventing an automatic bottle-making machine:

it was a mold made of wood or metal into which hot glass could be blown. By 1910, 33,000 bottles a day were being produced and that figure rose yearly. The Owens-Illinois Glass Company originated from this invention.

Two Italian immigrants at the Italian Swiss Colony winery, Pietro Rossi and Andrea Sbarboro, took up where Niebaum left off and marketed much of their wine in the East in glass. The *Wine and Spirit Review* editorialized:

> One of the most satisfactory features of the situation as regards California wines is the steady and marked gain that is being made by our best wines in glass, under a genuine label and marketed by responsible business houses.[4]

Those "responsible business houses" were also watching ever more closely what went into the wine bottle. It was not enough to produce average wine anymore; to compete with European wine the quality standard had to rise. If California wines were to maintain their sales lead even in San Francisco, quality would be the key. It was no longer enough to be a native wine. Those loyalties were being abandoned.

Wine quality could be improved significantly by adding pure yeast, suggested the Board of Viticultural Commissioners in their annual Report of 1888: "The best for the purpose is the compressed yeast, sold in small cakes throughout California, although any well-washed yeast will do."

Professor A. P. Haynes had urged the use of yeast in wine fermentation in 1896. A decade later Professor Frederic Bioletti issued a University circular describing the process in detail. Because the University Professors did not want their opinion to be simply theoretical, they convinced the California Wine Association to experiment with yeast in tanks of 5000 gallons at their Geyserville plant.

The industry as a whole paid scant attention to the results, which were very positive. But when Rudolph Jordan began using pure yeast at the Streich winery in the Napa Redwoods, some of the old attitudes began to change. Jordan was given complete freedom for his experimenting. He kept copious notes and described his success in a 1911 pamphlet called "Quality in Dry Wines Through Adequate Fermentations."

Jordan also wrote about his work and the need to upgrade wine quality in the May 1912 issue of the *Wine and Spirit Review*. His was the first application of pure yeast in a small family winery in California. His work influenced a half dozen or so vintners like de Latour, Julius Beringer and Felix Salmina, but the rest of the industry was slow to learn. Still, the movement toward higher wine quality was justified by the awards won in one wine competition after another, from Portland, Oregon, to San Francisco, including the great Panama Pacific Exposition of 1915, honoring the opening of the Panama Canal.

THE GREAT EARTHQUAKE AND FIRE

But Mother Nature dramatically interrupted this new concentration on quality advancement. An earthquake centered north of San Francisco on the morning of April 18, 1906, succeeded indirectly in destroying two-thirds of the wine supplies of the state. For a long time afterward, the sole concern for the wine industry was to replace that supply.

On that fateful morning, San Francisco was the wine capital of the state. There were as many as two hundred wineries in Sonoma, and almost the same number in Napa and Alameda counties. Nearly all were single-family ventures of perhaps ten to thirty thousand gallons. Most of the wine was made in single-walled redwood structures with no protection against the intense summer heat. Italian immigrants owned many of these small cellars, barely surviving on the income from their wine, butter and eggs. The stone wine cellars such as Far Niente, Inglenook, Atkinson & Ewer, et al, composed only a small fraction of the wine storage in Napa Valley. Cellars built deeply into a recess of a hillside had some protection against the summer heat, but

At least 45 million gallons of wine were destroyed in the San Francisco earthquake and fire in 1906 when huge tanks burned. Had the wine been sprayed on the flames it could have saved hundreds of buildings. This picture shows that many wine tanks (left) did not burn.

there was no air conditioning or insulation in the walls of the family cellars.

But summer heat was not a problem in San Francisco, where cooling summer fogs routinely covered the city. Consequently, every large winery owner had a real wine cellar there, and huge wine warehouses bought up the entire contents of the small rural wineries long before the heat of June arrived. Several dozen vast wine complexes in the city held millions of gallons. Among them were Lachman and Jacobi, S. Lachman, Kohler and Frohling, Gundlach-Bundschu, C. Schilling, Schlessinger and Bender, B. Arnold, Chauche and Bon, and Theodore Gier. Many of the owners were active in the California Wine Association. Among the Napa wineries with San Francisco cellars were Chateau Chevalier, C. Carpy, A. Finke's Widow, Gier, Grimm, Inglenook (through B. Arnold), Oakville Wine Co., Dos Mesas-Cedar Knolls, and the Golden West Company of Georges de Latour. Although there is no way to know how much wine was stored in San Francisco that fateful morning, we do know that the C.W.A. alone had about ten million gallons. Some estimates put the figure at 45 million gallons. If wine stored in hotel basements (nearly all in barrels and puncheons in very considerable amounts), grocery stores, saloons, etc. were counted, the figure could easily have topped fifty million.

Ironically, there is little evidence of any direct damage to all of this wine or equipment in the earthquake. Few if any wine tanks were nudged or shoved off their supports. In the summer of 1926, the San Francisco *Argonaut* published pages of eye-witness descriptions of the quake damage — everyone from policemen to journalists. There is not one mention of red wine flowing ankle deep in the gutters.

More than fifty fires started immediately. At Third and Townsend, a Chinese laundry collapsed into the basement where a furnace set the rubble on fire. The fire quickly spread and within an hour an entire block was burning. This fire could have been extinguished with wine stored nearby. All water mains had broken in the quake, but across the street from the Chinese laundry the C.W.A. had two million gallons of wine stored. The Hercules gasoline pump had been widely adopted by these cellars to move wine, and each facility had hundreds, if not thousands of yards of canvas hose.

The cellars were located in an arc running from about Third and Townsend across the city's financial district and old produce yards to North Beach. The wine was kept in 5, 10, 15 or 20-thousand-gallon tanks. A hose could have been dropped in a tank, cycled through the Hercules pump and carried blocks to fight a fire. Why wasn't wine used, given the extreme urgency of the situation? Firefighters may have assumed that wine sprayed on the fire would explode or burn because of its alcohol content. The largely untrained firefighters, most appointed through political connections, did not know that wine, with an alcohol content of only 12% to 15%, was used frequently at wineries to fight internal fires. Almost exactly ten years earlier, wine had put out a major fire at the Korbel winery in Sonoma County.

Until the turn of the century Chinese laborers did nearly all the viticultural work in California. After 1900 Italian workers, and later some Japanese, replaced them. The unique inverted conical hats identify the Chinese in this picture.

For three and a half days San Francisco burned. The holocaust took wine cellars along with everything else. the heat was above 2,000 degrees. Just under five hundred blocks of houses and commercial buildings were leveled by the flames, many of which could have been saved by spraying wine on the fires. It would have been a poignant footnote to history had the C.W.A.'s ten-year-old Clarets been used to save the city. Many Clarets were made from Napa Valley Cabernet Sauvignon or Zinfandel.

U.S. Army forces stationed at the Presidio marched into downtown San Francisco within three hours of the earthquake to help keep order. Armed soldiers were placed in front of any building with alcohol. The fear was that people who had lost everything they owned might go on a binge of drinking and subsequent looting.

Some of this paranoia can be traced to the influence of Prohibitionists and other anti-alcohol crusaders who saw a very special opportunity. Every saloon was closed, but not before every bottle of alcohol was knocked from the shelves and broken. This was done in neighborhood markets, as well. But the fears of a public gone mad were completely unfounded. In fact, probably because so many residents were dazed and shocked by events, there was a quiet, orderly evacuation of the downtown area with very few crimes.

In Santa Rosa, fire following the earthquake destroyed wine operations, but there were no fires in Napa Valley. The Brun & Chaix cellar in Oakville lost 100,000 gallons of wine when tanks slid from supports and buckled. The *Napa Daily Journal* carried accounts of damage in Napa City, where many downtown buildings were wrecked. The Migliavacca winery, all of stone, was a disaster, although the stone Mathews winery came through without a crack, and soon became the focus of operation for San Francisco's A. Repsold Company.

Most of the large San Francisco wine emporia were not rebuilt. The C.W.A. moved to Point Richmond, Lachman & Jacobi to Petaluma. San Francisco ceased being the focus of the California wine universe, and there was no longer anywhere to ship wine when the summer heat came on.

On June 8, 1906, Edgar Sheehan was quoted in the *Star* claiming 40 million gallons of wine had been lost, although his winery survived. The coming harvest would bring a bonanza for the small grower and producer, as wine prices were already rising.

Records of the State Board of Equalization for 1904 show Napa County had 7000 acres of vines. The county was recovering slowly from the phylloxera and just beginning to take advantage of de Latour's importations of grafted vines. A year later there were 9,340 acres of producing vines, but an encouraging 6,200 new non-bearing vines. Percy T. Morgan of the C.W.A. provided this review in 1910 of the previous four years:

> Planting again progressed rapidly and 'all went merry as a marriage bell' until the panic of 1907. The consequent exodus of a large number of wine-drinking Europeans to their native lands, coupled with the wave of prohibition which swept over the country, caused a great curtailment in the, until then, rapidly increasing export trade, which by 1907, had reached almost 25,000,000 gallons of wine and brandy annually.[5]

The "Roosevelt" panic, or depression, reversed itself by 1910, claimed Morgan, and a very short European grape crop brought prosperity once more. Boom and bust: these periodic cycles were a plague to the wine industry.

One aspect of Napa's unique history in viticulture was a dedication to promotion and advertising. When the grape crop was going to be too big or the wine surplus seemed about to overflow, someone always proposed a solution.

One aspect of this promotion campaign was quite new: photographs. Horatio F. Stoll, a San Francisco journalist, hired photographers to go with him on his tour of the vineyards and wineries, shooting pictures of vines in spring, summer and fall. For the first time, photographs became a serious and integral part of wine promotion. During the fall crush of 1909, Stoll produced what was likely the first moving pictures made of a winery's operation. His film, soon shown in theaters across the country, included footage of each wine district in California. This film marked the first time Napa Valley had appeared in a motion picture theater.

An especially novel idea to advertise wine was the "California Car," a railroad car filled with products of the state, emphasizing wine. The car was part of an entire train which also had promotion cars from other states. "The California car is furnished in California redwood and a grape arbor is carried out in a realistic manner" noted the *St. Paul Press*. "The wine exhibit is one of the best made of California products and has opened our eyes as to the extent of that industry." Napa Valley wines were from Inglenook and Theodore Gier.

The growing consumption of California wine in the East, in large part due to an emphasis on quality by such brands as Inglenook, To Kalon and Parrott, inevitably engendered news stories. One such story in the *New York Herald* in the fall of 1909 quoted Edward M. Tierney of the Marlborough Hotel:

> American wines, through their growing excellence, are actually driving French wines from the home market. In the best cafes, hotels and restaurants patrons are now insisting upon

the American grown article — in fact, they seem proud to order it. This is in striking contrast to the condition a few years ago when the average diner would not dare to order an American wine above a whisper.

Tierney added that he thought some American champagnes were "vastly superior to those brought in from abroad." For some Californians who had previously had to put up with disdain for their local wines, Tierney's remarks were almost unbelievable. Had he been paid to write that opinion? Or had American wine really come this far?

In California wine production nearly had to double to keep up with demand for dry table wines during the latter years of the first decade. Consumption jumped from 16 million gallons yearly to 27 million. Sweet wine production had a three-fold increase, from 6 million to 18 million gallons.

The attention of the press to wine displays and competitions at world's fairs contributed to this success. It seemed that a new world's fair was held about every two years in the United States. Promoters had to work overtime to draw the large crowds needed to satisfy the sponsors and put the event in the black financially. Wine tastings, wine cafes, and fountains of wine were good draws.

The decade of 1900 to 1910 saw an epidemic of world's fairs. At the first of these in 1900, in Paris, a wine competition was held, but few Napa vintners sent wine. France took the opportunity to strike back at America for not forbidding the use of French wine names, especially Champagne. The judges would not permit wine entries such as California Burgundy, California Claret and so forth. One French judge said he would have admitted the wine had it been labeled "California wine, Burgundy type." Henry Lachman, considered by many to be the most knowledgeable wine man in the state, saw in the French attitude an implication that California wine was making French vintners nervous. California wines were attaining too high a standard of excellence, and the French had to put us down, he claimed.[6] But the Migliavacca winery of Napa won a Gold medal and W.S. Keyes of Howell Mountain picked up two Golds and two Bronze awards.

Buffalo, New York, made a valiant attempt to host a World's Fair in 1901. It was called the Pan American Exposition, and, unfortunately, is remembered for being the site of the assassination of President William McKinley on September 6. Not many Napa vintners entered the Buffalo wine event, but Charles Carpy did and picked up a Gold medal. W.S. Keyes, still heady from his fame won the previous year, also sent wine but won no awards. This competition was curious, because for the first time there was a separate section for wines of Southern California. This was due, no doubt, to northern wineries' winning most of the medals; or perhaps someone at Buffalo took seriously the frequent efforts to divide California in half.

The St. Louis Exposition in 1904, honoring the centennial of the Louisiana Purchase, was made famous by the song "Meet Me in St. Louis," and the introduction of the ice cream cone. The Olympics were held there at the same time. For the international wine competition, 21 judges were chosen, including Europeans. California wines, entered *en masse*, won more awards than those from any other state or country by a huge margin. The three Grand Prize winners were W.S. Keyes, Paul Masson and Dresel & Company. There was something special about the Howell Mountain soil after all. Krug and Brun & Chaix had claimed that back in the 1880s.

The 1905 fair in Portland, Oregon, celebrated the centennial of the Lewis & Clark Expedition. The wine display featured columns fourteen feet high, adorned with elaborate gilt moldings and heavily corniced tops, all entwined with artificial vines. The concept was to bring back a bit of old Greece, with its early preference for wine in the diet. Free samples were available and the crowds lined up each day. California wines were nearly the only entrants in the wine event, and almost everyone won a Gold Medal. A Portland wine medal did not mean much in subsequent years, but some dealers ignored that in their promotions.

Seattle honored its neighbors to the north in 1909 with the Seattle Yukon Exposition, but since the city had voted itself dry, at the urging of the Prohibitionists, not a drop of wine could be poured for fairgoers. The huge Spanish Renaissance-style building that California sponsored had tall columns of wine bottles immediately inside the front door, so that the wine exhibit could not be missed by any of the 12,000 daily visitors.

Though the public would not have a chance to sample wines, an international jury of wine judges was brought in for the wine competition and this time the awards had considerable merit. To Kalon picked up five Gold Medals, their fine wines apparently a holdover from Crabb's ownership. Theodore Gier won the same number of Golds, but no distinction was made as to which came from Napa and which from his other winery in Livermore. It is curious that after dominating wine competitions for the previous fifteen years, only two Napa vintners were honored in Seattle.

The diminished presence of Napa wine brands at the Seattle world's fair was partly traceable to the California Wine Association. It controlled significant amounts of Napa Valley wine through its operation of Greystone, Brun & Chaix, the Napa Valley Wine Company and others. In Seattle, the C.W.A. won fourteen Gold Medals, but place of origin for the wine was not specified. Many other wine districts of California, besides Napa, were hurt by this narrow-minded judging criterion.

THE PASSING OF WINE PIONEERS

One Napa Valley wine conspicuous by its absence at many of these events was Inglenook. Gustave Niebaum had devoted less and less time to his winery after 1902, when he was named President of the Alaska Commercial Company. The company was the source of his personal wealth, not Inglenook. In the last two years of his life, 1907-1908, he was ill, and the winery practically ceased operations. It closed after his death in August 1908 and remained without a crush for three years.

When Niebaum's will was filed for probate, the San Francisco newspapers jumped on the scandal it brought to light. Niebaum had always followed the rules of etiquette and decorum to the letter, in part perhaps because he had been a sea captain symbolically adopted by the wealthy Sloss and Gerstle families. He expected no less careful behavior from the nephew and niece of his wife, Susan, when they came to live with the Niebaums after the death of their parents. Louis Shingleberger and his sister were raised by the Neibaums in luxury; they were sent to the finest private schools and often spent summers at Inglenook with horses to ride, bathing pools and servants. Gustave and Susan had high hopes for the marriage of the children into proper San Francisco families, like the Sloss and Gerstle clans.

Instead, Louis ran off with a budding actress, who took him to Los Angeles. His sister married a man rumored to be the chauffeur. Niebaum was so disappointed with the young people that he cut them out of his will. This was irresistible gossip for the San Francisco newspapers, especially Hearst's. Shortly before Niebaum's death it was rumored he and his niece did make up.

Unfortunately, the really important contributions Niebaum had made were never brought to the public's attention. He had translated documents and accounts of explorations on the northeast coast of America by the Norsemen. Some of these were published by research societies. Scholars of major universities sought his advice. His important collection of Alaska and Canadian Indian artifacts, particularly totem poles, formed the nucleus of the collection begun by the new Department of Anthropology at the University of California, Berkeley.

There was no scandal associated with the death on February 11, 1910, of John Benson, founder of the Far Niente winery. There might have been, though. Benson had been a bachelor all of his 81 years. He moved to Napa Valley only after his favorite haunt, the Pacific Union Club, burned after the 1906 earthquake. His wine had been served almost exclusively there. Benson dutifully left everything, as would be expected of a conservative New Englander, to two nieces, Virginia and Josephine Johnson. The nieces spent summers in Italy, as Benson had, or in Bermuda. They had never visited California but did have friends in San Francisco. Their move to Napa Valley was quite a change, but San Francisco was reasonably close.

Why the two sisters did not sell Far Niente immediately is not clear. They must have felt they honored the family by keeping the estate. They spent much time in San Francisco; Virginia wrote children's books and must have known other writers. She had served as a young female model for magazine and book illustrations executed by her cousin, Winslow Homer. Since Homer and Virginia were cousins, Benson apparently was Homer's uncle as well. By 1910, Winslow Homer had become one of America's most famous illustrators and painters. His seascapes were much sought after by collectors. Benson was a patron of the San Francisco Art school on Nob Hill. His last will and testament was meticulous, containing long lists of wine barrels, fermenters, and the contents of his house, except for art work.

It is possible that Homer designed the first wine label used by Benson and Far Niente. No copy of the label was known to exist, but Arthur Schmidt of Napa insists there was such a label on bottles of wine brought home by his father in the 1920s. The winery had been broken into by thieves, and the bottles were found in a ditch.[7]

Schmidt clearly recalls that the Far Niente label had a hammock with a young girl lying in it. The model could have been Virginia Johnson. Eric Rudd of Falmouth, Massachusetts is a Homer scholar who recognizes the hammock as a trademark of the artist's early illustrations. He believes a 1910 photograph taken in the winery shows an out-of-focus bottle with the hammock label.

This Far Niente wine label would likely be the only American wine label designed by Winslow Homer. That would make it a priceless rarity. If Benson and Homer actually were related, he never spoke of his nephew, possibly because Homer was a homosexual. He never married, and was a recluse for much of his life. His attraction to the male physique, often depicted in his paintings, is well known. It also seems that Homer was ostracized by his family with no explanation. Perhaps Benson was afraid his nephew's sexual orientation might draw attention to his own. Did he have something he wished to hide?

Virginia Johnson died in January, 1916. Josephine sold the winery the next year and died a year later. Since neither had married, they left the proceeds from Far Niente to their numerous nieces and nephews.

There were other deaths of distinguished Napa winemakers in these years, most of whom were fondly remembered by close friends and relatives. Giacomo Migliavacca died in November, 1911, 78 years after his birth in Pavis, Italy. His pioneering efforts on behalf of the Sons of Italy rated a granite bust in a public square. Jacob Beringer died in October 1915, ending a 45-year career in Napa winemaking. He had received his California training, as did so many other later winemakers like Ernest Wente and Charles Wetmore, at the Krug cellar. The German native had been trained as a cooper as well, which set him apart from most of his contemporaries. He was always ready to debate the use of California redwood, French or American oak in wine production. With Beringer's death, the German influence in the valley declined considerably.

The Italian Influence

Between 1900 and 1915 there were nearly as many new wineries opened in Napa Valley as during the boom years of the 1880s. Many that would survive for decades to come were built of stone, but by far the majority were wooden, usually of redwood, and were built by Italian or Swiss-Italian immigrants. Unfortunately, most of these men did not receive any public recognition for what they were doing. The Italian population in California jumped from barely 15,000 in 1890, constituting about two percent of the labor force, to 63,601 twenty years later.

Luigi Domeniconi was typical of this influx of immigrants, coming from the Italian-speaking portion of Switzerland in 1894. He made chocolate at the Ghirardelli chocolate factory in San

Francisco, then put in some apprentice time at the Italian Swiss Colony winery in Sonoma County. In July 1902 he purchased fifty acres in the Stag's Leap area and promptly began building a house with a full stone basement devoted to wine production.

Domeniconi never entered his wine in any competitions, and none of it was bottled. He simply wanted to earn enough to support his family, and he did so, rather well it seems, by placing two puncheons in a horse-drawn wagon and peddling his white or red wine door-to-door in Napa. There is no record of what year he had his first crush, but it was probably 1902.

For twenty years Domeniconi succeeded remarkably well, increasing his cooperage and expanding his small wine operation. Much of the crushing was done by stomping the grapes, with neighborhood youth helping out. Thompson Parker returned home from this task, purple from head to toe, and shocked his wealthy San Francisco parents, who had just moved to Stag's Leap.[8]

Prohibition forced Domeniconi to sell, but rumors were rife in the area for years thereafter that the winery continued operating as before and the quality was exceptionally high. Supposedly, one could purchase wine there for years after Prohibition began. The new owners had purchased tanks filled with finely-aged wine. Gary Andrus reopened Domeniconi's cellar in 1978 and renamed it Pine Ridge.

Giuseppi Brovelli took over the Laurent winery north of St. Helena in 1909. He not only made fine wines which he shipped East to dealers, but sold just as much out the door on Saturday night at winery dances. Italians came from miles around to dance and enjoy themselves. Brovelli paid for the orchestra, and his family prepared the huge midnight suppers. He won the top prize nearly every year at the St. Helena Vintage Festival for his elaborate wine displays. This kind of participation in the local wine industry won for Brovelli and other Italian immigrants high praise and acceptance among longtime residents. Brovelli made a point, too, of mastering the English language. He also let the

Swiss-Italian Luigi Domeniconi started his life in America making chocolate at the Ghirardelli factory in San Francisco. When he had saved
enough money to buy land in the Stag's Leap area of Napa Valley, he
built a house with a basement wine cellar. He peddled wine, red and
white, out of a horse-drawn cart, beginning about 1905. One would
never suspect that Luigi Domeniconi's 1902 house was the beginning of
the Pine Ridge winery in Napa Valley, but the original cellar, with the
entrance shown at left, is still a part of today's modern structure.

local newspaper editor know every time he had been east on a
successful wine selling trip, and gave the editor a photograph of
his winning wine displays if the newspaper had overlooked him.

Many other Italians followed in these same footsteps: the
Bartoluccis of Oakville; the Fagianis, who purchased Mt. Eden
winery in 1911; Giuseppi Navone and his partner, V. Valente,
who purchased the Anton Rossi farm in Spring Valley; and Phillip
Conradi on Spring Mountain. Actually Conradi's family origins

LUIGI DOMENICONI

were in Germany, even though his name ended in an "i." Like the Justis of Glen Ellen, old Italian families sometimes left Italy and spent a generation or two in Germany before moving on.

Conradi was a cigar and newspaper vendor in Oakland who dutifully put away half of each dollar he earned. On January 27, 1904, high on Spring Mountain, he began construction of a stone wine cellar. He had had vineyards in production as early as 1892; he was included in the Priber survey of phylloxera damage. The shortage of Napa wines may have been what induced him to enter wine production so long after planting his first vines.

The stone for the two-story 85 x 50-foot cellar was quarried nearby by two Italian stone masons named Guigni and Bognotti, who deftly cut each stone by hand and fitted it snugly into place. Italian stone masons built most of the stone wineries constructed in the three decades previous to Prohibition, including Greystone. Robert Keenan restored the Conradi cellar to its former glory in 1977, after fifty years of neglect.

Charles Wagner, another German, settled east of Rutherford. Wagner cleared out "a large hay barn" for his first winery, according to the *Star* of October 8, 1915. Besides winemaking equipment manufactured locally by Henry Hortop, he installed electric motors to bring modern efficiency to his entire operation. His old-world relatives might have sniffed in disdain at such labor-saving devices; why, he could almost run his winery from a chair next to the electrical switch. World War II closed down the first Wagner wine cellar. Charles Wagner, a son of the winery founder, resumed family winemaking under the name Caymus Vineyards in 1971, not far from the original winery.

GETTING AROUND IN THE VALLEY

Napa Valley residents in this period came to think of themselves more and more as one community, spread out over thirty-five miles. It was possible sometimes to hear a neighbor's rooster crowing on the opposite side of the valley. The community decided to build a second railroad. It was to be run by electricity, a sort of electric streetcar, with frequent stops which ran often enough so that children could ride it to school. Although the primary emphasis was the rapid and frequent movement of people, the train would also carry fresh milk, eggs and butter.

An electric line had been built in Vallejo in 1902 from a wharf on Virginia street with plans ultimately to run to Napa City. An entire decade was needed to find the financing and solve other problems before the line was completed to Calistoga in 1912. Local business boosters hoped it might revitalize the town: "The completion of the electric road into Calistoga means much more for the little town; one may expect to see great progress made there in the new few years."[9]

A timetable for the "San Francisco, Napa and Calistoga Electric Railway" for 1915 indicates the trip from the upper end of the valley to a wharf in Vallejo took just under an hour and a half. There were 22 stops, but the engineer would halt the train almost anyplace if potential passengers were sufficiently demon-

In the early 1900s, teams of workmen often traveled from vineyard to vineyard to graft grape vines onto phylloxera-resistant rootstock. The phylloxera root louse wiped out 75% of the valley's vineyards between 1890 and 1898. Grafting vines onto native rootstock in the field was hard work; the men in the bottom photo chose the easy way in the shade.

strative (the frantic waving of a sweater or coat sufficed). There were seven departures a day from Calistoga to Napa City. Two steamers, the *Zinfandel* and the *St. Helena*, plied the waters between Napa City or Vallejo and San Francisco. That trip usually took less than an hour.

Traveling a dusty country road by horse and carriage from an outlying farm to shop in St. Helena was uncomfortable, but attempting to make the trip all the way to Napa was an ordeal, as the columns of the local newspaper made clear. Horses kicked up so much dust, especially in summer, that women had to cover themselves from head to toe, using heavy veils to protect themselves.

Napa County supervisors paid to have the main county roads watered once a day in summer to hold down the dust, but the water soon evaporated. What a relief it must have been to local residents when their newspapers began carrying stories about a new technique of laying oil on roadways. Within a few years the technology of "macadamizing" roads, which involved a thick layer of gravel mixed with oil, advanced so rapidly that it was being done to Napa Valley's highways. The firm of Lindow and Johnson sprayed oil on country roads as early as 1902, although the first experiment in this direction was carried out the previous year by L.B. DeCamp. Thirty-five miles of county road were designated by county supervisors in April 1903 to be oiled.

In 1910 the League of California Municipalities sponsored experimental work in Alameda to find the right combination of gravel and heavy oil which would harden into a durable road surface. J. L. Webber, a county supervisor, had done a test strip in Napa Valley the previous year. By 1913, the Napa Chamber of Commerce organized a "Good Roads" meeting in Napa. Hundreds of citizens attended, and experts were brought from Sonoma County, where oiled roads were already being laid.

A county bond issue of $263,000 to cover the cost of the new roads was one of the topics argued for hours at the Chamber gathering. The Good Roads committee included many winemakers and vineyardists: H.L. Johnson, Henry Brown, Jos. A.

Migliavacca, J.E. Beard, E. Light, Homer Hewens, Frank Pellet, E.A. Burge, D.A. Dunlap, H.C. Melone, Morton Duhig and W.J. Stearns.

A new highway route was also discussed at the meetings. The state wanted to build a major new highway from Napa into Marin County via Black Point. This would mean bridging the Petaluma River near the Sonoma-Marin border at the north end of San Francisco Bay. This highway would follow around a second point on the Sears ranch, just south of Sonoma. In many areas, dirt roadways already existed. From a terminus in Marin County, travelers could take any of a half dozen ferries across the Bay to San Francisco.

All of this concern with roads provided the opportunity for valley residents on the eastern side to speak up about their being slighted one time too many over the years. When was the county going to do something about the East Side Road? Locals rankled when others called it "the old back road." A committee to find a new name for the road, generally considered to run from Soda Canyon Farm Center to Calistoga, induced the *Napa Daily Journal* to carry a long article on this subject in the issue of April 21, 1921.

"No doubt it will be of interest to many of us to know that none of the roads in our county have official names" began the story. It was not enough just to repair the Old Back Road; locals wanted a formal name like "Silverado Trail." That was the most popular suggestion out of a half dozen names put forward.

An informal referendum was held, and "Silverado" was duly adopted by the Board. The resurgence of interest in Robert Louis Stevenson may have contributed to the name selection. A decade earlier, the New Century Club of Napa had set out to have Stevenson's cabin site on Mt. St. Helena marked with a granite tablet.

With the new road name in place, it was suddenly fashionable to read *Silverado Squatters* again and discuss it at literary meetings. Many residents who had never heard of Stevenson's sojourn in the valley thought it time to name a school, park or street after him. If a few hardy souls picked their way through the brush and avoided the rattlesnakes on Mt. St. Helena, seeking inspiration at Stevenson's shrine, this in no way compared to what was happening on nearby Howell Mountain.

A virtual flood of newcomers began arriving at the old Edwin Angwin resort, which first opened in 1874. Most came to worship at the new sanctuary of the Seventh Day Adventist religion.

Angwin had sold his hilltop retreat in the summer of 1909 to the Adventists, who wanted a site for a new religious college. That the institution would be located in the heart of wine country was of no importance to the Adventists, who never drank wine. The large Angwin Hotel served as the center of the new college. There were cottages for staff and students, a swimming pool, and barns for horses and stock raising. They would still have to build a church, but classes began at the new Pacific Union College in September 1912.

Walter's Springs Resort in nearby Pope Valley burned to the ground the same year that Angwin's closed. Napa Soda Springs was facing declining numbers of tourists, and White Sulphur Springs opened and closed very erratically. Calistoga was having a hard time hanging on to the glamour and lure it once held.

Thousands of summer tourists still came to Napa Valley, staying more often in cabins or homes rented out by families. This major shift was blamed on the automobile and the new oiled roads being built. Lots of vacationers now drove to the Sierras, to mountain lakes like Donner or Tahoe, or to Yosemite Park.

The automobile also made possible a minor shift in the distribution of wine. Visitors to Napa wine cellars who arrived by car often left with small casks or barrels of wine, or cases if it could be purchased in bottles. The first automobile with a flatbed projecting out the back end might have caused some open mouths. It was a weird-looking conveyance, with solid rubber tires and wooden-spoked wheels, which would shortly be called a "truck." Carefully loaded with puncheons of wine, the truck would soon have its own effect on the wine industry. It moved faster by far than horse and wagon and soon would replace them.

All that was needed now to deliver quality wine to the homes, hotels and restaurants in San Francisco or Oakland were bridges across the Carquinez Strait and the great San Francisco Bay. No more wine would be left standing on the wharves to soak up the sun. But it would be decades before the bridges were built.

SCIENCE COMES TO THE VINEYARDS

With the near destruction of Napa County's vines by the phylloxera, growers had a golden opportunity to plant new and better varieties of grapes. George Husmann, Jr. came up with the brilliant idea of establishing at least three experimental stations in California to test under scientific conditions the vines, climate and soil. Husmann was in charge of Viticulture research for the Department of Agriculture in Washington, D.C. He found an ally in this cause in E.W. Churchill, the cashier of the Goodman Bank in Napa and the new owner of To Kalon. Churchill gave twenty acres of land fronting on Oakville Grade Road to the Department of Agriculture for the Napa Valley experiment station. It was opened in March 1903, along with one in Fresno. Another site was planned for Southern California.

Churchill offered the services of his ranch foreman, Hans Hansen, at no charge, to oversee the experimental plots. Hansen was among the most respected farm superintendents in the county, in part because he had worked for Henry Crabb. Every variety of grape, including those for raisins, was available at To Kalon.

Barely two months after Churchill signed the agreement, he died. But the family honored his decision to have Hansen oversee the vineyards. Ten years later Hansen told a Napa gathering of winemakers that over 12,000 tests had been conducted to determine the sugar and acid content of the grapes at the station. For the first time, vintners who relied on taste buds or intuition had scientific data to confirm or refute old practices. Science had arrived in Napa Valley winemaking.

Hansen's reputation as a viticulturist earned him a high standing in the industry. He was also an amateur photographer who made many pictures of vineyard activities between 1900 and 1925. Many of the photgraphs in this book are his works.

Almost simultaneous with the Oakville Experiment Station came the funding by the California State Legislature of a new agricultural college and ranch. It would be operated under the direction of the University of California at Berkeley, but would be located in farming country. The site eventually chosen was Davis, California, barely qualifying in size as a village.

Between the Experiment Station and the University of California, including its new college at Davis, pressure began mounting to shift from the Zinfandel and Mission grapes to better varieties. There were already Cabernet Sauvignon vines in the Parrott Vineyard on Spring Mountain, at Salmina's Larkmead, and naturally at To Kalon and Inglenook. De Latour planted twenty acres of the grape in 1910, probably the largest single planting of the variety in California at the time. Beringers grew the grape too, beginning as early as 1900. Theodore Gier had small plots of the Cabernet grape in the Napa Redwoods. Morris Estee had grown it and produced Cabernet wine at Hedgeside, and Fawver was still growing the grape in the same vineyards where the Goodmans had planted it back in the 1880s.

There had been only two prices for grapes in the previous century, one for red and one for white, although a few producers paid extra for hillside grapes. Now red grape prices were split, with the bottom figure for Zinfandel and other lesser varieties and the top price for Cabernet. The Repsold winery advertised in the *Napa Daily Journal* in September, 1915, offering to pay the top price, $25 a ton, for "Cabernet Sauvignon and Cabernet Franc."

As early as 1909 Brun & Chaix of the California Wine Association advised it would pay $16 a ton for the "Choicest varieties such as Alicante Bouschet, Petite Sirah, Cabernet and one or two other fine varieties." The Alicante was a shining star being touted then as the best grape to grow for adding deep red color to wine. It was a hybrid developed a few decades previously in France when red varieties in that country, as later in California, were having problems with good color.

234

HANS HANSEN

Napa Valley led every other region in the state in the production of Cabernet Sauvignon wine by 1915, when the giant
Panama Pacific International Exposition opened in San
Francisco. The Panama Canal, which it honored, was opened
officially, but mud slides effectively prevented any ships from
passing through. No matter. The Exposition included the largest
wine competition ever held in the United States. Fairgoers tasted freely of the wine and ate tons of fresh grapes.

This was the first American wine competition in which
Cabernet Sauvignon was a major competitor under its own
name. Twelve medals were awarded in the category, only five of
which went to Napa Valley producers. A. Finke's Widow won a
Gold for its Cabernet, as did Salmina and A. Repsold. Beringers
and Krug picked up Silvers. A Gold also went to the California
Wine Association, whose entries were generally not identified by
locale, their "Cabernet Claret" being one example. The C.W.A.
won the Grand Prize for four wines identified as "Greystone,

Hock, Cerrito, Sauterne." It is uncertain whether all four were produced at Greystone.

Over two hundred wine medals were awarded to California wineries, somewhat diminishing the value. But A. Repsold & Co. was proud to announce in the *Wine and Spirit Review* of June 30 that it had been awarded fourteen Gold medals and two diplomas. "All the wines exhibited by the Repsold Company were produced in Napa County. The awards attest to the excellence of the wines of Napa County."

Other Napa vintners honored by the judges included Inglenook (twenty awards), the French-American Wine Company, and Theodore Gier, whose "Cabernet-Pride of Livermore" won a Silver. Krug and Inglenook were two of fifteen honorees in the Grand Prize or highest category. Still, Napa came out rather poorly considering its domination of past events.

The Italian immigrant winemakers may deserve part of the blame for this poor showing. Many did not care to become involved in such competitions, in part perhaps because they did not read English and spoke it poorly. With increasing numbers of wine cellars owned by Italians, that cut the percentage that were entering wine events.

Napa County's wine and grapes were a prominent part of the huge Panama Pacific Exposition, regardless of the number of wine medals. A three-foot-wide, eighty-foot-long bridge was built for the Napa exhibit, with waterfalls, miniature roadways and baskets of every fruit grown in the county, plus grain, grapes and wine.

If there was some disappointment at To Kalon, Krug, Beringer or the dozens of other wine cellars in the valley over the small number of wine awards in 1915, it did not compare to the concern over lagging wine sales. The market for California wine had stalled after the strong growth years in the first decade of the new century. In fact, in some years, including 1915, wine sales actually declined.

By the end of the second decade, dry table wine sales had risen, but sweet wine sales plummeted, thanks to higher federal taxes, from an average annual sales of fifteen million gallons to six million by 1918. Total production of table wines in California was ten million gallons below that a decade earlier.

It was not difficult to pinpoint the major problem: the swell of support for Prohibition. The Prohis, short for Prohibitionists, knew they were winning the war when the grape growers' association split apart in confusion and when the wine and beer industry sought to separate itself from distilled beverages. Warnings on Prohibition were published almost monthly in the San Francisco *Wine and Spirit Review*. As far back as 1902 the journal carried a story titled "Going Dry Too Fast," listing five states which prohibited alcohol sales: Kansas, Maine, New Hampshire, North Dakota and Vermont. Six more were close to total prohibition. Every state in the nation was on the *Spirit Review* list because it also included counties and cities across the country banning the use or sale or alcohol. By 1902 California had 175 cities or towns in this category.

In 1908 a move was undertaken to unite grape growers and winemakers in the common battle to survive. The Grape Growers Protective Association was formed, with Pietro Rossi and Andrea Sbarboro again providing leadership. Unfortunately, these Sonoma men had no counterparts in Napa Valley, which had provided the leadership in the past.

Some inspiration for this new group may have come from the astonishing election results that fall in Lake County, not normally considered a bastion for the Prohis. Lake County voted for a "local option ordinance" which allowed cities and towns within the county to ban all alcohol. Some of the best-known resorts suddenly found themselves without alcoholic beverages. In 1912 the county went completely dry. At this same general election, Napa wine men spent some sleepless nights hoping the same thing would not happen in three local supervisorial districts. The Anti-Saloon League had succeeded, almost without being noticed, in putting local option initiatives on the ballot. The Prohis were strong in the southern end of the county and up at Angwin.

The *Star* carried a full page advertisement, "A Warning to the Voters of Napa County," in its October 25 issue. Napa City newspapers carried long letters to the editors reflecting the anxiety of local wine producers, at last fully awake to what could happen. One letter quoted Joseph Migliavacca as pointing out that he annually paid $80,000 for grapes brought to his Napa winery. That money was largely spent in Napa City.

The "Drys" were defeated handily in all three districts. Every vintner and grape grower with a car had raced from precinct to precinct, looking for eligible voters who needed a ride to the polls. Still, the Lodi precinct, north of St. Helena, astonishingly voted 114 to 69 to go dry. Napa County faced a peculiar paradox: grapes and wine had been a mainstay of the economy for at least five decades. Now even the local voters were about to destroy this industry.

But Napa residents were merely reflecting the mood of the entire country. Everyone was looking for quick, simple solutions to complex problems in America. Labor problems had become commonplace. Large cities were overwhelmed by and unprepared for the huge numbers of new immigrants, many of whom had difficulty finding employment. And there was another new problem: alcohol abuse.

The quick-fix to all of these problems seemed to be the banning of both the production and sale of alcohol. Prohibitionists didn't understand that all social ills could not be solved by a society that was on the wagon. Still, frustrated citizens felt it was worth a try.

PART
TWO

Overleaf: The train station at Oakville early in this century, with puncheons of wine piled on the loading dock.

PROHIBITION

The word *Prohibition,* spelled with a capital P, never requires definition when wine is being discussed. Prohibition lasted from 1920 to 1933. Many Americans can still remember the Roaring Twenties, when the sale of alcohol in any form was illegal, but when it could be purchased on many street corners or back alleys. For vintners anticipating Prohibition in Napa Valley, California, 1920 was a time of utter despair. Their means of earning a living would be destroyed. They had been producing on average between three and four million gallons of wine a year. The grape crop totaled about 30,000 tons. These were not table grapes; they were useful only for the making of wine.

Many a grower and vintner walked around with his hands high over his head, muttering and cursing, asking himself why fate had treated this particular industry so cruelly. Yet in this description there is just one small problem: the time frame is off by six full months. Prohibition in America's wine producing regions really began at midnight on June 30, 1919, when wartime restrictions took effect. For some peculiar reason this footnote to Prohibition has long been overlooked.

The U.S. Congress decided in 1917 that all agricultural products should be used in the effort to win the war in Europe. No farm products could be used to produce alcoholic beverages. California's congressmen won a reprieve of sorts for wine, a delay of two years. Beer was tacked on at the last minute. With the signing of the Armistice in France on November 11, 1918, vintners thought they had survived the wartime restriction without a scratch. Now the war was over, and the wine industry could resume full production. Leaders of the Prohibition movement disagreed. President Woodrow Wilson, caught in the middle, was urged by winemen to sign an executive order immediately, ending the war before Congress might act. He refused. The two-year reprieve for wine and beer expired in mid-1919.

Curiously, the mood in Sonoma Valley, and the town of Sonoma in particular, was in sharp contrast to the despair in most of Napa Valley. Wine was flowing out of the wineries in cars, trucks, by rail and horse and wagon. The price had climbed to one dollar a gallon, and vintners lined up at the banks with deposits. The *Sonoma Index-Tribune* reported, two days before the restriction took effect:

> The last hours prior to bone dry days are feverish ones in the vicinity of the big wineries in Sonoma Valley, for the family trade suddenly awoke to the fact that they must stock up while the stocking is good. As a result our wine men are doing a land office business, particularly with the smaller orders for household use. A long time back the big wine buyers of the East foresaw the demand there and everywhere and sent in immense orders at wonderfully fine prices.[1]

A week later the same newspaper reported that anticipating "the drought, many people thronged the wine cellars, family liquor stores and bars in a last mad endeavor to lay in a supply of drinkables. There was a regular auto procession to the wineries." The mood was bright even up to the last. "At midnight with considerable levity every place where liquor had been dispensed closed its doors." No wonder vintners wore smiles, with pockets bulging with greenbacks. There are few similar stories in Napa county newspapers. The *Star* claimed in a small news item on July 4th, 1919, "Business Was Not Rushing" in local drinking establishments as the deadline came and went.

Sonoma's triumph was due to the foresight of an Italian immigrant, Samuele Sebastiani. His vision of the future of the wine industry was unique in California. Sebastiani traveled every year, often twice, to major East Coast cities where he had sold wine for more than a decade. The *Sonoma Index Tribune* in August 1919 carried this optimistic observation:

> If California wine makers are not permitted to make wine here, they can ship their grapes in refrigerator cars, declares Mr. Sebastiani, and New York's foreign population will do the rest. The hundreds of Italian families there all make their 200 gallons of wine, and grapes will be in big demand.

Millard Bailey, writing in *Sunset* magazine a year later, had seen for himself the proof of Sebastiani's prediction. He said he had seen tons of grapes being shipped to Eastern cities:

> What did it mean anyway? It meant just this. The enormous Latin population of New York and other large Eastern cities, clamoring for its old familiar sour wine, was willing to pay almost any price for California dried grapes to be delivered at handy stations whence they could be carried to the cellar or kitchen. . . and the juice fermented and bottled.[2]

After June 30, 1919, the gloom of Napa Valley grape growers did not last long. In the middle of July a buyer named Fred Mercer arrived and offered $37.50 a ton for grapes. No one accepted his offer. People suspected that he was going to ship them back east. They decided to wait and see. Sure enough, by mid-August there were more strangers in town, driving big cars, claiming to represent major Eastern dealers in fresh produce. Local growers Frank S. Cairns and F. J. Merriam claimed they were in the market for 4000 tons of grapes for a San Francisco wholesaler. The *Star* in late September headlined: "Grapes Being Shipped in Large Quantities." The only hindrance, noted the writer, was a shortage of refrigerated railroad cars. Nearly every Napa Valley winery suddenly threw open its door and announced "business as usual." No one tallied just who made wine the fall of 1919 and who did not; no one wanted to be named as a violator of the law.

247

By one count, California at this point had 700 wineries, with 256 in Sonoma County and 120 in Napa County.[3] The Sonoma County Grape Growers Association announced it would not heed the orders of Justus Wardell, collector for the Internal Revenue Service, who ruled that no one could make wine except for sacramental or medicinal purposes. But Wardell had little or no enforcement staff.[4] The Internal Revenue authorities, charged with overseeing wine production, did not at first object if winemakers filled their puncheons and tanks with wine, but they would not be allowed to sell it. Wine could be shipped to any destination outside the U.S. until the 18th Amendment kicked in. That was expected to happen in early January 1920.

Three days before this change actually happened a Napa newspaper complicated matters by seeming to join the "Prohis" — a derogatory term commonly used by wine supporters. The *Journal* ran a large cartoon editorial with the heading "A Has Been."

How could a local newspaper come down so hard on the principal industry in the county? If the wineries closed, where were the tax dollars to come from for running the county government? Optimists hoped the Supreme Court would invalidate Prohibition. This may explain why nearly every winemaker applied for a permit to operate in 1920, after the 18th Amendment was declared officially the law of the land on January 16.[5]

Only six days later the weekly St. Helena newspaper told its readers: "Higher prices than have been paid for years now being offered." When the harvest began that first official year of Prohibition, prices soared to $100 a ton. Arthur Forni wasn't worried about a market for wine. That fall he purchased a brand new grape crusher and a hydraulic wine press for the Lombarda Cellar. He planned to make 200,000 gallons of wine. "The Vintage Is On," declared the *Star* in September, 1920. "Wine making is progressing in practically every winery in Napa Valley, the scenes of activity being as marked as for other years." One

Many valley readers were puzzled when the *Napa Journal* ran this editorial cartoon just as Prohibition took effect in January 1920. Whose side was the paper on? Apparently not that of the local wine industry. At least "Ol' John Barleycorn" was not a derogatory nickname usually applied to winemaking. The women in the audience were all smiles, the men grief-stricken.

month later the newspaper warned, "Grapes are so valuable this year they are being stolen."

Napa vintners took risks which could have resulted in jail sentences or stiff fines. It wasn't as if the Internal Revenue agents had simply turned their backs on what was transpiring — or on headlines in the local newspaper. The *Napa Journal* claimed that the Internal Revenue Service had hired 3,000 special agents — immediately nicknamed "Prohis" — to enforce Prohibition across the entire country. For the San Francisco Bay area that meant only a handful of wine cops.

249

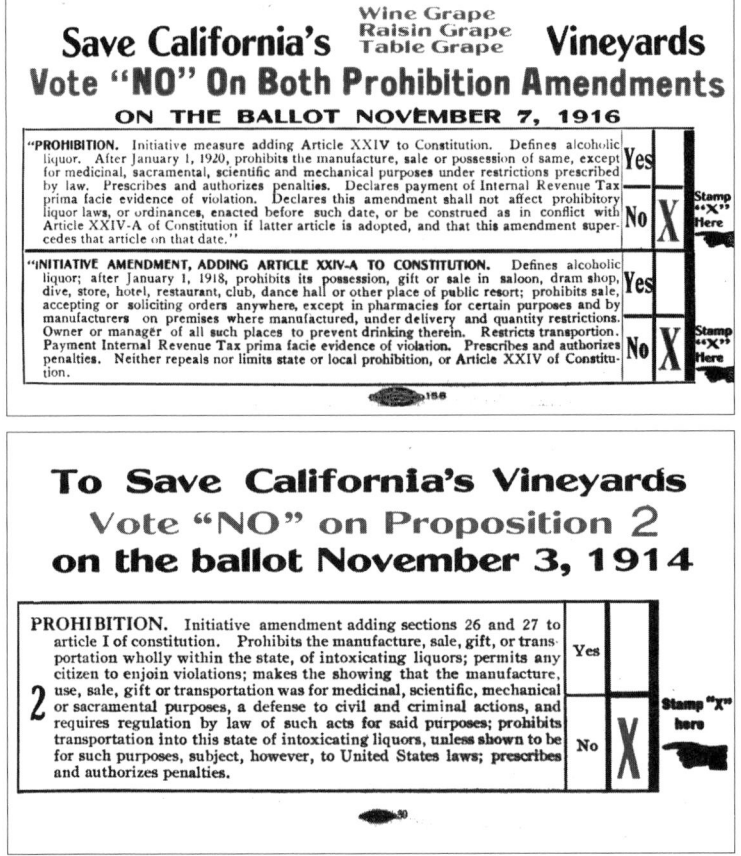

Handbills like these were distributed by the wine industry in an attempt to defeat state initiatives long before Prohibition began.

At first, arrests were made for making more than the legally allowed 200 gallons per family. Under the provisions of the newly passed Volstead Act, every American family could make wine for personal or sacramental use. Jewish families especially demanded this provision. It proved difficult to measure precisely whether a home vintner had 200 or 250 or 300 gallons. Revenue agents soon ignored so minor an issue but grocery stores, hotels or what had been local saloons were, however, watched carefully. Prohis soon began acting on their suspicions, and agents dutifully raided alleged violators, as friends and neighbors turned against each other. Often all that was found was a bottle or two of wine or grappa.

To Napa Valley's credit, the practice of neighbor spying on neighbor occurred far less frequently than in Sonoma Valley. For a time, the Sonoma newspaper carried such stories weekly. This was never true in Napa, possibly because Napa Valley was a more stable community with a higher percentage of resident property owners. Sonoma hosted many summer tourists. Baseball teams practiced in spring training camps, and big-name prize fighters trained in nearby Boyes Springs. Author Jack London had helped publicize Sonoma valley before his death only a few years earlier.

In Napa Valley nearly everyone was related, from the superior court judges to the sheriff to local vintners. This was clear when Internal Revenue agents sought a search warrant from a Napa court. As the agents left the courtroom, a sympathetic cousin telephoned ahead or sent word by fast car.

Vintners used other methods, too, to stay ahead of the federal agents. Wineries sometimes lost thousands of gallons of wine, "stolen" during the dark hours of the night. F.J. Merriam's winery was plundered of several barrels of wine in May 1921. The thieves were never caught. Four years later, the same men apparently returned, taking 300 gallons of fine aging red wine. They seemed to know exactly what they wanted and where it was stored. Some wineries were even set afire in order to conceal the midnight sale of the stock. One Calistoga vintner had all of his wine seized — what was left, that is, when Internal Revenue agents discovered that the amount of wine actually stored at the winery was far less than had been declared to the government. Usually such matters were handled far more discreetly. A wine tank somehow collapsed or broke apart after certain judicious alterations. That took care of shortages of wine which had been sold out the back door.

Healdsburg newspapers in the early years of Prohibition carried a number of stories on winery fires. Tramps were blamed.

Winery owners who were suspected of selling their stock illegally made sure one large tank or several puncheons of old Zinfandel or Alicante Bouschet were placed near the front. This was allowed to drain out the front door, proving that some wine had been inside before fire collapsed the tanks. If there was no red wine stain leading from the door, Internal Revenue agents suspected that a large quantity of wine had been sold before the fire. The questioning could go on for hours.

Sometimes thieves stole an entire railroad car filled with wine. If one incident had involved anyone other than Georges de Latour, suspicion might have pointed directly at the winemaker. But de Latour made wine only for the Catholic church, lots of it, and did not need to violate the law. There was a strange turn to this story, however. In December 1922, de Latour shipped a carload of wine east, via Texas. Somewhere in the Lone Star state, the barrels were drained and the railroad car went on. At the destination, even the seals on the barrels were intact. The case was never solved. A few weeks later, the Beaulieu winery was broken into and eight barrels of wine were taken. It would have required a large truck to cart away this booty. Yet no one, not even the night watchman, heard a thing.

Since grapes were in such high demand, the prices of vineyards or good vineyard land began climbing as well. Capt. John Naylor of Salt Lake City purchased the Schramsberg farm with 64 acres in vines. He brought his large family with him, presumably so they could help pick grapes. Colonial Grape Products purchased the historic McPike ranch on Spring Mountain and began enlarging the 100-acre vineyard. Joseph Ponti, superintendent and winemaker for Beaulieu, bought 40 acres of the St. Joseph's Institute ranch, east of Rutherford, for a new personal vineyard. George Brozovich, of Butte, Montana, purchased twelve acres of vines and a home on Inglewood Avenue, south of St. Helena, in early 1921. He paid $1000 per acre, double the price paid for the farm just one year earlier. Lafayette Stice and his two sons bought the Vann farm near St. Helena, with 40 acres in vines, in December 1921. The Bornhorst winery and

Within months of the start of Prohibition, hundreds of rail shipments of grapes left Napa Valley for eastern cities. Thousands of acres of new vines were planted in the early 1920's, until the last bubble burst from over planting. For many Napa grape growers, the early years of the decade were very prosperous.

vines near St. Helena High School sold in the spring of 1922 for $1000 an acre. A month later the Ephraim Light winery and vineyards at Calistoga were sold to buyers named Fiori, Giusti, Bianchi and Picard. The Lights had been in Calistoga since 1882. Arthur and C.B. Forni purchased the Angelo Milani farm, between St. Helena and Calistoga, in 1920, and then sold it two years later for double their price. Napa County newspapers carried dozens of such stories during the early 1920s. Had fine vineyard or farm land ever before sold for $1000 an acre? This was a strange turn of events to mark the early years of Prohibition.

W.D. Butler, horticultural commissioner for Napa County, estimated there would be a thousand acres of new vines planted in 1922. In a letter to the county board of supervisors, he told of 600 rail car shipments of grapes for the second year of Prohibition. The average price paid was $80 a ton, with the value placed at $750,000.[6] In California, vineyard plantings increased by 60% during the 1920s, many of the grapes being the prolific Alicante Bouschet, a hybrid developed in France forty years earlier to provide coloring to red wines which lacked pigment. The Alicante always brought the highest prices in the marketplace, for home winemakers believed that the darker the juice the better the wine. Zinfandel was also a favorite, but white wine grapes often had little or no market value at all.

MORE CHANGES COME TO THE VALLEY

Fires during the early 1920s radically changed the landscape of Napa Valley, covering tens of thousands of acres. The worst of these occurred in September 1923, when strong northerly winds and high temperatures combined to start several major wildfires simultaneously in mid-month. One fire, starting in Nunn's canyon, opposite Kenwood, burned eastward right up to the Gustave Niebaum home at Inglenook before it was stopped. The fire then reversed itself and burned back to Boyes Springs.

In Gordon Valley, fifteen square miles of landscape was blackened before 4,000 firemen, volunteers from surrounding towns, and soldiers from Benicia succeeded in controlling the flames. The fire by then had reached to within a few yards of the Solano County Hospital at Fairfield.

Napa Valley residents faced many worries besides the danger of fires. The post-war years brought sudden and often bewildering changes in transportation up and down the valley. Teenagers in Yountville had always taken the train to Napa High School, using a service that dated back forty years, to 1881. In August 1921 the Southern Pacific Railroad discontinued morning and evening passenger trains, and also stopped hauling local mail. Commuter trains between Napa and Vallejo, where one caught the ferry to San Francisco, also were halted. Seven hundred people once made that trip daily. Single-car electric trains — essentially rural streetcars using a separate rail line — took up the slack, running every two hours. Competition of a different sort for Southern Pacific came in the form of the new auto-trucks with passenger cabins mounted on the back. Rural residents could flag down the autobus, a convenience the rail services could not match.

Even more exciting than riding in an autobus was listening to a distant radio station. KGW, in Portland, Oregon, could be picked up clearly in St. Helena. Those who stayed up until 11 p.m. could join the station's Hoot Owl club. The local American Legion installed a radio in their club room, with Elmer Salmina and Mario Vasconi in charge of dialing in the distant voices. Elmer Salmina also arranged for the first broadcast in Napa Valley of state election results. Being an electronics expert, as well as a winemaker, he installed a radio set at the Rossi & Anderson store in St. Helena in November 1922. "Through the entire evening the clear, resonant voice of the announcer was plainly heard, announcing the returns as the *San Francisco Examiner* received them" reported one Napa journalist.

In the spring of 1922 the Mission Film Company of San Francisco came up to the Churchill ranch, formerly the Crabb place, to shoot a feature film called "Carry On The Race." The story had nothing to do with outdoor sports; the theme was white supremacy.

Some local residents, in the face of modern improvements, became interested in preserving the past. The Native Sons of the Golden West, whose members constituted a Who's Who of prominent valley residents, from Napa city to Calistoga, decided the deterioration of the historic Bale Mill, five miles north of St. Helena, had gone far enough. It was the oldest surviving man-made structure in Napa Valley, if local Indian hutches were overlooked. Another Salmina was involved in this project — Felix, Jr. — as well as Ralph Williams, Bismarck Bruck, Paul Alexander, Robert Brown and George Gosling. They persuaded Mrs. Sarah Lyman to give the Native Sons a deed to the Bale Mill and a half acre of land. They set an initial budget of $2500 for the mill's restoration and preservation. It is now a California State Landmark.

At Oakville, another emergency concerned the Viticultural Experiment Farm on the Churchill ranch. The land had been leased for twenty years to the U.S. Government, and the lease was now up. In the face of Prohibition, would important research into resistant root stock and vine diseases be discontinued? In March 1921 the U.S. Congress passed an appropriation bill providing for the purchase of the site; eight months later the deeds had been signed. The Prohis could not understand, of course, why the federal government should spend money on grape culture. The land was later deeded to the state of California; it is still used as a viticulture experimental farm.

On the east side of the valley, a public meeting was called at the Rutherford Grange Hall in January 1928 to consider whether a dam might be built on Conn Creek. There was strong opposition initially because a private water company was buying up the watershed, and many speakers at the Rutherford meeting felt the water runoff in the hills should be public property. Georges de Latour, N.P. Cole and Walter Metzner (all wine producers or grape growers) were named to the first Conn Valley Dam Committee, along with Dr. T. H. Stice and Herbert Sawyer of the Napa Tanning Company. Construction of a huge water reservoir on Conn Creek did not actually proceed until the 1950s.

Bismark Bruck, superintendent of the old Krug winery, led a campaign to design and build a new city park in St. Helena. The winery was owned by the socially prominent Moffitt family of San Francisco. The Moffitts had enough influence to bring famous horticulturist John McLaren, father of San Francisco's Golden Gate Park, to St. Helena in January 1925 to redesign the old, run-down Lyman Park. The renovation was completed by mid-summer, with most of the money contributed by winery owners and grape growers. McLaren also designed Fuller Park in central Napa. Neither park might have received the attention of McLaren if Prohibition had really destroyed the viticulture industry as had been forecast.

PROSPERITY IN NAPA VALLEY

A great deal of money was made — perhaps not all of it strictly legally — in Napa Valley during the early years of Prohibition.

Georges de Latour was the most successful vintner. He soon became a very rich man, probably the wealthiest in the entire county. De Latour, who had the right connections to the Archdiocese of San Francisco, obtained letters from Archbishop Patrick W. Riordan and later Edward J. Hanna recommending Beaulieu sacramental wine. Those letters helped sell Beaulieu altar wines all over the United States. De Latour had studied for the priesthood in his teen years in France; this may have given him an edge on some other sacramental winemakers such as the Beringers, who were also a Catholic family.

To meet the growing demand for his wine, de Latour purchased the Ewer winery in Rutherford, on the main county highway, with a rail siding to the front door. At intervals, about every three years, he enlarged the winery — first 40 x 60 feet on the left side, then a larger addition on the right. By 1928 Beaulieu could handle two million gallons of wine, but this was still not enough; de Latour contracted to take all the wine Wentes could produce in Livermore Valley. Wente Brothers became a "Beaulieu Bonded Winery" during those years to meet Prohibition regulations.[7] Some measure of de Latour's success can be gauged from the records of the Beaulieu Corporation during the Great Depression of the early 1930s. After all expenses had been paid, a dividend of $100,000 was paid each year to the two principals in the business, Georges and his wife Fernande.

Fernande may have had a better head for marketing wine than her husband. Long before Prohibition began, when the market for wine was either the wealthy set or poor immigrants, Fernande began joining key social societies in San Francisco. (The de Latours lived semi-permanently in that city: Napa Valley was only a summer home or as business required). With contacts made in high society Beaulieu wine could be served at the right occasions. The de Latours entertained often and lavishly as their income grew and permitted an ever widening circle of friends. It helped to be French — that was a prerequisite in those days — although Fernande was a Romer. Her father was a German businessman with "connections." Her grandfather had been a judge in the King's court in Berlin, Germany.[8]

Fernande and Georges de Latour rose to the pinnacle of San Francisco high society in 1924 when their daughter, Helene, married the French Count Henry Galcerand de Pins. Helene's wedding, as lavish as anything witnessed in San Francisco in years, was performed in St. Mary's Cathedral on Van Ness Avenue by Archbishop Edward J. Hanna. Helene thereafter divided her time between France and California, and so did the de Latours. Georges could always depend on his loyal Napa Valley superintendent Joseph Ponti to take charge, even in the midst of the yearly crush.

Georges de Latour had earned his reputation as a major player in the California wine industry long before his daughter had married a French count or he had made such a success of selling altar wine. He restored the California grape industry by importing millions of bench-grafted Rupestris St. George root stock vines between 1900 and 1915. Most of Napa Valley's vineyards were replanted with his French vines, as were other vineyard districts. Luck, or perhaps a smart decision back in 1908, also played a part in de Latour's financial success in the Prohibition period. Among the grapes planted in Beaulieu vineyards in 1908 were twenty acres of Alicante Bouschet. In order to pay his bills, de Latour sold all of those grapes, along with others picked from 80 more acres, to the California Wine Association. For most of his wine production prior to 1920, he purchased grapes at a far lower cost from other growers or other vineyard districts. The contract with the CWA ended with Prohibition. This freed his 20 acres of Alicantes, which some years produced eight to ten tons per acre. When the price of Alicantes reached $300 a ton, and even in some instances $400 a ton, de Latour could have conservatively earned $2400 per acre, or $88,000 for just the one grape. More than one-quarter of all Napa Valley vines were grafted over to Alicantes by the mid 1920s, following the lead of de Latour.

Having a permit to make sacramental wine made life easier for a vintner, because everything could be done safely and legally. It was not absolutely necessary, however. "Why are wineries running full blast," asked the *San Francisco Examiner* in early October 1924, "in these supposed days of dryness, and what do they expect to do with their surplus stores of liquor?" S. F. Rutter, Prohibition director for California, was asked the same question, and proposed an investigation. He claimed California produced 17 million gallons of wine in 1923. Yet there was now 40 million gallons on hand. The explanation was that the Internal Revenue Service continued to permit most wine owners to make wine when rail cars were not available to transport their fresh grapes to Eastern markets. It was assumed that some, part of, or most of this wine would be used for sacramental or medicinal purposes. Rutter rather innocently told the *Examiner* there was nothing illegal about producing wine, it just could not be distributed or sold except for religious or medical purposes. As long as a winery had empty cooperage, it could be filled with new wine.

The Alba Wine Company of San Francisco leased the E.P. Bellani winery on Spring street in St. Helena and expected to make 350,000 gallons of wine in 1923. In February 1925 six refrigerator rail car loads of wine were shipped from the LeBaron winery (formerly the Theodore Gier winery). In Sonoma County there were many wine cellars crushing grapes that year, with some four million gallons produced. No one knows how much of this wine was sold illegally. The huge and famous Greystone winery north of St. Helena was empty by the fall of 1924 and would not be refilled. There had been 200,000 gallons inside recently; the wine had been moved to bonded cellars in Richmond by the owner, the California Wine Association.

"The American people are drinking more 'hard liquor' today than they did before the Volstead Act became the law of the land," wrote John Held, Jr., in the June 21, 1924, issue of the popular *Colliers* magazine. "They consumed 30,000,000 gallons more in 1923 than they did in 1917," he reported, and this did not include "beer or wines, which are manufactured by home brewers and distillers from one end of the country to the other." *Literary Digest* writers joked about the advantages now advertised in newspapers of apartments with cellaring space "ideal for wine." Winemakers struggled to understand many conflicting and often confusing regulations. Maybe S.F. Rutter did not understand them either.

The Supreme Court had declared the 18th Amendment valid, so there was no escape via legal means. In November 1922 a state referendum called the Wright Act had been passed by a mere 30,000-vote majority. This gave muscle to local law enforcement to close loopholes in the Volstead Act. The Wright Act, more than any other law, finally began having an effect on the Napa Valley wine industry. It became increasingly risky to produce wine. Nearly 150 California wineries closed in 1925; 82 more in 1926. From then on, until 1930, more than 400 of the 700 cellars which were bonded at the start of Prohibition closed.

Another major factor was the over-planting of grapes. By the mid-1920s the bottom fell out of the grape market. Many, many growers who shipped their grapes to eastern cities ended up paying the freight with no return whatsoever. Tons of grapes rotted in rail sheds in New York, Philadelphia, Boston or Chicago. The Davis Agricultural Experiment Station counted 281 million grape vines in the State in 1925. Five years earlier that count had only been 175 million.[9]

To their credit, Napa County growers had seen the handwriting on the wall earlier than most other grape regions of the state, including neighboring Sonoma County. Napa growers pulled out 4000 acres of grapes by 1925, reported W. D. Butler, newly renamed the Agricultural Commissioner for Napa. Ironically, though only 21,000 tons had been produced that year, the value was placed at $1,260,000, up from the $750,000 value in 1920. Grape growers with quality grapes and connections could obviously still make money.

Actually, Napa growers deserved praise for continuing a tradition that had begun way back in the 1850s. When they saw the price of grapes sagging, they quickly decided to undertake an ambitious advertising program for "Napa Valley Wine Grapes." Bismarck Bruck and Charles Forni provided the initial energy and inspiration for the project when they decided to form a growers' organization. Even before the group began holding regular meetings, a "Mt. St. Helena Brand" was chosen as the label. "Napa Valley Grapes" would be printed in bold letters with space left for each grower's name. The first shipment of Mt. St. Helena grapes reached Eastern markets the fall of 1924.

How well this strategy worked can be measured by a quote from the *California Grape Grower* of October 1930:

> Last year Napa county rolled more cars of juice grapes to Eastern destinations than any other county in the Coast Region. It leads in the shipment of Alicantes (326 cars) and Petite Sirahs (245 cars).

Napa county was at or near the top in such shipments for many years preceding that statement, as well.

THE PRUNE INDUSTRY

When grapes weren't being discussed at meetings of local farmers, such as those led by Bruck and Forni, prunes were. On nearly every acre of vines pulled out, prune trees were planted. Some may have worried that this would soon be the valley of the prune, not the grape. The Prohis were no doubt ecstatic; their job would soon be far easier.

Prunes dated back in the Valley to at least 1882, when a hundred acres were set out near Calistoga. It was not until 1916 that the crop reached sufficient size for a Prune Growers Organization to form. There were then 6000 acres in prunes, but low demand for the fruit returned only a half million dollars to growers. Prunes had been grown in nearby Alexander Valley in Sonoma county for more than two decades, and farmers there made more money with the fruit than with grapes. Prunes had been planted there when the hops industry began to fail. The same pattern had never taken hold in Napa Valley, in part because hops never were a major crop. World War I changed the entire picture for the prune market and its juice. With Prohibition to be a virtual

Fermentation of wine at a Napa Valley winery previous to Prohibition was usually carried out in a shed attached to the winery, not inside. This photo is the John Wheeler winery on Zinfandel lane. Wheeler was so convinced Prohibition would never end he demolished the wine cellar in 1923.

certainty only a short while later, prune growing seemed an attractive alternative to grapes.

Only a real leader can alter the course of farming practices, and that leader was John H. Wheeler of St. Helena. His home just off Zinfandel Lane was one of the most imposing on the county highway. His friendship with Georges de Latour when they were both chemists at Stauffer Chemical Company in San Francisco helped convince him to settle in Napa Valley. Wheeler had been active in viticultural organizations early on, but in 1916 he began pulling out his grapes, having given up on some of the supposedly resistant vines he had planted. He planted a 92-acre prune orchard along with a large grove of walnut trees.

At the historic Lyman estate a Prof. E. Krunich was hired to alter the planting patterns drastically from vines to fruit trees. He laid a thousand feet of drain tile, planted more olive trees, and added thirty acres of French prunes. This all transpired in 1921. At the mid-point of the decade, farmers were earning about $800,000 yearly from the fruit. The threat that prunes might replace grapes in Napa Valley gradually became serious. By 1926, W. D. Butler in his annual report to the County stated that there were more acres of prunes in Napa County than grapes. The exact figure was 12,050 acres, with 10,990 in vines.

Prunes added something to the valley grapes did not — when these miles of trees bloomed, the view was indescribably beautiful. Fragrance hung in the air. For years afterward, the oldest residents talked nostalgically about this one aspect of their youth they could not forget.

Another reason the prune had such a profound effect on the valley was that large and small dehydrators were built everywhere. The prune, which ripens as a plum, has to be dried and soaked in a preservative before being sold. One of the major innovative advances in prune dehydrators took place on the Fred Ewer farm in Rutherford, next door to the old Ewer winery, now renamed Beaulieu. While trucks loaded with grapes passed nearby heading for Beaulieu, the drivers were treated to the odor of prunes laid in racks and being heated or dried by an oil furnace. Powerful fans carried the heat up and over the prunes, and of course, outside where prevailing breezes picked up the scent. The "T. K. Casey" dehydrator, invented during World War I, was patented to the native of Carneros, where it was first tested.

When the *St. Helena Star* celebrated its 50th anniversary on September 26, 1924, the prune was termed "One of Napa County's Greatest Resources." With Prohibition here to stay, the prune seemed destined to take over the mantle of the grape as the county's chief source of income and major agricultural crop. Other fruits were also being grown successfully in Napa County. W. D. Butler forecast, in the same anniversary issue of the St. Helena newspaper, "It would not be a wild prophecy to predict that the next ten years will see virtually all of the remaining grain lands within the county turned to the production of fruit." Butler listed four other fruits as being major crops in the county: apples (valued at $87,000 and ranking third in importance), cherries, pears, and plums. The primary grain-producing regions had by this date been relegated to Pope and Berryessa valleys.

Napa Valley had a very different look to it by the mid-point of Prohibition. If this one aspect alone were considered, the Prohis had succeeded dramatically. There were 17,000 acres now planted in various fruit trees in the county — most of those in Napa Valley. Visitors no longer were greeted by miles and miles of vines. There were still wineries scattered across the landscape, but more often than not, they were surrounded by and almost hidden by fruit trees. The vineyards were being lost in the trees too, which were taller, and in the springtime when in full bloom, much more dramatic.

By 1922, there were more than 300 Italians, both men and women, living in the county. It was very disconcerting to these Italian immigrants who arose in the morning and looked out not on their beloved vineyards, but on orchards. Oh, they could appreciate fine, fully loaded fruit trees too, but when the fruit was gone, eaten or shipped to market, it was not like having barrels of wine stacked to the ceiling. There was no winery to enter and breathe in the aroma of aging Cabernet or Zinfandel. Those barrels or puncheons or tanks of wine were like children. They needed care, constant attention. Wine rewards the caregiver by quietly, gracefully becoming a beverage like no other on earth.

PROHIBITION AND CRIME

Despite all that was published in Napa county newspapers about raids by the Internal Revenue agents, very, very few of these raids involved the wine industry per se. Despite the *San Francisco Examiner's* comment about widespread wine production up to 1924, the crushing was done under legal circumstances. In all the hundreds and hundreds of column inches published in Napa Valley alone about arrests during the 1920s and early 1930s, only a rare story mentions a winery or winery owner.

There is good reason for this. Immigrants, and especially immigrants from Italy, had found the good life in California. Why risk it by selling wine out the back door illegally? For every winery that did exactly that, ten or twenty others kept their wine year after year until, giving up hope that Prohibition would end, they had the Internal Revenue agents come and supervise the dumping of it. Still, the violations of the law that did occur cannot simply be overlooked.

William Caramella of St. Helena was arrested for a supposed shortage of wine only two months after Prohibition took effect. He claimed the shortage was a normal shrinkage and vehemently denied breaking the law. He appealed, and his case was sent directly to Washington, D.C. for review.

Theodore Gier, who owned wine cellars in Oakland, Livermore Valley and the Napa Redwoods, got himself into very serious trouble when he moved his wine from one location to the other without permits. He then sold some to an undercover revenue agent. As a result he served several months in jail. Later in the year, 20,323 gallons of wine stored in the Gier winery northwest of Napa city was ordered dumped. Because of Gier's business prominence, F.S. Higgins, deputy field director of the Internal Revenue service, personally supervised the draining of so much fine wine into nearby ditches.

Nathan Ghisolfo of Calistoga was fined $640 and penalties for misplacing 4000 gallons of wine in the summer of 1922. The *Star* reported that when a revenue agent inspected his cellar, Ghisolfo climbed up a ladder and took out a sample of one tank's contents. The agent tasted it and left. For some reason the agent returned later, and on inspecting the tank found a five gallon rubber bag of wine suspended from the top. His sample drink had been drawn from it. There was only water in the tank. Whether it was this case or another involving Ghisolfo, he made Prohibition history in September 1926 when a federal appeals court ruled his wine had been seized without a search warrant. This case made major newspaper headlines because twenty other California wine owners also had the contents of their cellars released.

It almost seems as if the courts were more often than not friendly to the wine industry. Or it may be that federal agents were too often poorly trained and ignorant of the law themselves. Two Calistoga winery owners were named in federal suits in May 1925 and charged with falsifying records to cover the sale of wine illegally. The *Star* did not give names. These may have been the same wine cellars whose violations — "mysterious so-called 'leakages' and misrepresentations of amounts on hand" — were described in a Healdsburg newspaper of August 27. The wineries were seized by federal agents.

Much of the wine produced in the first four or five years of Prohibition may have moved rapidly in and out of illegal channels. This was possible because there were too few Internal Revenue agents to police the industry. The Wright Act of 1922 helped correct this oversight. Some of the fault for poor enforcement of the law lies directly with the operations of the Internal Revenue service itself and the agents. The IRS agents spent most of their time, it would seem, tracking down individual bootleggers. These were men who made a living buying and selling liquor in small amounts. There were tens of thousands of bootleggers in the country, possibly a million or more. The ground war between bootleggers and revenuers was so widespread that Prohibition was doomed to failure.

Local newspapers often carried headlines like these: "Twenty-Two Are Arrested. Big Haul Made in Bootleg Raids and Thousands Collected in Fines." Or "Big Raid on Bootleggers. Napa Police Officer Parts with $850 and Also Loses Job."[10] Everyone arrested was named in the newspaper stories, and the names often were prominent Napa Valley residents. County Sheriff Joseph Harris arrested his own brother in one raid. Another raid netted a Napa city night watchman and policeman.

Almost all the arrests were for possession of illegal liquor, the distilled type. Some were for possession of wine in excess of 200 gallons. At an American Legion dance in St. Helena, the town marshal observed men going and coming rather frequently from two automobiles. The owners were selling hooch out of the back seat. In March 1923 the owners of the Italia Hotel in Calistoga and the Swiss Hotel nearby were arrested and handcuffed for selling liquor. The operator of the Hotel St. Helena was nabbed the same night. At a late night court appearance, each man was fined $400. Such hotel and restaurant raids numbered in the hundreds. Nine barrels of wine were part of the confiscated property taken in August in raids on hotels and clubs in the valley. Each person caught in the sting operation was fined, and the total just for one night came to $6,600.

The dwindling tax money from wineries was replaced by fines levied on bootleggers. This may explain why Internal Revenue agents spent so much time arresting them. Most paid quickly and did not hire lawyers to fight the arrest, as winery owners usually did. The *Healdsburg Enterprise* reported that Santa Rosa Justice Marvin T. Vaughn levied a total of $5,086 in fines in one month. That was just one court. The same story had to be true in other courts in Calistoga, St. Helena, and Napa. Yet the Enterprise claimed a great many violators of the law were getting off scot-free or with minimal fines: "It seems an axiom in Healdsburg that jury trials fail to reach conclusions favorable to the prosecution."

Raids on bootleggers gradually diminished, as this story from the *Star* of April 1926 observes: "It had been so long since there had been a dry raid in Napa county that it seemed like the bootlegging business had become unprofitable and therefore unpopular." Sheriff Harris challenged this claim when he and his deputies charged into the Yountville Inn on April 22, 1926. Proprietor Andy Zadro was taken into custody. Four others were arrested for selling liquor in flasks to residents of the nearby Veterans' Home.

As the decade of the Twenties progressed, the real excitement for law enforcement officers was in raiding carefully hidden distilling operations. High-proof alcohol returned more much money to the bootlegger than wine, because it could be mixed with flavoring agents to create cocktails such as Manhattans or Martinis.

For the revenue agents these kinds of raids were the real thing. Often there were lookouts posted, or watchmen armed with guns. Shots were fired back and forth. Such stories made front page headlines and probably netted promotions for the agents. It wasn't quite like Chicago's gangster shoot-outs with the cops, but for rural Napa County, life heated up when carloads of revenue agents headed out in the dead of night to raid a local still. Local people had something to gossip about for weeks.

Among the first people arrested for operating a still was a woman, and that may have raised local eyebrows even more — how could a woman be involved in this nasty business? Mrs. M. F. Evits was found just across the Lake County line tending two stills, one 20- and one 10-gallon. "She appeared not the slightest perturbed by the unwelcome visit by the Sheriff" reported a local newspaper. The case was turned over to Lake county officials since the stills were in their jurisdiction, but her home was in Napa County. What happened to Evits subsequently was not reported in the local press.

Domenico Barbaria thought his bonded winery would be the perfect place in Calistoga to hide his still. In April 1923 he was arrested and fined $1,000, plus losing the still, the "jackass brandy" produced and a large quantity of wine. A 250-gallon still was discovered in the Soscol district in late July 1924 — the largest still found up to that date. Ten men and a woman were arrested at the Hans Hansen ranch. Hansen (unrelated to another more prominent Hansen upvalley) claimed he knew nothing about the unusually large oil-heated furnace and still, even though his 18-year-old son was involved.

A still could be a very complicated piece of equipment. First there was an oil heater or small furnace, above which was a copper tub, into which water, barley, and sugar or molasses would be poured. When this mash had fermented, the heat was turned up, causing the alcohol to rise with the steam. When the steam and alcohol traveled through copper tubes and were cooled, the alcohol condensed and was collected. Stills gave off telltale hints of their presence by strong odors and smoke from the furnace, but if the still was well-hidden, it might not be easily detected. What could not be hidden was a large oil supply truck driving off to an obscure or hidden location. Revenue agents were constantly on the watch for such trucks. Wilbur Stewart of the Carneros had close calls many times during the 1920s. He drove for Flying A brands.

"Oh, I remember these deals," Stewart said. "There were five stills there in the valley where they used Flying A fuel to get their heat. I'd be the one to deliver; they didn't want everybody going in. I was working for Associated Oil Company."[11]

On one occasion a carful of revenue agents pulled up beside him, and one agent said, "You fellows in your tank wagons sure ought to know where [the booze] is."

"'Well I don't drink, gentlemen, I couldn't console you any.' The smoke was coming out of a bakery still [nearby]."

Stewart also flew many trips with whiskey from Vancouver, B.C., to various places in California and Oregon. His first flight was in 1917 when he was a teenager. Stewart claims he only went into flying illegal alcohol because the family dairy business was in such bad shape.

Less than five miles from his home was Stewart's closest oil delivery. Although he was hesitant to admit it, he certainly knew the details of the Von Strantz brother's illegal operations, but then so did most of the neighbors, and all kept quiet. Fred von Strantz was arrested in May 1925, according to the *Star*. He pled guilty and paid a fine of $500. On his property, and that of a neighbor, Joe Pelossir, officers found 90 gallons of wine, 70 gallons of moonshine whiskey, 1,000 gallons of moonshine mash and a complete still.

There was a raid on the Bruni ranch in Conn Valley, and another just inside the Napa County boundary at Fairfield. A still was found at the Ghisolfo ranch two miles east of Calistoga in early 1928. The standard $500 fine was levied on all those involved, and no one went to jail unless they could not pay the fine. In September 1930 a new twist appeared in the attempts to halt still operations. An Oakland dealer in electric motors was arrested for supplying motors to a still operation on the Henry Brandlin farm in the Napa Redwoods. Brandlin had leased the farm to another party.

Illegal stills were no longer small operations by the 1930s. A still found in Lovall Valley in December 1930 was worth $50,000, claimed the sheriff, and could produce 500 to 600 gallons of moonshine daily. There were 100,000 gallons of mash at the site ready to be converted to alcohol. Gunfire erupted as the Napa sheriff, deputies and Sonoma police arrived (Lovall Valley can only be reached by traveling through Sonoma.) Ugolino Prasso was shot while defending the still from the intruders. He died the next day. Antone Providently was wounded. Most of the others arrested were residents of San Francisco.

Twelve hundred sacks of sugar were found at a still in Knights Valley. This operation was partially hidden by a local cemetery. It required three large trucks to haul away the evidence from what had recently been the Foote ranch. Five men were arrested, with bail for each set at $2500. It was becoming more expensive to make hooch.

Social Unrest

With a large immigrant population and labor strife increasing across the country, someone in Napa city thought it timely to form a local chapter of the Ku Klux Klan. Two hundred klansmen arrived in late October 1923 to initiate the first Napa Valley members in a field near Napa State Hospital. The high point of the Klan's activities came the next year in a field just south of St. Helena. Word had spread rapidly that a giant cross would be burned. There were 2,142 automobiles and eight to ten thousand at the gathering — mostly sightseers. Dr. J. R. Bronson gave the evening's diatribe against Catholics, Jews, and blacks, and warned that if there were any bootleggers in the audience the Klan would get them. That remark almost certainly drew snickers, if not laughter. He may not have realized he was in Napa Valley wine country.

At Oakville, just in front of the closed Far Niente winery, George Hansen and others began building a runway for the greater Oakville Airport in December 1927. Hansen, like Wilbur Stewart, was fanatic about airplanes. Two Vought scout planes from the aircraft carrier *U.S.S. Langley* landed on the airport runaway in February 1928, causing a sensation. Local reporter

Arthur Schmidt wrote in the *Napa Register* that the motors were nine-cylinder Wright Whirlwinds and could fly the planes at the sensational speed of 150 miles per hour.

People who could afford to pay E. F. Cooper fifty cents had their photographs taken at his St. Helena studio. Cooper may have been hired in 1923 by the Napa Chamber of Commerce to shoot "33,000 square inches" of Napa county landscape. This was the first time that color film would be used to document what transpired in Napa county, on its fertile landscape.

OTHER EFFECTS OF PROHIBITION

Thirty-three barrels of fine, aging Napa brandy were moved out of the St. Helena Bonded Warehouse in February 1923 and the historic structure on Church street was closed. It had served wine men for forty-five years. The brandy belonged to A. Repsold Company of Napa and San Francisco.

The Migliavacca winery in Napa, for years the largest winery structure in the county, burned in July 1924. It was filled with machinery and freshly made grape juice owned by the Colonial Grape Products Company. That grape juice was sold in five- or ten-gallon cans and offered one more way to circumvent Prohibition. Of course, selling grape juice in whatever size cans was not illegal. The warning label was another matter. "DO NOT PLACE CONTAINER IN ROOM WITH A TEMPERATURE OVER 60° OR CONTENTS MAY FERMENT." This warning appeared on Colonial's cans of juice, which could be delivered right to your door. "DO NOT REMOVE CONTAINER COVER. CONTENTS WILL CONTINUE TO FERMENT FOR UP TO 36 DAYS." The instructions varied from grape juice company to grape juice company but it was clear — wine could or would be the end result with very little effort on the part of the customer. Colonial sold grape juice in small bottles for a time, as did Italian Swiss Colony and several major older California wineries. Either the market never caught on, or this was just a ploy to cover the ultimate goal — the retailing of five and ten gallon containers.

Joe Vercelli lived in San Francisco during the 1920s. As a young grape juice salesman, he hauled the cans of juice directly to the customer's door. "I looked around the house or apartment for a quiet place and yet warm enough to ferment the juice. I gave the customer clear instructions how to make the wine, clarify it after fermentation was complete and bottle the contents. Nothing was left to guesswork."[12] Vercelli sold thousands of gallons of grape juice, and he was just one of dozens of such salesman.

A more cumbersome process involved grape juice concentrate that was dried to form juice bricks. The *Literary Digest* of August 23, 1931, described their sale in a store on Fifth Avenue, New York City, where the salesgirl warned:

> You dissolve the brick in a gallon of water. Do not place the liquid in this jug and put it away for twenty-one days, because then it would turn into wine. Do not stop the bottle with this cork containing this patented rubber siphon hose, because this is necessary only when fermentation is going on. [This was to release the gases given off]. Do not shake the bottle once a day, because that makes the liquor work.

The *Digest* reported the arrest later in the day of the store owner and sales people, but the case was appealed to the Supreme Court. These "bricks of Bacchus" were not finished.

A refined variation of the canned juice was marketed by Fruit Industries of San Francisco. This group of eight pre-Prohibition wineries improved on Vercelli's five-and ten-gallon cans of juice by offering separate Sauterne, Riesling, Claret, Muscatel, or Port-type concentrated grape juice, so that the buyer could satisfy his particular taste. Philo Biane was in charge of the first national sales in Milwaukee and Chicago for Fruit Industries:

> We had three sizes you could order, 5, 10 and 25, and under certain circumstances we would do a 50 gallon. Seventy per cent was in the 5, 10 and 25 gallons. Under the law, each person could have up to 200 gallons of wine in their home. We sold millions of gallons of this juice concentrate.

Biane or his salesman would take a container of the juice to a home, bring along the necessary yeast and add water at the

destination. He sometimes added citric acid if necessary. A gallon jug with mineral oil was placed on the fermenting barrel with
a tube to vent off the gases. The salesmen would return once or
twice during the sixty days to check on the fermentation, then
come back to rack off the wine, fill the bottles and cork the contents. A five-gallon container of juice cost $18.85. Almost all
sales were handled through drug stores, the druggist getting a fee
for his work.[13] This "Vine-Glo" wine was of such high quality
that sales quickly went national. Ironically, the initial start-up
cost of $1 million at Fruit Industries was provided by the federal
government, which had spent $14 million the previous year to
buy up surplus grapes in an effort to salvage something of the
fresh grape industry. *Business Week* magazine for December 3,
1930, carried some of the details of this bold venture — some of
it was kept a secret.

While few Napa grapes may have gone into Vine-Glo, hundreds of tons went directly to San Francisco each year and were
custom crushed for the customer. *Sunset* magazine of April 1928,
in an article entitled "Grapes Crushed While You Wait,"
described the process in detail, including the now familiar warning about fermenting in a warm room. Author Eugene Block
wrote:

> The sign which makes the title of this article hangs on a once
> abandoned shed on the San Francisco waterfront. Men and
> women drive up — some in limousines; others in rattling fliv-
> ers. Some carry empty demijohns in their hands as they enter
> the 'office' only to drag them out, heavy, five minutes later.
> Others hop in empty-handed and leave with neat glass con-
> tainers.
>
> "How long must I wait until it's wine?" you ask.
>
> "How long must you wait until until it's ready?" he corrects,
> with a twinkle in his eye. "Four months — about that."

Block claimed that California had fifty bonded wineries producing sacramental or medicinal wine. Their total production came
to five million gallons yearly. This figure is important because of
hearings held in Washington, D.C. in 1931 to determine the

Directions for Making Three Gallons

SOAK five pounds of California Dried Wine Grapes in cold water. After 12 hours run the liquid off and keep for later use.

◆ Crush the grapes in a small mill or meat-chopper. The pulp is the soaked in water and pressed.

◆ Put all the juices in a three-gallon crock, fill with water to the top, add two pounds of sugar and let ferment at a temperature of 55- to 65- Fahrenheit for one week.

◆ Skim off and siphon into a cask or 3 gallon demijohn.

◆ Cork with a vent hole bung, (a bung with a hole bored through, allowing the excess gas to escape, at the same time preventing the entrance of air), and keep fifteen days fro after-fermentation.

◆ Add the beaten whites of two eggs for clarifying.

◆ Bottle, then immerse bottles with the mouth only projecting in a large vessel of water. Loosen the corks and heat the water to a uniform temperature of 180° Fahrenheit. Then remove the bottles, cork and seal tightly and place in an inverted position in the cellar.

BEBE COMPANY
233 Sansome Street

effectiveness, or lack thereof, of the 18th Amendment. Was Prohibition really a national joke, as many writers claimed in newspapers and magazines?

At the hearings held by the National Commission on Law Observance of the 71st Congress, investigators reported that, taking 1925 as a typical year, there were 60,687 rail car shipments of wine grapes to all markets. Each car carried 12.5 tons of grapes; each ton could result in 150 gallons of juice to be converted into wine. That meant 113,788,650 gallons of wine were being made at home in the United States annually. Legislators were told that half of table grape shipments ended up in wine; that five million gallons of sacramental or medicinal wine was produced each twelve months; and other grape shipments resulted in a reliable estimate of 156,602,247 gallons of wine fermented each year in the country. This figure compared with about 60 million gallons of wine produced in the United States in 1917-18, and another 10 million imported. The Congressional study had later figures for wine grape shipments, but not for some of the other categories given above.

All of the stories and recollections about circumventing Prohibition seem to pale by comparison to the ingenuity of Fred Abruzzini, who took over the management of the Beringer winery shortly before Repeal. What Abruzzini did was not illegal. In 1928, when Abruzzini was at the Cribari winery in Madrone, California, he and several friends came up with the idea of packing prunes and apricots in sherry or port wine. Both wines were made extra sweet with a special syrup. Quart fruit jars were first filled with the fruit, and the sherry or port was poured in until the container was filled. A bright label was devised with "Sonny Boy" as the brand. It read, in part: "This fruit is packed in compliance with all government regulations." The fruit was shipped to Young Brothers markets in Los Angeles, where attractive

---

Facing Page: Grapes for the making of homemade wine were available on many street corners in major cities during Prohibition. If you had never made wine, instructions were provided on a colorful 5x7 card with an enticing title.

movie extras were hired to demonstrate the product. They poured the wine off into small paper cups for customers to taste. "It was like a cordial with a kick" recalled Abruzzini.[14] Thousands of gallons of fruit and wine were sold. Other California wineries adopted the practice — quart jars of the cordial-like beverage lined back bar shelves even in grocery stores. We and others produced a lot of cooking sherry to; you added salt to the sherry to qualify it as a food product. A good chef quickly learned that the salt could be removed by heating the sherry and adding peeled fresh potatoes. They took out the salt," Abruzzini adds with a quiet laugh.

This expertise is one of the reasons the Beringer family hired Abruzzini in July 1932 to oversee its operations. They had a sacramental permit but did not produce more than five or six thousand gallons per year. The family also had thirty acres of prunes on a ranch just north of Napa, and forty acres in pears. There was little wine in storage, so Abruzzini brought 100,000 gallons with him from Cribari.

Fate stepped in to prevent Beringers from producing prunes pickled in port or apricots soaked in sherry. When Franklin Delano Roosevelt was elected President of the United States in November 1932, the end of Prohibition was not far off. Repeal was a plank in his platform. Abruzzini kept his sherry solarium in place, built a brandy distillery and prepared to re-enter the American wine market with Beringer wines.

If the Beringer family seemed to be in a state of panic when they hired Abruzzini in 1932, they had good reason. Abruzzini recalls the winery was about to go bankrupt. One look at W. D. Butler's annual report for 1930 and the reasons were perfectly clear. Napa's Agricultural Commissioner set the total value of the grape crop at $342,000. It had been a $1,250,000 five years earlier. Not only had the price plummeted; no one could see any bottom to it at all.

Napa did lead all its sister counties along the California coast in rail shipments of grapes; the Mt. St. Helena brand no doubt helped in selling wine grapes on the East coast, for the label had built a firm reputation for Napa Valley. Napa growers pulled out very few vines over the previous half dozen years. Butler estimated there were still 11,000 acres of grapes in 1930—the same figure as in mid-decade. A decline in prune prices also helped slow the removal of vines. Abruzzini packed most of Beringer's prunes in fancy lug boxes and gave a box to each church that would buy his sacramental wine. He recalls the price of prunes being only three cents a pound.

Since the repeal of Prohibition was so critical to the health of the Napa Valley wine industry, it would have been logical for local leaders to take up the cause. In years past, men like Charles Krug, Bismarck Bruck, Henry Crabb, John Wheeler or W. W. Lyman would have been in Washington, D. C., pushing Congress to pass the constitutional amendment. As far back as the mid-1850s, when California's first county agricultural society was formed at Napa, local winemen were at the forefront of change and progress. But this was not the case with Repeal. Napa winemen were strangely silent, or almost so. Fourteen years of Prohibition had taken its toll.

A "Napa County Association for Prohibition Reform" was organized in the Spring of 1933, with Chapin Tubbs of Calistoga as president. The directors included wine names like Salmina, Light, Ghisolfo, Beringer, Galleron, Gagetta, Fawver, and Cairns. In the June 1933 election, the ballot included lists of delegates, for or against repeal, to the state convention. The local Napa association urged every citizen to vote for repeal. There was less urgency on a local level to join the fight for Repeal because it was now a national political issue. Franklin Roosevelt made sure of that; it helped elect him to the White House.

The urgency in repealing the 18th Amendment was underscored by the shortcuts that were used. When Congress passed the Repeal amendment to the Constitution, the 21st Amendment, it did not leave the support of so sensitive an issue to conservative state legislatures. Rather, the 21st Amendment provided for state constitutional conventions. Convention delegates were more responsive to the needs and will of the people. The conventions approved the Repeal amendment in a record ten months. Ironically, it was the voters of Utah, mostly

Mormon and opposed to the use of alcoholic beverages through church law, that pushed Repeal over the top on December 5 1933.

Roosevelt's greatest appeal was to those hurt so harshly by the Great Depression, which began with the stock market crash in 1929. Unemployment at its peak reached 15 million men and women. Twenty-five thousand veterans with no jobs marched on Washington seeking relief. President Herbert Hoover ordered the Army to clear the tent camps, using tanks and guns on unarmed civilians, including women and children. Farmers were among the hardest hit, with income declining to one-third that earned in 1918. Farm mortgage debt rose from $7,857 million in 1920 to $10,785 million in 1930. Farm bankruptcies took an enormous toll, especially in Iowa and the Dakotas. During the first three years of the Great Depression, 5,504 banks closed. Bank holidays, instigated to halt the withdrawal of funds, became common occurrences. Napa Valley weathered this economic storm better than most sections of the country, with far fewer bankruptcies or other financial hardships. Many farmers with mortgages had paid them off during the good years of the 1920s.

W. D. Butler's farm statistics reported to the board of supervisors show that income had dropped drastically. The total value of all income from fruit raised in the entire county had been about $3.5 million in 1922; in 1930 it was slightly over $1 million, including grapes.*

Winemaking, or the potential for wine production, brought Napa County out of the Great Depression long before the remainder of the country. Families could go back to earning their principal livelihood again. Vintners could dream once more. There were wine barrels to be rebuilt, salvaged from years of drying out in dusty, nearly forgotten wine cellars. Grape growers

---

* Not a single oral history interview conducted in Napa Valley over twenty-five years and including hundreds of long time residents, mentions hardships or food shortages.

278

would have to replant. Prunes or other fruit trees would be removed, slowly at first. The Alicante Bouschet would have to go. Everyone knew it did not make a respectable wine compared to the Cabernet Sauvignon.

Winemaking is a labor-intensive industry. The grapes require a small army of workers to prune the long canes back in winter or early spring. There is suckering in early summer, and then the rush to pick before the sugar climbs too high or predicted fall rains arrive. In the winery, the annual crush is no place for the faint hearted. Canvas hoses snake underfoot everywhere, tripping workers who have worked late the night before and are not sure-footed. No one gets enough rest for weeks as the crushing continues well into the night. Wine is constantly being moved to make room to ferment the juice of grapes just brought in from an overly sensitive grower who wants immediate appreciation. Growing prunes or pears or apples in Napa Valley simply did not offer the same challenges, or the same potential for profit.

St. Helena's reliable weekly newspaper, the *Star*, tracked the excitement in a story it reprinted on October 3, 1933, from the *Wall Street Journal*:

> Business in the Northern California counties of Napa, Sonoma and Mendocino has been stimulated appreciably by the rehabilitation of wineries in anticipation of the repeal of the 18th amendment, according to Carl F. Wente, vice president of the Bank of America.
>
> The benefit to employment is demonstrated by the fact that in one day $3000 in new payroll checks was handled by the bank's branch in St. Helena.

Lumber companies on California's coast were adding more laborers to meet the demand by the wine industry, claimed Wente. Grape prices were rising. Prune prices were at $100 a ton, up from half that figure the year before. The Bank of America was happy because the Reconstruction Finance Corporation (RFC), newly created by the Roosevelt Administration, was advancing loans to restore wineries. The Attorney General ruled in September that long unsold wine could be used as security for such loans. Actually, much of that wine was newly made in the fall of 1933, while agents for the Internal Revenue Service turned their backs. Prohibition may have not been declared officially over until December, but 1933 saw a full crush of grapes at many Napa Valley wineries. The year clearly should not be counted when adding up the total years of Prohibition's effect on wine.

In March 1933, the president of the Crockett Bank purchased the Lombarda cellars from the Forni family. This included a cellar full of wine made by J. Gagetta — "the last vintage" — actually 1932. Thus the property qualified for an RFC loan, and could be resold as real estate prices climbed. In May, Louis Martini drove over from the San Joaquin Valley to purchase ten acres south of St. Helena. He announced plans to build a large winery on the site and to make Napa Valley his home. Thus was another Italian family added to the growing list (now more than 1,100 in the county).

At the Theodore Gier wineries, one just south of St. Helena and the other in the Napa Redwoods, production of vinegar was started in 1930 by Gideon C. Jones, of Berkeley. Three years later a group of wine men including Angelo Petri and Charles Forni leased the Gier St. Helena cellar as part of the Mt. Helena and Calistoga Wine Company. Cooperage to handle 500,000 gallons was installed. This would shortly become the Napa Valley Cooperative Winery.

Greystone cellars had been run by the Bisceglia brothers of San Jose since 1925, when they purchased it from the old California Wine Association. Sacramental wines were produced at Greystone for some years, but by 1930 it was empty. In October 1933 the Bisceglia brothers began restoring cooperage in the facility and bringing in new tanks. They then transferred several hundred thousand gallons of wine from San Jose to the St. Helena wine cellar. There was no crush that year at Greystone, but the wine certainly qualified the owners for a government loan. This clearly was not the primary reason for reopening Greystone, since a much smaller amount of stored wine would have been sufficient. Greystone was nonetheless an operating winery before Prohibition officially ended.

The story was similar at dozens of other valley wineries. Giuseppe Navone leased his cellar to Scatena & Company of San Francisco. (This would soon be the St. Helena Cooperative.) Inglenook reopened with great fanfare. A reception in the famous tasting room on December 8 brought guests from distant points. Carl Bundschu was superintendent for the Daniels family, descendants of Gustave Niebaum. Beaulieu was full of well-cared-for wine, over one million gallons of it. There had been a vintage in the cellars since 1923 when de Latour moved to the old Ewer winery.

"For grapes, improvements and for help, Mr. de Latour has expended a fortune this Fall," noted the *Star* on November 24, 1933. "He has furnished many men with work, paid good wages and contributed to the well-being of many families in the valley." He had helped ease the Great Depression in Napa Valley.

Perhaps not since 1889, when Napa Valley wines took the lion's share of awards at the Paris World's Fair, had there been so much publicity about wine, and Napa wines in particular. This time the publicity was on a truly national scale. William Randolph Hearst's Movietone Newsreels were taken at the major wineries. When the newsreel crews arrived in early October, the red carpet was rolled out at Beaulieu, Beringer and a half dozen other cellars. They filmed grapes being picked and even street scenes in St. Helena. Hundreds of thousands of movie goers saw how wine was made, particularly in California. It was education on a mass scale. Two years later a full-length sound movie was made by Arthur Berthelet on California's wine industry. H. F. Stoll, editor of the *California Grape Grower*, wrote the script. Footage shot at the Vintage Festival in St. Helena was included.

Standard Oil Company's monthly magazine, circulated widely in the United States, was devoted to wine in November. The Redwood Empire Association brought both still and movie cameramen to the Christian Brothers winery, Inglenook, Beaulieu, Beringer and Martini, to film the actual crush. Many national magazines hurried into print with wine stories. *Literary Digest* for December 2, 1933, described "Wines of Noble Vintage." *Fortune* magazine's issue of February, 1934 was "Wines of the U.S."

New wine books appeared on store shelves almost overnight. A young Baltimore journalist named Philip M. Wagner wrote *American Wines and How To Make Them*. He gave California wines a generous historical overview, but recommended no brand names. Julian Street wrote *Wines, Their Selection, Care and Service*. California was not well-treated in his first edition, but the book helped him sell articles on wine to mass-circulation magazines and that helped everyone indirectly. His article "Wine Cinderella of Repeal" was published in *Scribner's* magazine, in September 1935.

Douglas H. Riker's *The Wine Book Of Knowledge* practically ignored Napa Valley, but his text recommended drinking wine with meals. That too, helped everyone. Riker mentioned Paul Verdier, owner of the famous City of Paris department store in San Francisco. Verdier had provided a generous section in his store's basement for wine. He published his own booklet, *History of Wine: How and When To Drink It*, which was much kinder to Napa wines. Verdier gave away thousands of copies of the booklet to his customers. In 1933, D.T. Carlisle and Elizabeth Dunn published Wining And Dining with instructions for those who had "come of age" during Prohibition and needed some wine sophistication.

Only good weather during that final year of Prohibition was needed to make 1933 a banner year for wine. A good grape crop of fine quality was the prayer on everyone's lips. "The weather for harvesting of the grapes is ideal and everybody appears to be wearing his best smile," reported a local journal in mid-October. It wasn't just the lack of rain that brought smiles, grapes were bringing a healthy $35 a ton. They had been almost worthless in some recent years. And wonder of wonders, anyone with white

Napa women dearly loved to see this water wagon being pulled ahead of them when traveling to town for shopping or church. It meant they could put aside the heavy veils they wore in the last century to keep off the dust kicked up by their own horse and wagon. Roads were watered daily in the summer. Roadside advertising signs in the last century were so sparse that business owners in Napa Valley had to seek help wherever they might find it. J. Rutledge bought space on a county road watering wagon, as did George H. Beach. Rutledge sold artist's materials such as paints, oils and brushes.

grapes could ask up to $50 a ton. For the past fourteen years, those grapes had largely rotted on the vine, since home vintners wanted only red grapes. Now California grapes could be crushed and fermented in California wineries. "Not a single carload of grapes has moved from the Southern Pacific depot thus far this year and we have not heard of any Eastern buyers or shippers being in our midst," stated the *Star* of October 13.

How ironic that Prohibition should end with a whimper. The Prohis would not have succeeded in the first place without the banner of patriotism and World War I. Fortuitous circumstances aided in winning this battle, not sound judgment at the polling place. Still, Prohibition brought one benefit, for now Americans turned to the consumption of wine as never before in history. Previously, wine had only been a beverage consumed by immigrants or the very wealthy. The latter traveled abroad and learned from Europeans how wine enhances a good meal and aids in digestion and good health.

But Napa winemen had to face the fact that no matter how superior their wine might be to the homemade product, there was no money out there to buy it. In much of America, the Great Depression was still as bad as when Hoover was booted from office. Local vintners soon discovered that home winemaking was still solidly entrenched. That was the next, most unexpected obstacle to be faced.

WINNING BACK
THE HOME WINEMAKER

T hough wine consumption nation-wide had more than doubled during the years of Prohibition, from roughly 60 million to 150 million gallons, professionally-produced wine fermented in 1933 and 1934 was not selling very well. Robert Rossi, son of Italian Swiss Colony co-founder Pietro C. Rossi, learned that 13,054 rail-cars of wine grapes had been shipped from California to the east. Those rail cars of grapes translated easily into 23 million gallons of wine. (None of these came from the Napa Valley, which may explain why local farmers were so stunned when their wines didn't sell.) In the January 1935 issue of San Francisco's *Wines & Vines* magazine, Rossi wrote:

> Ever since repeal, the winemen of California have been wondering what has become of dry wine sales. Although legitimate wine sales are variously reported to average more than three gallons of sweet wine to one gallon of dry wine, dry wine is actually ahead of sweet wine in total consumption. But more than two-thirds of the dry wine consumed is being made in basements, by home winemakers and bootleggers.

"Bootleggers" was probably wishful thinking on Rossi's part, for their activities were illegal and might be controlled. But home winemaking was another problem altogether. Even stories about

285

illnesses caused by home brews of all sorts did nothing to deter citizens from making and drinking their own wines. The problem was so significant that it went far beyond a local solution by Napa vintners and vineyardists. A new, strong organization was needed with the finances to fight effectively. Someone suggested forming a wine institute. In the summer of 1934, Horatio F. Stoll began advocating a publicity bureau to promote California wines. He had been in the local wine business since 1910, when he worked for Italian Swiss Colony. In 1920, he took over *The California Grape Grower* (renamed *Wines & Vines* in 1935) and used his editorial space to advocate better publicity.

The California State Chamber of Commerce responded by calling for a state-wide wine industry conference at Monterey. The meetings, which began in June 1935, covered taxes, regulation of sales in individual states, tariffs, and promotion. From Napa Valley those in attendance included Charles Beringer, Carl Bundschu, John Daniel, Louis Martini, and Georges de Latour. De Latour was named to the executive committee. Four months later, in San Francisco, the California Wine Institute was created as a direct result of the Monterey meeting. A fifteen-member board of directors was elected, including Napa winemen Martini, Felix Salmina, Bundschu, and de Latour. Many of the members of the Institute were new to winemaking, but the first board president, Almond Raleigh Morrow, had been in the business nearly fifty years. He had been a member of the old California Wine Association before the new century had begun, and was now the highly-regarded dean of California vintners.

The Wine Institute included San Francisco journalists like Leon Adams, who served on the Publicity and Promotion committee, and whose task it was to win back the home vintner. They had help from Elmer Davis, who wrote in the December 1928 *Harpers*:

> There are probably few Italian-American families that do not make their own wine; but the wine they make, as a rule, can be endured only by stomachs toughened by a racial experience

of hardship dating back to the Punic Wars . . . The average home-made wine of today, sour or sticky-sweet . . . is nothing to make new converts to wine and beer among the younger generation.

In an early October 1931 edition of *Collier's*, Frank Taylor claimed that home-brewing fell off in popularity, except among the foreign-born element, which was still willing to give wine time to age. *Fortune* claimed in February 1934 that only inferior grape varieties were used for home crushing and that the wine produced was therefore low quality. But some critics believed that post-Prohibition wine sales would eventually do well. Julian Street wrote in his 1933 book, *Wines, Their Selection, Care and Service*: "It seems to me that I see hopeful signs . . . at no time in our history has the general interest in wines been so great. Few Americans know wines, it is true, but many want to know them."

Within a decade, most wine writers would agree. Frank Schoonmaker, a wine critic of high reputation, wrote in his 1941 book *American Wines*: "Unquestionably, most of the home made wine of the Prohibition era was bad; it was produced by people who knew little about wine making, and less about grapes." Horatio Stoll, writing in *Wines & Vines* in April 1935, said: "It is said that Prohibition probably did more to establish an appreciation of American vintages than did all the previous years of organized promotion work on the part of vintners." He believed that Americans who made their own wine learned for themselves that American and European grapes grown in this country "produced a very good quality of wine" if properly handled.

By the mid-30s there were hints that winemaking in Napa Valley was about to change drastically. For many old-timers there had been only two wines: red and white. But not much of the conversation in the industry was about wines named for one grape variety. Cabernet Sauvignon had won considerable recognition in the decade preceding Prohibition, and champions of the grape, like de Latour and Bundschu, now talked only of its fine-wine potential. Hopefully, it would rival the clarets of

France. Cabernet was honored with its own category at the 1934 State Fair, the first wine competition after Repeal. A newcomer, the Christian Brothers Order in the Napa Redwoods, won second place for their Cabernet wine.

In the 1935 State Fair, first place for Cabernet was won by Lombarda Wine Company of St. Helena, and second place went to a grand old name, Inglenook (Carl Bundschu). The year after, the Christian Brothers took the Gold medal (numbered wine honors were replaced) and Lombarda the Silver medal. Walter Martini, no relation to Louis Martini, owned Lombarda and was another valley newcomer. Zinfandel had long been honored with its own category, too. The first Napa Zinfandel medal in the 1930s was a Silver won by Inglenook in 1936. These awards encouraged vintners to believe that there was a future for several more varietal wines. The first Sauvignon Blanc wine medals came in 1938, also the Ugni Blanc, Barbera (Inglenook and Larkmead — the Salmina family premiered this one) and the old Golden Chasselas (later correctly identified as the Palomino).

Restaurant wine lists commonly contained no more than four or five red wines. Most popular was claret (any smooth red wine usually made of Cabernet or Zinfandel), followed by Burgundy, Chianti, Cabernet Sauvignon, and Zinfandel. The white wine selection was more old fashioned: Riesling, Chablis, and Sauterne. Many wine lists offered sweet wines, of course, and champagne.

Wine could easily be purchased in California at grocery stores or saloons. Ninety per cent of the wine sales were in bulk.[1] Customers brought their own glass jugs and had them filled from the shopkeeper's barrels. This was the era when meat was cut to order at the counter, and dry foodstuffs and most cookies were sold from large bags or boxes. Ice cream was scooped out of large insulated barrels into smaller containers. Wine in the Eastern states was more generally sold in bottles, but in nothing under a half gallon.

Napa wines could be found in barrels or puncheons lining the back walls of saloons or grocery stores. Each barrel was marked with the wine type, and cups were available for tasting. Tasting was good for sales but created a problem: if the barrel was not kept filled or tightly sealed, the wine could go bad. Shopkeepers didn't dispose of the wine until they were certain it was vinegar, or very close to it. It is not surprising that Napa growers and vintners became exceedingly restless. Varietals were popular and growing in number, but vintners now had to keep separate the wines of each grape. It was clearly time to organize. Napa Valley took the lead in forming wine cooperatives.

Repeal was only three months old when W.D. Tucker, of Calistoga, and a neighbor, G.W. Sauer, began discussing the formation of a Napa growers organization. At the first formal meeting in April 1934, Tucker was elected chairman of the Napa County Independent Grape Growers. The Growers immediately suggested a fair market price for the Fall grapes, even though wineries still had plenty of stored wines. H.J. Baade, the Farm Advisor for Napa from the University of California, suggested a solution: "It is all very well for growers to hold meetings and decide that they should receive a given price for their grapes but if the trade will not pay that price . . . growers should get together and form cooperatives for the acquiring of fully equipped cellars."[2]

Charles Forni was already on that track. After the Bisceglias at Greystone offered him only $7.00 a ton for grapes that had brought $100 a ton a few years before, he decided more cooperative action was warranted.[3] Forni, Angelo Pietri, Adam Bianchi and Louis Stralla formed the St. Helena and Calistoga Wine Company. Ephrain Light's winery was used for the first wine making that same fall in Calistoga. A year later it was renamed as the Napa Valley Cooperative Winery and was moved to the historic Bergfeld winery south of St. Helena. Thirty-five valley growers provided 5,000 tons of grapes for the 1935 crush. Felix Salmina, whose family owned the Larkmead winery, was the driving force behind the third organization formed in the valley, the Napa Valley Wine Industry. This was a vintner's group, formed to assist in marketing Napa wines. Its slogan was: "Use Napa Valley Dry Wines. Napa County Grapes for Napa Valley Wines."

There were still at least 25 million gallons of wine being fermented in homes, estimated *Business Week* in April 1935. Four years later, *Fortune* magazine claimed the figure had risen to 31 million. But Napa wine and grapes had had a distinguished reputation before Prohibition and even during the 1920s; now it was time to coax the American wine consumer to return to Napa vintages. Americans might continue making wine at home, but NVWI members hoped that an occasional purchase of a commercial Napa wine might turn into a habit.[4]

A fourth move to organize Napa's viticulture and wine industry came in the summer of 1938 when the Napa County Dry Wine Grape Growers Protective Organization was formed. Members of this group felt that dry wine grapes belonged in their own category. An enormous surplus of wine, table and raisin grapes had driven the price of all grapes so low that no farmer could make a profit. The state and federal governments stepped in to artificially prop up prices by diverting tons of grapes into brandy production and control plantings. But G. B. Edmonstone, the guiding light behind the Grower's Protective Organization, claimed there was no surplus of dry wine grapes. He believed that the market was saturated with too many table and raisin grapes, which ended up being used in wine production. Edmonstone also lent his organizational experience to St. Helena wineries, who formed their own cooperative a year later. The Cooperative purchased the historic Laurent winery at Highway 29 and Angwin Road.

Napa Valley's staunch determination to separate itself from the rest of California's grape industry was encouraged by the success of Georges de Latour and the Beaulieu winery. In several years of the Great Depression, de Latour declared a $100,000 dividend for himself and his wife and partner, Fernande. No other winery made such profits. But de Latour had built up a huge sacramental wine trade, primarily through the Catholic church. When Prohibition ended, his distribution was well organized and he had more than one million gallons of fine, aged "commercial" wine in his cellars.

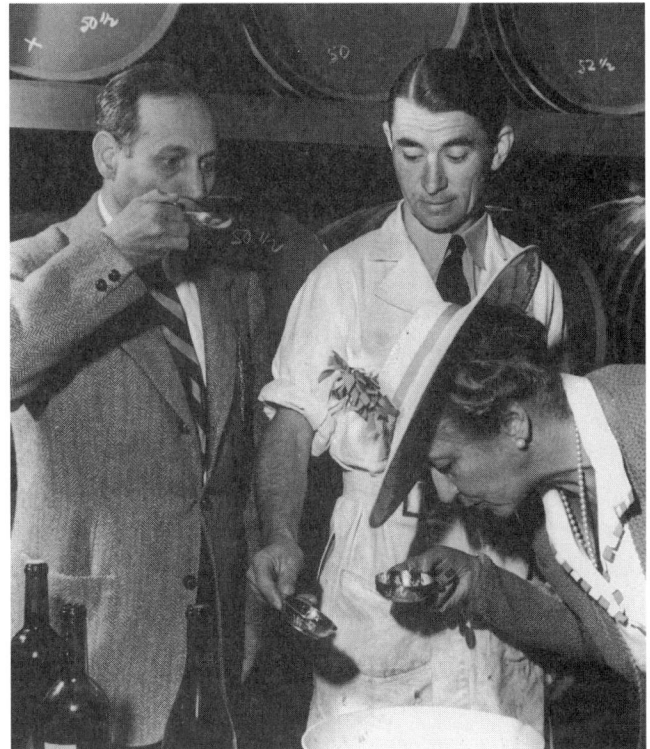

Fernande de Latour, wife of Beaulieu founder Georges de Latour, sampling wine provide by a very young Andre Tchelistcheff in 1942. He had only been with Beaulieu four years. Her son Richard is shown on the left.

Further, the public's general resistance to commercial wines didn't seem to extend to Beaulieu wines, which were virtually unknown nationally before Prohibition. What was de Latour doing that the others were not? He was bottling his wine and offering it to the public in a container sealed at the winery. When customers in New York tasted a bottle of Beaulieu Cabernet, they knew they were drinking very fine wine which would never be sour or off. And the wine was delicious. De Latour and his winemaker, an Italian immigrant named Joseph Ponti, cooled much of their wine before fermentation by pumping cold well water into coils surrounding fermenting tanks. Fermentation took longer, but produced a better wine. This "cold room" approach was perhaps the first in a California winery.[5]

In 1938, during one of his trips to France to visit his daughter, Helene, de Latour met and hired a full-time chemist. This was Andre Tchelistscheff, a Russian emigre who had been an assistant in a French wine institute in Paris and knew the latest oenological advances. And de Latour's wife, Fernande, had impeccable marketing instincts. She frequently invited prominent guests to the de Latour's Rutherford home; these visits would be covered by the newspapers. She also entered every California state wine competition from 1935 on. (Georges was already 75 years old; his death would come in 1940.)

The medals Beaulieu won propelled it into the front ranks of wine producers: Gold medals in 1935 for its Chablis, Sparkling Burgundy and Riesling; four more Golds in 1936 and 1937; and one in 1938. There were other honors at the Los Angeles County Fair.

The crowning achievement came in 1939 at the World's Fair on Treasure Island in San Francisco. Beaulieu wines won four Gold medals, and Beaulieu's Burgundy was among only two Grand Prizes awarded. The second was won by Wente. In a letter written decades later to *Wines & Vines*, Andre Tchelischeff said the Grand Sweepstake wine was a 1919 Burgundy, bottled in May 1923 and made by Joseph Ponti.[6] Beaulieu's success galvanized and inspired the entire Napa Valley wine industry. Inglenook began pushing hard to bottle more of its wine, keep its Cabernet Sauvignon and other varietals separate, and win medals. By 1939 Inglenook had won more wine medals in Napa Valley than any other winery, well over forty.

Beringer was not far behind Inglenook, winning more than thirty medals. Fred Abruzzini not only produced excellent, award-winning wines, he went after publicity as well. The Beringer winery was always the first or second stop when film crews such as Hearst's Movietone News were in town. Also,

Abruzzini had made friends with Perry Lieber, a publicity agent for RKO Pictures. Whenever a movie premiered in San Francisco, Lieber made a quick phone call to Abruzzini, who arranged lunch at Beringer and more publicity for the stars. With Prohibition so recently concluded, a lovely, operating winery as a backdrop had real news value.[7] Beringer's winery was exceptionally photogenic. Abruzzini had carved oak casks positioned at doorways with plenty of light for photographs. He set up tables inside the wine caves and served lunch to hundreds of convention delegates from San Francisco. His artistry extended beyond the winery boundaries: in 1936, Beringer displays won first place awards at both the Napa and Sonoma fairs.

Felix Salmina's Larkmead wines were serious challengers to the other major wine brands in the valley. Larkmead Cabernet won the Gold in 1937 at the State Fair, and the Larkmead name appeared on awards lists several dozen times during the 1930s, including five medals at Treasure Island. Larkmead was included in *Fortune* magazine's list of top California wines in 1941. The May issue recommended four red wines from Napa (Inglenook, Beaulieu and Louis Martini were the other three) and two Napa whites, Martini and Inglenook. Only nine state wines made this select listing.

CHANGES IN NAPA VALLEY

The rebirth of winemaking in Napa County probably accounts for the increase in population between 1930 and 1936. More than 2,000 newcomers raised the count to just under 26,000. In spite of the Depression, more and more people drove automobiles, with the result that the electric railroad between Napa and Calistoga was forced to close in 1938 after only 25 years of operation.

A Napa landmark, a beautiful home which had belonged to San Francisco socialite Lillie Hitchcock Coit, was destroyed by fire in 1938. The story of the fire rated front page news. Lillie

GEORGES DE LATOUR

Coit, who had died nearly twenty years earlier, had left funds to build a monument to San Francisco firemen; Coit Tower had just been completed. Her house north of St. Helena was sold to Ren and Al Bothe, who used it as as their Paradise Park lodge. (Paradise Park would later become Bothe State Park.)

Down valley and in the eastern foothills, engineers had finally begun surveying for the construction of Conn Dam. Proponents like Frank Mackinder, owner of the *St. Helena Star*, and Nathan Coombs, descendant of one of the founders of Napa City, were elated. More than a decade of disagreements had stalled the project, but the 1938 State Legislature authorized $300,000 for the new dam and reservoir. A few residents would have to move, and the Chiles Valley road would have to be raised. All of this would take years to complete.

Roads were also on the minds of valley residents because the Works Project Administration had federally paid workers available by the hundreds. WPA road crews fanned out over Napa county, building bridges and widening roads in all directions at once. The principal beneficiary was Silverado Trail. "The Silverado Trail is an accomplished fact!" announced the *Star* on October 28, 1938. "Last week the last shovelful of earth was turned on the project which has been the county's major road program for nearly four years."

County Supervisor Charles Tamagni could take most of the credit for completion of the highway along the east side of the valley, allowing cars to travel for the first time from Napa to Calistoga with reasonable comfort and safety. Over much of the old Silverado Trail, pot-holes had made driving dangerous. Most people rode or drove horses. Begun in the early 1940s, Spring Mountain Road was even rougher and more dangerous than the Silverado Trail. There had been a cow path to the top for decades, although some called it a buggy road. WPA crews tackled the steep hillsides, and the link to Sonoma County was soon completed.

Prior to the spring of 1939, dozens of Napa county roads bore no names, not even identification numbers. This was all changed before the summer was over, and many old-time local residents suddenly found their names posted at county intersections.

DEATH OF A WINE PIONEER

"Hundreds Attend Requiem Mass" headlined the *San Francisco Chronicle* of March 2, 1940. Though few of the attendees were from Napa Valley, everyone in the county read the details of the funeral for Georges de Latour. One member of the Wine Institute who attended said he had never seen four Catholic archbishops at a funeral before.[8] According to press reports, there were only two archbishops, but since there were also three monsignors and three regular priests crowding the dais in front of the altar, onlookers might have become confused.

"More than 500 of de Latour's friends attended the requiem mass, which was one of the largest and most elaborate in local Catholic circles in many years," added the *Chronicle*. Priests from the Dominican, Jesuit and Franciscan orders attended, as did priests from all of San Francisco's parishes. The list of honorary pallbearers included San Francisco Mayor Angelo Rossi, two U.S. Navy rear admirals, Frederick Koster of the State Chamber of Commerce, and many men prominent in the wine industry, including John Daniels, Herman Wente and Harry A. Caddow.

No death had been a greater loss to the Napa wine industry since Charles Krug's passing. The two men were opposites; Krug, an atheist, was friendly, outgoing; de Latour was conservative, elitist, wealthy and very religious. But they shared a commitment to improving the quality of Napa wine, and California wines in general. Krug did much of the work himself; de Latour hired experts, like Andre Tchelistcheff.

De Latour was driven by one goal: he wanted to produce a world-class wine equal to or surpassing those of France. He chose the most difficult wine of all, a red wine of the broad claret or Bordeaux category, a Cabernet Sauvignon. He had begun his quest for the best Cabernet years before Beaulieu's Burgundy won a Grand Sweepstakes prize in the 1939 World's Fair. A year after his death, Beaulieu Vineyard released the first "Georges de Latour Private Reserve" Cabernet. For decades it would be the finest red wine produced in California. Joseph Ponti deserves as much credit as his employer for all that was accomplished at Beaulieu. On de Latour's death, Ponti was rewarded for his loyalty by a modest bequest of $1,000.

Harvey Lewelling's funeral, on May 3, 1939, contrasted sharply with de Latour's. Lewelling was a Presbyterian. His funeral was in St. Helena; only one minister presided, and hundreds of Napa Valley citizens attended. He was president of the Bank of St. Helena, and he grew grapes, but he didn't make wine. He was a fixture in Napa Valley who added immensely to the rich diversity of local residents. And he was one reason a lot of people found the valley so attractive as a place to live.

Lewelling could have been successful at many different careers in many a big city, but he chose to remain in rural Napa

Valley. Some say the fact that he was blind in one eye put some restraint on his ambitions. "Harvey" as most people knew him, liked to tinker. His obituary in *The Star* described him as a mechanical genius. He installed the first telephone in St. Helena, between his home and his business, in 1881. He built a gas plant at his home to provide lighting, then promptly changed to electric lights with a gasoline generator. His was the first private electrical system on the west coast. He also built an automobile. But nothing compared to his photographic hobby. He had a large, cumbersome camera mounted on a tripod which he carried everywhere in the valley, even up steep hillsides to capture a beautiful view. Lewelling took hundreds of photographs, from landscapes to a portrait of the local barber. Many are among the earliest documenting life in Napa Valley of the 1880s. His photograph of the 1885 July 4th parade in St. Helena is particularly famous.

Several months after Lewelling's death, a close friend of de Latour died. John H. Wheeler had been a chemist with de Latour at the Stauffer Chemical Company in San Francisco more than a half century earlier. Wheeler served for a time as the Chief Executive Officer of the original Board of State Viticultural Commissioners. He also was one of the first grape growers to pull out his vines as Prohibition approached. His 400 acres eventually became the largest walnut orchard in Napa county.

The population of Napa Valley was extremely diverse. While most property owners grew grapes or made wine for a living, many pursued other dreams. Napa Valley wasn't just a farming community. Its proximity to San Francisco provided resources very distinct from those available in the San Joaquin Valley, for instance. There was something in the valley which nurtured the soul and imagination. It had been there even before the Civil War. It was still strong in the 1930s. The Christian Brothers, an order of the Catholic Church, were attracted by it in 1930 and moved to Napa Valley. On the surface at least, it doesn't seem likely that the valley's grape reputation had anything to do with the move. After all, the monastery produced good wines from its vineyard at Martinez.

The Christian Brothers had been in nearby Contra Costa County for half a century, making wines which had never been entered in wine competitions. But in the early 1930s, they were ready to move. A history of the local order suggested that the Contra Costa town of Martinez was growing fast and expanding into the privacy of the monastery.[9] The large wine facilities of Theodore Gier were up for sale; these included 100,000 gallons of fine, aged Napa wine. The Christian Brothers bought the Gier property and built a monastery and school, which were completed in April 1932. Brother Timothy, only recently out of seminary, had helped pick grapes from the Gier vineyards for the first crush at the Mont La Salle winery in 1930. He later recalled that the vineyards had been kept in good condition during the 1920s and even included some Cabernet Sauvignon vines.[10]

Brother Timothy had majored in chemistry in college. He was sent to the Christian Brothers Napa vineyard to help in the winemaking. He and others attended University of California classes on the use of commercial yeast in wine production. This method had been developed in France in the 1890s and was used experimentally in California before Prohibition. Rudolf Jordan, who had sold Gier his Napa Redwoods vineyards, had carried out major experiments with commercial yeast only a few miles away, at Castle Rock winery. The Christian Brothers adopted Jordan's ideas and became one of the first wineries in Napa to use commercial yeast consistently to make wine.

About the time Brother Timothy was dismantling wine tanks in Martinez and moving them to the new Christian Brothers Winery in the Napa Redwoods, another newcomer to the valley was looking into the possibility of reopening the Krug Winery, which was filled with cooperage that could be rejuvenated. Italian-born Louis Stralla had graduated from high school only a few years earlier in San Francisco, and had worked for several San Francisco newspapers. When he decided to go into the wine business he joined Charles Forni and Angelo Petri to form the St. Helena and Calistoga Wine Company. Stralla decided against linking with the new Napa Valley Cooperative Winery because he wanted to be on his own. By the fall of 1933, not long after the Moffitt family agreed to lease it to him, Stralla had revived the old Krug Winery, producing its first wine since 1922.[11]

By 1937, more than 40 wineries were operating again in Napa county, many founded by recent Italian immigrants: Calleri, Formento, Garibaldi, Luchetti, Molinari, Rossi, Tripoli, Varozza. A major partner in the old Sunny St. Helena winery was Cesare Mondavi, whose young son, Robert, was cleaning wine tanks, running the crusher and learning the art of wine making.

The Martinis were also in the wine business in just about every county where grapes were grown. Louis M. Martini, a highly opinionated, brusk man, was full of lofty ambitions. Before 1920 he and his father had made wine in San Francisco; Louis sold it door-to-door. During Prohibition, he had made sacramental wine at Kingsburg, California. Now that Prohibition was over, he wanted to produce high-quality, world-class wine. He bought land at St. Helena in 1933, and built a winery in 1934.

Martini did not enter his wines in a single competition prior to 1941. But his patience paid off when *Fortune* magazine in May 1941 included Martini's Zinfandel and Folle Blanche in their list of top American wines. Only seventeen wines from nine wineries made this prestigious list. With that vote of confidence, Martini began entering state fairs; in the late 1940s he matched his neighbors, wine for wine and medal for medal. He also played a major role in founding the San Francisco Wine Institute.

Napa's struggling wine industry was hit hard by the outbreak of World War II. Prohibition had ended only eight years earlier. Recognition of Napa's fine table wines was finally beginning to rebuild the industry. Now what would happen? For one thing, sons of winemakers would go off to war. There would soon be a shortage of labor for this labor-intensive industry. Who would

To-Kalon was one of the most distinguished wine brands in pre-Prohibition Napa Valley. The winery complex (shown above, circa 1900) was not far from where the present Robert Mondavi winery is now located at Oakville. H.W. Crabb grew hundreds of varieties of grape vines in adjacent vineyards. The winery burned May 28, 1939.

pick the grapes? And how would wine travel? Most railroad tank cars were quickly requisitioned for the shipment of oil and gasoline needed by the military. There would be no more bulk shipments of wine to the East Coast. All this would turn the entire wine industry upside down.

Even worse, the quality of wine was seriously at risk. Unscrupulous dealers diluted, or cut, the wine to meet the unprecedented demand. Only wine bottled in glass bottles, gallons, half gallons or fifths, with a cork, would be safe from tampering. Ironically, the U.S. government provided an incentive for the small wineries to set up their own bottling lines. While there were no available rail tank cars for shipping bulk wine, there were plenty of empty rail box cars: shipments of munitions came from the east to the west coast in box cars which could be filled with bottled wine for the return trip. Only a few Napa Valley wineries, like Beaulieu, Inglenook and Beringer, bottled their wine prior to World War II. Now, though it seemed absurd in the middle of a major world war, winemakers recognized the need for quality control. From one end of California to the other, wineries started bottling. *Wines & Vines* noted in March 1942:

> It has only been lately that the importance of bottling operations has been recognized by the wine industry. Previously, attention to this particular function was not very active, inasmuch as practically all wine business immediately following Repeal was based on tank car operations.

A bottling line was set up at the Italian Vineyard Company, in Guasti, using reconditioned machinery. At the Louis M. Martini winery no equipment could be found, so for the duration of the war, bottling was done by hand, a fifth or half gallon at a time.[12] At the Krug winery, the Cesare Mondavi family faced the same situation after their purchase of the facility in 1943. The Mondavis did find a brand new bottling machine, but it was "a simple bottling line, nothing very great."[13] They bottled half and full gallons which sold for nearly four times as much as the 28 cents a gallon for bulk wine.

The Mondavis had purchased the winery after Stralla pulled out. The facility needed some major remodeling, but $75,000 bought the winery and 140 acres, mostly in grapes. The Office of Price Administration had put tight ceilings on bulk wine prices by 1943, but not on the price of grapes. Thompson Seedless and Muscat grapes were requisitioned by the government for food; grapes suddenly were in short supply, and prices skyrocketed. The Mondavi family almost paid off their mortgage in a year, just by selling grapes.[14] They also had some very good luck: the winery really was in a terrible state of disrepair. The Mondavis had the funds to do the necessary work, but the war effort made it impossible to purchase lumber, cement to cover the original dirt floors, or steel beams to strengthen the structure overall. Robert Mondavi traveled nearly every day to San Francisco, where he haunted various government agencies that controlled the availability of such supplies. Finally, he was ushered into the right office where he told his story.

"I remember being told by a Mr. Henderson that the government allocated enough materials to keep a skeleton industry alive in each field. They knew that after the war, wineries would be needed. We were lucky. They decided, on the spot, to make Krug a winery which needed to stay open." Mondavi was given the approvals he needed.

Research into wartime uses of wine and brandy were begun almost immediately after Pearl Harbor. In February 1943 all wine tank cars were taken over by the government. *Wines & Vines* reported that these 1.2 million tank cars would transport "war alcohol being produced by the beverage industry this year for making synthetic rubber, munitions and other war essential materials." Former brandy distilleries moved into the business of fermenting molasses into alcohol.

REBUILDING AFTER THE WAR

Trade publications of the time rarely discussed it, but by 1943 it was clear that the war was a blessing in disguise for Napa vintners. Although no one knew for sure how much French wine had been carried quietly in flotillas to America before the German invasion, French wines would be a memory within a year or two. Once the supply of foreign wine was exhausted, there would be no new shipments to compete with American products.

A directory published in August 1946 listed forty wineries in Napa, the same number as before the war. Many had established brand names and sported bottle labels for the first time. Irving Marcus, editor of *Wines & Vines*, observed in April 1946: "Previous to the war, even those large wine companies which had their own brands and sold them commercially, considered the sale of bulk wine the backbone of their business."

Winemakers had not needed to advertise. With the notable exception of Italian Swiss Colony and Cribari, California wineries were rarely advertised in national magazines before 1940. The large eastern wine distributors, having bought bulk wine from Salminas, Beringer, Freemark Abbey, Garretto, Martini or the Mondavis, bottled it and attached their own labels.

Gourmet magazine changed all that. Its first issue, in 1942, appealed to the wine industry, and Napa brands such as Louis Martini, Beaulieu and Inglenook bought advertising space almost immediately. Other wineries followed suit, and many Napa wines were introduced to the public through this creative food journal. Still, the total amount of advertising dollars spent in such publications was small.

Grape prices topped $100 a ton by the last year of the war, and wine sales hit a new high in 1946. But by 1947, the wine industry was in a serious recession. An editorial in the April 1947 *Wines & Vines* explained: "There is more than a little evidence to show that during the war years the trade and consumers were under pressure to buy tremendous volumes of wine . . . This hidden volume of wine, not actually consumed but stored, finally reached such a peak as to defy measurement." Clearly, people would use their stored wines before they bought any more.

After 60,000 additional acres of grapes, including many table or raisin grapes, were planted in California that year, by September 1948 John A. Margolis called for a moratorium on planting. In his article in *Wines & Vines* Margolis also asked: "How can it be that the grape and wine industry lies economically prostrate, while at the same time our national economy is going through its wildest inflation in history?" Rumors that the Marshall Plan would buy up every available raisin to help feed hungry people in Europe proved untrue.

But in Napa, business was booming. Although the total acres planted in grapes had declined slightly during the war years, wine production in Napa was rising dramatically. Before the war, Napa's forty-odd wineries had produced about four million gallons of wine a year. In May 1947 the *Star* reported that the figure had doubled, to 8,041,000 gallons. The same week that Margolis was predicting disaster in *Wines & Vines*, St. Helena's weekly newspaper reported that "(wine) inventories in the valley are down 50 per cent from last year . . . making for a much more healthful situation." Napa Valley grape prices were up ten to fifteen dollars a ton, and it appeared that all the promotional efforts had paid off. Louis Martini was right, back in 1933: there would never be a problem for fine wines. Premium wines suffered least in recessions because wealthy people would always afford the best.

The California State Fair was flooded with entries when the wine competition resumed in 1947 after a hiatus of five years. There were almost one hundred medals given out in all wine categories, with the Wente winery in Livermore capturing six Gold medals. Three Napa wine brands won Gold, Beringer, Larkmead (Salminas) and Martini, and Napa collected 38 medals in all, more than any other county. Sonoma county was runner-up with 25 awards. That kind of domination at the State Fair attracted attention. Even little wineries in Napa Valley did well. Lee Stewart's tiny operation at Souverain won Silver medals for his Pinot Noir and Zinfandel. Young Robert Mondavi entered his family's Krug wines for the first time and won two Bronze medals, for Sauterne and Gewürztraminer, and three Honorable Mentions. Louis Martini left with a handful of wine honors, too.

This competitiveness set the stage for the next year's wine competition. "Top honors for a wine district easily went to the Napa Valley," observed *Wines & Vines*, in October 1948. Eight wineries won Napa's 46 awards; Inglenook won eleven, and Beaulieu won three Golds and five Silvers.

It wasn't much different in 1949 or 1950, for that matter. As usual, Napa County took more awards than any other, with a total of 48 from seven Napa wineries, as compared with 26 for San Joaquin County, followed by Alameda with 24, Santa Clara with 22 and Sonoma with 21, observed the wine journal. Ingelnook again won the most medals, including five Golds. Wentes were not far behind, and the Mondavi boys at Charles

Krug walked off with four Gold medals and also established themselves as the leading Rhine wine producers in the state.[15]

Napa's prestige was soaring, but there were complaints from within the local industry that with more than three dozen wineries in Napa, only a few won all the medals. The State Fair reacted by opening the 1950 competition to wines of all states and nations. Guess who won? Beaulieu accumulated the most points (based on three for Gold, two for Silver and one for Bronze). The *Philadelphia Observer* carried a story in September 1950 on Beaulieu's huge total number of wine medals won at Sacramento. Inglenook, Charles Krug and Louis Martini beat their competition. Napa picked up a total of fifteen Gold medals, the other competitors combined gaining fourteen.

Bickering among some of the competitors continued.[16] Dr. Maynard Amerine at the University of California, Davis, thought there might be merit to investigating why some large wineries ignored the State Fair. Almaden, for example, never entered. Christian Brothers withdrew. But the in-fighting stayed largely in Napa, and the public read only about the wonders of Napa Valley wines. People were particularly impressed by a luncheon for 650 members of Harvard University's Associated Clubs, served on the grounds of the old Bourn mansion south of St. Helena. To prepare the food, George Mardikian brought the entire staff of his Omar Khayam, then the top restaurant in San Francisco. The Napa Valley Vintners Association picked up the tab for the luncheon, a hefty $6,000. But the organization could afford it; everyone belonged, and the association had plenty of clout.

During the early years of the war most of the county's wine or grape-grower associations disbanded. Several of the wine men left in the valley, most of whom were too old to be drafted, met occasionally to discuss common problems. Louis Martini, who was a great talker and could expound for hours on all aspects of wine, set up the meetings in a local restaurant or at his home. At some point in 1943 he invited Charles Forni, John Daniel and Louis Stralla for lunch at his Monte Rosso vineyard in the eastern hills of Sonoma Valley. Martini said it was time to meet once a month to share and discuss common wine concerns.

In February 1945, *Wines & Vines* reported the founding of a formal organization of wine producers, the Napa Valley Vintners. Seven wineries joined the organization, with Martini as president, Daniel as vice president, and Robert Mondavi as secretary. Thereafter, anything of consequence affecting wine in the valley had to have the Vintners' approval, and no one suggested it should be otherwise. The Vintners immediately went to work to promote Napa Valley wines. One promotion which earned an enormous amount of good will was adopting a San Francisco cable car in 1949. The cable car system was in deep financial trouble and falling apart. The Vintners picked up part of the tab for the cost of operation for a full year. When Idwal Jones' popular book, *Vines In the Sun,* was published the same year, the Vintners offered promotional backing. And why not? Napa Valley wineries were profiled more than any other region's. Jones' history was frequently inaccurate, but the interviews and folklore added much to the valley's mystique.

The only woman to join the Napa Valley Vintners was elected a director: Fernande de Latour. Perhaps she discussed with the Vintners her plan to take Beaulieu wines to Paris for a tasting in August. She spoke French, of course. Her daughter was married to a French count. The winery was founded by a Frenchman. How could the Hotel George V refuse to arrange a tasting? Madame de Latour's reputation preceded her. She had been featured in *Country Life* magazine in 1942, and was written up in *Vogue* in 1947, with a full-page photograph accompanying the story, for her unusual stature as a woman successful in a field totally dominated by men. Fifty prominent members of the French wine industry tasted her Beaulieu wines and were highly complimentary. No one would have dared to be otherwise. Madame de Latour had a commanding presence, in America and France. But Beaulieu's success in Paris was not well received by Napa winemen. There were few toasts to Madame de Latour's good health. Few sent congratulatory telegrams.

Appearances of a winery had little to do with wine quality in the early years. The Stanley winery in the Carneros once produced some of the finest wines in all of Napa Valley and California. This fire gutted the structure in 1936, but it was never very picturesque.

While Beaulieu was doing well in Paris, the American market for fine Napa wines was once again taking a nose-dive. Now what had gone wrong? If a group of Napa growers and vintners had traveled to middle America and quietly observed sales of wine, they would have been astonished. More bottles of "Mogen David" kosher wine were being sold than any other brand. Why kosher sacramental wine? The label clearly suggested it was for Jewish religious holidays. It was very sweet. Irving Marcus at *Wines & Vines* suggested: "Undoubtedly, the Concord flavor in 'kosher' wine is a strong selling point. To a big proportion of U.S. citizens the most familiar grape taste is that of the Concord. When a housewife thinks of grape juice, she thinks only of that flavor."

Marcus was aware that Concord grapes, in the familiar wooden baskets with wire handles, were sold each fall in every grocery store in America. Welch's grape juice and jellies were immensely

307

popular. Concord grape-flavored sodapop was coming close to equaling Coca Cola in sales. Some critics suggested that the Wine Corporation of Chicago (Mogen David producers) and Monarch Wine Company of New York (Manischewitz) had just added alcohol to the grape soda to produce their wares. "Kosher wine has become a marketing phenomenon," declared Marcus. "Producers old and new are rumored getting ready to grab a share of the blossoming business."

Still, most of Napa Valley's wine cellars really did not have to worry. Kosher wine production could not gear up quickly enough to serve a 140-million-gallon U.S. market. The premium producers naturally were concerned, but it was the jug wine salesmen who might lose their jobs, and maybe their shirts. Roma Wine Company, California's largest winery, knew its jug sales were endangered. Some quick market research showed that more and more women were deciding what kind of wine to buy for their homes. So in the fall of 1949, Roma introduced its answer to Mogen David, directed toward the female purchaser: Jo-Ann Concord wine. Gallo Brothers of Modesto followed suit with Gallo-ette, accompanied by advertisements featuring a young woman. Cook's Early American Wine, of St. Louis, also had a Concord base, but it was gender-neutral. The California wineries had to use all their political clout to change a state law which did not permit the production of wines with as much sugar as was found in Mogen David.

Roma solved its sluggish sales of Jo-Ann Concord by buying out the Monarch Wine Company. Manischewitz would now require inspection by a Jewish rabbi at Fresno, as well as in Brooklyn, to make sure the wine was kosher. With its major competitor now in California, the Wine Corporation of Chicago also went after a larger share of this market. In only four years, Mogen David sales doubled. Back in the midwest, the *Omaha World Herald* studied the wine buying habits of its readers: three of every four wine-drinking families preferred Mogen David wine.[17]

Some wine makers followed the lead of the Christian Brothers in Napa Valley. They had an abundance of Muscat grapes: why not put the sweet Muscat flavor into competition with the Concords? Christian Brothers premiered their Sauterne-colored Chateau LaSalle in March 1960, in a bottle shaped like a bowling pin. Gallo-ette had fallen on its face as rapidly as Jo-Ann, so Ernest Gallo introduced "Thunderbird." Petri Wine Company brought out Silver Satin, Chateau Martin in New York came out with Jet, and Roma introduced a new wine called Rocket.

Economist Louis Gomberg of San Francisco had already seen that the kosher wine boom was waning. It had been something very close to a phenomenon, having grown from two million gallons to ten million a year, just in the United States.[18] Now the demand was leveling off. But if the bloom were indeed off the kosher rose, as Gomberg hinted, to what beverage would these consumers now turn? Might they be persuaded to refine their tastes? Why not a Napa Valley Cabernet with prime rib?

Or would the wine market have to go through another major readjustment as happened after World War II? The sixteen-year period between 1934 and 1950 was perhaps more difficult than the fourteen years of Prohibition. There had not been a single year when events were really favorable to the winemaker. Wine production was increasing yearly in Napa Valley, but grape prices fluctuated widely. No one was getting rich, not even Fernande de Latour. Inflation had sent the cost of equipment much higher, while the price of a fine bottle of wine was still under one dollar.

On top of everything else, the 1940s ended with four years of near-drought conditions. On the other hand, Napa Valley residents had a white Christmas in December 1948, for the first time in many years. There were eighteen inches of snow at Angwin and nearly as much on Spring Mountain. But the vines weren't affected in the least; they were in a deep, deep sleep.

From 1950 to the late 1960s, between 60% and 75% of the wine produced in Napa, Sonoma, and Mendocino Counties was sold to E. & J. Gallo and bottled under the Gallo label. This advertisement from the *St. Helena Star* is dated October 19, 1961.

A WINE BOOM AT LAST

S ometime during the month of June 1949 Ernest
and Julio Gallo stopped in unannounced at the
Napa Valley Cooperative winery in St. Helena to
taste the cooperative's wine. The cooperative was
in deep trouble. Sales were lagging; payments for what had been
sold were terribly slow. There was far too much wine still in storage, with the annual crush only weeks away. The Gallo name
meant nothing to the receptionist; it was just another Italian sur-
name. The plant foreman recognized "Gallo" as a winery in
Modesto, but he had little idea of its size, or whether the Gallos
might be interested in purchasing bulk wine. Ernest and Julio
were given the royal treatment nevertheless.

It is understandable that the Gallos were not well known in
the Napa Valley in 1949. They ranked about twelfth in size
among all California wineries. The Gallos could store 8.5 million
gallons of wine. Roma, the industry's largest, could store 32 million; Fruit Industries of San Francisco handled 29 million; and
Italian Swiss Colony, 24 million gallons. No deal was made at the
cooperative that day, and none would be made for some time to
come. But the two brothers would not forget what they had tasted. These Napa wines, though not always produced from the best
grapes — too many Golden Chasselas, Burgers or Alicantes —

were just what they needed to improve the quality of their San Joaquin valley wines. They would be back.[1]

The wine industry, in general, had a lot on its mind. American tariffs on wine had been dropped to aid in the rebuilding of the European wine industry. Late spring frosts in Napa vineyards meant a vastly reduced harvest. Some thought that was not a good omen for the future. Some old-timers, like James Beard of St. Helena, worried when the first diesel train arrived on the morning of September 5th, replacing Southern Pacific's old steam locomotives. The *St. Helena* Star described Beard's long face as he witnessed the event: steam trains had carried him up and down the valley for decades and dated back to 1868. An era seemed to be ending: one had to be flexible or be overwhelmed.

And there was the threat of nuclear war. In the late 1940s, this was a distraction that bordered on hysteria. Then on June 25, 1950, when North Korea invaded South Korea, many people thought World War III was about to begin. President Harry S. Truman ordered American air and naval forces, then ground troops to Korea. The United Nations was asked to join the U.S. in repelling the invaders, who were fighting with Russian rifles, artillery, tanks and jet planes.

Still, with large numbers of men again being inducted into the services, wine purchases in 1950 matched the record set in 1946, the first full year of peace after World War II, an astonishing 140 million gallons. As the year went on, grape growers were paid almost double for a ton of grapes compared to the previous year. They had averaged $45 a ton in 1949; now they were selling for $75 to $130 a ton, because frost had cut the crop by nearly half. But any celebration was premature. Three years after the end of World War II, only a half million gallons of wine had been imported into this country. France's vines were in bad shape, and those in Germany and Italy were even worse. But by the end of 1951, imports of dry table wines into the United States had climbed more than 200%, and each succeeding year was setting new records. The amount of imported wine came to only about four million gallons, but the threat to the American wine industry was real. Alfred Fromm, partner in the major wine distribution company, Fromm & Sichel, put it succinctly: "While it is true that foreign wines account for less than ten per cent of all wines sold in the U.S., they represent 75% of all table wines sold here in the premium class."[2]

During the late 1940s the Mondavis, Christian Brothers, Louis Martini, Beringer, and others had entered the premium wine market, and they intended to stay there. In 1953, Robert Mondavi analyzed the premium table wine market and discovered a 13.26% increase in sales, while bulk wine prices were plummeting.[3]

Whether it was the effect of foreign wine imports, the hoarding of wine for later use, or psychological effects of the Korean War, wine consumption nationally dropped more than 20 million gallons in 1951. A far more dismal figure is the share of the U.S. market held by California and Napa wine: California wine producers lost about ten per cent of the American market, and Napa Valley was particularly hard hit. Without the Gallo brothers, it would have been far worse. They were hardly the largest players in the California wine market, but they were growing steadily. Julio was in charge of wine production, and Ernest handled sales and marketing. Ernest analyzed every fact he could collect on the California wine business. He knew that many newcomers to the state came from nearly dry states in the Midwest; they loved the freedom to buy and drink California wines. As a matter of fact, though California wine wasn't doing well nationally, wine sales in the State had climbed from a quarter million to a million gallons each year.[4]

The Gallos could not produce wine fast enough for the local market; they had to buy more. So why not purchase medal-winning wines from Napa Valley? The Gallos made their first major purchase of Napa Valley Cooperative wine in April 1951. They bought 60,000 gallons and paid the enormous price of 62 cents a gallon — about twenty cents above the going rate. The Cooperative had storage space for 2.5 million gallons of wine and could crush up to 12,000 tons a year. They had been producing at less than half their capacity.[5] But the following year the Cooperative crushed 4000 tons of grapes and the Gallos agreed to purchase all their wine, as well as all of the wine made that year at the small St. Helena Cooperative just north of the city.

In February 1954 the Cooperative and the Gallos entered into a ten-year contract. The fall crush was doubled. By 1955 the winery was almost up to capacity.[6] At the St. Helena Cooperative, more Gallo wine tanks were added to increase production by a quarter million gallons. Ernest Gallo told his brother he could sell even more wine if he could make some spot purchases from other Napa wineries, so Julio began buying from Christian Brothers, Beaulieu, Charles Forni and others. By mid-decade Napa county wine production was again increasing. By 1955-56, about six million gallons was being produced, and Ernest and Julio Gallo were buying nearly 65% of it. When production again reached the 7 million gallon plateau, Gallo was purchasing more than half of everything Napa Valley produced. This situation lasted well into the next decade, and, quite literally, averted disaster in Napa Valley.

A MINI-BOOM IN WINE

Ernest Gallo was a genius at marketing wine, a talent which was missing at both Napa cooperatives. In the 1950s, Gallo began buying wine distributorships outside California, and in due course the Gallos had organized the first truly national wine distribution system. None of their competition could even come close to the Gallo operation. Ernest Gallo also knew that California's wine boom would spread across the country. For one thing, wine tastings were catching on fast.

In Boston, Massachusetts, in September 1957, an entire week was devoted to introducing California wine, sometimes at tastings involving hundreds of wine novices. Such events had long been popular in San Francisco and Los Angeles. During the first week of January 1958, nearly 2,000 people attended a five-day tasting of California wines in St. Louis, Missouri. The news

media in these cities were lavishly courted by California vintners. Wine flowed and gourmet food was in abundance, and no
wine company was too small to host an event. Jack Taylor and
his wife, owners of the tiny Mayacamas Vineyards in the Napa
Redwoods, arranged a private wine luncheon in New York where
even the Richard Nixons showed up (he was not yet President).
The Chicago Daily News was moved to lift its 50-year-old ban on
wine advertising.

Elmo Roper had conducted a private survey of wine drinking
habits in the mid-50s which came up with two startling conclu-
sions: women were more likely to buy wine for home consumption than men, and people would buy more wine if it were readily available.[7] In 1957 Ernest Gallo came out with what was
described in *Wines & Vines* as the "first specialty wine," aimed at
pleasing the maturing tastes of the American public. The name
of the wine was "Thunderbird."[8] It was linked through advertising with high fashion and was sure to attract the attention of
women.

Christian Brother's "Chateau La Salle," introduced in 1960,
was a muscat grape wine just sweet enough to please new wine
drinkers, and it did not seem to be harmed by the addition of ice
cubes to the glass. That was important to a country that drank
huge amounts of soft drinks, always cooled with ice. There were
no muscat grapes in Napa Valley, of course. Years later, Brother
Timothy recalled that Julio Gallo had complained long and hard
to the Cooperative members about upgrading Napa varieties.
Gallo's urging had produced little change. But, while some members didn't like it, a few long-overdue changes did occur.[9]

Vintners in the valley could not agree on the direction the
wine industry should take. Most growers, numbed by years of
erratic and often poor prices, just wanted to be left alone. But
people like Beaulieu's winemaker Andre Tchelistcheff, Robert
Mondavi and his brother Peter at the Krug winery, Leland
Stewart of Souverain, the Taylors of Mayacamas Vineyards, and
Fred and Eleanor McCrea of Stony Hill Winery, wanted to
upgrade all Napa wine. They saw no reason it could not match

The Robert Mondavi Winery at Oakville, here shown under construction in 1966, was only the third new winery to be built in the Napa Valley since Prohibition.

the best French chateau vintages. These people and several others from nearby wine counties formed the Chateau Wine Growers of California in January 1951. Regular tastings were held of each member's wine to guarantee it met certain standards. Each bottling that passed muster would carry a member's label guaranteeing quality. Contrary to long-standing regulations by the Bureau of Alcohol, Tobacco and Firearms, which controlled the wine industry for the U.S. Treasury Department and required only 51 percent of a wine be from the principal grape used in the varietal, the Chateau Wine Growers decided that 85 percent was necessary for varietal classification. Several years earlier in St. Helena, Mondavi and Tchelistcheff had set up the

Napa Enological Center Laboratory to test wine yeasts, must samples and other aspects of wine making. Now they had another organization with some clout, one which promised to move wine quality further ahead.

Three years after signing their contract with the cooperative, the Gallos did not seem to be making any progress with members on improving grape varieties. Mondavi and Tchelistcheff had no success either. *Wines & Vines* reported in July 1957 that a mere 100 acres had been replanted in Napa county. "Some of the older standard varieties are slowly being pulled out," reported the magazine. "Among these: Alicante Bouschet, Grand Noir, Golden Chasselas, Green Hungarian, Mission and Black Malvoisie." Nearly thirty years after Prohibition had ended, Alicantes were still being grown in Napa Valley. And even worse, Mission grapes. At least Burgers were not mentioned — maybe the editor was too polite. Even as late as the mid-1960s, grape growers were still dragging their feet. Petit Sirah was more widely grown in the valley than Cabernet Sauvignon, which ranked fifth. The Carignane grape also beat out Cabernet, as did Gamays and the perennially popular Zinfandel.

Premium grape prices were always higher than the older common varieties, sometimes by as much as $50 a ton. This should have been incentive enough to replant, but it wasn't. And there were compelling reasons not to replant. The price of grapes went up and down like a yo-yo. In 1953 *Wines & Vines* carried a bold chart showing that farmers growing wine grapes earned less money than almost any other fruit farmer. Wine grapes returned on average $150 per acre. Cherries, lemons, peaches, pears and even dates earned figures three to five times as much.[10]

Many farmers held steadfastly to their prune orchards. They had good reason. Growers could earn a hundred dollars more per acre from prunes than from grapes. Still, prunes were on their way out in the Napa Valley. By the start of the 1960s prune trees covered only 6,500 acres, down from more than 13,000 at the beginning of World War II. Nathan Fay was one farmer who changed from prunes to grapes. In 1953 he purchased 205 acres with a small prune orchard from Thompson Parker in the Stag's Leap area. Fay was advised by the University of California to pull out the prune trees and plant as much land as possible in vines. "They were growing prunes then in the Sacramento Valley, up around Oroville. They were bigger than ours and in a cellophane bag looked better, although we always believed Napa prunes had better quality."[11] In the early 60s, when Robert and Peter Mondavi promised to buy whatever grapes he raised, Fay's prunes finally gave way to Cabernet Sauvignon grapes.

There are two curious historical sidelights to the demise of the Napa Valley prune: St. Helena native Fred Knipschild invented an automatic prune dryer which he took to Yuba City in 1948. His idea was to dry green lumber when prunes were not being processed. It appears that some prune growers followed Knipschild out of Napa Valley, never to return. Hungarian-born John Nemeth claims that in the mid-1950s prune growers in his home land took over the English market for California prunes. The Hungarians produced the prunes at a far lower cost. [12]

Prunes were not the only part of Napa's disappearing past. Across the Mayacamas mountains, in the easternmost region of Napa County, nearly 20,000 acres of prime cattle grazing land was under water — perhaps for the first time in history. A Mexican adobe and rancho in Berryessa dated back long before the discovery of gold in California. About the time the American Civil War was ending, E. A. Peacock and Abraham Clark began the area's first town, Monticello. Ranchers and wheat farmers quickly settled in and Berryessa became a stopover for quicksilver miners heading further north to Knoxville. Louie Stralla planted several hundred acres of grapes in the valley in the late 1940s, but no one else followed his lead.

The idea for a dam and lake had been around for decades. Shortly after World War II, the Bureau of Reclamation revived the concept because water was needed to irrigate nearby Solano and Yolo counties. Local residents, barely 350 in number, fought back, as did Napa County Supervisors, but none of the heated arguments did any good. In July 1953 bids were let for the dam, estimated to cost $47 million. It was completed four years later. They named the lake Berryessa; the dam was called Monticello, after the small community now resting ninety feet below the surface. Lake Berryessa soon became a major recreation area for Napa County, supervised by the National Park Service. It would take a major drought to drop the water level low enough to see again the pioneer town of Monticello.

The use of the automobile also threatened enormous change, but resistance to a four-lane freeway covering the entire length of Napa Valley was much stronger than the efforts put forth against Monticello Dam. The State had announced the freeway plans in October, 1953. The strongest resistance came in and around the city of St. Helena, where the valley narrowed significantly between the mountains. A major freeway could destroy much of the scenic beauty of the town. Freeway construction south of Napa and north as far as Yountville was completed in 1969. But it never extended any further. California highway engineers might have met with armed resistance had they not halted further work.

These intrusions on the landscape may explain why Napa voters approved Proposition 3 on the state ballot in 1966. The proposition required that assessment of farm land be based solely on agricultural uses of that property, and not on business or commercial potential. This meant that vineyards near a city could not be taxed out of existence simply because the potential was there for business development. The new state law also allowed counties to set up agricultural preserves, which Napa did immediately. Farmers were thus guaranteed no tax increases for ten years; and no parcels under 40 acres were allowed. The Napa Valley Vintners Association was among the earliest backers of this "green belt" legislation. Jack Davies of Schramsberg Winery, Hanns Kornell, Michael Mondavi, Thomas May and Louis Martini, Sr. served on committees related to the measure.

Others also wanted to see the valley protected from overdevelopment. A headline in the San Francisco *Examiner*, May 8, 1966, proposed: "Napa Valley Vineyards — National Park

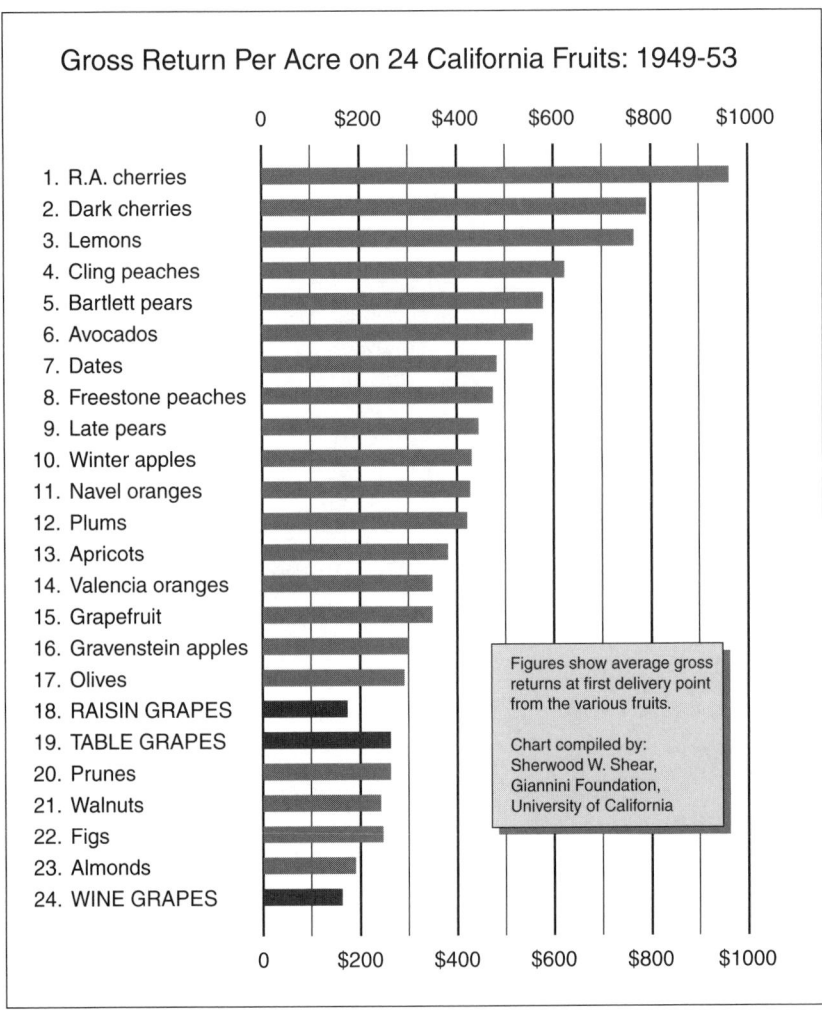

Gross Return Per Acre on 24 California Fruits: 1949-53

	0	$200	$400	$600	$800	$1000

1. R.A. cherries
2. Dark cherries
3. Lemons
4. Cling peaches
5. Bartlett pears
6. Avocados
7. Dates
8. Freestone peaches
9. Late pears
10. Winter apples
11. Navel oranges
12. Plums
13. Apricots
14. Valencia oranges
15. Grapefruit
16. Gravenstein apples
17. Olives
18. RAISIN GRAPES
19. TABLE GRAPES
20. Prunes
21. Walnuts
22. Figs
23. Almonds
24. WINE GRAPES

Figures show average gross returns at first delivery point from the various fruits.

Chart compiled by:
Sherwood W. Shear,
Giannini Foundation,
University of California

	0	$200	$400	$600	$800	$1000

Source: *Wines & Vineyards*, September 1956

Heritage." Environmental writer William Bronson suggested setting up a "national vineyard" designation for the valley, similar to national parks. The federal government could acquire title to much of Napa Valley, and farmers would continue what they had been doing for generations — raising grapes and making wine which would become part of our national heritage. A symposium on the idea was held at Calistoga. Napa residents were flattered by the attention but few took the idea seriously.

By the mid-60s nearly everyone living in Napa County was aware that a wine boom of perhaps spectacular proportions was on its way. An official at the historic Krug winery reported that 70,000 tourists had visited the winery in 1964, up from 50,000 in 1960.[13] Well dressed people in shiny new cars were visiting the area for longer than just weekends, and realtors were driving them up and down back roads, looking at vineyards and wine cellars. There was an unmistakable air of intrigue in Napa Valley. Almost everyone knew someone who knew of a winery deal about to happen.

And there was a shortage of grapes. Americans everywhere, not just in California, were drinking so much wine with meals or for entertaining that wine consumption of all types had doubled in one decade.[14] Those wine tasting parties in the '50s had obviously paid off. San Francisco's Wine Institute had increased its advertising budget significantly, with full-page color advertisements in national magazines. In an increasingly affluent society, wine was desirable as a part of the good life. Also, it helped enormously to have a friend in the White House. In June 1965 President Lyndon Johnson directed that only American wine be served at State functions and American consulates. But now there wasn't enough to go around; at least not the kind everybody wanted. "No, we don't have any more wine," became the frequent answer to customers calling wineries. The Krug winery took out an ad in various magazines, including *Wines & Vines*, in November 1965: "There's a drought at Charles Krug. To put it simply, we don't have enough of certain types of Charles Krug wines to go around."

The rest of the nation was following a new trend in California toward table wines. Until 1950, dessert wines, including kosher wines, outsold dry wines four to one. In 1965, Americans consumed roughly 74 million gallons of table wines compared to 84 million gallons of sweet wines. But only four years later, the

321

figures were upside down. Wine consumers were drinking 112 million gallons of table wines and only 77 million of sweet wines.

California was setting lots of new trends in the '60s: the free-speech movement at U.C. Berkeley set a precedent for student protests across the country; the gay movement in San Francisco inspired the Stonewall protests later in New York; the earliest anti-Vietnam protests involved Californians of every age, race, and economic status; even west coast restaurants were trend-setters with new dishes and fresh produce from California's rich farmlands. A California native-son won election to the White House, and the beautiful California weather inspired a population boom of 100,000 new residents a year.

A professor at California State College, Fresno, spotted the wine trend early. Joe Heitz had helped set up a department of viticulture at the college; then, restless to be more involved in the profession, he quit teaching and went to work for Beaulieu Vineyard at Rutherford. He spent seven years as production manager at Beaulieu and left in 1961 to go out on his own. He purchased a small wine cellar south of St. Helena, but that was only the beginning. Three years later he acquired the old Rossi winery in tiny Spring Valley. The old stone winery dated back to the turn of the century but had not been used since Prohibition: it needed a complete renovation. The vineyards had been sadly neglected, too. Most of the work was completed when Heitz had the good fortune to meet two relative newcomers to Napa viticulture, Tom and Martha May.

The Mays had acquired their Napa home, west and slightly south of the historic Far Niente winery at Oakville, in 1963. Twelve acres were planted with Cabernet. They immediately expanded the vineyard to 50 acres, which Tom honored his wife by naming "Martha's Vineyard" (no connection to Cape Cod). Martha's Vineyard would soon become one of the most famous in California. The first serious harvest from Martha's Vineyard came in 1965, and Heitz took it all. May wanted the wine to be kept separate from any of his neighbors', but Heitz felt the quality wasn't yet good enough. In subsequent years he did keep it separate, however. When he released the first Martha's Vineyard Cabernet in 1971, it caused a sensation.

"Wine writers began sitting up and taking special notice of the Cabernet," recalled May, and this was especially true of his 1968. "I remember *Town & Country* magazine carrying a full-page photograph of the vineyard with the label from the wine bottle. Harry Waugh praised it strongly even before it was released."[15]

Heitz's reputation as "master winemaker" was about to be made, not only for the Mays' wine, but for the others he had shepherded from vine to cask. So he decided to honor the Mays by putting the "Martha's Vineyard" name on the label. He had also done this with a "McCray Vineyard" designation on a 1967 Pinot Noir released in 1969. This label recognition was another first for Napa Valley and California. Ridge Vineyards and Winery of Cupertino carried vineyard label designations as early as 1966 but the designation was "Vineyard at 1100" [feet] or "Late-picked raisined grapes, Geyserville"; no family names were given.

No one could quite explain the exceptional quality of the May Cabernet. Andre Tchelistcheff thought the slight hint of mint came from a stand of eucalyptus nearby. He had noticed the same thing at Buena Vista in Sonoma.[16] Or perhaps the secret was simply that May insisted from the first that his grapes not be blended with others. Such a demand seemed arrogant, perhaps, but it is exactly why Rene di Rosa's "Winery Lake Vineyard" grapes became the most expensive in the entire state and country.

Di Rosa arrived in the Carneros region of Napa county in late 1960. He worked for the *San Francisco Chronicle* as a reporter after trying to write the great American novel in Paris, where he met Gertrude Stein and Alice B. Toklas. He developed an interest in modern art and began collecting it. His family had money and connections.

He picked Napa over St. Helena, then the center of the county's wine industry, thinking he might raise hay, or even sheep. He was drawn to this Basque way of life because he liked the Basque people he'd met in a North Beach restaurant. But there had been vines on his land before the phylloxera arrived, and di Rosa's home was an old winery — the von Strantz place. He was told he was crazy to plant grapes on his land. Even the University of California suggested something other than vines — perhaps an overnight camper's site. But di Rosa had always followed his heart, and by 1966-67 he had grapes to sell. ZD winery bought some, Burgess Cellars, Schramsberg, McCrea's Stony Hill, Souverain and others. Robert Mondavi became a major buyer in 1971. Di Rosa demanded that Mondavi crush his grapes and keep the wine separate from that of any other grower. Without any hint of Burger or Carignane or Petite Syrah in the 100% Pinot Noir, "Winery Lake" was soon on the way to wine stardom.

"The word was spreading by the time my grapes came into production that the Carneros grapes made all the others look bad," recalled di Rosa. Beaulieu and Louis Martini were producing Carneros grapes, but di Rosa had the only grapes from the Carneros for public sale. "I decided to set my price twenty-five per cent above what the North Coast Grape Growers recommended, and I got it," said di Rosa. Domaine Chandon winery was almost built on di Rosa's property, and, says di Rosa, "I was lucky they did not." [17]

Like Heitz and Gallo, Hanns Kornell had a vision of the future of wine. Born in Germany, he moved to Napa Valley in 1958. His father had died in a German concentration camp, but with help from friends and a lot of luck, Hanns escaped and fled to England, then to the United States, where he got a job with the Fountain Grove winery at Santa Rosa. When he moved to St. Louis, Missouri, to go to work for Cook's Imperial Champagne, he found his true path. Kornell wanted his own winery, his own brand of champagne. With borrowed funds and a small savings he leased a little winery near the center of Sonoma. When the Mark Hopkins Hotel in San Francisco agreed to handle his champagne, Kornell knew he was on the right track. He moved to Napa when the Safeway chain bought his Sonoma property for a new store.

Originally built in 1889, the Schramsberg house still stands, as grand and elegant as ever. Jack Davies, now deceased, and his wife Jamie restored the building in the early 1960s.

Champagne sales had been skyrocketing in the U.S. In the space of only six years, from 1951 to 1956, Americans almost doubled their consumption of sparkling wine. Sales of champagne during the 1960s grew at an even more astonishing rate, and because a large portion of the new champagne was Charmat or bulk-process produced, the price could drop sharply as consumption rose.

Kornell purchased the historic Larkmead winery just north of St. Helena. (The Salmina family was unhappy when Kornell changed the name of the winery from Larkmead to his own.) The Larkmead facility was built like a fortress. The bottling line was dated and noisy, and visitors felt like they were going back in time. This was champagne-making the old fashioned way. Kornell guided many of the tourists through the cellars himself.

Jack Davies wanted to make champagne too. He and his wife, Jamie, came to Napa County from Southern California, where Jack had been an executive with a paper box manufacturing business. They had salted away enough money to invest in a venture he could run personally. Wine making was the main source of interest at business seminars and dinner tables, so Davies looked into it.

Schramsberg was Napa County's second oldest winery, west of the St. Helena highway and a thousand feet up the hillside. The California Champagne Company out of San Francisco had purchased the property in 1942 and named the place Mt. Diamond Cellars. Douglas Pringle bought the cellar a decade later and had to replant the entire vineyard and modernize the equipment. Fortunately, the Chinese-built wine caves were as sound as the day they had been carved out of the hillside rock.

Davies purchased the facility in 1965, and seven years later a minor miracle occurred: thirteen cases of Schramsberg champagne was flown to Peking, China, when President Richard Nixon made his historic visit there in February 1972. No one ever found out who on the White House staff had made the selection, but when President Nixon and Premier Chou En-lai lifted their glasses in a friendly toast, along with hundreds of other guests at a State banquet, Schramsberg Napa Valley champagne was sipped. Photographs of the event were carried in many major American newspapers, and phone calls for interviews kept Davies busy for days. Wine connoisseurs were jolted out of their seats. Napa Valley had no reputation for champagne. It had always been known for fine red wines, and almost no one there even made sparkling wine. But Davies and Kornell were changing that.

Changes in the wine industry weren't lost on Otto Beringer. He decided his family had to make further preparations for the predicted boom. But he would have to convince his elderly aunts, Bertha and Martha Beringer, daughters of Jacob Beringer, who held the purse strings. In 1959, the two sisters had bought

JAMIE DAVIES

the Holmes ranch in Knight's Valley, west of Calistoga, where land was much cheaper than in Napa Valley. A year later, Otto planted 25 acres of vines and prepared ground for another 300 acres. The winery had been named Los Hermanos by a neighbor, Señior Tiburcio Parrott. Los Hermanos means "the brothers," an ironic name for a winery later purchased by two sisters. Otto Beringer presided at a luncheon at the winery in May 1967, when it was designated a state landmark.

On the other side of St. Helena, Louis Martini had a new wine warehouse built in 1966, then added a tasting room and retail area a year later, along with four 15,000-gallon, temperature-controlled, stainless steel tanks. Like Beringer, Martini left Napa Valley proper to buy 900 acres in Chiles Valley for the expansion  of his privately-owned vineyards. A portion of the property had been owned at the turn of the century by pioneer George Husmann. Remnants of his stone winery were still there.

Inglenook, too, fell victim to wine fever. John Daniel, grand-nephew of founder Gustave Niebaum, sold the winery in 1964 to United Vintners. U.C. Berkeley graduate Daniel was an iconoclast. Tall, handsome, athletic, and wealthy, he was active in the Vintner's Association, progressive, and extremely well-liked and respected. His first passion was flying airplanes, and he was happy to have a small airfield nearby. After Repeal, he and winemaker Carl Bundschu pushed varietal wines instead of generics and produced some of the best post-Prohibition Cabernet Sauvignon. Two years after United Vintners took over Inglenook, they built a brand new 80 x 100-foot bottle storage facility, tucked off to the side so that the magnificent view of Inglenook from the highway would remain. Their winery was perhaps the most photographed building in the entire valley.

Brother Gregory, head of the Christian Brothers winery in the Napa Redwoods, and his chief winemaker, Brother Timothy, may have paused occasionally after daily prayers to wonder if they spent too much time on their knees. Christian Brothers wines were selling faster then they could produce them. They reported to *Wines & Vines* in January 1960 that sales had climbed 18% in the last year. They had expanded their vineyards on the valley floor in 1956 by buying 520 acres from Charles Forni. Two years earlier they had begun making champagne by the Charmat method. Since there was little room to expand at the old Greystone winery, Brother Gregory selected a site south of St. Helena for a new bottling and wine storage facility in 1964. This was not going to be a modest undertaking. The building would be 150 feet wide by 400 feet long; 108 stainless steel wine tanks would be added, bringing Christian Brothers' total capacity to 3.5 million gallons. Profits from the wineries funded the many schools operated by the Brothers.

In September 1968 the Christian Brothers were the first to buy a mechanical grape harvester, which would drastically change forever the way viticulture was practiced in Napa Valley. An operator inched the machine along a row of grape vines while hard rubber "beaters" dislodged grapes. The grapes were caught, funneled onto a conveyor belt and carried to a truck which kept pace with the harvester. The harvester had been built by Up-Right Harvesters of Berkeley under a license grant-ed by the University of California, which held the patent.[18] The machine required many improvements in future years. The beat-ers sometimes took a heavy toll on the grape vines. In addition, vines had to be pruned differently, starting when the vine was in its first year. And the harvester did not operate on steep hillsides.

Another change in vineyard management was directed toward controlling frost damage. Frost was a frequent headache to Napa grape growers in the 1960s. There were vine-damaging frosts in 1961, 1964 and 1965, with a low of 25 degrees being recorded at the University of California Experimental vineyard at Oakville in 1964. L.N. Bianchini introduced the concept of spraying the vines with water to control frost damage. He was manager of the Louis Petri vineyards on Big Ranch Road, just north of Napa city. A sprinkler system was put in place at Petri by early 1961 and Bianchini recalls the system practically paid for itself that cold spring.[19] Al Forni, nephew of Charles Forni, produced a film showing the technique for sprinkling vines in 1964, and thereafter this method of fighting frost took hold rapidly. It was not cheap, however, for the sprinkler systems cost between $400 and $700 an acre. An average of 45 gallons per acre was needed for the sprinkler systems, so ponds were built to store water.

Weather of a very opposite nature took center stage in the val-ley the same year as the severe frost was recorded at Oakville. As hot, dry, searing winds swept over the hills the last weeks of September 1964, fire was inevitable. "Greatest Fire in History Ravaged Napa County," headlined the *Star*. The fire started on the flanks of Mt. St. Helena on a Saturday morning. Winds of 70 miles an hour drove it toward Calistoga, which was largely evac-uated that night. The next day hot embers blew across the val-ley's main highway to the western hills where the fire quickly burned into Sonoma County as far as the outskirts of Santa Rosa.

Another section of the fire burned to the St. Helena Sanitarium and on to Angwin. Tons of ash fell on San Francisco for days.

The next year it happened all over again. The first fire in September 1965 broke out in Chiles Valley, then raced out of control toward Soda Canyon to the south. Two other fires rapidly grew into fire-storms in the Knight's Valley region and Middletown of Lake county. The latter headed south to the area burned the previous year. Some of the fires were set by children playing with matches, but others were from power lines downed by the strong winds. With temperatures near 100 degrees and low humidity, the heat from a farm machine's engine could just as easily bring flames to life when driven through high grass. There were harrowing tales of escapes from the flames, homes saved with garden hoses and pets rescued at the last minute. But many homeowners lost everything.

The media didn't need to depend on nature for good copy about the wine industry, however. In March 1960 the *Los Angeles Times* carried a 13-page section on wine, its first of many subsequent wine features. *Look* magazine did the same in July, 1961. *Time* took notice of the wine boom the same summer, and in London Ridley's *Wine and Spirit Circular* for July 20th issued a glowing report on California wine. Articles about wine also appeared in *Holiday*, *Life*, and the *Los Angeles Herald Examiner*. In January, 1964, *Wines & Vines* published a piece called "The Story of Wine in Print," which listed nearly fifty publications with wine feature stories; this summary covered only the previous twelve months.

Beginning in 1960, the weekly *St. Helena Star* issued annually a special section devoted to wine. The *Star* was read by everyone in central Napa Valley, and the paper covered everything that could possibly qualify as newsworthy in the industry. No man fit the image of a country weekly editor better than Starr Baldwin. Already in his late 60s, he was of medium height, heavy-set, stooped; he had a great mane of white hair, and was as cantankerous or warm and jolly as he felt like being. He had run the newspaper for nearly half a century.[20] Though it probably never occurred to him, Baldwin was recording the history of the wine industry.

There were 36 bonded wine cellars in Napa county by 1969. Two years earlier, the consumption of wine in America passed the 200-million-gallon mark. It seemed impossible, but investors believed the numbers, and wanted a piece of the action. In 1967, Charles Carpy headed a group of seven investors who leased the old Freemark Abbey Winery. Carpy's great-grandfather had begun making wine in Napa city in the 1870s, though he had been a resident since the Civil War. He had operated the Uncle Sam Winery, one of the largest wine cellars in the county. Then he moved his business office to San Francisco and became a major wine dealer.

The Carpy family kept their vineyards in Napa Valley but hadn't made wine since Prohibition began. Charles distinguished himself in the Korean War as a young infantry lieutenant. He won a Purple Heart and Bronze Star, and was featured in a photographic story in the *Saturday Evening Post* in May 1952. Carpy and his group restored the Freemark Abbey winery, but only the lower portion; a candle factory and restaurant operated on the upper floors. In 1968, the winery did a small crush of grapes from the John Bosche vineyard.

That same year, almost within sight of Freemark Abbey, but halfway up the Angwin road to Howell Mountain, Lee Stewart began enlarging his winery. "Boutique" barely described Stewart's small operations at Souverain Cellars. He had arrived in 1943, and started winning numerous wine medals late in the decade. Almost 25 years later Stewart addded a 2,000-square-foot building for aging, bottling, laboratory and office.

Stewart was a genuine maverick in the Napa Valley wine business. No one worked for him very long — he was too independent — and he was downright parsimonious. He did things his own way, but he won so many medals, out of a winery far, far from modern, that he engendered some outright jealousy. He was not particularly sociable. Warren Winiarski liked visiting with Stewart, but "once he put on his classical music, socializing stopped. I've never known an individual like him. He lost interest in visitors when dinner was over and the music started."

Legh Knowles at Beaulieu was Stewart's exact opposite. He was so affable he could have sold the Brooklyn Bridge to the Napa Board of Supervisors to span the Napa river. He loved a good laugh, and didn't mind if it was at his own expense. Knowles had a great voice and made radio spots for Beaulieu wines in the 1960s and '70s. He so successfully touted "Rutherford dust" as the ultimate source of quality for Beaulieu grapes and wine, that others in the industry began talking of a Rutherford appellation.

Knowles had begun his adult life as a trumpet player and worked with some very well known dance bands, including Glen Miller, Charley Spivak and Red Norvo. After his military service in World War II, he went into sales work and in 1948 joined the San Francisco Wine Institute and Wine Advisory Board. He worked out of New York. Then in 1962 Helene de Pins, daughter of Beaulieu founder Georges de Latour, asked Knowles to join her team.

During the mid- to late 40s, there were few state dinners, or banquets for war heroes, that did not include Beaulieu Private Reserve Cabernet. Beaulieu was still, in the 1960s, a major supplier of altar wines for the Catholic church. But now Beaulieu was having problems, many of which dated back to the previous decade, when distribution was often hit-and-miss. In spite of all the medals won by Beaulieu, their wines were still not available in enough states. Knowles spent more time in major cities selling wine or acting as a wine ambassador than he did at home, at least in his early years with Beaulieu. His hard work paid off so well that in 1965 two new structures were added to the winery. One was a huge aging and storage warehouse. The second brought some much-needed grace to the winery. From the stone of an 1880 distillery on the site, a new visitor's pavilion was built. Prior to that date, visitors were hosted in a small cubbyhole next to the general offices. In 1969, Heublein, a corporate conglomerate from Hartford, Connecticut which also owned

Kentucky Fried Chicken and a vodka distillery, acquired Beaulieu. Around 20 years later, Knowles would be honored as one of 12 "Living Wine Legends of California" in a San Francisco ceremony.

But if things were happy and bright with Knowles, they were stormy and dark with the Mondavis. Some years earlier at the Krug winery, there had been a family quarrel, with shouting well into the night. After a supposed fist-fight between the two brothers, both of whom were over fifty, Robert Mondavi was given the boot from Krug by his mother, and younger brother Peter took over.

Robert sued Peter, his mother and a sister for his share of the value of the Charles Krug winery and their differences became public. Peter charged Robert with being too free-spending, and Robert accused his brother of being too conservative in a time that required highly innovative approaches to marketing wine. Peter had always been content to make fine wines without bragging. Like many Italians, he believed that earning a good living was its own reward. But Robert thrived on competition and public contact. He entered Krug wines in judgings and was elated when they won gold medals. Robert wanted his winery to produce the finest wines in the entire world. As a matter of fact, he wanted all Napa Valley wines to be superior.

Robert was a founding member of the Napa Valley Vintners Association in 1944, and helped form the Napa Enological Center in 1948. Three years later he supported the founding of the Chateau Wine Growers of California, whose principal aim was to improve and guarantee wine quality. He wrote in *Wines & Vines* in early 1953 that quality table wine sales were increasing every year in California; he predicted correctly that the trend would go national. Mondavi turned the Krug winery into a visitors' center in the early 1950s, hosting every convention delegation he could to introduce Napa wines. His contention was that once Napa wines were tasted, there would be no need for follow-up calls. In 1968 Mondavi saw "Napa Valley [as the] Focus of the World of Wine," and said so in the *Star* of October 31st. He

LEGH KNOWLES

lectured on the relationship between wine and food, hoping to prove that Napa wines equaled those of France.

Robert often said after the legal wrangling had ended that the family dispute was providential. He was free not only to build his own winery, but to continue enhancing his role as a major wine ambassador. Mondavi received some criticism for seeming to seek the limelight, but the truth was the news media preferred to build wine stories around individuals. Before he could build his own winery, however, he had to figure out a way to support his wife and family, though his eldest son, Michael, had just finished college and planned to go to work in the Krug winery that summer. He would be the first member of the third generation of Mondavis to make his fortune in the wine business.

Robert Mondavi soon found work as a consultant. He discovered that his long-time close friends were willing to help him establish his own winery. Bill and Ina McCormick Hart were the first to offer cash: nearly $100,000. Hart had inherited his family's investment in Kern County oil, and it took a full day to walk the McCormick land holdings on Spring Mountain. Fred and Diana Holmes also joined in funding the new winery. Mondavi selected land, which was already a producing vineyard, owned by Ivan Schoch, who became Mondavi's partner. Schoch had been foreman for Martin Stelling, a San Francisco steel producer, who owned 600 acres of vines before his untimely death in 1950. Mondavi chose his site well. There would be no competition along Highway 29 this far south of St. Helena. Mondavi's was only the third new winery built since Prohibition. The early California architecture was stunning, and included a bell tower. So many visitors turned in for winery tours that ten per cent of his production went straight out the front door.

Although the *Star* reported the new Mondavi Winery as the first in over 30 years, it was actually the third. Louis Martini's had been the first. Then Fred and Eleanor McCrea built a new winery in the hills west of St. Helena, with a first crush in 1951. Their winery was called "Stony Hill," for obvious reasons. The McCreas sold none of their magnificent wine in stores; it was all shipped out or carried out by devotees. The Chardonnay grapes, stressed in hillsides with little soil and lots of rock, won a Gold medal at the State Fair in 1960. There were also Gewurztraminer and Riesling grapes in the vineyard.

While Robert Mondavi was establishing his own winery, Peter made some changes at Krug. The main office was remodeled to handle an increasing sales force and office staff. Guests were welcomed in a new and very elegant reception area: a former Southern Pacific railroad passenger car 73 feet long, parked on steel rails, with a full wine-tasting bar. Vineyard expansion included 100 acres near Yountville, and 500 acres of the old To Kalon vineyard at Oakville, acquired in 1962. There was also a new Willmes press — no more pre-Prohibition relics for Krug. Peter also purchased new stainless steel tanks, with nearly a half-million-gallon capacity, as well as 540 French oak barrels, a quality-control feature Robert had insisted upon before he departed.

Forty wineries in the valley, lots of new equipment, higher quality wines. Certainly there was reason to feel complacent. But the Napa Valley Vintners knew that change was constant in their business. Once a month the Vintners held a luncheon in an old, green and white, one-room school house north of St. Helena. Everyone belonged to the Vintners and nearly every one came to the luncheon to swap wine news. Each month a different winery provided the wine. Journalists were not invited: "It is a very private thing with them. The vintners are all good friends, despite the competition of the marketplace, and they often help each other out with production problems. This is really a brotherhood." [21]

Wine makers enjoyed the new respect earned by the wine industry. To those who had been in the business for a long time, like Louis Martini, Sr., who had sold wine door-to-door in his youth, this was the most important achievement of the period. Robert Mondavi explained: "When I was a teenager this business of making wine was not popular like it is today. In fact, many people looked down on the Italian families because they made wine. Now they send their sons and daughters to UC Davis to become winemakers. It is quite a respectable profession."

NEW WINERIES BLOSSOM -
NAPA WINES BEAT THE FRENCH

I n late March the California poppies announce the arrival of Spring by covering Napa County's hillsides with bright orange and gold. By the end of the 1970s, new wineries seemed to be almost as abundant on the hillsides as those poppies. Sixty new or refurbished wine cellars came into being in ten years. That kind of phenomenal growth had been seen only once before in Napa's history — during the 1880s. The influx of new residents was like a stampede, and the dust, quite literally, did not settle for years. Old roads leading up steep hillsides to once-abandoned wineries were straightened and paved. Vines were replanted on land that had not been cultivated since the phylloxera scourge of the 1890s killed off nearly fifteen thousand acres of wine grapes.

The decade was ushered in with the news that the venerable Beringer winery had been sold to the Swiss chocolate firm of Nestle. The very floor of the valley seemed to tremble. Inglenook had been the first landmark winery to be sold to outsiders, but most valley residents had looked upon the sale as a fluke. With another major winery going to foreigners, the insular community of Napa County was shaken. Nestle, then worth over $5 billion, did not look upon Beringer simply as a prestige investment. It wanted profits from the winery to pay off its $6.5 million price tag. Beringer winery equipment was badly out-of-date and needed improvement so that wine output could be increased. The new owners decided to build a brand-new crushing facility across the main highway, right next to the Mondavi clan's old Krug winery. Peter Mondavi took one look at the $25 million plans and consulted his lawyers.

Mondavi's main objection was aesthetic: he didn't want huge new stainless steel tanks and warehouses right next to the beautiful lawns where Mondavi held wine tastings and other outdoor events. The rural ambiance would be lost. Guy Kay, winery manager at Beringer, was perplexed by the growing hard feelings. Nestle spent a half million dollars restoring the Rhine House and landscaping the grounds. Revered winemaker Myron Nightingale was coaxed away from Cresta Blanca Winery to upgrade Beringer's wine production. Five thousand French oak barrels were installed for aging the wine. The bickering with neighbors went on for years. Nestle finally got some relief from public attention when word leaked out that a French champagne house wanted to invest in Napa Valley vineyards. The Napa wine industry was not favorably disposed toward the French, and with good reason: Californians couldn't sell their wines in France, and now the French wanted to buy into the valley.

John Wright had been asked by Moet & Hennessy to quietly purchase a few hundred Napa Valley acres for vines. No one really knew what was happening until Moet & Hennessy Vineyards had been incorporated, and had acquired hillsides in the Napa redwoods and vineyard land in the Carneros and at Yountville. The Yountville location was chosen for the winery or champagne house. It would be a large and original project — the ground would be scooped away deep into the hillsides, cement walls would be built, and the dirt would be replaced over the top of the facility. Trees and native plants would grow as before.

In the June 1973 issue of *Wines & Vines*, editor Phil Hiaring, Sr. wondered how the French could make champagne in California. After all, they had insisted for centuries that champagne came only from the Champagne District in France. And would the French be entitled to join the Wine Institute and the Wine Advisory Board? If so, wasn't there a potential for conflict about marketing issues? Wright quickly made the company's conditions clear: Moet & Hennessy would market sparkling wine, not champagne. The French were willing to export their dollars to invest in Napa Valley; they would even allow their best vintners to travel frequently to California to guarantee it was all done correctly; but beyond that, certain inalienable rights would have to be retained: Champagne was a French beverage; in California it must be called sparkling wine.

THE ESHCOL WINERY

France's first California champagne — the word has been legal in the U.S. since 1911 — was made in the fall of 1973 in one of Napa Valley's oldest wineries, Eshcol, recently revived by the Trefethen family. Six months later the cuvee for this bottle-fermented champagne was moved to the partially completed new cellars at Yountville.

Some valley residents might have recognized Eshcol as an earlier name for the winery which had long since fallen into disuse, but no one knew the name Trefethen; they were not local people. Eugene Trefethen was the recently retired president of Kaiser Industries of Oakland. The society pages of the San Francisco newspapers frequently included news of the family. He was on the board of directors of the San Francisco Museum of Modern Art, and he and his wife both hailed from old-line California families. Eugene got his start with the Kaiser companies in the mid-1920s. He grew walnuts as a pastime in Walnut Creek until his orchard was forced out by home subdivisions. In 1968 he purchased the historic Eshcol ranch. His son John, who did not follow in his father's footsteps at Kaiser Industries, took a special interest in replanting the old vineyards at Eshcol, and both father and son began to consider reopening it. There had not been a crush in the facility for decades: the Beringers had long

JANET TREFETHEN

used it for wine storage. In 1973, the year John married Janet Spooner (she was from an old rice-growing family in Colusa County), Trefethen winery had its first crush, along with the grapes Moet & Hennessy trucked in from their young vines. John and Janet took over the winery with great enthusiasm, partly because they were working with one of the great French champagne houses. No one else in the Napa Valley had such a unique opportunity.

THE SPURRIER TASTING

The general hostility from valley residents toward the French and Moet & Hennessy evaporated almost overnight because of one of the most bizarre events ever to transpire in wine relations between California and France. In Paris, an English wine merchant named Steven Spurrier came up with the daring idea of organizing a blind tasting of California and French wines. He operated the Academie du Vin, a wine shop and school for both locals and tourists who were curious about foreign wine. He would hold the tasting in late May 1976. It was to be a small, private affair. The wines to be sampled and judged were limited to Chardonnay and Cabernet Sauvignon — the two finest wines on both sides of the Atlantic. Among the Napa Valley wine brands selected were Chateau Montelena, Spring Mountain, Freemark Abbey, Veedercrest, and Stag's Leap Wine Cellars. Chalone and David Bruce were California wines chosen from outside the valley. From France came wines from Meursault-Charmes, Beaune Close des Mouches, Batard Montrachet, and Puligny-Montrachet.

No one recorded how much time the French jury took to judge the wines, but there would have been no reason to hurry. This was Paris, after all, on a warm spring day late in May, and no one was in doubt about the results. But the results were startling: Chateau Montelena's Chardonnay and Stag's Leap's Cabernet Sauvignon took the First Place honors. "California Wines Triumph in Paris" chortled the headline in the Santa Rosa *Press Democrat*.

The resulting publicity for Napa wine was almost as good as that a century previously at the 1889 World's Fair in Paris, when the French, pleased that their phylloxera disease had been wiped out with American rootstock, allowed California wines in large numbers to be entered in the international judging for the first time. Of some forty-plus wine medals given to U.S. entries in Paris that year, Napa took the lion's share. The resulting publicity for Napa Valley was enormous. Now, in 1976, American wine consumers all over the country found out that French wine judges had given their nod of approval, in a blind test, to California wines. The two upstarts whose wines bested the French in Paris, Stag's Leap Wine Cellars and Chateau Montelena, were nearly as mysterious to old-time residents as newcomers like John Wright or the Trefethens. There had been a winery called Stag's Leap for nearly a century, but the addition to the name seemed to confuse people. Chateau

Montelena was older still, but rumor had it that Los Angeles people were running the place.

Warren Winiarski had founded Stag's Leap Wine Cellars in 1970, after working for six years in the valley wineries as a cellar laborer. He'd had no experience at winemaking, having spent his career as a teacher of political theory at the University of Chicago. Winiarski never considered going back to college to learn winemaking formally. He'd had enough of universities: this was to be a complete change of scene. At times he must have questioned his sanity, especially when working with Lee Stewart at Souverain. Stewart was difficult to work for, but he had the same wine goals as the ex-professor from Chicago, and that was all that mattered.

After two years at the new Mondavi winery (he was there for the first crush), Winiarski chose land in the Stag's Leap area for his Cabernet vineyards. The decision was so carefully considered, in Winiarski's characteristic manner, that he simply ignored land any place else. He produced his first wine in 1970. For the first five years it was all work and little pay for Winiarski. Getting recognition for his new brand was not easy. But thereafter, his fate seemed to be in hands other than his own. Unbeknownst to him, Spurrier and his partner Patricia Gallagher visited Napa Valley in the summer of 1975 and tasted Stag's Leap Cabernet Sauvignon. They liked it so much they put it on the Paris tasting list.

The nearly one-man operation at Stag's Leap that year contrasted sharply with Chateau Montelena, at the other end of Napa Valley. That venerable old cellar, long closed, had been purchased in 1968, but it was four years before a crush took place. Everything from wine barrels to hoses needed replacing. That took money. Los Angeles real estate developer Ernst Hahn and lawyer James L. Barrett invested in Montelena. Winery owner Lee Paschich then hired a Yugoslavian winemaker, Mike Grgich, to oversee the crush, with special emphasis on a white wine called Chardonnay. Grgich had been in the valley for several years, working in various wine cellars, including Souverain.

Winery co-owner Jim Barrett just happened to be in France in May 1976, when the Spurrier wine tasting was completed. He was called away from dinner by a *Time* magazine writer wanting his reactions to the Chateau Montelena Chardonnay winning first place over its French competitors. Barrett had difficulty trying to respond; he didn't even know his wine was in a competition. Mike Grgich, who had immigrated from Yugoslavia just six years earlier, was even more dumbfounded by the news, and by the sudden media attention to his winemaking. Was this the payoff for all those years of hard work in Napa Valley cellars? If so, America, and especially Napa Valley, was proving to be a great place to live.

THE LOS ANGELES TASTING

Another blind tasting excited the locals just as much as the verdict from Paris, but with little national attention. It had taken place three years earlier at the Buena Vista winery in Sonoma. Robert Lawrence Balzer was a wine columnist for the *Los Angeles Times* in 1972. He was aware of the wine boom's furious momentum, and wanted somehow to be a part of it. He was one of the judges at the Los Angeles County Fair wine competition, and was aware that the criticism of that Fair — for too many medals — was causing a void in wine judging events. (The California State Fair wine competition had ceased several years previously amidst great controversy over supposed favoritism.)

Balzer came up with the idea of bringing together the top vintners in the state, so that they might judge who produced the best Cabernet Sauvignon. It took guts and clout to persuade the people he wanted to attend, and some no doubt turned him down. He brought together the venerable Andre Tchelistcheff, Louis P. Martini, Otto Meyer, Frank Bartholomew, Dan Mirassou, Joe Heitz, Brother Timothy, Joe Concannon, Myron Nightingale, Robert Mondavi, and Rodney Strong to join him in a blind tasting on the grounds of the oldest wine cellar in California, Buena Vista in Sonoma. Members of the press were highly intrigued by what Balzer was attempting. Two weeks before the event, Balzer purchased Cabernets of 27 different wineries from store shelves. Three bottles from each vintner were used, in case one bottle was off for some reason. The wine rested quietly in the naturally cooled caves at Buena Vista.

Robert Mondavi's Cabernet came out the winner, though just barely above Louis Martini. Beaulieu won third place; Chappellet was fourth. The San Francisco Bay Area media reacted as if the ultimate judgment had just been made on California wines. Mondavi Cabernet quickly replaced Beaulieu's as the preferred red dinner wine for many wine consumers, who were bowled over by the tasting's results. Mondavi's wine medals and honors seemed to flow endlessly thereafter, although he was not chosen by Spurrier to compete in Paris four years later. The Chappellet wine's good showing was proof to Donn Chappellet that he was on the right track. He made big Cabernets that needed to be aged for several years before drinking. His grapes came from the steep hillsides of Sage Canyon, on the east side of the valley.

Donn had moved to the valley with his wife in 1967, after spending most of his life in the Los Angeles area. His father, one of the five original founders of Lockheed Aircraft Company, advised his son not to follow in his footsteps, which freed Donn to pursue his own goals. He made a small fortune in the vending machine business, then sold out, and decided to pursue a career free of the anxieties of life in a large city. Chappellet had begun collecting wines in his college days; now he thought the wine business would be perfect for him. Like Winiarski, Chappellet knew exactly what type of vineyard he wanted, and it was not on a valley floor. In 1967 a real estate agent showed Chappellet a 60-acre vineyard high in the hills above Conn Dam. It was exactly what he wanted. Three years later his first crush came as he struggled to complete his very modern winery. For years after, Chappellet wines were collected mainly by wine connoisseurs — people who also knew exactly what they wanted.

On the opposite side of the valley, a short way up Spring Mountain road west of St. Helena, Jim Frew and Greg Bissonette reopened the old Chateau Chevalier winery. There wasn't a wine barrel on the property, and the vineyards were dead or overrun with weeds. It would take time and money to restore them. Chateau Chevalier had been shown to nearly every investor who drove over the hillsides of Napa Valley. While the vineyard's rich history held a certain appeal, buyers with deep pockets wanted to start from scratch and build their own vineyards.

English-born Peter L. Newton was one of these. He owned pulp paper mills in a half-dozen locations around the world and had established his headquarters in San Francisco. He chose a rather imposing knoll half way between St. Helena and Calistoga for a Mediterranean style winery with an English name, Sterling. When it was completed in 1973 the structure at the very crest of the knoll caught everyone's attention, even at some distance. The stark white building glistened in the bright sun. Though there was a small road to the winery, visitors were transported to the top by a thrilling ride on an aerial tramway. Many locals believed that all wineries should resemble the old stone Chateau Chevalier, or Greystone, or Beringers. They were critical of the radically modern new winery. And no one liked the fact that a lovely green hilltop had been transformed into a tourist attraction. In time the winery might become part of the landscape.

Those who grew grapes but did not own a winery also enjoyed the new prosperity in the valley. In 1972 the price for select lots of Cabernet and Chardonnay reached $1,000 a ton for the first time. Of course the grapes had to be very distinctive to achieve that lofty price. Rene di Rosa, the first to earn it, demanded his grapes be fermented separately. The resulting wine proved the superiority of his grapes. John Bosche, who owned vines next door to Beaulieu, believed some of the acclaim for the Georges de Latour Private Reserve Cabernet should be shared with him because his grapes also went into that wine. When he switched to Freemark Abbey winery, the wine made from his grapes was so good that Freemark put his name in a vineyard designation on the label.

Diamond Creek Vineyards, near Calistoga, produced hillside grapes, as did York Creek on Spring Mountain, and both soon came to be regarded as first growth grapes, worth top prices. Tom and Martha May, of Martha's Vineyard, were similarly rewarded for the special quality of their grapes. Milt Eisele's grapes, grown near Calistoga, and Nathan Fay's grapes, from the Stag's Leap area, were recognized early for their distinctive character and earned higher prices. It is peculiar that the vineyards that achieved such prominence were widely separated, and none of their closest neighbors achieved comparable success. There was no simple explanation for what set these growers apart, but they did insist that their grapes be crushed and fermented separately. Some believed that "clones" made the difference; each clone provides distinct grape flavors.

While grape clones were one way to produce exceptional Napa wine, W. Andrew Beckstoffer suggested another, by improving farming practices, which had not changed in decades. Initially, Beckstoffer knew little about raising grapes. He was born in Virginia and had earned a degree from Dartmouth College. He was stationed at the San Francisco Presidio when he was in the Army during the early 1960s, and soon discovered California wine.

Beckstoffer, who came to the valley with the Heublein Corporation, believed that some beneficial changes, like drip irrigation, could be incorporated into the Heublein farming techniques. He also believed closer spacing of vines and trellis systems would improve grape quality. He took over operations of the vineyards in 1973, when a separate farming company, Vinifera Development Corporation, was formed. But change came slowly in large corporations, so, a year later, Beckstoffer convinced Heublein to sell out to him. He knew he could grow higher quality grapes, and knew that Heublein would be happy to divest themselves of their vineyards, even though the price of grapes was rising steadily. Heublein didn't even ask for much cash up front. Beckstoffer rounded up the best experts he could find on vineyard culture, people like Robert E. Steinhauer and Roy Harris. Then he hired Andre Tchelistcheff as a consultant, and he was in business. It would take some time before he saw any profits, however.

It was little wonder that grape prices should climb dramatically, considering that two of California's largest banks were predicting that soon there would not be enough wine to satisfy consumer demands. Wells Fargo Bank claimed Americans would be drinking 490 million gallons of wine by the end of the decade. Bank of America put that figure at 650 million gallons.[1] But only two years after these forecasts were made, the market actually seemed to be sagging. Consumption leveled off at a still healthy growth rate of 7% a year, but wine production was three points higher at 10%. Wine surpluses began appearing everywhere, although less noticeably in Napa Valley than elsewhere.

Weather also affected crops in the mid-1970s, with one of the most severe droughts in California history. Normal rainfall for the twelve months ending June 30 for St. Helena averages about 30 inches. But on that date in 1976 rain gauges showed only 12+ inches — the driest year of the century. The next year's rainfall came to only slightly more, 13.61 inches. Grape vines put down deep roots; twenty feet or more is not uncommon. The size of the clusters decreases in a drought, and a single grape may consist of the seeds, a tiny amount of juice, and the skin. Such were the products of many vineyards by the summer of 1977.

But there is always a worse fear in California than shortages in agricultural production when rainfall is so short — wildfires. When hot, strong winds come up during Santa Ana conditions, everyone, including residents of Napa Valley, watches the hills for signs of smoke and fire. "In the midst of last Saturday's torrid afternoon it happened," began the story in the *Star* of August 4, 1977: "Shortly after 3 o'clock a car caught fire near the Conn Valley-Old Howell Mountain road junction. The nearby tinder dry grass and brush erupted into a crackling, hissing, roaring inferno of flame and smoke." Temperatures were at 110 degrees before the fire started. Humidity was dangerously low, as it always is in Santa Ana wind conditions.

Fire crews from a hundred miles away were summoned to fight the rapidly spreading flames. Hundreds of residents on Howell Mountain fled their homes. The town of Angwin was directly in the path of the huge fire. Aerial tankers dropped tons of flame retardants through Sunday, and by nightfall the 2,000-acre fire was checked. Smoke hung so heavily over Napa Valley that driving was difficult. Not one home was lost, though the flames often burned frighteningly close. Long-time residents insisted a wet year always follows dry years, and this time they were right: 1978 recorded almost 49 inches of rain. The Napa River rose to its banks on at least one occasion, but there was no flooding.

Despite some pessimism traceable to the possible over-production of wine, no one canceled plans for winery construction. In fact, the Napa County Planning Department was swamped with architectural drawings for new wine cellars or remodeling of old ghost wineries which had not been used for decades. Robert Mondavi's prime location on Highway 29 caught the attention of Bernard D. Buttig, who began rounding up investors in 1973 for something similar just north of Rutherford. Buttig called his winery Franciscan Vineyards, after the Franciscan priests who had founded the California missions two centuries earlier. Like the Sterling winery atop its knoll, the modernistic Franciscan winery did not fit into the landscape. People hoped that trees surrounding it would help, a decade in the future. One year after the winery was built, it went bankrupt. New investors quickly arranged plans for a fall crush. A year later, with money still short, Raymond T. Duncan and former Brother Justin Meyer, who had been with the Christian Brothers winery, announced plans to purchase the impoverished Franciscan winery.

With so many strangers moving in next to old-line Napa families, there was almost a sigh of relief among locals when the *Star* disclosed that the Raymonds would build their own winery. Roy

Raymond, Sr., left high school in the Great Depression and got a job in 1933 as a cellar laborer for Beringer. He married into the Beringer family later in the 1930s when he wed Martha Jane. Their sons, Walter and Roy, Jr., were star athletes in local schools, then took degrees in Viticulture and Enology at the University of California, Davis. (Few newcomers in the valley could boast of a Davis degree, but they often hired Davis graduates to oversee their wine operations.)

The Raymonds had bought land on Zinfandel Lane, a portion of the old Wheeler property. The old walnut trees went up in smoke faster than you could say "salute." Their first crush, from purchased grapes, in a pre-fab Butler building on the property in 1974, was not auspicious. They built their winery four years later, a quarter mile east of the highway, painting the buildings in a dark green color which almost camouflaged them. With the Raymond vintage of 1974, Roy, Sr., could count nearly four continuous decades of involvement in Napa Valley wine production. Only Brother Timothy, whose work in his Order began in 1935, could come close to Roy's long years in the local wine industry.

Local residents also welcomed the new winery built by the Wagner family, who had been in the valley since the 1906 earthquake. Charles Wagner, Sr., opened a small winery in a converted barn on his property in 1915, producing about 20,000 gallons a year. The wine was sold in bulk to San Francisco wine houses until Prohibition began. Like many of his neighbors, Wagner did not believe Prohibition would last more than a few years. He was forced to keep his last year's production in bond until 1927, when revenue agents assisted in dumping it. He wasn't able to reopen his winery until 1934. Two years later, near the end of the Great Depression, the winery was again closed. The family farm was finally sold three decades later.

Charles Wagner, Jr., purchased what would eventually become Caymus Vineyards, east of Rutherford, in 1941. There wasn't a vine on the small property; Wagner planted Burger grapes two years later. When asked years later why he planted the lowly Burger, Wagner recalls: "I got ten tons to the acre — in those days you survived by quantity because the price was so low."[2] Burger was one of the first wines Wagner made at Caymus when his new winery was ready for its first crush in 1972. He also produced Cabernet Sauvignon, which seemed to have unusual potential. No one said anything about the unusual pairing — Burger was still in relatively good favor.

Wagner did not have to wait long for success. *Wines & Vines* magazine reported in June 1976 that his 800 cases of 1973 Cabernet quickly sold out after the wine scored high in two private tastings. "The Wagners have seven acres of Cabernet Sauvignon grapes on a piece of their vineyard a little higher than the rest, and possessing — they firmly believe — a micro climate of its own. The vines are spaced 6 x 10 feet, and the yield after thinning is about six tons per acre . . . The grapes make a big fruity wine with real Cabernet Sauvignon character," reported the wine journal. It appeared Wagner had a vineyard to match Bosche, May, Eisele and the others as a first growth. The slightly elevated ground may have provided better drainage, curbed frost danger and eased the influence of hot weather.

Charles Krug had claimed a century earlier that just a slight elevation resulted in soft breezes that kept weather problems to a minimum, but Legh Knowles claimed it was the "Rutherford dust that produced superior wine." In a series of radio commercials in the late 1970s, Knowles posited that Rutherford dust was the secret of Beaulieu's famous Cabernets. Though Knowles's remarks were tongue-in-cheek, the public took him seriously, as did many winemakers. More than likely, the secret to Beaulieu grapes and wine, and Wagner's early success, was the underlying gravel stratum. This soil formation was known to begin just west of St. Helena and extend southward almost to Yountville. How far inland the gravel subsoil went was a little uncertain, but if Wagner's wines proved out over the long run, it must have reached as far as Caymus Vineyard. Inglenook's rare vintages were attributed to this same gravelly soil.

Prime locations near Rutherford interested many winemakers who planned to build new facilities in the 1970s. Mike Grgich, still flush with his success in Paris, found an interested partner in Austin Hills, scion of the famous and wealthy San Francisco family which founded Hills Brothers Coffee. Grgich-Hills Cellars opened July 4, 1977, just across the railroad tracks from Rutherford, in a very modest building. The first crush, mostly Chardonnay, wasn't large. That was the wine everyone wanted from Grgich, the wine which had won him so much attention at Spurrier's Academie du Vin.

There was a French infiltration into Napa Valley before John Wright and his Moet & Hennessy connection arrived, but Bernard Portet kept such a low profile few realized he was even here. Portet chose the less obvious east side of Napa Valley for his winery, on land which would soon become described as the greater Stags Leap region. The money behind his Clos du Val winery came from Francophile John Goelet, an American who lived in France. Portet was a graduate of the University of Montpelier, and his father was long associated with Chateau Lafite. The young Frenchman crushed Cabernet the first year his winery was open, 1972, and chose to add Zinfandel wine to his repertoire. That was a curious choice for a Frenchman who may not have known the grape before coming to California.

So many other winery names were added to the signposts along Silverado Trail and Highway 29 that automobile drivers had to halt to read them or miss a favorite brand. Joseph Phelps, a building contractor from Greely, Colorado, built his winery on Taplin Road, up a small ravine southeast of St. Helena. He had supervised the construction of Souverain Cellars and decided to stay in the area. German-born Walter Schug was in charge of the first wine made in 1973 at Phelps' new winery.

One area of Napa County that had seen little of this wine rebirth was Spring Mountain, west of St. Helena, though the area had been home to vineyards for a long time. For more than a hundred years, there had been vineyards along the somewhat treacherous winding road which eventually led to Santa Rosa. The historic Conradi winery was built two-thirds of the way up Spring Mountain Road at the turn of the century, but had been abandoned for a long while. The remaining cooperage inside was in shambles, but the native stone winery looked almost as good as the day it was built. In 1974, San Francisco insurance executive Robert Keenan was taken on a wild ride up the road and shown the long-abandoned winery. He purchased it immediately. Keenan had to replant the surrounding vineyards; he had enough Chardonnay for winemaking in 1977. The views from the 45-acre vineyard surrounding the winery are awe-inspiring, even if the terrain is just a little steep.

Just slightly below Keenan's vines are those of two brothers, Stuart and Charles Smith. They were from Southern California too, but chose Berkeley for their university studies. Both admit that decision was fortituitous, for it was an easy weekend trip to Napa Valley to taste the local wine. Unlike Keenan, the brothers did not find a long-forgotten winery waiting to be reconditioned, but instead chose steep hillside land on which to plant Cabernet, Riesling, Pinot Noir and Chardonnay. They built the winery themselves and opened it in 1977. It was christened Smith-Madrone Vineyards.

Nor far below Smith-Madrone was an old wine relic waiting for a buyer, one with very deep pockets. The old Tiburcio Parrott estate consisted of wine caves and a truly elegant, and habitable, Victorian house, but the 120 acres of vineyard were totally wild. Cabernets from this vineyard site had won wine medals as far back as 1894 at the San Francisco Mid-Winter Fair, but no wine had been produced here since before Prohibition. Michael Robbins rounded up investors to buy the estate, and had everything in place by 1974. The following year, major restoration of the house was begun. Large wine tunnels on the property were in good shape and would be an appealing tourist attraction. All that was needed was a small crushing and fermenting building in the front. One of the investors brought in to help finance the construction and renovation was Sid Greenberg, chairman of the board for Standard Brands Paints in Los Angeles. Young Chuck Ortman became the winemaker.

A half dozen years later a location scout for Lorimar Productions of Hollywood saw the restored Parrott house and offered Michael Robbins a contract. His company wanted to use the house and grounds as the backdrop for a television series set in the wine country, tentatively titled "Falcon Crest." The proposed television series caused Napa County Supervisors to call a halt to all new winery permits in May 1978. Sterling had built an aerial tram for tourists at their facility, and supervisors were worried about changes in the character of the valley. The *Napa Register* published a story headlined "Napa Winery Disneyland."

The fire under this bubbling political cauldron really had more to do with the fact that too many wineries were being built. There was legitimate concern that the valley's economy was now dangerously close to being limited to only one product — wine. One look at the county agricultural commissioner's report clearly supported such a conclusion. Agriculture, the principal business of the county, accounted for gross revenues of nearly $53 million, by far the greatest tax base. "Most of that revenue was from wine grapes," reported Commissioner Aldo Delfinio.[3] Livestock and poultry accounted for $6.5 million annually; floral and nursery crops, $2 million; and field crops, just under $1 million. The tourist industry was growing rapidly, but was almost completely dependent upon the wineries. What if a major recession hit the wine industry? The Supervisors needed to create some balance in Napa County's economic base. No one had a quick solution to this problem.

Residents of Napa County who preferred gossip to economic controversy had plenty to talk about. Robert Mondavi's lawsuit against his brother Peter came to trial in Napa in late 1976. The old county courthouse was being renovated, so visiting judge Robert Carter (local jurists disqualified themselves) held court in a small portable building. The press reported how uncomfortable this courtroom was for parties to the lawsuit, who had to sit in very close proximity to each other. Robert had been left a 12% interest in the Krug winery by his father, Cesare, who had died in 1959. Robert wanted his mother, his brother, Peter, and sister, Mary, to buy him out so he could use the cash for his own winery. His sister Helen took his side, but Peter was against the arrangement; he didn't want Robert to use the Mondavi name on his wine labels.

Grandmother Rosa Mondavi, no longer active in Krug's management, still cooked Italian food for her close-knit family. And even though Robert had his own winery, he still lived in a house on the grounds of the Krug winery and was on its board of directors. But when it was suggested that Krug's profits be reduced so that Rosa could transfer her shares in Krug to her grandchildren without their paying hefty inheritance taxes, Robert objected strenuously. He didn't want his stock value to decline. He was also against any restructuring of stock ownership which would decrease his net worth. Just before the trial started, Rosa Mondavi died at the age of 86.

Newspapers in California had a field day with the details of the Mondavi family's dispute and the ensuing trial. Other wine families had had their problems: the Keck family at the Korbel winery in Sonoma had just gone through a similar legal battle. Judge Carter listened patiently, and in the end agreed with Robert and his attorneys. If brother Peter would not pay a fair market value for Robert's stock, the Krug winery had to be sold and the profits split. Two years later Peter and his sister Mary bought out Robert's and Helen's share of the winery. The delay was necessary to allow time for lawyers to examine tax implications, etc. Robert and his sister each received between $4 and $5 million. The Krug winery went deeply into debt.

Robert used the money to buy back shares in his own winery from Rainier Brewing Company of Seattle, which had purchased 82% of Robert Mondavi winery stock early in the decade, when capital was badly needed for expansion and equipment. Robert had taken a big gamble then, and could have lost everything.

Instead the Mondavi winery was now healthier than it had been for years.[4]

Louis Martini, Sr., died two years before Rosa Mondavi. Nathan Chroman's wine column in the *San Francisco Chronicle* on June 26, 1974, was headlined, "A wine king is dead." An accompanying photograph of Martini showed him as a tired old man, but that was not the way most people remembered him: he had always been stubborn, long-winded, and usually right when pontificating on wine. Martini and his neighbor de Latour had brought attention to Napa Valley wine before Mondavi was dry behind the ears, before Richard Nixon took Schramsberg wines to China, and probably before Steven Spurrier was born. Martini Zinfandel and Folle Blanche were selected by *Fortune* magazine in 1941 as among the best wines produced in the entire country. Louis Martini was also the energy behind the formation of the Napa Valley Vintners in 1944; that alone would have been sufficient as his epitaph. The Vintners were an exceptionally strong force in the Valley in the 1970s.

In 1971 Vince Gracin, the only surviving cooper in the valley, died in Napa. He had been there for decades, almost taken for granted. Some thought a cooper like Gracin was an anachronism, especially as more and more wine barrels and puncheons were coming in already assembled. But when many barrels arrived with staves and metal hoops tied in neat bundles, people began to realize how badly Gracin would be missed.

Michael Mondavi was credited by *Wines & Vines* with helping the rebirth of coopering in the valley. According to the issue of December '73, he enlisted the help of three young men, Keith Robert, Donald Surplus and Stoddard Lane, in assembling a shipment of French oak. After Souverain, Heitz, Spring Mountain and other wineries put out the word they needed coopers, the trio founded Barrel Builders. With the cost of French oak escalating and a shortage of new barrels, Barrel Builders quickly developed the art of shaving the inside of used barrels, making them as good as new. This was done in particular to former whiskey barrels (by the hundreds) to reach the oak wood which had not been permeated with the taste of distilled beverages. In time Henry Work, a former submarine officer turned school teacher, joined Barrel Builders, and the rapidly expanding company moved to Lodi Lane. One by one the former three founders departed for other challenges, and Work took over the company.

THE CARNEROS REGION COMES OF AGE

Change in harvesting methods was a hot topic during the early 1970s. At a monthly meeting of the Napa Vintners Association there was increasing talk about the new mechanical harvesters. Vintners were skeptical of the claims that the machines worked best at night, and indeed that was not the case. However, the quality of juice seemed significantly better, especially on very hot harvest days, when the grapes were harvested at night. Experiments had been tried at Christian Brothers a few years earlier on Grenache, Colombard and Rubired varieties, and the results didn't cause a rush to buy one of the large, cumbersome machines.[5] This was largely due to the fact that Napa Valley vineyard plots were so small. Vineyards would have to be almost totally redesigned before the machines could be used. But in the newly evolving Carneros region, bordering the San Francisco Bay, potential vineyard land could be had in 40 acre pieces, although the best of it might have some hilly sections just a trifle steep for machine picking of grapes. Rene di Rosa was in the Carneros long before mechanical harvesters were even dreamt of. By 1962 he was planting grapes and harvesting enough for wine to be released three to four years later.

Andre Tchelistcheff convinced Madame de Pins at Beaulieu to invest in 150 acres in the Carneros, and plantings were begun on former dairy lands in 1963. He wanted Pinot Noir and Chardonnay grapes because the climate was so much cooler than up valley. Tchelistcheff told a writer for *Wines & Vines* that different micro-climates in the Carneros could be only half a mile from each other, depending on the lay of the lands. Beaulieu's vines had a southwest exposure, but nearby Buena Vista's vineyards, facing directly to the south, were warm enough for Cabernet.[6]

Martini, Sr., may have been first in the Carneros area. He had purchased vineyards in the area west of Stanley Lane in the late 1930s. Rene di Rosa recalls: "It was said their Carneros vineyards made the wine from other areas look good."[7] In other words, blend poor wine with Carneros wine and the result was wonderful. By 1976 the owners of the small ZD Winery believed that a 100% Pinot Noir from the St. Clair vineyards in the Carneros was so good that a "Carneros" designation on the label was justified. This had not been done before; even Beaulieu had never included Carneros on its label. John Wright and his French investors decided early that in order to obtain the cuvee they wanted for their sparkling wine, Carneros would be an appropriate growing region.

Meanwhile, another controversy arose in the Napa Valley. Heublein decided to build a new wine warehouse directly in front of the venerable Inglenook winery. Inglenook had been a landmark for almost a century (construction was started in 1883) and sight-seers on Highway 29 always slowed down to take a good look at the winery. The locals were furious about Heublein's plans. The *Star* put it politely by stating the structure was "the target of considerable criticism."[8] But the real culprits were the County Board of Supervisors and the County Planning Commission, who approved the building without consideration for its visual impact or the history of the Valley.

As usual, the shifting tastes of wine consumers continued to bring change to the Valley. Sometimes the industry had to scramble to keep up with those changes. This was especially true with the shift from red to white wines. It may seem far-fetched, but the shift had some relationship to the growing consumption of soft drinks. The editor of *Beverage Digest* pointed out that between 1955 and 1975 sales of soft drinks had nearly doubled. Good-tasting diet soft drinks was one of the factors.[9]

Now wine consumers wanted something sweet, but with a zing. They put aside red wine and began to buy sweet or slightly sweet white wines. Women had always preferred white wine over reds. The *Ladies Home Journal* had been aware of this trend for more than a decade. A study commissioned by the *Journal* in 1977 reported: "Someone in each family makes the decisions about serving wine. . . We find that fewer husbands are making the decision to serve wine at a meal and which wine to serve."[10] While the sampling number was small (only 100 women) it was a broad cross-section of the nation and showed that 66% of the time a woman picked the wine for the evening meal. Ten years earlier that figure had been 50%. Men chose the wine only 17% of the time, or it was a co-decision 12% of the time. Even though few viticulturists or winemakers read the *Journal* , it was clear that a change would be necessary if the trend continued. And it did. In 1979, U. S. white wine shipments had increased 17% while red wine shipments declined 8.4%.[11] In July, 1981, a major supplier of bench-grafted root stock for Sonoma and Napa counties reported that 80% of the requests were for white grape varieties, particularly Chardonnay.[12]

Grape growers in Napa, trying hard to keep up with the demand, were planting 2000 new acres a year. Late in the 1970s vines covered over 24,000 acres. Although most of the new acreage was for white grapes, red wine grapes maintained their dominance by a major margin. Napa Valley soil still produced the finest Cabernet Sauvignon in the nation, and it beat out the French in '76. One does not pull up those vines.

Francis Mahoney had given little thought to these new trends in wine when he and Balfour Gibson co-founded Carneros Creek Winery shortly before the white wine boom began. When he was in college in the 1960s, Cabernets from Louis Martini, Beaulieu, and Mayacamas were the center of most wine discussions. Even at Connoisseur Wine Imports, San Francisco, where he began working after giving up thoughts of teaching history, French red wines were most often tasted and evaluated. It was here he first met owners Balfour and Anita Gibson, and something clicked between them. This new friendship cemented around a shared appreciation of Mahoney's essentially homemade Pinot Noir and Riesling in 1971. He had no training in wine production and wasn't precisely sure of the steps in the process, but he read a lot. And from all the tastings at Connoisseur he had learned what qualities made fine wine, especially when French vintners were in town selling their wines.

When Mahoney's '72 wines tasted as superb as the previous year, Gibson decided his friend was wasting his time selling wine at their shop. "Go find us some land in Napa Valley," he said, "and we'll build a winery." After talking to Tchelistcheff, Mahoney's only concern was that the land in the Carneros be well drained. He was introduced to Bernard Portet, who needed a place to store wine. He agreed to provide the storage in exchange for Portet's teaching him what he knew about French wine methods. Carneros Creek winery was built in 1973, just in time for the fall crush. A year later vineyards were planted. Mahoney had difficulty controlling his enthusiasm after visitors began commenting, "Your wines really resemble those of the French Burgundy." Those comments may have reflected Portet's influence, but it is just as likely that Mahoney received the compliments because of the evolution of his own sensory training. Cabernets still intrigued Mahoney, and he added Zinfandel to his repertoire along with Chardonnay and Sauvignon Blanc. By the late 1970s, with more and more customers carrying white wine out the front door, it was becoming increasingly difficult to know just which grapes to plant or buy or ferment.

Another newcomer to the valley who helped co-found a winery, Norman de Leuze, wasn't intimidated by the industry's confusion. For many years, de Leuze had worked in his father's Oakland store selling wine. He could recall the fifths and jugs they sold in the 1940s, and learning about varieties from restocking the mostly Gallo bottles.

"Wine was always on the dinner table," says de Leuze, "because of our French background." He attended the University of California at Berkeley, graduating with a degree in mechanical

FRANCIS MAHONEY

engineering. At Aerojet General in Sacramento he met Gino Zepponi, who had grown up with his father's homemade wine on the table. In 1967, at the home of Zepponi's parents in Sonoma, the two men borrowed the senior Zepponi's wine making equipment and experimented on their own. Like Francis Mahoney's first efforts, theirs turned out extremely well, and the die was cast. They rented space from a neighbor, and for ten years, according to de Leuze, gave up holidays, weekends and vacations to make wine while both still worked at outside jobs. The wine improved each year, especially after they bought some of Rene di Rosa's Carneros grapes. They asked his permission to be the first to put "Winery Lake" on their wine label, but di Rosa refused. He still wasn't sure their wines matched his quality standards. In 1979 the two men purchased land in Napa Valley along Silverado Trail and moved their ZD Winery from Sonoma Valley. "ZD wines would have remained in Sonoma," recalls de Leuze "if we could have found the right location without all the zoning restrictions. Napa just by chance offered all these in one place — it wasn't the attraction of the name."[13]

To concentrate on only one variety of wine, and particularly the Cabernet Sauvignon, must have been the dream of many winery owners. Justin Meyer could act on that dream when he opened Silver Oak Cellars because his financial backer, Colorado oil man Raymond T. Duncan, agreed totally with him. Meyer needed someone like Duncan for his entrepreneurial and economic skills. He had joined the Christian Brothers teaching order in 1957 and planned to devote his life to education. One decade later, Meyer was chosen by the Order to move to Mont La Salle in the Napa Redwoods and become assistant cellarmaster. Meyer claims he hasn't the slightest idea why he was chosen, since he knew nothing about wine. He was sent to U.C. Davis to obtain a Bachelor's degree in Viticulture and Enology. With persuasion from Dr. Harol Olmo, who became his mentor, Meyer also got permission to earn a Master's degree. Finally at Mont La Salle, he not only assisted in wine production, but wrote a history of winemaking by his Order in California.

Meyer met Raymond Duncan in 1972, shortly after making the decision to leave the Order. Duncan had already purchased 500 acres in the Napa and Alexander Valleys and needed someone to supervise the planting of grapes. Their relationship meshed from the first day, and both began planning for a winery at some point in the future. Silver Oak wines originated the same year Meyer left Christian Brothers and were produced at Mont La Salle. A year later an old dairy barn, part of Duncan's vineyards just off Oakville Cross Road, became the first Silver Oak wine cellar. Cabernet was the only variety. Plans were made for a modern new wine facility. In the meantime, Duncan and Meyer purchased the Franciscan winery and operated it until selling the entire complex to a West German company.

The highly individualistic Lee Stewart sold Souverain to four investors, headed by Thomas Burgess, a native of Ohio. He had majored in aeronautics in college, then trained to be a pilot in the Air Force. With every flight to Europe he learned a little more about wine. He drove to Napa Valley whenever his orders took him to Travis Air Force Base in Fairfield, California. He recalls driving through Napa Valley one February day when the mustard was in full bloom and the air so clear it was "luminescent." There were few cars. At Beaulieu he and a fellow pilot tasted a late 1930s Beaulieu Cabernet that was left over from a party. If that wine was and example of what Napa could produce, he wanted to be a part of it.

"I could never live in a city," he admitted. He was ready for a career change after flying private aircraft for the IBM Company. The change was formalized June, 1, 1972, when he signed the purchase agreement for what was left of Souverain. (The name had already been sold.) There were a half dozen varieties of grapes in the vineyards bordering the Angwin road. By the end of the decade Burgess had pulled out everything except Cabernet, Zinfandel and Chardonnay. He decided to use his own name for the winery, in keeping with the history of the place, where each of the owners since the original stone cellar was built in 1880 had used his own name — with the exception of Stewart.[14]

Leland Stewart had his idiosyncracies, but he had been influential in Napa winemaking for many years, and he knew his craft. He had made wine for the first three years of operations for the historic Stag's Leap Winery. Carl Doumani and a group of investors had just purchased the Stag's Leap Ranch when Stewart came to buy some Petit Sirah (or Syrah) grapes, one of the varieties grown on the 400-acre parcel. Doumani knew Stewart's abilities and asked him to oversee making wine of the same grape for him for the next three years. The fermenting was done at a new Souverain winery on Silverado Trail.

Fire had long ago destroyed the wooden interior of the Stag's Leap Winery. The stone walls were still intact, but they were in precarious condition. The wine tunnels just needed cleaning and airing out. "The place was in sad shape," recalled Doumani. "None of the houses had been lived in for some time. The original manor house had a third floor which needed removal. There were even Alicante Bouschet grapes still in the vineyard."[15]

These may have been the last of the once famous Prohibition grapes in the valley.

Carl Doumani was a Los Angeleno, born and bred. He had been in the restaurant business and in home construction, and had invested in a meat company, all in Los Angeles. By 1970, he wanted a new challenge and a change of scene. After visiting Schramsberg with a former investor in that winery, Doumani found himself admiring the genteel life of the winery's owners, Jamie and Jack Davies. He wanted a piece of that life, a place to build a home and settle his family, and a new business interest.

"I'm a great starter." says Doumani. "I like to start up businesses." To resurrect Stag's Leap would take someone who liked challenges, and wouldn't mind a good squabble. Winiarski over at Stag's Leap Wine Cellars sued Doumani over use of the name "Stag's Leap" on his label. Winiarski had got there first and trademarked the name. Doumani dug in his heels and hired a lawyer. When several of his neighbors petitioned the Bureau of Alcohol, Tobacco and Firearms for a "Stag's Leap Appellation," Doumani was on the front line again. He was an extremely likable man, but he wanted what was his. The disagreement with Winiarski would drag on for years, and the appellation fight would come in the next decade.

"I really wanted to turn Stag's Leap into a country inn or manor house," said Doumani, but when he tried to get county approval for a bed and breakfast operation, there were more problems. The neighbors complained there would be too many cars on the small back road leading to Stag's Leap. Stag's Leap winery was formally reopened in 1979, and the Cabernet produced there, along with Petit Sirah, Chenin Blanc and several other varieties, turned out to be exceptional. And it sold quickly. "Having been in the restaurant business helped me sell nearly everything we had" said Doumani. "Besides, I think I know half the restaurant owners in Los Angeles."

But those restaurant owners did not need an introduction to Napa Valley wines from Doumani. That was being provided by more and more national publicity. On November 27, 1972, *Time* magazine did a cover story on California wine, and included a photograph of Robert Mondavi, Brother Timothy and Louis Martini at the Balzer tasting at Buena Vista. "The wine boom is evidence of a growing ease and worldliness in American life-styles," observed the publication. British author Hugh Johnson was quoted as saying: "Wine needs no apology. It is one of the good things of life. While hard liquor is drunk for its effect, wine is drunk patently for pleasure."

Many major east coast newspapers came to the conclusion that they needed a wine column in their weekly food section, and wine-loving reporters were drafted to become the new wine critics. Even *National Geographic* decided to do a story on wine. Moira Johnson was hired in 1978 to write the story. Charles O'Rear would shoot photographs. The May, 1979, issue included 24 pages devoted to the subject, with color photographs of life in the valley so compelling they would draw tourists for years.

U.S. News & World Report also covered the subject in their August 13 issue, with photographs which looked surprisingly similar to those in the *Geographic*. There were the hilltop manor and vines of the Draper family, Calistoga at the northern end of the valley, and the obligatory photo of Andre Tchelistcheff. By 1980, *Time* decided the wine industry had earned another cover story; this time Napa Valley was highlighted. This emphasis was also obvious in other magazines' coverage of the industry. Results from those famous wine tastings made it clear that the important wine news was coming from St. Helena, or Rutherford, or Stag's Leap.

Tourism grew dramatically. Although there were all sorts of maps and guides published locally, the oldest was the *Star's* annual Vintage Edition, usually printed in October. Editor Starr Baldwin reminded readers that there was a time when wine was not king:

> To most people, especially those of the younger generation, wine growing has always been the big crop here. But in fact, this has not been been exactly true. For many years, for instance, Napa Valley, particularly the upper part and its tributary areas, grew enough wheat to support two grist mills.[16]

Baldwin was determined not to ignore Napa County's history. Napa city's principal newspaper, the *Register*, initiated a Vintage issue in the early 1980s, complete with color covers, enormous photographs, and a very crowded winery map.

A major influence on the eastern media's interest in California wines was the Heublein fine wine auctions. They began quietly in Chicago in 1969. Then in 1971 they came to California and San Francisco for the first time. Tastings were held in three or four major cities to drum up interest and crowds jammed the auction locations. The wines were primarily European, but the Heublein-owned Beaulieu and Inglenook ranked, once again, right up there with rare Chateau Lafite Rothschild vintages.

High prices for rare bottles of wine were routine in Europe — especially in London, where auctioneer Michael Broadbent had worked — but not in this country. In 1970, one bid reached $1400 for a case of French Bordeaux. The next year, a Boston wine merchant bid $5,000 for one bottle of 1846 Chateau Lafite. But auction prices of California wines escalated each year, with mixed cases of pre-World War II Inglenook wine bringing nearly $1000 each in the 1970s. Buyers usually were people who liked publicity; they often sold the wine by the glass at local charity events.

Heublein began to draw criticism for depleting the wine library of Inglenook and Beaulieu. A.C. McNally of Heublein admitted that at the 1979 auction 20% of the total bottles of wine sold were from Inglenook. But then 1979 was a special year for Inglenook — its centennial. "In 1969 wines from Inglenook and Beaulieu were mostly curiosities," said McNally somewhat later, "the interest was in French wines. The market didn't know California."[17]

Frank Prial, writing in the *New York Times*, observed: "Being a once-a-year event, [the auction] cannot really have much effect on the U.S. wine market. But it has brought wine to the public's attention. Each year it is heavily covered by newspapers and television."[18] But the wine auctions contributed to the enormous rise in recognition for California wines. And the idea for wine auctions in general really caught on. Robert Mondavi, inspired by an auction he attended in France, was the first to suggest the idea for a Napa Valley Wine Auction. The entire industry was delighted and happy to participate.

The first annual Napa Valley Wine Auction in 1981 was elegant and sophisticated. Bidding paddles, required for entrance, cost $500 each. The event was held under tents on the plush greens of the Meadowood Golf Club; all visitors were bussed in. Ladies purchased gorgeous new ensembles for the event, and large, colorful sun hats were everywhere. Even with the 100-plus degree temperatures, the event was an astonishing success. Prices soared, and people were amazed. Wine columnist Harvey Steinman tried to make sense of it all:

> This whole business of wine auctions is getting out of hand. What is to be made of such things as $46,000 paid for a bottle of 177 year old Bordeaux at the Heublein auction in Los Angeles? Or $7,000 for a 1969 Chardonnay packaged in an assortment of bottles, the top bid at the [1983] Napa Valley Wine Auction? [19]

California newspapers and television stations picked up the story, which eventually went national. Gil Nickel was directing his family's wholesale nursery business in Oklahoma when the high prices at the Heublein wine auctions began making local headlines.

Nickel had taken a degree in science and had worked in a missile guidance laboratory before concluding he wanted to go back to horticulture. He liked the outdoors, and there was money in plants, especially after the nursery had become among the half dozen largest such operations in the United States. After his father's death, Gil and his brother John took turns running the business. In 1976 Gil moved to San Francisco to see what investments he might make with his personal fortune. A yacht for the choppy waters of San Francisco bay was one. Another was the historic Far Niente winery at Oakville. There had been some activity at the winery right after Prohibition, but it took a major effort to preserve the stone walls. Nickel brought in the best experts to modernize the interior with fine hardwoods. The winery's castle-like appearance soon made it a popular landmark, easily visible from Highway 29.

Retired Bechtel Corporation president Jerome Komes liked to play golf at Silverado Country Club near Napa. He soon purchased a condo there. In 1977 he bought from the Louis Martinis the old Rennie home and winery. When his daughter Julia and her husband, John Garvey, visited, they fell in love with the place and soon made the decision to move to the Valley. Her brother John and his family soon followed. There was plenty of work to do, and some major decisions to be made: the blackened walls of the old stone winery, from a fire in 1900, had never been cleaned or repaired; and the Brockhoff winery nearby would make a better home than winery. All of this would take a small fortune. But Jerome could afford at least part of the cost. He had created the international division for Bechtel, which quickly became one of the largest construction companies in the world.

"My father never took us to the country, not even on picnics," recalled Julia. "He did not like the country; we had no experience in agriculture."[20] But the Komes children learned fast, and when their newly-named Flora Springs Winery was opened in 1979, the wine drew rave reviews.

Another Bechtel alumnus who came to the Valley was John Buehler, a West Point graduate who had served twenty years with the Army Corps of Engineers. On his retirement from the Corps, he joined Bechtel. In 1952, along with another Bechtel executive's family named Yates, Buehler invested in Castle Rock vineyards in the Napa Redwoods. They had little interest in grapes at the time, but the house and grounds made an excellent location for company retreats. It was impossible to spend time at Castle Rock without becoming interested in wine. The Buehlers purchased hillside land in the somewhat remote Greenfield Road area in the eastern foothills of the valley. Vines were planted in 1972, and the Buehler Winery had its first crush six years later.

This was the façade of the Far Niente winery Gil Nickel found in 1977 when he began restoring the old winery relic. It had been built in 1885 but with founder John Benson's death in 1910, wine had been made there but rarely.

John, Jr., decided which grape of the varieties would be planted (mostly Cabernet and Zinfandel) and oversaw the design and construction of the beautiful French-chateau style buildings. In its remote setting among hillside vines, with Conn Dam below, the winery is breathtaking. The cost? Millions of dollars.

Money was also available to the granddaughter of Bank of America founder A.P. Giannini. Ann McWilliams and her husband James had been taken to Chateau Chevalier, Stag's Leap, and a dozen other locations before deciding on the historic Mt. Eden ranch on Oakville Crossroads. Even though the family was Italian, wine had not been a routine part of Sunday dinners at Ann's grandfather's house in San Francisco. Jim was a native of Colorado. Both had attended Stanford University, but they had not met until becoming involved in investment and securities houses in San Francisco.

When the investment in Napa property was proposed, Ann wanted, first of all, a place to raise horses. But her husband insisted their investment should make money: raising horses might not be profitable, but the old Mt. Eden winery, dating back to 1884, had fifty or so acres of grapes which could be sold immediately. They quickly restored the old wine cellar. Their first wines won gold medals, and by the mid-1970s they decided to add "Villa" to "Mt. Eden" for their brand in order to prevent confusion with another Mt. Eden winery in Santa Clara county.

Not far south of Ann and James McWilliams property, Stanley and Carole Anderson purchased 29 acres of fallow land ready for planting. Stanley, a dental surgeon in Pasadena, had learned about Napa wines during his years at the San Francisco College of Physicians and Surgeons in the 1950s. His father had been a doctor, and in spite of being Seventh Day Adventists, the family used wine with meals. Carole Anderson studied winemaking at the University of California, Davis. She and Stanley were especially intrigued with champagne production. They had been buying French champagnes for years and drank them regularly with dinner. Out of deference to the French, they made "sparkling wine" when their winery opened in 1979.

Less than a dozen miles east of Anderson's, just a stone's throw from both Stag's Leap wineries, an Illinois publishing executive, John Shafer, replanted an old vineyard and founded his own winery as the decade of the 70s ended. Winemaking was a midlife career change for Shafer, as it was for many of his neighbors. He had spent 23 years working for one of the largest publishers of textbooks in America. At the age of 47 Shafer gave up his safe future as a corporate executive, sold his expensive Chicago-area home and headed west with his family. He had never grown grapes and knew nothing about winemaking, except that the future for the industry looked very bright. Everyone he knew talked about and sampled wine with meals.

He read every publication available on growing grapes, then learned to run the farm equipment needed to work the vineyard he was replanting to Cabernet, Zinfandel and Chardonnay. Like the Komeses at Flora Springs, the McWilliamses at Villa Mt. Eden, and other newcomers in the valley, Shafer hit it big right from the start when he began wine production. His first Cabernet won both the San Francico Vintner's Club and Chicago Winefinders Guide tastings. Recognition of such accomplishments was not difficult to come by, with the tremendous number of wine writers and wine columnists publishing all over the country. Mike Lonsford, of the *Houston Chronicle*, thought his Texas readers would be fascinated with Shafer's story and detailed it in his wine column. People like Shafer and Carole Anderson found themselves overnight celebrities in an industry headed for the stars.[21]

AN APPELLATION –
FOOD AND WINE TOGETHER

W ith a wine boom of spectacular proportions in Napa County by the 1980s, the time had arrived to set limits on what would and would not be considered Napa Valley grapes. As far back as 1934, Napa Valley vintners had adopted the slogan: "Napa County grapes for Napa Valley dry wines." That meant grapes grown anywhere in the county could be used to produce wine with the label "Napa Valley." But growers in the little eastern valleys, such as Pope, Gordon, Wooden or Berryessa, had always sold to valley wineries. Now there was a movement to terminate this long-standing tradition. "A valley is a valley is a valley," said the more literate advocates. But how high up the hillsides should the boundary of Napa Valley extend? To the top of the highest nearby peaks? Finally, someone suggested that the watershed of the Napa river be used as a boundary. That would include all the surrounding hillsides.

But Andy Cangemi, superintendent for the owners of Pope Valley Vineyards, cried foul. Butte's Gas & Oil Company of Houston, Texas, purchased the old Ten Lakes ranch in Pope Valley in 1972 with the idea of planting vineyards. By 1978 their first vines were in the ground and expansion plans called for 2200 grape acres. Their projected profit margins specifically depended on sales in Napa Valley. Robert Mondavi didn't like the watershed idea any better. His winery depended heavily on Wooden Valley grapes, which were trucked to his Oakville winery and were considered essential to the blending process. Several more small vineyardists also opposed a definition of Napa Valley which left out the small auxiliary valleys. The watershed of the Napa Valley wasn't nearly as important as making a profit. Further, they could point to the history of the wine business in the area which was established by grandparents who hauled grapes in horse-drawn wagons from valley to valley.

Finally, the Bureau of Alcohol, Tobacco and Firearms (BATF) announced guidelines in 1980 for American "viticulture appellations." As in France, once an appellation, or grape region, was established by law, its use on a wine bottle label would be a guarantee to the consumer that the grapes originated there. Public hearings would be held before any decision was made on boundaries.

Napa Valley vintners endorsed the idea wholeheartedly. No one really wanted grapes from outside Napa County used in Napa wines. But grapes from other valleys within Napa County might not be considered improper. Opposition to the so-called "outside valleys" collapsed quickly. Both the Napa Valley Vintners and Napa County Grape Growers approved a "Napa Valley appellation" that took in much of the county.

The packed and sometimes tense hearings were held in Napa in April 1980. Robert Mondavi hoped "Napa Valley" would be the first American appellation. Brother Timothy of the Christian Brothers expressed the hope that an acceptable consensus would be reached. During the hearings an historian presented copies of the 1973 and 1974 local phone books to the BATF panel. The 1973 phone book cover, labeled "Napa County," showed a map of the entire county on the back, indicating the geographic coverage. The 1974 phone book cover was labeled "Napa Valley," with the identical back cover map.[1] The Pacific Telephone Company had been urged at public hearings in 1973 to adopt the Napa Valley name to promote Napa Valley wine.

Food writer M.F.K. Fisher lived in this cottage in St. Helena from 1954 to 1970. She was enticed to the Napa Valley from Whittier, California, by Krug's Bottles & Bins editor Paco Gould. They founded the St. Helena Wine Library in 1961.

Barely a month after the Napa Hearings, the BATF announced that the first American appellation, in Missouri, would be called "Augusta." Mondavi could still hold out hope for Number Two. In its decision of March 31, 1981, the federal agency agreed to make the Napa appellation extend to as large a region as possible, under its guidelines. Thereafter, at least in most California cases, the broadest possible boundary lines were drawn. Once again, Napa had set a precedent in the California wine industry.

Foreign investors, who were already a force in the Valley, were delighted with the appellation agreement. Swiss owners already controlled Beringer; French money built Domaine Chandon; and Franciscan was the property of the Peter Eckes Company in Germany. Although some foreign money was strictly invested in part ownership, many wineries were bought outright. Harvey

Steinman reported in the *San Francisco Sunday Chronicle Examiner* of June 29, 1980 that the small Calistoga winery, Cuvaison, had been sold recently to another Swiss investor. "The foreign taste for state wineries" was the headline on his article, accompanied by a large map. Buena Vista winery in nearby Sonoma was a recent German purchase. The new owners abandoned most of the old historic buildings and built a brand new facility out in the Carneros. The view of San Francisco Bay was much better, among other advantages.

Jack and Jamie Davies came down off their mountaintop to ink an agreement with the Heriard-Dubreuil French family to build a brandy distillery/winery in the Carneros region in September 1982. Brandy consumption was on the upswing in the U.S. but there had never been a major producer of the beverage in Napa Valley. Before Prohibition, most major wineries had small brandy distilleries to take care of wine when the market was glutted.

French investors could have held a party along Highway 29 in those years, there were so many crowding the valley. Francis Dewavrin-Woltner joined William and Mary Collins in ownership of Conn Creek Winery, which had been founded in 1974. Dewavrin-Woltner were owners of Chateau La Mission Haut Brion in the Bordeaux district. Credentials did not come much better than that, unless your name was Rothschild and you owned Chateau Mouton-Rothschild, whose vines ranked among the top five "first-growth" in France. Rothschild accepted an invitation from Robert Mondavi to investigate a joint venture. Rothschild toured Mondavi's Oakville complex to see if it was up to his standards. Then, in April 1980, the two signed an agreement to build a separate Napa Valley winery and market a wine called "Opus One," which they hoped would sell for more than $100 a bottle.

It would take several years more before the great French Champagne house of G. H. Mumm came to the valley. No one was much surprised when this illustrious French name arrived; it was owned by the Seagram whiskey family, which had already purchased Sterling Vineyards. By mid-decade plans were being made for a 100,000-case-per-year facility. The low-key wine cellar would be sunk partially into a hillside along Silverado Trail.

Investment money also began to trickle in from across the Pacific Ocean. Sonoma Valley's Chateau St. Jean and Ridge Vineyards in Cupertino were the first in California to be owned by Japanese. Brooks Firestone in Santa Barbara County soon followed suit.[2] By mid-decade Sopporo Breweries of Tokyo were owners of St. Clement Vineyard (winery) at St. Helena. Kirin Beer sent a check for $18 million to the Raymond family for a portion of their winery, and the owners of Whitehall Lane winery accepted a $5 million buyout. Alan Steen and Art Finkelstein had less than ten crushes at Whitehall before they sold the winery.

Bruce Markham took his money and moved to Nevada when he sold the Markham winery in October 1987 to Sanraku, Inc. Had Markham disposed of his winery a decade or so earlier, around the time Nestle or the first French investment came into the Napa, there might have been major opposition from local people; the Markham winery dated back to the 1870s, when it was founded by French immigrant Jean Laurent.

Shortly before World War II began, the St. Helena Cooperative was formed to take over the winery, and from 1939 on, dozens of Napa growers sold their grapes to the organization. About 1950, Ernest and Julio Gallo contracted to take everything the co-op produced, even bringing in truck loads of used stainless steel tanks for fermenting and storage. Co-op members began arguing over the grape prices being paid by Gallo in the late '60s, and the membership voted to sell to Allied Grape Growers. Ten years later, in November of 1977, advertising executive Bruce Markham bought the property. Gallo's huge storage tanks almost completely obscured the view of the cellar. No wine had been produced there for years. It was not exactly an inviting tourist attraction. But Markham had plans. Bryan del Bondio, from an old-line Napa family, joined Markham in operating the cellar, and hired Robert Foley as winemaker. They had received degrees from U.C. Davis only months before, Foley majoring in enology, Del Bondio in viticulture. They were young, but they had a chemistry that suggested success would not be far off. The Japanese investors who bought the property retained both men.

It was anticipated that investments in the wine business might be returned a hundredfold. Income from grapes had increased 23 percent over the previous year, reported the county agricultural commissioner, "an increase of $10,113,000."[3] That did not include income from wine sales, a figure rarely available because wineries did not release it. Napa County now ranked eighth in California in personal income, a thirteen percent growth rate over the previous twelve months. Some of this boost in income could be attributed to the demand by Napa growers for higher grape prices than those paid in neighboring counties. For more than a century, Napa grapes had brought higher prices than those from Sonoma, Mendocino or Solano. Prices had evened out during Prohibition, fluctuating slightly. In 1964 the North Coast Grape Growers Association was established, in part, to recommend prices for wine grapes in all north coast counties. But in 1981, the Napa Valley Grape Growers demanded prices 30-40% higher than their neighbors. Napa wines were selling for higher prices than those from other regions, and the growers wanted a greater share of the profit.

The public's taste for white wine caused a 60-40% ratio now in the acreage devoted to red grapes as compared to white varieties. With a ton of Chardonnay now nearing $1,300 and Cabernet at $800 (up $200-$300 a ton), the wine industry wanted to assure plenty of open space and agriculture-zoned land for more vineyards. They needed to make sure available land wasn't squandered on housing. A county ballot measure, Proposition A, addressed this slow-growth issue. Vineyard owner Bill Jaeger argued against the measure, saying that some growth was necessary to expand the tax base. Jack Davies and others claimed the new Board of Supervisors just might dismantle the Agricultural Preserve and cease protecting the vulnerable hillsides. Proposition A passed, but it seemed nothing had been settled.

Heated wrangling broke out, and people took sides. True to predictions the County Supervisors decided to withdraw the tax advantages for farmland, instituted years earlier by the Agricultural Preservation Act and the related Williamson Act.

Milt Eisele was one of the founders of the Napa Valley Foundation, formed to preserve the "unique agricultural, scenic and small-town characteristics" of the county. The new "Upper Napa Valley Associates" had the same goals. These strong grassroots organizations helped force the county supervisors to do some long-range planning. By the end of December, 1982, a new general plan had been drawn up preserving open space and restricting housing to urban areas set aside for that purpose. It halted commercial projects (other than wineries) outside city limits.

Six years later the Associated Press carried a startling story which supported the concerns of local status-quo advocates: "California Farmlands Rapidly Being Lost" was the headline in one local newspaper. "California's soils are being paved over, polluted with salts and toxic chemicals and eroded at a rate that threatens the future of the state's agriculture . . . Of the state's crop land, approximately 1,785,000 acres are shedding soil faster than nature can replace it," ran the wire story.[4] Although the focus of the story was the San Joaquin Valley, it tied in with numerous articles in Napa newspapers about hillside erosion. St. Helena residents worried constantly about their major water source, Bell Canyon Dam, because it was in danger from vineyard planting above and around it. Scars on the hills from new vineyards alarmed some people, although quickly planted vines allayed most concerns.

Newcomers to Napa Valley wanted only to settle high in the hills and plant vines, as Donn Chappellet had done. One of these was William Hill, an Oklahoma transplant who obtained his MBA at Stanford University in 1969. He went to work for an investment company in San Francisco, then suddenly shifted his entire life's focus to wine. Hill was barely thirty years old in 1974 when he put together the financing to purchase what became

Diamond Mountain Ranch, high in the western hills between Schramsberg and Calistoga. One wall of the old stone wine cellar was threatened by the roots of a huge pine tree growing alongside it. But Hill liked the rustic nature of the place.

Hill and his investment partners planted part of the hillsides to grapes, then sold Diamond Mountain Vineyards to the Sterling winery and Coca Cola Company. "I wanted to move farther south in the valley, to a cooler climate," said Hill. He wanted land on Mt. Veeder or Atlas Peak, with shallow soils which would stress the vine to its maximum. That was the recipe for the best grapes — and he was committed to producing the best wine. "The vineyard determines the real character of the wine," said Hill. "At that time the emphasis was on technology and the input of the winemaker. I did not go along."[5]

Jacob Schram may have originated the theories, in Napa Valley at least, that Hill espoused. Professor Eugene Hilgard at the University of California, Berkeley, credited Schram in 1878 with having "the honor of being the successful pioneer of hill-vineyard cultivation."[6] Until Prohibition began, hill-grown grapes were always worth a dollar or two more per ton than valley grapes. In the Yearbook for 1898 of the U.S. Department of Agriculture, George Husmann wrote: "The deep lands of the river bottoms will produce the greatest quantity of grapes, while the hillsides will yield the best quality."[7] This theory doesn't explain why wines like those at Inglenook or Larkmead or Martini or Crabb's To-Kalon, all from valley grown grapes, won so many medals.

Only months after purchasing Diamond Mountain ranch, William Hill was looking for land on Mt. Veeder. Before the year was out, he bought one parcel already containing 56 acres in vines. Before 1980 Hill had carved out an unusual niche for himself in local wine circles. He had become the leading exponent of mountain-grown grapes. "I wasn't the only one to hold these ideas," he adds, "winemaker Rick Forman held the same strong beliefs." When Hill began making wine, his national advertising slogan was: "The quality and character of a wine is determined

medals are not = quality [handwritten margin note]

primarily in the vineyard." The so-called Rutherford dust didn't impress him, however.

A Swiss investor touring Napa Valley about this time agreed with him. Donald Hess was looking for a vineyard investment opportunity that might have the same returns as did his family's business back home. Their bottled spring water from a Swiss hillside was sold in every city in Europe. Hess purchased all of the Mt. Veeder vineyards and hillsides that Hill controlled and then talked Robert Craig into jumping ship. Craig had been an early ally of Hill; both men had been converted to hillside vineyards after tasting wines from the grapes grown at Mayacamas. Craig held an MBA, too, from the University of Chicago. He was an Arizona native raised in Texas. "I believe in the mountains. I like the intensity of the wine," declared Craig, one of the most likable people in the world.[8]

Most of the land Hess initially purchased, in 1979, had belonged to the Partrick family, which had been in the valley almost for as long as anyone could remember. No grapes were growing on their property, and may never have. They had made candy in a family store in Napa for generations. As the Mt. Veeder vineyards expanded, Hess looked for a location to make wine. Originally, he had in mind a grand valley vista with a stunning architectural masterpiece. Instead, in 1986 he obtained a long-term lease on the nearby Christian Brothers Mont La Salle winery. Many Napa residents were stunned.

The Christian Brothers had been in the valley only since 1930, but they had become such a fixture that nearly everyone assumed they had always been there. Tall, quiet, likable, sincere Brother Timothy had been nearly as active as Robert Mondavi in the vintner's association. He had become a legend, traveling the country to sell wine and showing off his corkscrew collection. His name was on most of Christian Brothers' wine labels, his photograph in many magazine advertisements.

But Christian Brothers wines were not doing well in the marketplace. There was an enormous money crunch generally. Vineyards needed replanting with prime varietals. Their

Greystone winery in St. Helena had to be closed for seismic upgrading, which had to be put on hold for financial reasons. The winery had not even adopted vintage dating on labels. It was time for a change. Brother Timothy and the other brothers would keep their Mont La Salle dormitory and, of course, the large Catholic church. But a central road dividing the property made it easy to assign and lease all the commercial winemaking buildings on the western side to Hess, including the formidable stone Gier Winery.

Hess ordered architects to redesign a portion of the interior of the winery for an art gallery, and renovation was begun in the summer of 1988. He would bring some of his personal art collection from Switzerland. When his plans were announced, they were met with no resistance from others in the Valley; it seemed Napa's fears of foreign investors had simply faded away. The vineyard development on Mt. Veeder was accomplished without much concern over erosion or other damage to the environment because one could not see the contours being carved into the mountain from Napa Valley's Highway 12. The Napa Redwoods, which included Mt. Veeder, were considered isolated, especially during winter's heavy rains. No trees were removed for the development.

Knoxville, in Pope Valley, was isolated too, in the far northeastern corner of Napa County. No one really paid much attention to the little town until gold was discovered there in the 1970s. This was not, however, a typical gold discovery: the gold was discovered in huge piles of debris taken from quicksilver mines a century earlier. The gold was so fine it could only be recovered by a complex chemical process. Homestake Mining Corporation of San Francisco leased or purchased 30 square miles of land around Knoxville. It would cost about $400 an ounce to recover the gold, but as long as the price of gold was above that figure the estimated 3.2 million ounces could earn a tidy profit. The mine was called the "McLaughlin." By 1987 miners had managed to purify 173,000 ounces of gold. Homestake didn't earn much of a profit, since development expenses had been so high, but Napa County had its first bonafide gold mine, about 135 years after the Gold Rush of 1849.

Gold digging as a means of accumulating wealth in Napa Valley appealed to very few people. Nearly everyone wanted to own a winery, but that required almost as much start-up money as the McLaughlin mine. If you arrived in the valley with only few hundred thousand dollars in your pocket, you might consider opening a restaurant. Food was the latest fad. The largest wineries were opening private kitchens and hiring pedigreed chefs. When Domaine Chandon opened its restaurant in 1976 with a world-renowned chef, Udo Nechutnys, at the helm, even San Francisco diners had reason to stay for an evening meal instead of hurrying home after a day's wine tasting. Five years later came Auberge Du Soleil, Mustard's, the French Laundry, the Calistoga Inn — the list grew almost exponentially as the years passed.

Mondavi, as usual, was the first to install an elegant kitchen and dining room in his winery, in 1966. The American southwest architecture of his winery, spare and stunning, was perfect for a dining room which opened onto the vineyards and nearby hills. Diners could also choose to have their meals outdoors on a comfortable patio. Mondavi's Swiss-born head of public relations, Margrit Biever, initially served as chef. Then in 1976 she talked Robert Mondavi into buying a program called "Great Chefs of France" and importing in rotation some of the best cooks France had to offer. Thereafter, lunch at the Mondavi winery on any particular day might be prepared by a chef from Lyons or Bordeaux or Paris. These meals were not open to the public but served a never-ending stream of guests from the media, wine industry and the world of politics.

Margrit's daughter Annie took over the Mondavi culinary kitchen shortly thereafter, and Michael Chipchase, another graduate chef, was soon added to the crew. Each day's lunch was a surprise cuisine from one country or another. Incidentally, if the road to a man's heart is really through his stomach, Margrit Biever's cooking must have played some role in winning the heart of Robert Mondavi. In time he divorced his wife and married Margrit.

Robert Mondavi seemed always to set the standard for what happened in the wine industry in Napa Valley. But before long, in the 1980s, the crew at the Beringer winery created its own bandwagon. Tor Kenward, director of public relations, had always liked to cook. In 1979 he spent a summer touring Europe and tasting the cuisine of various regions, as well as the local wines. Kenward came back fired up, and spoke to Mike Moone, then president of Beringer. Why not bring young American chefs to the winery and experiment with preparing dishes to match Napa Valley wines? The program was begun in 1980. The young chefs came from the California Culinary Academy in San Francisco. Beringer already had a fully-equipped kitchen, but Kenward had in mind something on a grand scale: an entire building devoted to a state-of-the-art kitchen. Here young, inexperienced chefs could be trained by the great chefs of America, and later, of Europe. Moone talked Nestle into setting aside a few million dollars for the project. "Mike brought this into being; he deserves much of the credit," acknowledges Kenward.[10]

The building was the historic but badly run-down Hudson house on the property, once the home of Jacob Beringer. The house, built in 1852, was restored completely by 1988. Beringer and Kenward then scored another coup: they persuaded chef Madeleine Kamman to come to the winery to teach at what they had named the Great Chefs Of America Cooking School. Kamman had authored a dozen books on cooking, several translated into English from her native French. Her credentials were impeccable. Former *San Diego Tribune* food editor Antonia Allegra was hired by Beringers to oversee the cooking school's business, leaving Kamman free to watch over simmering sauces and decadent desserts.

From the start, the emphasis at the school was to develop a California cuisine to match local wines — especially Beringer wines. "We have a fused cuisine in this state," observed Kenward, "with no clear identity, at least as of the moment." No winery in the state has done more to come up with a solution to that problem. The winery also sponsors competitions to identify wines in blind tastings, in order to honor the best *sommeliers* (restaurant wine stewards).

Monticello Cellars, on Big Ranch Road north of Napa, opened a culinary kitchen in 1984. A year later they hired chef Richard Alexei, and for five years gave him free rein to roam Europe to come up with unusual menus for luncheons or dinner. "We employ Alexei now only as we need him for special dinners," says Kevin Corley, son of founder Jay Corley. "We've had food classes, everything, but the cost of such a culinary kitchen is expensive. There isn't a direct dollar return except that it can be measured in good public relations," adds Corley.

Louis Martini has also emphasized the relationship of wine and food, especially since fine dining was a pastime of considerable dimensions with his father. Louis told an interviewer for the PBS documentary "Secrets of the Wine Country" that his father would buy a fresh fish, for example, take it to a restaurant they frequented and tell the chef how to cook it. "He got away with that in the old days."[11] In the mid-1980s Martini arranged with various restaurants around the country to prepare special full-course dinners to go with Martini wines. Members of the media, like Harvey Steinman of the San Francisco *Examiner*, were often bowled over by the meals: "As each course went by, we sampled all five wines with the food. Roast quail with the Pinot Noir was especially memorable, but the main message I took away from the experience was that Martini's wines often seem light and thin, even a bit acidic, next to some of the brawnier examples of California winemaking. With food, they turn supple and warm."[12]

Martini copyrighted a fabulous new idea: a wine/food compatibility scale. Jim Gordon of the *St. Helena Star* attended a dinner at the Martini home, where he tasted five wines with each course served at dinner. He liked a Martini Cabernet when served with roast beef but not with spinach cannelloni. He liked the Chardonnay with the spinach cannelloni but not with the after dinner cheese. "We make wines in the European tradition, to complement food, not for competition," Gordon quoted Louis Martini. "Intense, highly tannic or powerful wines may make a strong impression at competitive tasting, isolated from food, but they are not necessarily pleasant with food."[13]

This theme really caught on. Dan Berger, in his column for the Los Angeles Times the first week of July 1984 observed: "Wine makers throughout California have been trying hard the last few years to persuade the world that they make food wines. What, you may ask, is a food wine? It is a wine that is made to go with food, which, in my sphere of things, means a wine that is moderate in alcohol, moderate in acid and has decent varietal character."

It could have been too, that the ideas of Mary Francis Kennedy Fisher were finally being given their due. No one in America wrote more lovingly of food and wine than Fisher, who had been doing so since the 1930s. M. F. K. Fisher moved to Napa Valley in 1954 from Whittier, California, where she had lived infrequently since 1929, when she went off to France with her first husband. She had lived in Switzerland for a year with another husband; a third died after only a few years of marriage. When her father died, she and her sister Nora sold the family newspaper business in Whittier and moved north.

Fisher began writing about food for the New Yorker magazine. She wrote her first book, Consider the Oyster, in 1941, and followed it the next year with How To Cook A Wolf, which established her as a best-selling author. Why Fisher should select Napa Valley for her home after experiencing so much of Europe, is somewhat difficult to fathom. In her 1988 book, Dubious Honors, she wrote that she wanted a quiet, rural countryside in which to raise her two daughters. Still, Napa Valley was somewhat remote, and cooking and fine cuisine were not general topics of conversation at the time. Francis "Paco" Gould may have been her inspiration for making the move. Paco Gould had founded a monthly consumer publication, Bottles & Bins, for the

Krug winery a decade earlier, in which he wrote enthusiastically about wine.

"We met her in Pasadena, I think in 1951," recalls Romee Gould, his wife. "We went down to visit friends and attend a Shakespeare play. He gave her a bottle of wine and kissed her hand. She was impressed."[14] Gould invited Fisher to Napa Valley: she came, she loved it, and she stayed. There is no definitive bibliography to tell us how many books, magazine and newspaper stories Fisher wrote during her sixteen years in St. Helena. *An Alphabet For Gourmets* and *The Art of Eating* were published in 1954. *The Story of Wine in California* came in 1962, then *Map of Another Town; A Memoir of Provence, The Cooking of Provincial France, With Bold Knife and Fork,* and *Among Friends*. The latter was published in 1971 but certainly was written in St. Helena.

Fisher and Gould's friendship certainly contributed greatly to the Valley. They had often shared books on wine and food, in 1961 they decided the Napa Valley needed a Wine Library. Both of them contributed books, but the core of the library came from duplicates from the U.C. Davis's library, arranged by Department of Enology and Viticulture chairman, Dr. Maynard Amerine. The Library held yearly tastings on the grounds of the old Spotteswood mansion, attended by everyone in the industry, including Fisher and Gould.

Fisher had a sharp wit and equally sharp tongue. Asked once why another author had sold so many books and she so few, she replied: "Because he is an author, I am a writer." She recalled with delight wine being served in her home during Prohibition. "We always drank wine during Prohibition. In fact, we had some good wines during that time. They came from vineyards at Riverside and San Gabriel. We made some ourselves," recalled Fisher.[15] Her family was Episcopalian, but most people in Whittier were Quaker. Quaker families would not allow their children to associate with her, and she was understandably hurt. She felt her judgmental Quaker neighbors were rather short on brotherly love. In 1970, Fisher accepted an offer from

Francophile architect David Pleydell-Bouverie for a rent-free home in Glen Ellen. Her fame continued to grow — for example, there was a PBS special interview with Bill Moyers in 1990 — and visitors were constant. But illness gradually caused her to lose her ability to speak. She died in 1992 at the age of 83.

The *Napa Register* is a Scripps newspaper, and by the 1990s, with food such a hot topic, it was a natural that the Scripps newspaper chain might think it time to provide the valley with a wine and food magazine. Betty Scripps liked the word "appellation" and thought it belonged on the cover. (The *Register* had published an annual guide to the wine country using that name.) Fortunately, a woman with the right background and enough energy to handle editorial chores was living in St. Helena. She knew everyone in the wine industry and hobnobbed with the social set. Antonia Allegra had left Beringers and was the only one interviewed for the job. She was perfect. The *Napa Valley Appellation* debuted in November 1993. It was splashy, colorful, ritzy and in tune with where Napa Valley was headed for the next century. The food layouts were Allegra's specialty. One of the bimonthly issues in 1995 featured Joe Montana and his wife Jennifer on the cover. They had put money down on a ranch hideaway in the valley, then withdrew the offer. Rumor had it they were now looking in Sonoma County, but Allegra went ahead with their story — they did eat frequently in local restaurants.

Allegra was the guiding light behind the Napa Valley Culinary Alliance, along with Karen Mitchell of the Model Bakery, and chefs Richard Alexei and Jamie Morningstar. "It resembles the old guilds of Europe," said Allegra. "Anyone can join who is in food production, catering, a chef or food writer."[16] Allegra often carried the ball in the fight to bring the Culinary Institute of America to the valley. Nearby Sonoma County also wanted the famous cooking school to set up shop there. But the decision was ultimately made in Napa's favor, and the venerable Greystone winery was chosen as the site. Even Brother Timothy could not have come up with a better use for the building which the Christian Brothers had once occupied.

The Culinary Institute is one of America's most prestigious teaching centers for careers in food preparation. Based in New York state, the Institute decided to establish a western branch in 1991. Napa's attraction was obviously stronger than Sonoma's, although Sonoma grows far more of the foods used in nouvelle California cuisine.

Heublein, Inc. virtually gave the huge building to the Culinary Institute: the Institute paid $1.68 million for the winery, which could have sold for $10 million. Seismic upgrading and renovation were finished barely in time for an opening in August 1995. Today tourists flock to the school, to sample the students' cuisine and to tour the huge third-floor kitchen. The institute often draws as many visitors as nearby wineries.

THE WINE TRAIN

Multi-millionaire Vincent DeDomenico could have purchased several abandoned wine cellars when he sold the family business, Golden Grain Macaroni Company, to Quaker Oats for $275 million. Instead, he seized on an opportunity like no other in the valley: he purchased the Southern Pacific railroad right-of-way and took over a faltering concept called "The Wine Train."

From its conception in the early 1980s, the wine train was highly controversial, though no one remembers why. The Southern Pacific railroad stopped using the Napa line in 1985, and trucks took over the freight business. The railroad company wanted to abandon the rail line. Some people tried to get the county to buy the line and continue to operate the service. Instead, John McCormack and a group of investors bought the line with the idea of a "wine train" which would carry 300 sightseers per trip. McCormack believed this unique way of touring the area would appeal to people who would rather ride than drive, and would also decrease the number of cars on local highways. The investors, however, ran short of money. DeDomenico heard they were looking for additional partners, but he was more interested in owning the project outright. He wanted to make the wine train a fabulous dining experience for tourists as they rumbled slowly past vineyards and wine cellars. There would be baked salmon, coquille St. Jacques, Caesar salad, locally made French bread, blueberry tarts and assorted locally made cheese. Oh yes, and lots of Napa wine.

Mayor Lowell Smith in St. Helena turned pale when he was told each trainload of passengers would be allowed to disembark and shop in his town. Three hundred tourists running wild, maybe several times a day? Plans were immediately made to condemn the railroad right-of-way, preventing the train from entering the town.

Even some wineries did not like the idea. If DeDomenico's prediction of 450,000 travelers annually proved true, controlling crowds would be difficult, if not impossible.[17]. Local newspapers soon carried full-page advertisements supporting or condemning the project. One ad listed the names of the 1,100 Napa residents against the Wine Train. Each side hired lawyers. Those against the project appealed to the California Public Utilities Commission to take jurisdiction and stop the train dead on its tracks. The battle dragged on for years, but DeDomenico was not particularly dismayed. He bought a half dozen 1915 rail coaches from a Denver ski train and had them transported to Oroville for restoration. He also purchased two former Canadian National Railway diesel locomotives.

The State Public Utilities Commission finally decided it did not have jurisdiction over the Wine Train and kicked the dispute clear across country to the Interstate Commerce Commission. Both sides in the local dispute grew feisty: the Wine Train threatened to fence off everything ten feet from the center of their tracks and right-of-way, cutting off access, and in a few cases actual construction, for some businesses. Residents along the tracks insisted that the Wine Train erect expensive warning lights and arms at every railroad crossing.

By the summer of 1988, the diesels had been repainted in the burgundy colors of the Wine Train. Engineers gently guided the quiet engines over the 21 miles of track. Six months later the luxuriously refurbished dining cars were ready for test runs, too. The Interstate Commerce Commission threw the controversy back into the lap of the State Public Utilities Commission, but it didn't seem to matter anymore. Both sides had won arguments, and everyone was satisfied.

The Wine Train runs fifteen times a week during peak season. Passengers board the train in Napa at a brand new station and do not leave the cars during the entire trip — not that anyone would want to. The food is prepared on the train by highly qualified chefs and equals the best restaurant fare in the valley. Outside the windows, some of the most beautiful country in the world passes by, and one may see workers pruning vines in the spring or gathering grapes in the fall. It is on-site education in living color, without cold winter wind or summer heat.

LABOR IN THE VINEYARDS

Disputes generating as much energy as did the Wine Train are relatively rare in Napa Valley. Life here is tranquil. Especially during the tourist season, people do their best to avoid major controversies. Still, controversy does occur. Labor disputes are nearly always between the United Farm Workers, representing a group which includes mostly Mexican field workers, and the large wineries like Krug, Heublein (when it operated both Inglenook and Beaulieu), Christian Brothers and perhaps Trefethen or the Napa Valley Cooperative. Unlike conventional picketing with homemade cardboard signs, the UFW workers carry the large and colorful red and black flags of their union. Most of the morale-building singing is in Spanish. First-time visitors sometimes are confused, thinking they might be witnessing an ethnic or religious parade.

"With their familiar red and black banners unfurled, more than 150 members of the United Farm Workers picketed Inglenook Winery in Rutherford last week," began a story by Kim Marcus in the *Star* of June 2, 1983. This was all part of a "national boycott of the winery's products." Boycotting fresh table grapes in the local supermarket was by then a familiar UFW tactic, but urging the public not to buy wine was new. It is difficult to know whether the boycott actually had any impact on Inglenook sales, but both sides accepted binding arbitration less than a week later.

Generally, the UFW had far fewer problems to address in Napa Valley than in other areas of the country. Most winery owners seemed to have a genuine concern for the health and well-being of their workers. Mondavi's, for example, had long provided housing, although maybe never quite enough. A 1991 survey found nearly 4,700 migrant workers employed in the local wine industry at peak harvest times. Earnings ranged from $9,776 yearly for migrants to $18,105 for permanent employees.[18]

Profits from the annual Napa Valley Wine Auction have in recent years gone to Clinic Olé, in Yountville, the free medical clinic for Mexican farm workers. The two major local hospitals, Catholic-run Queen of the Valley in Napa, and the Seventh Day Adventist St. Helena Sanitarium, are also major beneficiaries. The auction has raised $1 million for each of several years.

"*Quinceañera*" ceremonies help bridge the culture gap for Mexicans living in Napa Valley. The ceremony is the most important celebration in the life of a young person. It celebrates the 15th birthday and the coming of adulthood. The day begins with a Catholic Mass. The honored boy or girl dresses in formal clothing. After the Mass, a procession leads to a hall where a grand party is held. All family friends are invited — everybody. Luckily for Napa Valley, many Mexican families have settled permanently in the area, and those of us who might never have known about *Quinceañeras* are now honored to be included. About ten *Quinceañeras* are held each year, although many families take their children back home to Mexico so that grandparents can be present for the festivities. The first dance is always a waltz. Youngsters practice for several weeks before the party to be sure they're at ease on the dance floor.

Another important reason Napa Valley is relatively free of labor problems is the new harmony between grape growers and winemakers. The Napa Valley Grape Growers Association (NVGGA) can take much of the credit, along with the Napa Valley Vintners. Prior to the Grape Growers' organizing themselves in June 1975, their only voice was through cooperatives such as the Napa Valley Co-op Winery. For decades, growers were not even advised until the following spring of the price they would be paid for a ton of grapes delivered the previous fall. This was the case in other grape regions; most Napa Valley winery owners were not so callous. But even in Napa, things could have been better. Tired of the dissention, Ren Harris and Andrew Beckstoffer founded the Napa Valley Grape Growers Association. Early members included Bill Jaeger, Ed Westgate, Ed Brovelli, Nathan Fay and John Trefethen. The men met to chart a new course for the growers side. Harris claims the NVGGA signed up 80% of the independent vineyardists that first year, representing some 12,000 acres, perhaps half of all the vines then in the county. These numbers are ample testimony to the urgent need that was addressed.[19]

NAPA VALLEY APELLATIONS

The most significant achievement of the organization was to win higher prices for Napa grapes, especially as compared to other regions of the North Bay. The North Coast Grape Growers in Ukiah set prices (which were often ignored), but they failed to reflect the much higher land costs in Napa Valley. When all of the expenses were itemized and publicized, most Napa wineries fell into line. They were, after all, getting higher bottle prices than other counties. Grape prices climbed to nearly astronomical heights during the 1980s and '90s. Rene di Rosa in the Carneros sold his grapes for $2,000 a ton and higher. Still, some growers were barely breaking even, thanks to major inflation in every segment of viticulture, which had taken place the previous decade.

Relations among the membership of NVGGA were seriously strained when sub-appellations were suggested in Napa Valley. A "Rutherford Bench" appellation at first seemed like a brilliant idea. Inglenook and Beaulieu wines were testimony to the greatness of the Rutherford soil. But no one could trace precisely the origins of a Rutherford "bench." The phrase was recent, a few decades old at most. When boundaries were drawn, especially east of Highway 29, leaving out this or that vineyard, some vineyardists were really angry. Suggestions for a "Yountville" appellation, one for "Oakville" and maybe even "St. Helena," did not placate the opposition. Augustin Huneeus, president of Franciscan Vineyards, was so irate that he mocked the Rutherford proposal by building a huge wooden "Rutherford Bench," twelve feet long and nearly seven feet high, sitting on a foot-thick block of cement, at the entryway of his winery.

With nearly a dozen appellations approved by the BATF now within Napa County and more proposed, there is a growing fear that the original "Napa Valley" appellation will soon be meaningless. Perhaps it may go the way of the "North Coast" appellation which was approved in the early 1980s but used rarely today. If the geographic region is too large, the defining principles behind the appellation are lost.

Napa County's second appellation, the Carneros, offers a curious study in historical conflict. Historically, the Carneros was an area in Napa County, defined as that lower portion of the county bordering on San Francisco Bay to the south, the Napa river to the east, Sonoma County on the west and north, a boundary stretching from Milliken Peak to Napa City. The phrase was never applied to any portion of Sonoma County until very recent times.

Only John Stanley's winery ever achieved any major status in the region before Prohibition. The phylloxera disease destroyed most of the vineyards in the Carneros before the year 1900. Few were replanted until recently. When Louis Martini, and then Andre Tchelistcheff, began bragging about Carneros grapes and wine, the region became very popular. The unusually cool climate near the bay produces what many regard as the greatest Pinot Noir grapes in California. Many of the finest grapes used for Napa's champagne come from here.

Beaulieu Vineyards, Legh Knowles and Tony Bell were the first to petition the BATF for recognition of the Carneros. Sonoma Valley growers saw an opportunity to link up with Napa County and requested the BATF to unite the two regions. Sonoma growers were able to convince the BATF hearing panel that they had the same climate and the same soil, even though U.S. Geological Survey maps, etc. did not specifically include them under the Carneros name. The appellation was approved in September 1983. Growers from the two counties have since shown a remarkable ability to work together to enhance the reputation of Carneros wine.

Napa County has been divided up into nine appellations, pending or approved, and there is talk of more still. One area most wine consumers will probably not visit is the remote Wild Horse Valley appellation. The road to it is narrow and twisting, and likely to terrify tourists. Wild Horse Ranch is a well-known equestrian center whose name derives from a small herd of horses that turned wild about the time of the American Civil War.

Dr. John Newmeyer and James Birkmyer were the principal backers of this appellation, though together they own less than 50 acres of vines in Wild Horse Valley. No one will argue that they haven't a right to a separate identity; this distinctive region is isolated high in the hills five miles east of Napa, and rainfall is more than abundant. There once was a Vorbe winery in the region, but its rock foundation long ago caved in and is now home to families of rattle snakes. Anyone who questions the decision to grow grapes in such a remote area need only talk to Warren Winiarski. He has crushed Birkmyer's Riesling grapes for years and put the name on the wine label. In 1983, when Queen Elizabeth visited San Francisco, she hosted a birthday dinner for then President Ronald Reagan at which Birkmyer Riesling was served.

Mount Veeder and Napa Redwoods

On the opposite side of Napa Valley is another appellation with many similarities to Wild Horse Valley. "Mount Veeder" derives its name from the elegant 2,677 foot peak in its center. It is also called the Napa Redwoods; abundant rainfall here is conducive to the growth of the redwood tree.

Winemaking in the Mount Veeder area goes back to the 1860s. There have been numerous small wine cellars, including the current Mayacamas Winery, but only one large cellar, the Christian Brothers, now leased to the Hess Collection Winery. The steep hillsides generally produce big red wines, especially the Cabernet. Production is often barely two tons per acre, but the small crop is generally considered to a reasonable tradeoff for the special quality of the grapes. Some very prominent Napa residents cultivate vines on these slopes: John Wright of Domaine Chandon; Elaine Wellesley, who founded the original Quail Ridge Winery; Lore and Linn Olds of Sky Vineyards; James Konrad, and Al Buckland, president of the Napa Valley Grape Growers.

Two names are prominent in the long history of Mount Veeder's place in the winemaking tradition of Napa Valley: Rudolph Jordan and Theodore Gier. Jordan's Castle Rock winery, founded by German immigrants in 1884, is tucked deep into the hills just beyond the Hess winery. The earliest on-site experimentation with commercial yeast in wine production was carried out here by Rudolph Jordan in 1896. Commercial yeast was not generally adopted by the wine industry until after Prohibition. One German immigrant, Theodore Gier, built the large stone winery which today forms the oldest part of the Hess winery. Gier came to the Redwoods at the encouragement of over a dozen other German immigrant growers and winemakers. In May 1930 the Gier winery was sold to the Christian Brothers.

Even though the Christian Brothers abandoned winemaking in the Mount Veeder area in 1986, they still maintain their original monastery buildings and magnificent Catholic church there.

A dormitory is open to all former brothers of the Order, and Brother Timothy makes the facility his home. There is probably no more picturesque mountain site in all of Napa County than the 60-year-old monastery. Some day, a life-size statue of Brother Timothy will surely grace the grounds here. He may not have brought champagne to life, as did Dom Perignon, the French monk, in the late 1600s, but he did much to put Napa Valley securely on the world wine map.

Brother Tim, as he is affectionately known, arrived in the Napa Redwoods in the early 1930s. He helped make many of the wines that won numerous gold medals for his order over sixty years. He served as President of the Napa Valley Vintners several times, and his name on Christian Brothers wine labels soon made him a legend. One small measure of Brother Tim's stature is the 50th anniversary party accorded him in December 1985. The central court of the DeYoung Museum in San Francisco was vacated so that tables could be moved in to accommodate hundreds of guests. BBC Television chef Ken Hom was flown in to oversee the dinner, which began with Chinese Green Ravioli swimming in Black Truffle cream. The wines were all made by Brother Tim, including a 1980 Cabernet and a Port made of very ripe Zinfandel, his personal favorite. The following year he was out of a job when Donald Hess leased the old Gier winery. A Mount Veeder appellation was approved by the BATF in February 1990.

Only one Napa County viticultural appellation really led to hard feelings, and that was Stag's Leap. Warren Winiarski brought the name back to life with the founding of his winery in 1972. His success at Paris in 1976 focused the spotlight on the area, and suddenly he had lots of new neighbors smiling, waving and plowing up the land for new vineyards. That this area should have a viticulture reawakening was inevitable. But Winiarski somewhat justifiably felt he had been there first, and he wanted to protect what he had accomplished. He sued Carl Doumani to keep him from using the same name on his wine labels. Then he hired lawyers to maintain a strict historic boundary in the Stag's Leap appellation petition to the BATF. But everyone wanted to get in on the act. Stanley Anderson, clear over on Yountville Cross Road, demanded to be let in. The Pasadena dentist had both the demeanor and build of a football player. He was tenacious. The polite Disney family, just down the road, asked to be included; they were building their Silverado Winery. Across the Silverado Trail, Robert Sinskey did not want to be left out, either.

In 1985 the BATF held hearings at the nearby Veterans' Home. On some days, there were more lawyers than witnesses. One estimate put the cost of legal advice at $150,000.[20] One subject of the debate was how far the cooling summer fog and breezes extended. There were low hills between Winiarski and Anderson. Did the fog and breeze reach Yountville Cross Road one day, three days, or nearly every day during the summer? Some argued that residents in the old Stag's Leap area were part of Napa because their mail came out of Napa City. Yountville Cross Road residents got their mail from Yountville, so they couldn't be part of the Stag's Leap area.

For two full years the BATF was inundated with paperwork on all sides of the issue. As with nearly all BATF hearings in which controversy arises, the federal officers chose the larger parameters. While historical evidence for the name was a requirement for the appellation, much of the conflicting history was conveniently ignored by the hearing officers. This was true in many other petitions as well, for example in Carneros and Alexander Valley. Stag's Leap viticulture appellation was approved in February 1989. Since then, Spring Mountain has been recognized as a viticultural appellation, as have Howell Mountain, Oakville, and Atlas Peak and Rutherford.

Will appellations really matter very much in two or three decades? Some people, like Andy Beckstoffer, believe not. The estate designation may be the crucial factor, however, for only an owner-farmer can control grape quality, the key element of the wine. Designations of First Growth or Second Growth vineyards have no relationship to appellations.

It is curious as well, that within Napa appellations, few wineries achieve as much prominence for their wines as the most highly recognized wine brand in that appellation. "Rutherford dust" has helped many wine labels, but few can match Caymus Vineyards' rise, in only a decade or two, to become one of Napa's top labels. But appellations and designations are of minor concern to grape growers when compared with the resurgence of the dreaded old disease, phylloxera. It is back in force, destroying vines randomly from one end of Napa Valley to the other. The destruction of patiently cultivated prime grapes is sometimes enough to make grown men cry.

Roy Raymond, Jr. thinks the great flood of 1986 is at fault. Over two feet of rain fell on the valley floor during the third week of February, and Raymond believes the phylloxera vine louse was simply washed from one vineyard to another. Within two or three years vines began dying where no phylloxera had ever been seen. No more than 800 acres were identified as being infected prior to 1990, but since then phylloxera has infected vines at about the rate of about 2000 acres per year. The disease has been labeled as type B phylloxera, and the commonly used Axr-1 rootstock has little or no resistance to it.

The cost of replanting can reach $10,000 or more per acre. Many growers have elected to go slowly before replanting: production from an infected vineyard can vary greatly from year to year. Strong vines, moderate weather and rainfall, and proper nourishment can enhance production, but there are no guarantees once phylloxera has been at work. Pulling out an entire vineyard can be beneficial, especially where improvements have not previously been made. Trellises, irrigation, and improved frost protection systems can be installed before the vineyard is replanted.

In 1995, Francis Ford Coppola purchased the Inglenook winery and approximately 90 acres of vineyard, which he knew would require replanting. His interest in Napa dates back to about 1969, when he spent months shooting his film, "American Graffiti," in Petaluma. Whenever there was a break in filming, he and others visited wineries, sampling both Napa and Sonoma wines. After moving his film company, Zoetrope Studios, to San Francisco, he wanted to find a country retreat to pursue his writing. Coppola and his wife, Eleanor, also wanted a quiet, more rural setting to raise their children. Eleanor, who has a degree in Applied Design from U.C.L.A., began finding creative projects in the Bay Area.

By 1972, the Coppolas had decided to look for a place in Napa Valley. They had in mind a small cottage and a few acres, but eventually purchased the enormous, grand old Victorian Niebaum house and 1500 acres. Most of the land was steep hillside on the western side of the valley. With more than a hundred acres of grapes, Coppola began seriously considering wine production. Of course, he could easily have sold every ton of these Rutherford dust grapes, but his Italian heritage kept whispering "make wine." In 1978, with the help of Russ Turner as winemaker, the first "Francis Ford Coppola Family Wines" came about. Production was a mere 2000 cases.

The financial success of "The Godfather" had enabled the Coppolas to change their focus from the small cottage to the grand estate. His success with ensuing films would increase Coppola's involvement in the wine arena as well. Coppola wine was made in what had been the old Niebaum carriage house, which was built to last. Actually, the timbers and caulking made it resemble a ship. Niebaum had been captain of a sailing ship for the old Alaska Commercial Company, and later rose to became its president.

When Coppola hired John Skupny as the general manager of his wine estate, their private talks drifted frequently to the historic Inglenook winery, just a stone's throw away. It had all once been part of the original Niebaum estate, owned for decades by John Daniel, Niebaum's grand nephew. Heublein now owned Inglenook. Coppola, hoping to reclaim the original Niebaum lands, asked Skupny to make inquiries of Heublein. For several years, nothing happened, but in 1994, Skupny heard the winery had been sold. Coppola was distraught. Then a telephone caller informed Skupny that the only the Inglenook brand had sold, and "If Francis Ford Coppola wants the winery, he can have it."[21] The agreement to purchase Inglenook was signed in February,

1995, and when the local newspapers picked up the story on the front pages, there was a huge collective sigh of relief. Inglenook was back in the hands of a (semi) local person.

Coppola certainly belies the image of the big-time movie director who spends weekends at his country place. In fact, he and Eleanor have become real locals, hosting dinner parties, being invited out regularly, becoming a part of the Napa scene. They usually take in valley wine events. When Inglenook's centennial was feted in 1979 at a grand black tie dinner in the Garden Court of San Francisco's proud old Palace Hotel, the Coppolas were there. They had already begun to make friends with residents of the valley.

"Niebaum-Coppola Wine Estate" is the new name for wine produced at the majestic Inglenook winery by winemaker Scott McLeod and consultant Tony Soter. The vineyards in front have been replanted to mostly Cabernet Sauvignon grapes. They are searching for the old Inglenook clones, trying to restore the wine's greatness. Coppola may accomplish this goal if at some point he can also bring the name "Inglenook" back home. It won't replace what he will build with his "Niebaum-Coppola" brand, but those buildings, that 113-year-old winery filled with spirits from the past, deserve an identity as lovingly familiar as the word "Napa."

The '90s seem to have brought with them a modicum of stability in the Napa Valley. A case in point is the Charles Krug winery. Peter Mondavi steadfastly held on to the Krug winery when it would have been far easier to sell. There are calmer pursuits in the valley than running a winery. He was in hock up to his ears, but if he had sold, it might have broken his heart. "We have had growing pains," recalls Mondavi. "This was true especially from about 1981 on. We built our biggest building then. We sort of lost control of our wine. Eight years of work and we are finally catching up. I'm pulling lots of loose ends together now; that's what I do on a day-to-day basis. The boys, Marc and Peter, Jr., run everything else. You know computers are supposed to be so great, but they sure have made a lot of extra work."[22]

Indeed, many winery owners aren't convinced that they really need 24-hour-a-day input on every nuance of their operations.

Peter and his staff are now concentrating on upgrading Krug's wines. Thousands of new French and American oak barrels now age the wine, imparting qualities so subtle they can't be measured, even by those computers. There is also a surprising new label: a solid, dark green background with the name "Mondavi, Napa Valley." The "CK Mondavi" emblem is directly above, but never before has Peter featured his family name so prominently.

Calm has also been restored at Sutter Home Winery, which has finally stopped expanding. It has been difficult to keep up with this wildly successful operation during the past twenty years. Bob Trinchero has made a mega-winecellar from what was once a very small family winery. If there is any complaint from neighbors, it is that few of the grapes used at the winery come from Napa Valley. Sutter Home, built in 1874 by John Thomann, is among the oldest wineries in all of Napa Valley. The Sutter family renamed the facility when they purchased it in 1904. It was closed during Prohibition. A year after World War II ended, two brothers named Trinchero came from New York and purchased Sutter Home. Sutter Home would have remained small, perhaps, if White Zinfandel had not been rediscovered. Bob, the oldest son of one of the Trinchero brothers, tasted a 1965 Zinfandel from Amador County and was smitten. Why not concentrate only on Zinfandel? Or maybe a White Zinfandel?

White wine from the Zinfandel grape has been around for a long, long time. Old timers still occasionally talk of it. White Zinfandel was the principal wine in Arpad Haraszthy's famous Eclipse Champagne a century ago. Charles Wetmore, the first president of the State Viticultural Commissioners, referred to the wine at the Second Annual State Wine Convention in 1883. For decades prior to Prohibition, White Zinfandels were always produced somewhere in the state. When the white wine boom began in the early 1970s, Trinchero seized an opportunity. By mid-decade, Sutter Home production had climbed dramatically to over 25,000 cases a year. Barely ten years later, the winery was producing 2.5 million cases.

Since vineyard land was so expensive in Napa County, Trincheros expanded to Lake County, then bought 640 acres in Glenn County, and finally the small Monevina Winery and its vineyards at Plymouth, California. They also own acreage on Zinfandel Lane, which is where they actually make their wine. With the addition of 33 acres of the Galleron ranch on Zinfandel Lane, Sutter Home has been able to increase its production to over three million gallons, making it the largest winery in Napa County. No grapes are crushed, and no wine is made in the old Thomann/Sutter Home wine cellar. That facility is only for tastings, sales and small storage.

Almost next door to Sutter Home is the Napa Valley Cooperative Winery. Portions of it, too, have been there for a long time. The old stone Peterson winery dates back to 1885. A family named Bergfeld operated it for years at the turn of the century. In 1934, a cooperative purchased the Peterson/Bergfeld winery, and within a few years greatly expanded the facility. The Napa Valley Cooperative winery often lacked marketing expertise in selling its wine, until Ernest and Julio Gallo came along in 1950-51.

With the advent of high grape prices in the late 1970s, the Cooperative went its own way. It was even decided to bottle and market its own brand, choosing the old "Bergfeld" name in honor of the long history of the wine cellar. Marketing remained a problem, however, and sales were not as good as was hoped. The parking lot in front of the new tasting room remained mostly empty. It did not even seem to help when a Cooperative Cabernet Sauvignon was awarded "Best of Show" honors at the California State Fair in 1991.

Membership in the Cooperative was declining steadily, down by half in twenty years. When Golden State Vintners of Cutler, Tulare County, offered to buy the winery and 33-acre site, the deal was signed in record time. Golden State has continued operation of the historic cellar. Cooperative wineries are now a relic of the past. In March, 1953, *Wines & Vines* required four pages to describe the more than 30 cooperatives in California. Now there are less than a handful of such cellars. Napa Valley had two at one time, the other being the St. Helena Cooperative. Without them, dozens of small growers would have had no home for their grapes. Times have changed, but tears were shed when the Cooperative was sold.

There was some uneasiness too, when the Raymond winery was sold to Japanese investors. The winery could trace its roots, through the Beringers, back to the 1870s. But Roy, Jr., and his brother Walter have maintained a minority interest and have a long-term contract to operate the winery. The Japanese investment has made it possible to greatly expand wine production at Raymond. There is a new barrel storage building with 7500 mostly French oak barrels. (Enough French oak has been added to valley wineries in the past decade so that the entire valley should float the next time flooding occurs.) Production at Raymond has jumped to over 200,000 cases yearly, made possible by a new fermentation room and crushing room.

Raymond wines are among the most sought after by wine consumers, in part because they win so many awards. They won "Best of Show" over 408 entries at the National Restaurant Wine Classic in Chicago in 1988. A year earlier *Wines & Spirits Buying Guide* named their Cabernet American Champion at an all-Cabernet competition. The honors continue to accumulate impressively.

What the Raymonds might have done for the Beringer winery, had they taken over its operation before it was sold to Nestle, is prime dinner-table speculation now. An investor with deep pockets was needed to restore the fading giant. How many millions of dollars Nestle poured in is anyone's guess.

Before Beringer was sold, and Beaulieu, and Inglenook, and Christian Brothers, Napa Valley ownership might have been preserved had someone provided different direction in the seeking of investment capital. Robert Mondavi certainly picked up the funding he needed rather easily, though for real expansion he had to sell stock to Rainier Brewing Company. New corporate owners have poured millions and millions of dollars into Napa wine cellars. Some, like Heublein, have sold off vineyard assets (of Beaulieu) or brand names (as in the case of Inglenook) and have recovered initial investments easily.

Some measure of local control may be returned to Beringer now that Nestle has sold the winery to Mike Moone and a group of investors he has put together. Moone was president of Beringer for more than a decade and certainly understands how it operates. The winery deal was for an estimated $350 million, and that kind of money is just not lying around Napa Valley, looking for a home. An equity fund called Texas Pacific Group, of Fort Worth, is involved.

Some type of sweetheart deal with investors might have saved Hanns Kornell from bankruptcy. His story is one of the saddest in Napa history. Hanns fled the Nazi regime in Germany and worked for more than two decades in Missouri and California wineries or champagne cellars before finding the old Larkmead Cellar. He set up shop in the late 1950s and began what was then the only Napa Valley champagne house. "I make champagne the old fashioned way," he boasted proudly. Visitors loved his warm smile and felt honored to be given a wine tour by the owner himself.

The old-fashioned way, however, sprang a leak in the 1970s. His equipment was outmoded. Costs of buying grapes rose significantly, and he owned only a small acreage in vines. The winery needed to expand to keep pace with expenses. Hanns borrowed from banks to build new storage buildings. The interest alone was a huge drain on his income. Competition from neighboring champagne producers was stiff, especially the large, foreign-owned wine cellars down valley. They made Hanns look like small potatoes, and he was. His hand-made product could match any other, but his prices could not.

Illness and a stroke in the midst of all of these problems exacerbated a difficult situation for Hanns. Finally, in November 1991, the winery had to file for bankruptcy, hoping to buy a little time to reorganize. Three years later, with the Kornells' home about to be taken away as well, Robert Mondavi came to the rescue. He bought the Kornell residence, then told Hanns and Marielouise, his wife, they could stay amidst their family treasures and memorabilia the remainder of their lives. In July 1994, Hanns Kornell died, at age 83.

There are more than two hundred separate wine cellars in Napa County. Keeping track of them has become nearly impossible, even for the Napa Valley Vintner's organization. Only about fifty percent now belong to that trade group, in large part because newcomers don't understand the value of organizing for the common good. If they knew the history of the Vintners, there would be no such reluctance. Many of the smallest wineries receive very little media attention at all. Take tiny Mayacamas Vineyards, on the side of Mount Veeder. Production is barely 5,000 cases a year. The road to it is narrow, yet there is a never-ending flow of cars and visitors. Bob Travers produces big Cabernet Sauvignon wines that require aging at home. And people want them. That comes from having a secure reputation and a long history of high quality.

Travers received national television exposure when a CNN news team came to film what turned out to be a four-minute interview in September, 1995. CNN included in their piece a film clip from the movie "A Walk in the Clouds," which showed people stomping grapes. The scene was shot at Mayacamas, as was a long shot of a tree-shrouded road where two lovers were walking. Travers doubts that grapes were ever crushed that old-fashioned way at his winery, but it was picturesque. Other portions of the film were shot elsewhere in Napa Valley.

Lakespring Winery on Hoffman Lane, Yountville, is another name that has had little publicity. Frank Battat and others in his family at Liberty Gold Fruit Company, San Francisco, founded the cellar in 1980. Frank provided most of the guiding energy. But there was just too much to do. "It just took too much time" observed Battat, "and if I had charged Lakespring for all my personal time there would have been no profit at all."[23] This is the reason the brand name of "Lakespring" was sold in 1995 to their distributor, Frederick Wildman & Sons, of New York City. The Lakespring facility is now owned by two different sets of investors: Michael and Kathyrn Havens, John Scott and Russell Lane, of Havens Wine Cellars, and Peter Franus of the Franus Wine Company. Havens has had a small wine storage facility in Napa city for the past eleven years.

Battat says his winery suffered from other problems as well. Distribution was the main headache. "There are fewer and fewer wine distributors, each with a longer and longer list of wine brands to sell," says Battat. "That mix did not work for us, we finally concluded."

The story is the same for many absentee winery owners. When your winery produces only around 20,000 cases a year, you can't hire a large staff. As owner, you must do most of the work yourself, especially the sales and marketing. If you don't have a background in wine sales, you face a highly challenging learning experience.

Selling Lakespring was a major disappointment for Frank Battat. Wine had been a part of his San Francisco upbringing since childhood. When he was thirteen years old, at his Bar Mitzvah, his father had told him he could help select wine or a liqueur, and together they would taste and experiment. "We did a great deal of sampling," recalled Battat. "In 1958, my father and I were invited to take a trip to Los Angeles aboard the *President Cleveland*, the flagship of American President Lines. At the dinner table we were served wine. The ship had an impressive cellar of California and French wines. My father discussed the wine with [Ralph] Davies. (His wife later provided the financing for Davies Symphony Hall.) I resolved to collect wine."[24] Lakespring was, in essence, a spiritual gift to the senior Battat by his eldest son and family. The father had died just one year before the first crush in 1980.

Mario Perelli-Minetti has spent much of his life in the wine industry. When he founded his own small winery on Silverado Trail in 1988 he thought it was going to be a retirement pastime.

All the talk about problems of wine distribution seemed unimportant. He believed there was little anyone could tell him that he had not heard before, because his family had been in the wine industry for years.

Perelli-Minetti is a much-honored name in the California wine industry. When Antonio Perelli-Minetti died in 1976, at the age of 95, newspapers honored him as the "dean of California wine-makers." From 1927 on, the family owned a winery and a vast acreage in vines at Delano, California. Eventually, they acquired the remnants of the California Wine Association. Antonio was Mario's father.

Mario could have taken his retirement savings and family inheritance and sat in his Hillsborough, California, home sipping wine and dining on Italian cuisine. But like his father, who worked in the vineyards until the day he died, Mario wanted one more challenge. Napa Valley offered that challenge. The family had never been associated with the premier winemaking region in California, but Mario had always been fascinated by the possibility. In 1979 he began purchasing bulk wine in the valley and had it bottled by Rutherford Hill under the "Mario Perelli-Minetti" label.

Several years later, Mario found the Napa address he wanted, just off Zinfandel Lane and Silverado Trail. In 1988 his winery was completed. Now three years short of his 90th birthday, Mario still handles the day-to-day selling of his wine for Northern California. Dean Sylvester makes his Cabernet and Chardonnay for him — 6000 cases a year. Mario doesn't pay himself a salary for selling his wine. As was the case at Lakespring, there would not be any profit left over if he did. Earnings are reinvested immediately in the winery, and he's happy with the situation. He wants to leave his name and family legacy in Napa Valley, and he hopes and prays some grandchild will soon take over. "There is a lot of work to making wine. The romance in wine is not in the making of it, or in the selling of wine," admits Mario, somewhat wistfully. "It is in the drinking of it." [25]

Mary Novak has had far different problems from the Battats and Perelli-Minettis with her Spottswoode Winery. The wine

BETH & MARY
NOVAK

almost sells itself. That may be because of the underlying gravel soil, or Tony Soter, her remarkable consulting winemaker. But Novak has had to fight city hall for even the smallest permits needed to build and operate her winery. Her husband began the battle twenty years ago; he tried and failed many times before his untimely death. A part of the unique problem faced by Novak is that Spottswoode is one of the truly grand old homes in all of the valley, and especially in St. Helena. The house sits on the western edge of the city, and there are neighbors on all sides except the west, which is vineyard. Spottswoode is where the Napa Valley Wine Library held its first fund-raising wine tastings. This generated not only money for the library but put some new wine brands on the map. It is where Rupestris St. George root stock first proved the salvation of valley vineyards when they were being destroyed by the phylloxera in the 1890s. Indian arrowheads are buried in the soil, and perhaps even Indian burial grounds.

Spottswoode wine production actually dates to 1982, but its grapes were fermented and bottled at other facilities. All of it was aged in her basement. In 1990 Mrs. Novak acquired the stone Kraft winery, just a half block to the north, and crushing has been carried out there ever since. In the December 31, 1988 issue of *Wine Spectator* magazine, Spottswoode wine was ranked #8 in the World's Top 100 wines for their 1985 wine. In the following two years, Spottswoode wines ranked in the Top 100 again. Their 1986 and 1987 released wines both fell within the Top 20 ranking.

Mary Novak's son, Matt, has taken a Master's degree in viticulture from UC Davis and works in the vineyards. Daughter Beth is general manager, and Lindy is in sales. Any time their mother wants to relinquish her swivel chair and desk as the chief at Spottswoode, there are three heirs apparent. They are all undoubtedly grateful that they will never have to take on city hall, as she did, to get permits.

Tony Soter, who sprinkled some magic dust over those *Wine Spectator*-recognized wines, is a bit of a maverick, like Mrs. Novak. He doesn't hold a degree in enology from UC Davis. His B.A. is in philosophy from Pomona College, Claremont. He had thought of being a lawyer — not too seriously, fortunately. For a summer-time job in 1974 he tried selling wine in an Orange County liquor store. Many customers were there on serious business, and wanted to know which wines he recommended, and why. No one asked him about philosophy. His curiosity was piqued, and he suddenly wanted to learn all he could about wine.

Soter denies he was born with a special palate: he believes that comes with wine tasting and training. That training could best be had by working in a winery, so he headed north to Napa Valley. There was no thought of going to UC Davis; he did not want to take the time. By a strange circumstance, he found a "cellar-rat" job at Stag's Leap with Winiarski, who had also put philosophy aside and turned to wine. Soter helped make the 1973 Cabernet which won the 1976 Paris tasting. From there, Soter moved on to various valley wine cellars, including a six-year stint as winemaker for Chappellet. He did finally take courses in chemistry, enology and viticulture at Davis. When he began consulting for Spottswoode, he insisted on having as much input into the management of the vineyard as in the winery. He had learned that fine wine begins in the vineyard. That has been a cardinal rule for him ever since. When he accepts a new consulting job, the two tasks must be linked.

Tony Soter has earned himself a truly enviable reputation in Napa Valley by making award-winning wines for many of his clients. He has even signed an agreement with Francis Ford Coppola to restore the reputation of Inglenook, or what once was Inglenook. Soter has also leased a small, unused winery from Monticello, on Big Ranch road. There he makes "Etude" Pinot Noir and Cabernet Sauvignon. His activities are being watched like a hawk by wine connoisseurs. Will he be as successful with his Etude wines as at other places?

There is another, more profound reason to track Tony Soter. He and a small group of winemakers who did not earn degrees in enology are having tremendous success. Francis Mahoney at Carneros Creek, Charles Ortman (who spent years in Napa Valley before moving south), and John Stuart at Silverado Vineyards are such winemakers. These men have caused the wine industry to begin asking questions about the value of degrees, and just how a great palate is developed.

Charles Ortman began working for Heitz Winery in 1968, when there were few trained enologists available. He had graduated from the School of Arts and Crafts in Oakland, California. His Chardonnays, made for Spring Mountain winery between 1973 and 1975, were regarded by wine writers as the best on the market. He brought the same attention to Far Niente Chardonnays, which enabled owner Gil Nickel to price them above all others. Unfortunately, Ortman left the valley in the late '80s for the Meridian Winery, at Paso Robles, California.

John Stuart, winemaker and general manager for Silverado Vineyards, graduated from Stanford with a degree in English. He went back to school to pick up science courses, then to UC Davis for a Master's in Food Science. In early 1980 he was hired by the Disneys to run their new wine cellar. The International

Wine and Spirit Competition, which takes place in London, named Stuart "Winemaker of the Year" seven years later, the first American to win the award. His honors and wine medals have piled up at an impressive rate ever since.

There is no denying that university training is important in the winemaking process, but there is more than one path to success in the field. Robert and Peter Mondavi did not take degrees in enology. They grew up in a family whose life was wine. Louis Martini the younger has a B.S. from Davis, a rarity for his generation. Heitz is college trained. Al Brounstein is not.

Andre Tchelistcheff received his training in universities in Russia and France before coming to the United States. He was the first chemist hired by a Napa Valley winery, in 1938. He admits that the wine that won the Grand Sweepstakes award, which Beaulieu picked up in 1939 at the World's Fair on Treasure Island, was made by Joseph Ponti, whose background was in stone masonry and family winemaking. All of Beaulieu's award-winning wines prior to Tchelistcheff's arrival were made by Ponti, with advice from Georges de Latour.

Were the combined talents of Ponti and De Latour, a trained chemist, the explanation for Beaulieu's impressive list of awards from 1935 onward? When Tchelistcheff took over de Latour's duties during his early years, while Ponti was still in charge of wine production, did the wines change significantly? No one has undertaken research to answer such a delicate question. Ponti has been accorded little credit for his work. Brad Webb was one of the rare university-trained chemists in the wine industry as far back as the mid-1940s. He was a partner in Freemark Abbey's restoration in 1967 and has long provided expertise that comes from decades of work in the wine field. Much of the credit for Freemark's fame belongs to Webb.

Unfortunately, the general public is not often aware that the name on a label is not usually that of the person who actually made the wine. Even members of the wine media contribute to the confusion by interviewing winery owners when they should be talking to the winemaker. Winery owners are a very diverse

Anyone driving into the Napa Valley for the first time is awe-struck by the Domaine Carneros winery, sitting alone, elegant, very French, on a small hillock just east of the Sonoma-Napa county border. Taittinger Champagne owns it. Eileen Crane helped design it, and is general manager.

and colorful class of entrepreneurs today, deserving of public attention, but the winemakers are crucial to the quality of wine. Everyone who loves Napa Valley wine should know, at the very least, names like Theo Rosebrand, Bill Dyer, John Richburg, Michael Weis, Rick Forman, Robert Foley, Jack Cole, Chuck Wagner, Ed Sbragia, Nels Venge, and Tom Selfridge.

WOMEN WINEMAKERS

If many male winemakers have been ignored or overlooked by the media, women winemakers have been treated even worse — or at least they were until the past few years. Today some of the top winemakers in the valley are women, and their influence is growing.

Eileen Crane, general manager and winemaker of Domaine Carneros, has graced the cover of one or two wine magazines recently, but in the early 1980s she had difficulty getting wine writers and editors to return her phone calls. Her career began as

EILEEN CRANE

an assistant winemaker at Domaine Chandon. By 1982 she was working with the architects to design the Gloria Ferrer winery in Sonoma County. That is where the Taittingers found her six years later when they came from France to establish a champagne cellar in the Carneros district. Before long she was again sitting at the drawing table with architects, explaining why the bottling room had to be placed here, and the crushing facilities there. Domaine Carneros, a spectacular addition to the southern Napa Valley, had its first crush in 1988.

Eileen Crane's champagnes score in the 90s (on a scale of 1-100) in magazine ratings, proving that she has a superb wine palate, besides being an able administrator in the front office. Her quiet demeanor can be disarming to others in the male-dominated wine business. But in expressing her ideas and opinions on issues in the industry she can be formidable. She refuses, naturally, to argue the question of whether she produces sparkling wine or champagne. The French still insist that true champagne can only come from the Champagne region of France. American courts have held since 1911 that the word "champagne" is legal on the label as long as the geographic region of origin is clearly designated.

Another woman winemaker is Janet Pagano, who makes champagne for Codorniu, the Spanish wine company, on a scenic hillside high above Domaine Carneros and just to the north. The winery opened in 1991. Pagano, after graduating from UC Davis in 1980, began work as an enologist for Domaine Mumm. She had planned a career in medicine, then switched to winemaking. Never in her wildest dreams did she think she might help to plan a champagne cellar, from choosing the location to overseeing construction and planting of the vineyard.

Pagano and Crane may have exchanged ideas on winery construction at meetings of Women For Wine Sense, an organization founded in Napa Valley in 1990, but encompassing the entire state of California. Active members of the group are Michaela Rodenlo, president of St. Suprey Winery; Julie Williams, co-owner of Frog's Leap Winery; Jamie Davies of Schramsberg; and Janet Garvey, co-owner of the Komes Winery. Dozens of women now belong to Women For Wine Sense — including Carolyn Martini, Janet Trefethen, Mary and Beth Novak of Spottswoode, and Heide Peterson Barrett, a consulting enologist. Membership is not limited to winemakers. Lynne Carmichael, a Napa attorney, is president of the group. Margaret Biever, head of cultural affairs for Mondavi, is on the advisory board.

WINE FOR HEALTH

Even more important than the provenance of a wine is the question of the health of the consumer. Is wine a healthy beverage? Mediterranean cultures have long held that wine aids in digestion. One would think that two or three thousand years of wine consumption should be taken seriously. But modern science is making us look again at the health question. Two segments on the CBS Television program "60 Minutes" have claimed that the French suffer far less heart disease than Americans because of their heavier consumption of wine. An ingredient in red wine in particular, phenol, may be responsible for the benefit.

An even more recent study in Denmark reached substantially the same conclusion. In the "Copenhagen City Heart Study," conducted from 1976 to 1988, researchers followed the health of 13,000 men and women between the ages of thirty and seventy years. The study found that the risk of death from heart disease dropped by half among people who drank wine in moderate quantities. What gave this study more credibility is the fact that wine consumption in Denmark jumped substantially after 1976, with the relaxation of import controls associated with the Common Market. Wine was suddenly much cheaper.

Several similar studies conducted in the United States have been attacked by anti-alcohol groups. The Center for Science in the Public Interest, for example, refuses to recognize what other scientists have discovered. Mothers Against Drunk Driving fights tenaciously the entire alcoholic beverage industry, even though wine is rarely involved in drunk driving arrests because it is most often consumed with foods. MADD certainly has worthy goals in trying to keep drunk drivers off the road, but as one physician put it, "Should we outlaw cars because some people drive recklessly?"[26]

The wine industry, as well as other producers of alcoholic beverages, have long pondered what role they should play in the prevention of alcohol abuse. Returning to Prohibition certainly isn't an option: it didn't work. Robert Mondavi organized many of his vintner friends in 1988 to support a "Wine and Food Cultural Fund" to fight any return to Prohibition. "Wine feeds not only the body but the soul and spirit of man," he contends.[27] The Century Council, formed in Los Angeles in 1991 from all segments of the alcohol beverage industry, has a huge budget to target abuse of alcohol. It produces television ads and purchases print advertisements to aid in the fight, particularly among Spanish-speaking segments of the population.

Naturally, the wine industry wants to do what it can to prevent drunk driving, but it also believes our society needs to work on problems involving untrained drivers and unsafe vehicles. The industry realizes also that poverty, social isolation, joblessness, lack of education and drug use frequently go hand-in-hand with alcoholism, and all of these need to be actively addressed. Still, every increase in wine taxes which helps to pay for alcohol abuse programs punishes the industry.

Farm pesticide use is another difficult problem which seems, however, to be close to a solution. Pesticide use is dropping each year, particularly in Napa County. The Santa Rosa *Press Democrat*, a *New York Times*-owned daily, gave front page coverage to a story on the subject on November 26, 1995 with this observation:

> Napa County, which like Sonoma County has about 36,000 acres of vineyards, used about 2.8 million pounds of chemicals, a decrease of about 25 per cent from the year before. Agricultural officials said the decrease indicates the trend toward reduced pesticide usage in Napa Valley vineyards and the decline in vineyard production caused by the phylloxera root louse.

The chemicals discussed in this article include the two most widely used — sulfur and methyl bromide. Sulfur has been used for centuries in all of Europe as the best protection against mildew. Without sulfur on the vines during the summer, especially when the summer is cool and moist, grapes would rot long before they could mature for picking. Sulfur is approved for use in organic farming, and although only about 19% of the 76,000 vineyard acres in the North Coast follow organic farming procedures, more and more farmers are choosing to do so. One of the largest of these is the E&J Gallo vineyards in Dry Creek, Sonoma County.

In Napa County, the Hess Collection Vineyards have followed modified organic farming procedures for years. In some vineyards, the soil is not tilled. Rather, the groundcover is allowed to grow so that insects will survive which thrive on eating vineyard pests. Insects which are beneficial to vines have actually been introduced when they are not naturally present.

In some vineyards methyl bromide is injected into the soil before planting, to kill an oak tree fungus and other enemies of a young vine. Some vineyards would never recover the cost of planting if methyl bromide were not used, because production would be so low. The chemical is not used after vines are planted. But after the year 2001, methyl bromide use will be banned because it is believed to contribute to the depletion of the ozone layer around the earth. California's State Office of Drinking Water tested 450 water wells in Napa County as recently as 1993 and thankfully found no evidence of pesticide contamination.

American health consciousness has played an important role in ridding agriculture of chemicals that are harmful to the environment or people. Grape growers are farther ahead in this matter than their counterparts in other segments of farming, not least because most of the people who own vineyards live in houses where vines are only a few yards from their front doors.

To many of the long-time residents of Napa Valley the biggest worry is not farm chemicals, labor problems, or even the abuse of alcohol, but how to handle the growing influx of visitors. Tourists love Napa Valley; they clog the roads from early spring to late fall. The San Francisco *Examiner* carried a story on tourism in Napa Valley back in January 1990, with a graph projecting over two million visitors by the year 2000. Just three years later the Napa Valley Conference and Tourists Bureau claimed over four million visitors. The figure will likely reach five million in 1998. Wine sales have been soaring, in part because so many visitors leave with at least one bottle of Napa wine. The Napa Valley Vintner's Association did a survey of members in 1994 and found sales had jumped 18% over the previous year. There is no reason to believe sales will decline.

The wine stories on CBS Television's "60 Minutes" have helped wine sales enormously, because they document the healthfulness of drinking wine on a regular basis. Documentaries like "Secrets of the Wine Country," shown during September

1995 on PBS, show clearly that no place on earth has quite the attractive qualities of Napa Valley. Colorful layouts in magazines every few months do the same thing.

Jon Fredrikson tracks wine sales annually for his San Francisco-based Gomberg, Fredrikson & Associates. He says that while sales of wine nationally were down for the period just prior to 1990, premium wine sales rose 14 per cent. "This is really a premium table wine revolution. Napa Valley wines continued to enjoy solid growth in the 1990s, with a $1.1 billion growth rate in only ten years," said Fredrikson.[28] It is easy to see why the economy of Napa County is booming.

Much of Napa's wine doesn't leave the State of California. Per capita, Californians drink about twice the national average. An estimate in 1990 claimed 2,516,000 people moved to the state in the prior decade. Wine is part of the good life here, and many newcomers quickly adopt the ritual of dining with wine. One winery tourists can't visit is the magnificent Opus One, almost directly across the highway from the Robert Mondavi winery at Oakville. There are no public tours. Still, that doesn't keep the winery from selling out each year. Visitors can taste the wine at $10 a glass at the Mondavi winery, or they can pay $55 to $75 for a bottle at retail shops. Opus One is one reason Napa Valley wines stand out above all the competition. The total cost of the winery is estimated to have been $26 million, with an additional $3 million now being spent to replant vineyards damaged by phylloxera. Because only 30,000 cases of Opus One wine are produced annually, it may take a half century to pay off the debt. None of this really bothers Robert Mondavi or his family, or the French Rothschilds, their partners. If a cork is popped at Opus One, someone from the media is there to cover the story. More flattering words have been used to describe Opus One wines than just about any other label, and in only a few short years of existence.

All of this suggests there is something magical about Napa Valley, something that sets it apart from other wine regions. Vineyards stretch nearly unbroken for the entire length and most of the breadth of the valley. Wineries are everywhere — some architectural masterpieces, others curiosities simply meant to draw attention.

If L. Frank Baum were alive to write another sequel to his Wizard of Oz books, he could easily set it in the Napa Valley. Dorothy could visit a real castle — the Beringer house — take an aerial tram ride to Sterling Vineyards, pause next door to gaze at the Greco-Roman Clos Pegase, walk the original wine tunnels dug by the Chinese at Schramsberg, or stand before the Acacia winery with the rippling waters of San Francisco Bay almost at her feet.

CHAPTER TWELVE

EPILOGUE

S preading across Napa Valley's vineyard landscape each spring is a weed whose blossoms send photographers into states of ecstasy. When the wild mustard is in full bloom, any time in March, the low rolling hills of the valley are covered with a brilliant yellow. It grows only on cultivated ground, extending as far as the eye can see. This weed can reach heights of four to five feet leaving many vines, still dormant from the winter, lost in its lush foliage.

Wild mustard is similar to what many epicures delight in eating as mustard greens, but it has a different parentage. Commercial mustard greens are cultivated for the dinner table. Napa Valley's mustard, *Brassica rapa*, is officially classed as a weed. It just grows and multiplies, vying for the attention of tourists with the California poppy, which prefers the more hostile environment of hills or roadsides.

Brassica rapa is believed to have arrived in California about the time of the Gold Rush of 1849. Ann Howald, of the California Exotic Pest Plant Council, says field mustard (as differentiated from the edible kind) arrived first in San Francisco and then spread outward. It may have come in the soil used as ballast in sailing ships.

Ed Webber, University of California Extension agent in Napa County, says mustard helps to prevent soil erosion on hillsides during heavy rains. It also sends down a deep tap root which breaks up and loosens soil for the roots of young vines. It does not provide nitrogen or have any food value for the grape vine, and some growers would prefer not seeing its bright yellow each spring.

"Field mustard has one natural advantage over all the other vineyard weeds," says Webber. "It blossoms early, so that the seeds are spread before the vineyard is cultivated. Discing kills many weeds, but the mustard seed just enjoys being bumped about by the discing and sprouts early the following spring." Mustard seed can remain dormant in the soil for years, awaiting an opportune time to sprout.

There is no native California mustard of the *Brassica* family, but a domestic variety easily spreads out of a garden into surrounding soils. A memorable dinner, served at the old home of Jack London by his grand-nephew Milo Shepard, included local wild mustard greens. They have a very sharp taste.

ANDREW BECKSTOFFER - MASTER GROWER

Environment is critical to the grape vine, a lesson which farmers in Napa Valley have only begun to learn in recent years. For the past century, grapes have been grown just about anywhere in the valley, with little or no regard to temperatures, soils or elevation, on hillside or valley floor.

It is now well understood, for example, that the southern or Carneros region of the valley is significantly cooler than up valley because it lies close to San Francisco Bay. The Pinot Noir grape flourishes here. Heat reflected off Mt. St. Helena makes Calistoga significantly warmer; Pinot does not do so well there. The valley floor is warmer than the higher hillsides, which are cooled by breezes from the bay or ocean. Vintners are still learning about these climatic differences, and adapting their vineyards accordingly.

For these reasons and others, the next two decades will witness a near revolution in viticulture practices. Each year technology brings major advances in the field of wine production. Yet many believe that Napa wines cannot be further improved, since they are already world class. The best certainly rate that distinction.

Andrew W. Beckstoffer has taken a major role in bringing about change in vine cultivation. When he first came to the valley at age 28, he had his sights set on a corporate post with Heublein, Inc., of Hartford, Connecticut. A native Virginian with an MBA from Dartmouth, he had never even walked through a vineyard previously. Sent to California by Heublein to scout possible investments in winemaking, he returned to Hartford with some exciting ideas. He told Heublein to buy Inglenook and United Vintners. A short time later, when Beaulieu came on the market, he helped negotiate the sale.

As Beaulieu and Inglenook expanded production, Beckstoffer discovered that Napa growers could not fill the need for fine wine grapes. He started a farming company to buy land, plant Cabernet or Chardonnay grapes, and attract investors who would bear the cost instead of Heublein. When Heublein decided to divest itself of the farming company, as previously planned, Beckstoffer somewhat hesitantly took it over. His dream of a corporate position at Heublein was derailed.

The typical Napa Valley grower-farmer at the time was born to the profession. Vineyard dust had sifted through windows to cover his baby crib. Few growers had considered any other calling. Beckstoffer was a newcomer, and he knew it. He had to convince the great Andre Tchelistcheff (retained by Heublein) to share his knowledge of grape culture. Beckstoffer arose at 4 a.m. when frost threatened the vines, lit the smoke pots, and sipped hot brandy with the field hands when the job was done.

That was during the 1970s. Beckstoffer is now the owner of more vineyard acreage than any other individual in the valley. None of his land is on hillsides. Why not? "It has never made sense to me. Why go up there and buy forty acres and get six for

ANDREW BECKSTOFFER

grapes? What we find is that grapes grown on well-drained valley soils are the grapes on which the Napa Valley reputation has been made, forever."[1]

Microclimates for the growing of grapes became an obsession with the ex-scout for Heublein. Tchelistcheff, his mentor, was a major influence. Beckstoffer discovered that vines would grow well in the Carneros, but only with water during the growing season. This would not be irrigation in the traditional way, with open ditches; the water, piped through miles of small black hoses, dripped slowly down to the roots of the vines.

Irrigation had always been anathema to Napa grape growers. Beckstoffer, with his highly trained professional staff, has changed all that. "The idea that irrigation is bad is totally debunked now. We know that the proper time and the amount of water are crucial."

"We put in the first drip irrigation in Napa County in 1971," Beckstoffer says. "In 1970 we spaced vines six feet apart, with ten feet between rows. The old spacing was 8 x 12. By 1974 we were experimenting with trellising."

The Cabernet Sauvignon grape is a Beckstoffer obsession. He recalls a company seminar in 1988:

> It is from this meeting that we moved into the new age in viticulture. We did not want the same old University-of-California-Davis Clone #7, which has been planted for 20 years. We replanted Beaulieu Vineyard #3 to what is called Clone #4. It is disease free, but a non-heat-treated clone of Cabernet from Argentina. It was discarded back in the '60s because its yield was low.

He also brought Clone #6 from the old University of California Field Station, in Jackson, in the Sierras. He has not stopped his search for new grape clones. For that matter neither have any of the other major grape growers. The most successful growers now tramp the vineyards of Europe, searching for a clone which will top everyone else's.

"We are not selling an agricultural commodity, we are trying to sell a specialty product," Beckstoffer claims. "What I want to sell is Beckstoffer Vineyards, Napa Valley Cabernet Sauvignon grapes! *Terroir;* distinction, not just grapes." (*Terroir* is a term new to the valley, meaning the overall character of a vineyard, which contributes to the quality of the fruit.)

THE HESS COLLECTION VINEYARD

Donald Hess disagrees with Beckstoffer about the value of hillsides for vines. Being a native of Switzerland may account for his attraction to the Napa Redwoods and Mt. Veeder when he began buying vineyards in the 1980s. He now owns 900 acres on the southern flank of Mt. Veeder. Instead of building a winery on the valley floor, he chose to lease the historic Christian Brothers winery in the Redwoods, far off the beaten path for most valley tourists. Some people regard him as eccentric, in a flattering sense of the word. Many of his new releases are in the $20 range. Clem Firko, president of Hess Collection Wines, explains why:

DONALD HESS

"Donald wants wines that the public can afford to buy. He is not after some niche in the upper stratum of the wine world. Our Hess Select wines are specifically targeted for the wine mainstream."

Hess, one of the largest bottled-water purveyors in Europe, has vast resources. That has no bearing, however, on the price of a Hess wine. The Napa company is completely self-supporting, according to Firko. In 1997, Hess Collection purchased 500 acres of ranch land in Pope Valley for vineyards. The company owns 50 acres in Napa Valley's Jameson Canyon, and also has 350 acres in vines in Monterey County. "We did not ask Donald for a dime; we borrowed from a bank to finance it all. Our credit is good."

Firko, formerly a wine distribor in Colorado, has been at the helm of Hess Collection since 1990. He has adopted Donald Hess's casual approach to dress (Hess dislikes the stuffiness of

STEPHANIE PUTNAM

European business etiquette) by wearing monogrammed Hess
Collection sport shirts at work. He oversees every department at
the winery, with a wary eye always on the budget. The company
has made a profit each year since he joined it.

Stephanie Putnam, of the Hess Collection Vineyard, is one of
the growing list of women winemakers in the Napa Valley. She
joined the staff at Hess in 1991, after graduating from UC Davis.
She became assistant winemaker in 1994, and in 1997 was pro-
moted to chief winemaker.

Much of Hess's private collection of European and American
art work is housed in a new museum on the grounds of the winery. No other American winery can boast of such an attraction.
There is no contemporary art collection anywhere near this size
north of San Francisco.

But art has nothing to do with the operation of the Hess winery. There is no attempt to promote the Hess art museum through

the winery; they are distinct and separate entities. A tasting may be held in the gallery, but the wine is the attraction, not the art.

Hess did not collect modern art with the idea of helping to sell his wine. When he sees a painting or a sculpture, he takes his time making up his mind. He buys only the work of living artists, and doesn't stop with one or two pieces; he may purchase half a dozen.

Many visitors are struck by the paintings by Franz Gertsch in the gallery. Most are huge, upper-body portraits, eight feet high, so real they look like photographs. The eyes follow the viewer about the room. Robert Motherwell's painting "Open No. 88" is five feet wide, an almost solid blue surface with a lighter blue mid-section. No trees, no human figure, no landscape, yet it is a landscape for the mind to penetrate. "What does this painting mean? That is essentially unanswerable," Motherwell has said.

Hess needs no explanation for what he sees:

> I rely on my own eyes, on my own intuition. The work must awaken a profound response in me. It is very important for me to have a personal relationship with the artist. I love sharing my passion for art.

Hess relates fine art to fine wine, as some people do with fine food; the one enhances the enjoyment of the other. At the Hess winery this special experience may be fully realized, because the art goes far beyond a few paintings on a tasting room wall. There is a message here. A few minutes of silence and it all becomes abundantly clear. The world is a far better place because of the vision of an artist, whether he paints with a brush or makes wine.

THE ROBERT MONDAVI TOUCH

Robert Mondavi, and especially his wife Margrit, share Hess's attitude toward art, and they extend it to music as well. Sculpture is scattered about the grounds of the Robert Mondavi winery, and there are fine art works inside. Margrit is a principal supporter of the Napa Symphony.

ROBERT MONDAVI

Kay Ryman of Calistoga claims the first concerts on the grounds of a Napa winery began in 1964 at the Charles Krug winery. While the idea was hers, Robert Mondavi provided much of the enthusiasm, as well as the funding. Regular "August Moon Concerts" became a part of Krug's promotion two years later, and the concept quickly spread to other wineries throughout California.[2]

Robert is staying far ahead of everyone else, though, by proposing the "American Center for Wine, Food and the Arts" in downtown Napa. He tossed in a cool $3 million to get the project started; it will ultimately cost $45 million. Ground breaking is set for the summer of 1999.

Mondavi, of course, has long touted the idea that the good life includes wine with food, and that wine should be a part of the daily life of the average American. The new complex will include a master kitchen for the training of chefs, as well as a restaurant for the public to sample their cuisine; after lunch they

MICHAEL MONDAVI

can tour an art gallery. There will also be a performing arts center. Napa has long needed such an attraction for tourists and locals alike.

Mondavi may have had something to do with the mission statement for the proposed center; it will be "a cultural institution, museum and educational center dedicated to exploring the distinctively American contribution to the character of food and wine in close association with the arts and humanities."

Having passed his 85th birthday, Robert Mondavi can afford to sit back and ponder philosophical statements like the above. He has wisely turned over the operation of the winery to his two sons and daughter: Michael (president), Tim, and Marcia Mondavi Borger. Over 100 employees work at the central office, in an industrial complex south of Napa. Robert and Margrit still maintain offices at the original winery at Oakville.

The Robert Mondavi winery is now so vast it has affiliates spread across the globe. In 1997 it announced a merger with the Eduardo Chadwick family of Chile in a venture to produce ultra-

428

TIM MONDAVI

premium wines, retailing at $50 a bottle. The Vichon label, owned since 1980, has been taken to southern France, in the Languedoc-Roussilon region. The wines produced there will be shipped back to Napa Valley for finishing.

A co-venture in Italy with the Frescobaldi family began with a Sangiovese-Merlot blend. Opus One wine, made with the Rothschilds of France, is already well known. In Santa Maria County, 640 acres developed by Ken Brown are now owned by Mondavi. To this can be added the Woodbridge winery, which produces 4.8 million cases annually. The Mondavis readily admit that the profits from Woodbridge have financed many of their investments elsewhere. Their wines are relatively inexpensive but of exceptionally high quality, in the Mondavi tradition.

All of this change at Mondavi has altered forever the marketing of wine. Robert Mondavi was once the most approachable person in the Napa Valley. He usually made decisions at his desk at Oakville, instantly. Now the corporate structure makes seeing Michael very difficult.

PETER MONDAVI, JR.

PETER MONDAVI AND THE KRUG VINEYARD

Peter Mondavi is a year and five months younger than his brother Robert. He still has not turned over the operation of the historic Krug cellar to his two sons, Marc and Peter, Jr. Marc is president of the company, but the changes that perhaps are long overdue, and would come with a younger generation, seem to be mostly daydreams.

But a few major changes have been made in bottle labels, for example. A recent label has a dark green background with the name "Mondavi" printed boldly in the center, the omni-present "CK" emblem but a whisper near the top. It is one of the handsomest wine labels in the nation. Some of the old standard wines at Krug have been pushed aside in favor or more modern wines. Chenin Blanc bit the dust in the fall of 1997.

The hesitancy on the part of Peter, Sr., is understandable to anyone who has followed the Krug story since the breakup in the

MARC MONDAVI

Mondavi family in 1966. Peter assumed enormous debt to buy out his brother's interest and that of one sister. Not wanting to be left behind while the wine boom of the '70s and '80s roared on, Peter took on more debt to expand the winery. While those dark days of financial uncertainty have mostly been left behind, they can't be forgotten.

"We are at a major turning point," said marketing director Larry Challacombe, just before abandoning Krug in January, 1998. "We are going in the right direction, profits of recent years prove that. We've adopted new packaging, new wine varietals, but are we moving fast enough to keep pace with the industry? We need a family vision to bring this all together," he added, somewhat wistfully.

Challacombe agrees with Peter, Jr., that a wine boutique concept is badly needed to upgrade the Krug and CK Mondavi lines. Peter, Jr. would like to renovate the historic Krug cellar (now nearly abandoned) to produce such wines. It could house badly needed office space and provide tours in a structure that is one of

With an amphitheater next to the Napa River seating 300 persons, the American Center for Wine, Food and the Arts is scheduled to open in downtown Napa in 2001. In part the brainchild of Robert Mondavi, its goal is to explore the American contribution to the character of wine and food, while celebrating the arts.

the oldest winery buildings in the valley as well as in California. It reeks with age, but not in the olfactory sense. Wines are still aged on the bottom floor. The nose there is well-treated.

Challacombe wisely thought to utilize the winery's history in future marketing and had great ideas before deciding to leave. While the history under founder Charles Krug is important, the more modern chapters contain gems as precious as emeralds and diamonds. *Life* magazine in 1954 named the Krug Traminer "the best white wine in America." In 1981, the *Wine Spectator* named Krug's Cabernet Sauvignon the best in California. Steve Heimoff, writing in April 1996 in the *Wine Enthusiast,* called Krug's Cabernet "California's most classic Cabernet Sauvignon."

At the luncheon served by Vice President Richard Nixon for the visiting Queen of England and Prince Phillip in 1958, the wine was Krug's Cabernet Sauvignon, 1951. In those years, the media did not jump on wine stories, unlike 1972, when President

Nixon took Schramsberg champagne to China. By then the wine boom was in full flower.

What saddens the heart most, at least for anyone who loves wine history, is the neglect of the archives at the Krug winery. None of this history predates 1943, when the Mondavis purchased Krug, but on the third floor of the old cellar are boxes piled on boxes of every weight slip, every invoice, every employee time card, and copies of every letter signed by Cesare, Robert or Peter Mondavi. The *Life* magazine cited above was recently found lying in dust in a corner.

No wine cellar in California has preserved its history in such detail. Time cards or weight slips might seem ephemeral, but not to some future historian in the year 2020. Peter gave strict orders that this all be preserved, and he deserves the credit. But Providence may not protect these records much longer.

Mystery at the Old Far Niente Vineyard

Providence unfortunately did not do so well in preserving bottles of Far Niente wine with an original label. Owner Gil Nickel has been looking for such a label ever since he purchased the property in 1976. He assumed he would merely reproduce an old historic label for his own wine.

Years of detective work by historians failed to turn up an original label, but one finally came to light quite by accident in March 1998. A bottle of Far Niente "Sweet Muscat" wine had been preserved in a Marin county wine cellar, and the elderly owner called a relative to come and select any wines he might wish. The relative was a friend of Nickel and knew of the search.

Even more intriguing, the label may have been designed by one of America's foremost artists, Winslow Homer. This aspect came to light in the summer of 1986 when Eric Rudd of Falmouth, Mass., visited Napa Valley. He was working on a book about Homer's life and wanted more detail on his uncle's life in California. Homer's uncle was John Benson.

Rudd's search was greeted with some incredulity at first. Benson's background had been thoroughly researched when Nickel purchased the winery. Benson had been a founding patron of the San Francisco Art Association (then housed in the Hopkins mansion, at the site of today's Mark Hopkins hotel) but there was no other connection. On his death, Benson left his estate and winery to nieces who were cousins of Winslow Homer.

There would still have been little to link the two men except that Rudd saw a photograph, taken inside Far Niente, of a table with glasses and a bottle of Far Niente wine. A calendar on the wall was for the year 1910. Rudd could just barely make out a portion of the wine label, enough to clearly see a hammock. That was a trademark of early Homer commercial art work. Could it be that Winslow Homer designed the label? Having seen photographs of the newly discovered label, Rudd now firmly believes it was designed by Homer. Very likely it is the only wine label in America drawn by the artist, who incidentally died the same year as Benson. Additionally, the bottle of wine has a neck label with the year 1886. No bottle of Napa Valley wine is known to predate this recent find. It may even be drinkable, since the wine is a "Sweet Muscat" and could age gracefully all those years. There is no ullage, or it was topped off and recorked at some point.

A MYSTERIOUS FLAVOR

Another Napa Valley mystery, just a stone's throw from the Benson winery, apparently defies solving. Do the eucalyptus trees bordering Martha's Vineyard add that special flavor which makes the wines Joe Heitz produces exceptional? Martha's Vineyard Cabernet Sauvignon sells in the range of $65 to $80 a bottle, one of the most expensive wines in California.

Martha's Vineyard was begun in the early 1960s by Dr. Bernard Rhodes, with bud-wood from the nearby University of Califoria Experimental Vineyard. Tom and Martha May purchased the property in 1963 and immediately began expanding the vine-yards. May recalls the first real harvest came two years later, but Heitz did not like the quality, so 1966 was the first year for a bot-tled wine from the vineyard. It was released in 1971.

Rhodes begins this story by recalling that Andre Tchelistcheff told him, when he began planting, that the grapes would have a "minty" taste since there was a row of eucalyptus trees nearby. It was the same situation as at a small Buena Vista vineyard where he was a consultant. Andre was sure the Rhodes grapes would carry the same taste.

Rhodes forgot this advice until Heitz one day asked him to barrel-sample three Cabernets. Heitz believed the mint taste is a characteristic of all Cabernets, and this does seem to be true, Rhodes adds.

Some years later, Rhodes told this story to Tim Mondavi, who sat bolt upright in his chair. "Come to our winery tomorrow. I want you to sample some of our Cabs," Tim said. "He lined up a number of glasses of wine for me to taste. The mint flavor was very strong in the first and became progressively weaker until the last glass was tried."[3]

Tim explained the grapes for the wine came from a Mondavi vineyard directly across a small stream from Martha's Vineyard and on the other side of the eucalyptus trees. He had the grape pickers select lugs of grapes from close to the trees, then at some distance, and spaced out regularly as far as the main road. He kept the wine separate for each lot. Rhodes recalls that the mint taste was strongest in the lot nearest the trees, and that it declined dramatically by time the last lot was sampled.

Tim Mondavi believes the eucalyptus flavor reaches the grapes through the soil, especially if the eucalyptus trees are of great age. If it is a natural flavor in Cabernet, as Heitz believes, it may be lost through blending. Martha's Vineyard Cabernets are not blends.

This anecdote does not explain why the Mays' Cabernets are among the finest in California. Heitz would suggest that his winemaking just might be the major factor. Rene di Rosa's theory is that if you keep exceptional grapes separate and don't blend them with average grapes, you will produce exceptional wine.

May has less than fifty acres in grapes, nearly all Cabernet. Some of Mondavi's exceptional Cabernet Sauvignon comes from a nearby vineyard but hardly all of it. Inglenook produced extremely fine wines from vineyards having the same position in relationship to the western hills. The same was true of some Beaulieu Cabernets. Warren Winiarski's Stags Leap Cabernets, equally highly regarded, come from the other side of the valley. What accounts for the high quality of wines from these small, separate locations?

One thing is certain, Tom and Martha May do little to enhance the image of their wines. They both shun publicity. The drive to their rural chateau is purposely left as a gravel road which appears rarely used. From 1993 through 1995 there was little travel on the road. All of the vineyard was replanted because of the phylloxera, and so was out of production.

Yet Tom May is the most jovial person in the valley, and Martha is a supreme hostess. Perhaps that is a part of the explanation for their high quality Cabernets — Tom treats his vines like children. He is never cross, always understanding, smiling as he wanders down row after row of vines. His smile may, of course, come from thoughts of the next vintage and of what he will earn from those grapes.

DAGMAR DE LATOUR SULLIVAN

Napa Valley is filled with characters — that is, people with real character, in the best sense of the word. Dagmar de Latour Sullivan is one of these. She was born into the wealthy, socially prestigious de Latour family. Her father was a French count of the old school; he still owned the family's French estate. She owns what is left of the de Latour estate, which once included the Beaulieu winery and extensive vineyards.

Dagmar Sullivan prefers not to live in the sprawling de Latour home built in 1912. Her mother and grandmother entertained lavishly in the house: literati, opera singers, journalists, senators, admirals, archbishops and entrepreneurs were their guests. She lives in a small cottage on the estate with only a secretary for company during the day. She prefers country life, spending part of the year in Toulouse, in southwestern France.

Most of the Beaulieu estate is gone now, sold in 1969 to Heublein. Dagmar still owns Beaulieu Vineyard #1, all planted to Cabernet Sauvignon grapes. Her prayer is that her children will keep what is left of the estate in the family, and of course the French chateau — all or mostly planted to wheat and grain crops, no grapes. Her children are Paula Sullivan Escher, Walter H. Sullivan III, Erica S. Sullivan Fuller and Dagmar Sullivan II.

Dagmar Sullivan is quite unpretentious. What a contrast to her mother and grandmother, who were grande dames of San Francisco society. They were frequently pictured wearing large white hats and gloves, dressed always for the noble occasion, including high heeled shoes. This is not Dagmar's style. At times, she could be mistaken for the family cook.

Like the Mays, she shuns publicity. A locked gate thwarts unwanted company. Dagmar feels she does not need to prove the quality of the grapes she sells, or even to publicize Napa Valley. Her family has been doing that for nearly a century. The de Latour name alone is still worth a small fortune.

THE RAYMOND FAMILY

Roy Raymond, Jr., and Walter Raymond, are always quick to point out that when they were teen-agers, winemaking had little romance to it. Hard work was routine, with meager rewards, even though their father had married into a distinguished early winemaking family. Jacob Beringer went to work for Charles Krug in 1870, almost 130 years ago. The boys' mother, Martha Jane Raymond, was a granddaughter of Jacob Beringer, who founded the Beringer winery. Roy, Jr., and Walter are great grandsons of that distinguished gentleman. Like the de Latours, the Raymond family has such a rich history they have no need to seek publicity. The Raymond name itself has a wine lineage of 65 years.

In 1933 a very youthful Roy Raymond, Sr., went to work for the Beringer winery and eventually married into the family. No one still active in winemaking in the valley has that kind of longevity. Today the elder Raymond readily admits that he skips the hard work around the winery; he likes to drive a small tractor, pulling a plow to weed the vines. The Raymonds still conduct their business with a personal familiarity that was once typical of the whole valley.

Roy, Sr., asked a few years ago about newspaper predictions of a poor grape crop, said, "I pay little heed to newspaper stories about the poor crop. After we have a big crop, we can expect the grapes to produce less. This happens every fourth or fifth year; the vines get tired. It doesn't have so much to do with weather or rain, but it goes in cycles. This is not very scientific; I just note it." His observation comes from six decades in the industry.

A visitor to Roy, Jr.'s office one day overheard one end of a telephone call from someone looking for a wine sales job. Roy, Jr., listened intently to the qualifications for several minutes and then said: "We don't have anything right now, but keep calling every few weeks. It never hurts to phone repeatedly and ask." How many job seekers get that kind of response on the first call?

Since Raymond wines often earn ratings in the 90s (on a scale of 1 to 100) in tastings held by wine publications, they are among the valley's elite labels. When the Raymonds released their first bottle of Meritage, made in 1989, the bidding at the Napa Valley wine auction drove up the price in minutes to $2,600, and the successful bidder admitted never having tasted the wine. He bid only on the basis of the maker. Chardonnay, Cabernet, Merlot and Pinot Noir are the four principal wines by Raymond.

If there is any question as to why winemaking is so attractive, and why the Raymonds have stuck with this profession despite some very difficult years financially, Roy, Jr., knows the answer. In the spring of 1993 he was asked to write a piece for the winery quarterly newsletter. He decided to describe what he sees out his executive office window:

I look north up the valley. It's a wonderful spring day. The sun is shining and the Chardonnay vines are just starting to bud. The Cabernet is still sleeping, but will also come to life again within the next few days. Mt. St. Helena in the distance and the surrounding hills are emerald green from this year's ample rainfall. What a beautiful picture — I marvel at it each day and never tire of it. I see many beautiful places in my travels around the country while representing our winery but none ever compares to this Napa Valley.

He also mentions seeing his son Craig driving a tractor through the rows of vines, and knowing a third generation is already preparing for a turn at the helm. The Raymond family is close, all three generations. Is family tradition critical to the success of the Raymond winery and the quality of its wine? It surely seems to help, especially if all the family members love what they do for a living.

A NEW PHYLLOXERA SCOURGE

The second week of February 1986 brought disastrously heavy rain to Napa Valley. Rainfall during that week varied from 22 to 30 inches — close to the total for an average year. Dormant vines are not hurt by the water, but the flood waters spread the eggs of the phylloxera vine louse throughout the valley. Roy Raymond, Jr. was one of the first to realize, a year later, that the phylloxera showing up in so many vineyards, including his own, had come with the cold rushing waters.

Napa County has about 35,000 acres in wine grapes. During the past ten years, many of Napa Valley's vines have unceremoniously been pulled out, even the clones gathered in Europe or at an old Sierra field station. Not all vineyards suffered from the disease at the same pace. Vines on a phylloxera-resistant root stock called AXR-1 had to be replanted. Surprisingly, vineyards growing on the old standard resistant rootstock, Rupestris St. George, survived; Peter Mondavi had planted a significant portion of the Krug vines on the St. George. Ed Webber, of the University of California Extension Service, agrees with

Raymond, that the'86 flood was to blame for distributing the onerous plant louse. He estimates that as of last year, sixty per cent of the replanting has been completed. The cost of replanting an acre is not cheap. Growers must spend $12,000 to $15,000 an acre to replant. A forty- to fifty-acre vineyard would cost about a half million dollars to replant.

AXR-l has been the choice of most vineyard planting in the past four or five decades because the vine reaches full maturity faster. No one is rushing back to the St. George, however; most prefer to try several new resistant rootstocks. A dramatic shift has occurred in varieties of grapes being planted as phylloxera destroyed old vines. About two thirds of the replantings, as well as new plantings in Napa and Sonoma Counties, are Cabernet Sauvignon, Chardonnay or Merlot. These grapes often bring prices above $2,000 a ton, twice the prices paid for many older varieties.

AXR-l rootstock did not actually fail as a phylloxera-resistant vine, but rather the phylloxera evolved into a new, hardier strain. "Type B phylloxera" was first identified in a Napa Valley vineyard in 1983, three years before the flood.

RUDY VON STRASSER AND DIAMOND MOUNTAIN VINEYARD

The microscopic vine louse has not spread nearly as rapidly on the valley's hillsides as on the valley floor, lending credence to the theory that the '86 flood was a major factor in its spread. Grapes grown in the valley's newest appellation, "Diamond Mountain," seem hardly disturbed by the disease. Rudy von Strasser says most of his vines are on AXR-l rootstock, but he sees little or no evidence of phylloxera. Some of his vines were planted as far back as 1970.

Rudy and his wife Rita have been in the Diamond Mountain location since 1990, when they purchased the Bill Roddis vines and winery. Von Strasser is the energy and driving force behind the prospective Diamond Mountain appellation. Many residents of Napa Valley have never heard of Diamond Mountain, either

RUDY VON STRASSER

as a topographical feature on a map or as a winemaking region. Al Brounstein's great wines have helped earn the area some notoriety, but he is so modest that only avid wine collectors know of his Diamond Creek brand.

Diamond Mountain is located just one mile south of Calistoga in the western hills. The peak itself is mostly in Sonoma County but the eastern flank lies in Napa Valley. There was a Diamond Mountain school as far back as 1904, but it took a major fire to put the region on the map. "First Forest Fire of The Season," headlined the *Calistogan* on August 24th, 1950. The fire burnt over from Sharp's Road to various farms on Diamond Mountain Road.

Major vineyards on this road go back more than a century. Richard Schmidt planted his first vines circa 1883, and built a stone and wood wine cellar in 1888. He had 65 acres in grapes up near the county line. Adele Furniss built a winery a mile below in 1890. In 1910 a very famous Calistoga resident, Jacques Pacheteau, constructed his cellar nearby. Pacheteau Springs was

CAROLYN MARTINI

a very well-known hot water spa from the turn of the century to World War II. Pacheteau bought and sold Napa Valley wine in that city up until Prohibition. He was French, of course, and apparently liked the quality of grapes grown on the Diamond Mountain hillsides.

Rudy Von Strasser was born in New York. His father, who had fled the Nazis in Austria during World War II, worked in the stock market and was a correspondent for an Austrian newspaper. He has since become a recognized expert in antique glass. Rudy had no desire to follow in his father's footsteps. He liked agriculture. He tried raising apples in Vermont. On a whim, he came to Napa Valley in 1981 to work at the Robert Mondavi winery. Once here, he was smitten with the valley; he shifted gears and went for a degree in Fermentation Sciences at the University of California, Davis.

For the following six years, Rudy worked at one wine cellar after another: France's Chateau Lafitte Rothschild as an intern in 1986, two years with Trefethen Vineyards, and three years at

Newton Vineyards. In May 1990 he bought the Bill Roddis wine cellar and vineyards on Diamond Mountain road.

It is curious that a newcomer to Diamond Mountain Road should be the person to bring together a viticultural focus on the area. The historical background Rudy Von Strasser needed for an appellation clearly shows a long tradition of raising grapes and making wine, although both were on a small scale. The appellation will extend to Schramsberg winery, in part because Ritchie Creek is the northern boundary of the Spring Mountain appellation, and in part because Schramsberg was called "Diamond Mountain Cellars" in the 1930s and 1940s.

Rudy Von Strasser is a dynamo of energy. He likes his business dealings to be frank and direct. If he takes time off for pleasure, he goes hunting or fishing. He has the only fly-fishing wine label in the country, Freestone. He commissions an artist each year to paint a different fishing fly for the centerpiece of the label.

Most interviews about wine are with men, who consequently receive most of the attention in published accounts of winemaking. This is true of the interviews for this book, as well. Rita Von Strasser is in some ways a typical wife of a winemaker, absolutely vital to the winery's operation.

Rita runs the office. She knows what wine has been shipped, how much is in storage, what bills need paying, what BATF records require completion and by what deadline. She handles the minutiae associated with wine production, than which no agricultural pursuit requires more precise records. There is a government form to be filled out nearly every day.

Some sort of professional title is needed which would not only describe the work but honor the woman who is the right hand of the winemaker. Such women have been ignored too long. Rita probably knows more about the day-to-day operation of the Von Strasser Winery than Rudy does. He concerns himself with priorities of the moment.

This epilogue is about people, places and events (and wild mustard), and only occasionally about wines per se. But one wine has a truly unique history: Louis Martini's Moscato

Amabile. If any wine might deserve the title "Elixir of Life," it would be this one. It travels so poorly, however, that it can be purchased only at the winery; the demand is such that there is a waiting list.

The name Moscato Amabile gives a hint of its origins. Made from the muscat grape, it is sweet, to be consumed only when chilled. Louis Martini, Sr., claimed several barrels of the wine were once stacked in the back of his winery and forgotten until spring. He tasted the wine only to find it had a slight sparkling effect, like champagne. It took some time to duplicate the process, but the winery produces it yearly.

Many winemakers now duplicate or try to produce a wine something like Moscato Amabile. Christian Brothers brought out Chateau La Salle in the 1950s and it became one of the winery's all-time best sellers. Because it is not a dry wine, in the sense of a Cabernet Sauvignon or Chardonnay, wine snobs often turn up their noses at it. Yet it is not a sweet wine, like Sherry or Port.

Louis P. Martini long ago took over the operation of the Martini winery, but his oldest child, Carolyn, is now president. Louis died in September 1998, shortly before his 80th birthday. His son, Michael, is vice president in charge of production and chief winemaker.

Those involved in the making of wine never quite give it all up. Until his death Louis Martini attended Wine Institute meetings, winemaker dinners and the annual Wine Auctions. "The transition to my taking over his duties went smoothly" observed Carolyn. "My father was far easier to get along with than my grandfather." Louis, Sr., was legendary for being hard-headed.

Being a woman in a still heavily male-dominated industry doesn't bother Carolyn in the least. "I have no problems doing my job." She has no regrets about not following a career in art, which was her major field of study in college. She had little opportunity actually. When her father suffered a major heart attack she moved into the winery and never looked back: "I find the wine industry fascinating. I doubt there is anything I could have done to match this."

THE NAPA VALLEY WINE TRAIN

Napa Valley's Wine Train is celebrating ten years of operation, having chugged from Napa to St. Helena for the first time with tourists on September 16, 1989. Many people opposed the venture at first, but most of the opposition has evaporated like the morning fog. The train makes two trips daily, lunch and dinner runs, with a brunch run on weekends. The Wine Train has been profitable from its second year of operation with about a twelve per cent growth in use over a decade.

Plans for modest expansion include new stations at Yountville, Oakville, Rutherford and St. Helena. Four more stops will be made at wineries along the route. Passengers can debark at Grgich-Hills Cellars and spend an hour touring the winery and tasting wine before being picked up on the return trip to Napa.

It is expensive to ride the wine train. A lunch special runs about $63 per person, although there are many package trips which can lower the cost. Plans are in the works for a train ride which will not include amenities such as the wine tasting car or dining car.

Anyone driving Highway 29 regularly must now wonder what all the fuss was about in the first place. The five- to eight-car trains with the diesel locomotives travel very quietly. The rail line crosses the main highway at only two places, at Trancas Road in northern Napa and just north of Rutherford. There is no danger, since the train moves slowly and ample warning lights have been installed at both crossings.

Railroad travel and railroad trains were so much a part of American life that the Wine Train is a refreshing throwback to a more sublime time when the pace was less harried. The Wine Train is history that moves, and history is an essential part of the wine industry in the valley. History sells wine. People who are interested in wine want to know, for example, about the Chinese role in the industry, and the part played by the first Italians, and the more contemporary Italian-American contribution. They want to know about Prohibition. The wine boom that came with the 1970s. Even the wrangling over the Wine Train is history in the making.

AN HISTORICAL MYSTERY

One historical mystery that has plagued Napa Valley historians for decades seems about to reach its conclusion. More than a century ago a book published in 1878 about the history of Napa Valley contained this highly puzzling paragraph:

> In 1776, a fort was erected by the Spanish Governor Felipe de Neve, a short distance northwest of Napa on an elevated plateau. Part of the original fort is now standing, the wall being of adobe and three feet in thickness. It is situated on the Rancho Viljo, and is occupied as a residence and wine cellar by J. J. Sigrist.

The late historian and co-founder of the Napa County Historical Society, Jess Doud, use to drive the roadways northwest of Napa looking for such an adobe but with no luck. He finally concluded the information in the *Illustrations of Napa County, California* was totally erroneous.

In March 1998, former San Francisco Supervisor Thomas Hsieh and his partner Raymond Hanson arranged to have research undertaken on their vineyards and property on Dry Creek Road, just north of Redwood Road, Napa, exactly where Doud use to search. Hsieh wanted to know something about the quality of grapes grown over the years on his property and whether the old wine cellar on the site had ever produced award winning wines. He knew the winery had been built by a man named Barth. Barth did build a winery on the Hsieh property in 1878, and part of the stone walls still remain, though the building has not been used as a wine cellar since long before Prohibition. That same year Barth had purchased a smaller wine cellar and vines belonging to J. J. Sigrist.

One year later the *Napa County Reporter* carried a brief story on Barth's efforts: "Mr. G. Barth, the new proprietor of what is known as the Sigrist place, situated about three miles west of

GUNTHER BARTH

Napa, has been making improvements . . .The grounds in front of the old adobe residence have been enclosed by a handsome fence and artistically laid out." (Issue of April 18, 1879.)

A decade later, because he was ill, Barth sold his property to Emanuel Goldstein of San Francisco. When the *Napa Register* visited the farms along Dry Creek road in June 1895, the reporter briefly described the orchards, vineyards and "two wine cellars" plus this observation: "An adobe, over 100 years old, stands on the premises, a monument to the silent past."

Research back through the deeds to this land shows that Jacob Sigrist and his brother Frederick purchased the property from Salvador Vallejo in 1857. It was all a part of the Rancho de Napa, granted in 1837 to Salvador Vallejo, and once covering over three thousand acres.

Vallejo built an adobe home on his property a year before he was actually granted his request for the Rancho de Napa land grant. Or at least this is the speculation of Professor G.W.

Hendry of the University of California, Berkeley, who researched the subject extensively in the early 1940s. Writing in an unpublished manuscript entitled *The Spanish and Mexican Adobe and Other Buildings in the Nine San Francisco Bay Counties, 1776 to about 1860*, Hendry states:

> The Salvadore Vallejo Adobe Dwelling Site. 1837. It stood about 500 feet north of the Mill Creek branch of Napa Creek and about 1200 feet west of Napa Dry Creek road, at a point 1.3 miles west of Union Station which in turn is 2.2 miles Northwest by road from the Jefferson street bridge.
>
> It stood on the present Goldstein ranch and near the Barth winery. The house is marked on the diseno [map] of the fall of 1838 and is indicated as standing in this area. The testimony in the land case states that the house was built in the year of occupancy. Permission to occupy the land was granted by General Vallejo in June 1837; in all probability the house was begun that summer and completed to the extent that it could be placed on the diseno to accompany the petition to the Governor on February 28, 1838.

In the land case involving ownership of Rancho de Napa, in 1853, George Yount testified the house was of adobe. Napa resident Hensley Davis recalled the house as late as 1887 and reported that the 1906 earthquake damaged it severely.

Remnants of this 1837 adobe were still present in the 1930s when Floyd Thomas purchased the land. He recalled being told the final portions of the old adobe were cleared from the land three years before his purchase. He also remembers Napa high school history teacher D. T. Davis bringing his students on annual visits to the site before World War II.[4]

If the adobe was built in 1837, it would have been the second adobe built in Napa Valley, following that constructed by George Yount at Yountville. The site is long overdue for historic recognition as the second oldest site occupied by modern man in Napa County. As for that one paragraph in *Illustrations Of Napa County*, someone with a vivid imagination must have written it. San Francisco was founded in 1776; Napa was not even explored until the 1820s. Nearby Sonoma was founded in 1824 as a bulwark against any potential invasion by the Russians, who settled on the California coast in 1811.

An acre of vineyard in Napa Valley now sells for an astronomical sum, especially if the grapes have a record of producing exceptional wine. Thomas Hsieh has an historical site and wine cellar remnants worth even more to the citizens of the valley. No value can really be placed on saving an historical site that has been long lost, or at least long overlooked. Napa Valley's history is a very precious resource.

CHRONOLOGICAL LISTING OF NAPA VALLEY'S PRE-PROHIBITION AND OLDEST WINE CELLARS

When I first started researching wineries more than three decades ago, much of my work dealt with accurately dating the founding of various old wine cellars. With Beaulieu Vineyards I ran into an almost insurmountable headache. The owners, Heublein, liked using "1900" as the founding date. This date had long been in use by the de Latour family.

There was no Beaulieu winery in 1900 when George de Latour had begun buying bulk wine and shipping it to San Francisco. Then he purchased land at Rutherford. His made his first Napa Valley wine in 1905 at the rented Sutter Home winery. His first wine cellar on his home place was a barn which he cleaned and renovated in 1907.

In 1921, de Latour leased the Ewer winery, where the date cut into the stone over the front door is 1885. All de Latour's wine-making since 1921 has taken place in the old Ewer winery. Can the owner absorb the previous history made by the Ewer family and use 1885 as the founding date for Beaulieu?

At the Charles Krug winery, a founding date of 1861 has been in continuous use, including the years of ownership by the Peter Mondavi family. Not one piece of wood from the original 1861 winery remains. The oldest structure still in use is the Redwood cellar or Krug cellar, dating to 1880-81. Adjacent structures were built by the Mondavis in the 1980s. Since winemaking has been

Listing (by Age) of Napa Valley's Oldest Wine Cellars

Age Rank	Name	Date Established	Other Names
1.	Charles Krug	1861	
2.	Schramsberg	1865	
3.	El Molino	1871	
4.	Vine Cliff	1871	(Burrage & Tucker)
5.	Sutter Home	1874	(No winemaking at site) (Thomann)
6.	Markham	1875-76	(Laurent)
7.	Beringer	1876-77	
8.	Alta	1877	
9.	St. Clement	1879	(Rosenbaum)
10.	Niebaum-Coppola	1879	(Inglenook)
11.	Burgess	1880	(Ponchetta)
12.	Woltner	1883	(Brun & Chaix) (Howell Mtn.)
13.	Hanns Kornell	1884	(Larkmead)
14.	Villa Mt.Eden	1884	(moved to new location) (Meyers)
15.	Jaeger	1884	(Williams)
16.	Ehler's Grove	1884	(Ehler)
17.	Far Niente	1885	
18.	Hedgeside	1885	
19.	Beaulieu	1885	(Ewer)
20.	Freemark Abbey	1885	(Tychson)
21.	Golden State	1885	(Napa Co-Op) (Peterson)
22.	Trefethen	1886	(Eshcol)
23.	Chateau Mt.Helena	1886	(Tubbs)
24.	Christian Brothers	1887	(Greystone)
25.	Storybrook	1888	(Grimm)
26.	Mayacamas	1886-1887	(Fisher)
27.	Spring Mountain	1889	(Parrott)
28.	Flora Springs	1890	(Rennie)
29.	Chevalier	1891	
30.	Nichelini	1891	(cellar under home; winery 1896)
31.	Spottswoode	1891	
32.	Deer Park	1891	(Ballantine)
33.	Stag's Leap	1893	(Winery)
34.	Schafer	1895	(Ohl)
35.	Heitz	1898	(Rossi)
36.	Pine Ridge	1902	(Domencioni)
37.	Hess Collection	1906	(Gier winery)

more or less continuous from 1861 to the present, except for a few years when the vineyard was closed during Prohibition, no one is inclined to challenge the 1861 founding date for the Krug winery.

Most people would agree that no cellar owner should be penalized, when longevity is being measured, for having to close his facility during Prohibition. Many wineries in Napa Valley operated during the first four or five years of Prohibition, anyway.

This kind of problem extends to all of the neighboring counties to Napa. Hugh Johnson, in his 1971 *World Atlas of Wine* observed: "Chateau is the word for a wine cellar in Bordeaux. Its overtones of castle or stately home are rarely justified. In most cases the biggest building at the chateau is the *chai*, the long shed, often half underground." A French "chateau" or wine cellar may be nothing more than a series of sheds or outbuildings, no doubt with a history rather loosely defined. Given this predicament, I have come to the following conclusion: A winery is as old as the first winemaking on the site, regardless of whether any of the original buildings still exist, and regardless of whether the ownership has changed over the years.

If a wine brand is moved a significant distance, such as taking the Cresta Blanca brand from Livermore to a Ukiah vineyard, then the owners are not entitled to use the original founding date. The jury is still out on Buena Vista, which was moved eleven miles from Sonoma to the Carneros. Buena Vista claims to be the oldest premium winery in California. However, it was closed from 1879 to 1945, a period of six decades.

History sells wine. An old founding date certainly benefits subsequent owners of wine cellars.

ALPHABETICAL LISTING OF
TAPED ORAL INTERVIEWS

An alphabetical listing of taped oral interviews conducted by the author between 1973 and 1997, with Napa county residents or persons with historical information on Napa wine and viticulture.

Name	Location	Interview Date
Abruzzini, Fred	Beringer Winery	May 23, 1980
		Feb. 7, 1984
Adams, Leon	Wine Institute	Oct.14, 1982
Anderson, Stan	Anderson Vineyards	June 22, 1984
Andrus, Gary	Pine Ridge Winery	June 6, 1984
Barrett, James	Chat. Montelena	Apr. 4, 1984
Battat, Frank	Lakespring Winery	May 25, 1983
Beckstoffer, Andrew	Beckstoffer Vineyards	June, 1993
		Dec., 1995
		Feb., 1996
Bellani, Everett	Bellani Trucking	Nov. 6, 1989
Benkeiser, Justus	Napa Redwoods	Feb. 1, 1986
Berkowitz, Zach	Hagafen Cellars	Dec. 6, 1985
Bissonette, Greg	Chateau Chevalier	Aug. 5, 1982
Brandlin, (bros.)	Napa Redwoods	Mar. 29, 1986
Brother Timothy	Christian Bros.	Sept. 8, 1980
	Napa Redwoods	Jan. 20, 1986
	Gier Winery	May 19, 1989
	Napa Valley	Jul. 29, 1992
Bronfman, Sam	Seagrams/Mumm/Sterling	Oct. 21, 1987
Brounstein, Al	Diamond Creek Vineyards	Jan. 18, 1984
Brown, Harmon & Mrs.	Spottswoode	Feb. 14, 1984
Brown, Robert	Codorniu	July, 1989
Buehler, John	Buehler Winery	May 14, 1985

Buller, Dale	Hedgeside Winery	Apr. 1, 1986
Burgess, Thomas	Burgess Cellars	Aug. 7, 1986
Cain, Jerry	Cain Cellars	June 11, 1984
Chappellet, Donn	Chappellet Winery	Oct. 3, 1983
Chevalier, Robert	Chevalier Winery	Feb. 23, 1985
Clark, Lilburn	Wooden Valley/Pope V.	Apr. 20, 1979
Clark, Spencer	Amizetta Vineyards	Dec. 17, 1985
Corley, Jay	Monticello Vineyards	Oct. 6, 1983
Costello, John	Costello Vineyards	Sept. 14, 1984
Craig, Robert	Napa Redwoods/Hess	May 17 1985
Crivelli, Walt	Carneros/Talcoa	May 1, 1985
	Domaine Carneros	Jan. 22, 1988
Dal Porto, Sattimo	Napa Valley Co-op	Dec. 18, 1990
Davies, Jack	Schramsberg	Nov. 10, 1983
Del Bondio, Bryan	Markham Winery	Nov. 9, 1989
de Leuze, Norman	ZD Winery	Feb. 1, 1984
di Rosa, Rene	Winery Lake Vineyards	Aug. l, 1984
Doble, William	A.R. Morrow	Dec. 9, 1982
Doumani, Carl	Stag's Leap	Dec. 15, 1983
Duffy, Owen	Yountville, VineCliff	Nov. 11, 1988
Duhig, Stewart	Carneros/Talcoa	Nov. 27, 1980
		May 1, 1985
Ehlert, William	Prohibition Grocery	Aug. 8, 1986
Eisele, Milt	Eisele Vineyards	May 19, 1988
Falk, Ben	Alta Vineyards	June 5, 1984
Fay, Nathan	Fay Vineyards/Stag's Leap	Mar. 19, 1986
Forni, Charles	Beaulieu/Napa Co-op	Feb. 13, 1984
Galleron, Virgil	Napa Valley Co-op	Feb. 7, 1984
Gantner, John, Sr.	Spring Mtn.	Sept. 10, 1991
Girard, Stephen	Girard Winery	Aug. 10, 1982
Gosling, George	Pope/Wooden Valley	May 26, 1979
Gramlow, Otto	Beaulieu Vineyards	Dec. 11, 1973
Graves, David	Saintsbury Winery	Feb. 28, 1984
Grgich, Mike	Grgich-Hills Winery	Sept. 25, 1984
Groth, Dennis	Groth Winery	July 19, 1984
Guigni, William	Keenan Winery	Apr. 4, 1978
Harlan, William	Harlan	Apr. 20, 1989
Harrington, Max	Whitehall Lane Vineyards	May 23, 1989
	Hassenmeyer Winery	Nov. 6, 1989
Harrington, Wm	Beaulieu	Jan. 30, 1974
Harris, Roy	Beckstoffer Vineyards	Dec., 1995
Hart, Ina	Chateau Chevalier	Feb. 26, 1985
	Spring Mountain	
Haus, Sam	Pope Valley/Haus Win.	Apr. 23, 1979

Harrison, Frank	Winery Construction	Mar. 3, 1978
Hazen, G. P.	Chateau Chevre	May 17, 1985
Heid, George	Eschol/Trefethen	July 8, 1975
	Stag's Leap	May 5, 1989
		Oct. 23, 1987
Heitz, Joe	Heitz Cellars	July 6, 1983
Hewitt, William	Brun & Chaix	June, 1993
Hill, William	Napa Redwoods/Hill	Mar. 20, 1984
Hills, Austin	Grgich-Hills	Nov., 1993
Hocken, Herbert	Wild Horse Valley	July 28, 1986
Holdene, Edith	Domeniconi/PineRidge	Jan. 20, 1981
Howell, Chris	Cain Cellars	June 28, 1991
Jaeger, Wm. & Lila	Jaeger/Williams Wny.	Apr.10, 1985
Jensen, A.	Coca Cola/wine-1930s	June 18, 1980
Johnson, Mabel	Lewelling/Napa Valley	May 1, 1975
Johnson, Reverdy	Johnson-Turnbull Wny.	Nov. 3, 1984
Keenan, Robert	Conradi/Keenan Wny.	Nov. 8, 1984
Kiser, Fred	Carneros	Jan.30, 1988
Klubelcheidt, Louise	Inglenook/St. Helena	Mar. 19, 1973
Knowles, Legh	Beaulieu	Arp. 23, 1974
Kolf, Robert	Leopard Trading Co.	Sept. 2, 1987
Komes, John, Julia	Flora Springs Winery	Aug. 25, 1983
Kornell, Hanns	Kornell Cellars	July 21, 1983
Lamoree, Robert	Georges de Latour	May 7, 1974
Laufenberg, Charles	Knights V./Napa Valley	Jan. 26, 1982
Laurent, Ted	Markham/St. Hel.Co-op	Apr. 19, 1989
Learned, Babe	Spring Mountain	Mar. 11, 1988
Lewelling, Vera	Far Niente	Apr. 4, 1978
	Martha's Vineyard	Aug. 16, 1988
Luper, Jerry	Bouchane/Freemark Ab.	Feb. 16, 1983
Lyman, William	Napa Valley/Niebaum	Mar. 19, 1973
	Inglenook	Apr. 2, 1973
	Beaulieu/Napa Valley	Dec. 27, 1973
Lyons, William	Wooden Valley	Apr. 19, 1979
Mahoney, Francis	Carneros Creek Wny.	Jan. 28, 1982
Markovich, Frank	Lewelling/Martha's Vdy.	Nov. 14, 1988
Matheson, Henry	Mt. Veeder Winery	Apr. 15, 1984
Matle, Mario	Carneros/Talcoa	Jan. 22, 1988
May, Tom	Martha's Vineyard	Feb. 22, 1988
McManus, Inez	Arighi/Pope Valley	May 25, 1979
McWilliams, Jim& Ann	Mt.Eden Cellars	July 19, 1984
Meyer, Justin	Silver Oak Cellars	Dec. 9, 1983
Mihaly, Louis	Silverado Vineyards	June 29, 1984
Mondavi, Peter	Krug/Mondavi Winery	June 14, 1980
		March, 1997

Mondavi, Marc	Krug/Mondavi	June 21, 1984
Mondavi, Robert	Mondavi Winery	Feb. 21, 1984
	Lee Stewart/Souverain	Sept. 27, 1990
	Early Krug History	March, 1997
Mondavi, Michael	Mondavi Winery	Feb. 23, 1984
Mosley, Aaron	Napa Valley Cellars	Dec. 12, 1985
Navone, Ernest	St.Helena Co-op/Gallo	Apr. 26, 1989
Newlan, Bruce	Newlan Winery	Mar. 2, 1984
Newton, Peter	Sterling/Newton Vineyards	Mar. 26, 1984
Nichelini, James	Nichelini Winery	Aug. 11, 1982
Nickel, Gil	Far Niente	Mar. 23, 1983
Nickel, John	Chateau Chevalier	Apr. 25, 1985
Parker, Thompson	Stag's Leap	Dec. 16, 1980
	Stag's Leap	Nov. 4, 1987
	Parker Ranch	Apr. 19, 1989
Pecota, Robert	Pecota/Napa Valley	July 29, 1982
Penland, Phillip	Martha's Vineyard	Nov. 2, 1988
Pepi, Robert	Pepi Winery	Aug. 25, 1983
Perelli-Minetti, Mario	Perelli-Minetti	Nov. 4, 1982
	A.R. Morrow	
	Perelli-Minetti	Mar. 10, 1986
Phillips, Robert	Vine Hill Ranch	Nov. 18, 1988
	Wine Train	
Pina, Dave	Pina Vineyards	Feb. 17, 1984
Plam, Keneth	Plam Vineyards	May 20, 1987
Ponti, Joseph	Beaulieu	Nov. 15, 1973
Portet, Bernard	Clos du Val	Feb. 3, 1986
Prager, James	Prager Port Works	Jan. 24, 1984
Preston, William	APM Cork	Sept. 30, 1987
Raymond, Roy, Sr.	Beringer/Raymond	Apr. 9, 1982
Raymond, Roy, Mrs.	Beringer/Raymond	Apr. 9, 1982
Raymond, Roy, Jr.	Beringer/Raymond	June 3, 1982
Raymond, Walter	Beringer/Raymond	June 3, 1982
Regusci, Livina	Occidental Winery	Sept. 22, 1984
Rhodes, Barney/Bell	Napa Valley/Rhodes	Mar. 22, 1988
Riordan, Tom	Domaine Carneros	Mar. 6, 1988
Richmond, Michael	Acacia Winery	Aug. 22, 1983
Robbins, Michael	Spring Mtn. Vineyards	Mar. 21, 1984
	Falcon Crest	
Rombauer, Koerner	Rombauer Vineyards	Feb. 2, 1984
Rossi, Ray/Louise	Rossi Winery	Dec. 12, 1989
Sattui, Daryl	Sattui Winery	Dec. 21, 1984
Schafer, John	Schafer Winery	Dec. 1, 1983
Scharbaro, Ramo	Beaulieu/de Latour	May 20, 1974
Schmidt, Arthur	Far Niente	Apr. 4, 1978

Schoch, Ivan	Schoch, Far Niente	Aug. 13, 1986
Schulze, Jack	Napa Creek Winery	Feb. 7, 1987
Shown, Richard	Shown Vineyards	July 21, 1983
Shrem, Jon	Clos Pegas	June 10, 1987
Skupny	Niebaum-Coppola	Nov., 1995
Steen, Allan	Whitehall Lane Wny	Oct. 21, 1983
Steinhauer, Robert	Beckstoffer Vineyards	Dec., 1995
Stewart, Wilbur	Carneros,Prohibition	July 30, 1980
Stralla, Louis	Pope Valley Wines	Aug. 1, 1977
		June 2, 1977
		Apr. 23, 1979
		June 25, 1979
Streblow, Jack	Streblow Vineyards	July 9, 1987
Streich, Robert	Napa Redwoods	Feb. 26, 1986
Stuart, John	Silverado Winery	Dec. 19, 1983
Stuart, Stuart	Smith-Madrone Vineyards	Feb. 17, 1984
Smith, Charles	Smith-Madrone Vineyards	Feb. 17, 1984
Sullivan, Dagmar	Beaulieu/de Latour	July 17, 1991
Sullivan, James	Sullivan Winery	Feb. 2, 1984
Tollini, Theresa	Beaulieu	Dec. 4, 1973
Travers, Robert	Mayacamus Vineyards	July 13, 1983
Trefethen, John & Janet	Trefethen Winery	July 2, 1984
Trinchero, Louis	Sutter Home Winery	Oct. 15, 1985
Tudal, Arnold	Tudal Winery	Jan. 24, 1984
Varozza, Charles	Spring Mountain	Sept. 4, 1987
	Rutherford Bench	
Venge, Nels	Groth Winery	July 19, 1984
Vierra, George	Vichon Winery	Nov. 11, 1983
Vose, Hamilton	Vose Vineyards	Jan. 18, 1984
Vizkelety, Imre	St. Andrews Winery	Mar. 27, 1984
Wagner, Charles	Wagner Winery	May 2, 1989
Webb, Brad	Webb/Freemark Abbey	Dec. 10, 1987
Weichers, James	Leopard Trading Co.	Sept. 2, 1987
Weir, Ernie	Hagafen Cellars	Dec. 6, 1985
Westgate, Edward	Westgate Vineyards	June 3, 1988
Wichels, John	Yountville/Stag's Leap	Oct. 21, 1987
Wilcox, Arthur&Elma	Conn Valley	July 19, 1986
Wilson, Sheldon	Chimney Rock Winery	Sept. 13, 1989
Winiarski, Warren	Stag's Leap Winery	Mar. 4, 1983
		July 13, 1983
Work, Henry	Barrel Builders	Sept. 24, 1987
Wright, John	Domaine Chandon	Dec. 6, 1985

AN ALPHABETICAL LISTING OF
NAPA VALLEY WINE CELLARS

The following list comprises the wine cellars in operation as of January 1, 1999. Wineries come and go so quickly that the author cannot vouch for accuracy in every case.

Acacia, Napa
Aetna Springs, Pope Valley
Alta Cellars, Calistoga
Amizetta, St. Helena
Anderson Conn Valley, St. Helena
S. Anderson, Yountville
Araujo Estate Wines
Vincent Arroyo, Calistoga
David Arthur, St. Helena
Atlas Peak, Napa
Avatar Wine Partners, Napa

Beaucanon, St. Helena
Beaulieu, Rutherford
Beringer, St. Helena
Bouchane, Napa
Buehler, St. Helena
Burgess, St. Helena

Cain, St. Helena
Cakebread, Rutherford
Caporale, Napa
Carneros Alambic Distillery
Carneros Creek, Napa

Casa Nuestra, Napa
Caymus, Rutherford
Chanter, Napa
Chappellet, St. Helena
Charles Krug, St. Helena
Chateau Boswell, St. Helena
Chateau Chevalier, St. Helena
Chateau Chevre, Yountville
Chateau Montelena, Calistoga
Chateau Potelle, Napa
Chateau Woltner, St. Helena
Chimney Rock, Napa
Clos du Val, Napa
Clos Pegase, Calistoga
Codorniu, Napa
Conn Creek, St. Helena
Corthay, St. Helena
Cosentino, Napa
Cuvaison, Calistoga

Dalla Valle, Napa
Deer Park, St. Helena
DeMoor, Oakville
Diamond Creek, Calistoga
Domaine Chandon, Yountville

Domaine Carneros, Napa
Domaine Charbay, St. Helena
Domaine Montreaux, Yountville
Domaine Napa, St. Helena
Duckhorn, St. Helena
Dunn, Angwin
Dutch Henry, Calistoga

El Molino, St. Helena
Evenson, Oakville

Farella-Park, Napa
Far Niente, Oakville
Flora Springs, St. Helena
Folie a Deux, St. Helena
Forman, St. Helena
Franciscan, Rutherford
Freemark Abbey, St. Helena
Frisinger, Napa
Frog's Leap, St. Helena

Girard, Oakville
Golden State Vintners (Napa
    Co-op), St. Helena
Grace Family, St. Helena
Graeser, Calistoga
Green and Red, St. Helena
Grgich Hills, Rutherford
Groth, Oakville

Harrison, St. Helena
Heitz, St. Helena
Helena View, Napa
Hess Collection, Napa
William Hill, Napa
Honig, Rutherford

Jaeger Family, St. Helena
Judd's Hills, St. Helena

Kate's Vineyard, Napa
Robert Keenan, St. Helena

La Jota, Angwine
Lakespring, Yountville

Lamborn Family, Angwin
Larkmead, St. Helena
La Vieille, St. Helena
Liparita, Angwin
Livingston, St. Helena
Llords & Elwood, Yountville
Long, St. Helena

Macaulery, St. Helena
Markham, St. Helena
Marston, St. Helena
Martini, Louis, St. Helena
Mayacamas, Napa
Merryvale, St. Helena
Peter Michael, Calistoga
Milat, St. Helena
Robert Mondavi, Oakville
Mont St. John, Napa
Monticello, Napa
Moss Creek, Napa
Mount Veeder, Napa
Mumm, Rutherford

Napa Creek, St. Helena
Napa Valley Port Cellars, Napa
Napa Valley Wine Co., Napa
Napa Wine Co., Oakville
Newlan, Napa
Newton, St. Helena
Niebaum-Coppola, Rutherford

Oakville Ranch, Oakville
Opus One, Rutherford

Pacific Star, Napa
Pahlmeyer, Napa
Pecota, Calistoga
Peju Province, Rutherford
Pepi, Oakville
Mario Perelli-Minetti,
    Rutherford
Phelps, St. Helena
Pina, Rutherford
Pine Ridge, Napa
Plam, Yountville

Pope Valley, Pope Valley
Bernard Pradel, Napa
Prager Port Works, St. Helena
Pride Mountain, St. Helena

Quail Ridge, Rutherford

Raymond, St. Helena
Revere, Napa
Ritchie Creek, St. Helena
Rombauer, St. Helena
Round Hill, St. Helena
Rustridge, St. Helena
Rutherford Vintners

Saddleback, Oakville
Sage Canyon, Rutherford
St. Andrews, Napa
St. Clement, St. Helena
St. Suprey, Rutherford
Saintsbury, Napa
San Pierro Vara, Calistoga
V. Sattui, St. Helena
Schramsberg, Calistoga
Sequoia Grove, Napa
Shafer, Napa
Chas. Shaw, St. Helena
Signorello, Napa
Silver Oak, Napa
Silverado Hill, Napa
Silverado Vineyards, Napa
Robert Sinskey, Napa
Sky, Napa
Smith-Madrone, St. Helena
Soda Canyon, Napa
Spottswoode, St. Helena
Spring Mountain, St. Helena
Stag's Leap Wine Cellars, Napa

Stag's Leap Winery, Napa
Star Hill, Napa
Steltzner, Napa
Sterling, Calistoga
Stonegate, Calistoga
Stony Hill, St. Helena
Storybrook, Calistoga
Stratford, St. Helena
Streblow, St. Helena
Sullivan, Rutherford
Summit Lake, Angwin
Sutter Home, St. Helena
Swanson, Rutherford

Phillip Togni, St. Helena
Trefethen, Napa
Truchard, Napa
Tudal, St. Helena
Tulocay, Napa
Turnbull, Oakville

Van Der Heyden, Napa
Viader, Deer Park
Vichon, Oakville
Villa Helena, St. Helena
Villa Mt. Eden, Oakville
Von Strasser, Calistoga

Wermuth, Calistoga
White Rock, Napa
Whitehall Lane, St. Helena
Whitford, Napa

Yverdon, St. Helena

ZD Wines, Napa

AUTHOR'S PREVIOUS
HISTORICAL RESEARCH STUDIES

Privately commissioned historical research studies, on wine and viticulture subjects, 1970 through 1997, undertaken by the author. Arranged in chronological sequence.

88. Napa Valley's Oldest Winery-The Charles Krug Winery and A Half Century of Winemaking History in The Valley By The Mondavi Family. 1997.

87. A History of Beckstoffer Vineyards, St. Helena and Napa Valley, California. For Andrew Beckstoffer. 1996.

86. Hops Growing in Sonoma Valley, California. 1900-1960s. For The Benziger Family. 1996.

85. Samuele Sebastiani, and The Founding of Sebastiani Vineyards and Winery, 1900-1940, at Sonoma, Ca. 1993. For The Sebastiani Winery. 1993.

84. Eden Dale—An Historical Overview of The History and Ranch Now in Part Known As "Sangiacomo Vineyards". For Sangiacomo Vineyards. 1993.

83. Charmat. A History of The Large-Bottle Process of Producing Champagne. For The E & J Gallo Winery, Modesto, Ca. 1992.

82. Winery Fires in California. A Brief Examination of Their Potential and Use of Wine in Fighting Fire. For Fetzer Vineyards, Hopland, Ca. 1992.

81. Report of Research into The History of The Ignace Paderewski Vineyards, San Luis Obispo County, California. For Chimney Rock Vyds, Paso Robles, Ca. 1991

80. Napa Valley's 'Spring Mountain' - A Wine and Viticulture Region With Its Own Special Identity. For Spring Mountain Appellation Committee. 1991.

79. A Historical Perspective on Mountain Winegrowing. Paper Prepared For Delivery at The "Mountain Winegrowing Symposium," Gauer Estates Vineyards. 1991.

78. An Historical Overview on The History of Brandy Production in California, Covering The Period From Brandy Making at The Catholic

Missions Founded in 1769 to The Shift From Coastal Counties to The Interior Valleys of The State in The 1940s. For RMS Vineyards, 1991 Plus Photocopy Appendix Historical Items.

77. The Founding of The Norton-Rossi Winery, St. Helena, Cal. in August 1884. 1991.

76. A Brief History of The Napa Valley Cooperative Winery, St. Helena, California and The Winemaking Facilities That Have Occupied The Site Since Wine Was First Made in 1885. For Napa Valley Cooperative Winery. 1990.

75. Biographical Background to J. Leland Stewart, Founder of The First Souverain Winery. For Chateau Souverain. 1990.

74. Historical Background to The Joseph Patten/Cheotti Ranch Property, Dry Creek Valley, Sonoma County, Ca. For The E&J Gallo Winery. 1990.

73. A Brief Study of Grape Varieties Grown and Wine Varieties Produced in Sonoma County, California, 1900- 1920. For E & J Gallo Winery, 1990.

72. A Brief Historical Overview of The Maddux Ranch, Fulton, California — Now The Farmery Inc. Also Known As The Duke Ranch. For Rich and Saralee Kunde. 1990.

71. Hops, Hop Barns and Kilns on Mark West Creek-Circa 1900 & The James Clark/Lizzie Woodward Ranch. For Rich and Saralee Kunde. 1990.

70. An Historical Review of The Hassenmair-Cook Ranch, St. Helena, Ca. Covering Especially The Hassenmair Winery Founded in 1883 and Vineyards Which Date to The 1870s. For 585 Ranch Partners. 1990.

69. Milliken Peak, Carneros Valley and The Carneros Background For The Site of The Codorniu-Napa Valley Champagne Cellars. For Codorniu, USA. 1990.

68. Missionaries and Soldiers of Catalonian Origins in Early California, 1769-1823 (The Mission Period). For Codorniu, USA. 1990.

67. Ten Oaks Vineyard, The Warfield Winery & Kate Warfield, Glen Ellen, California. For Lewis and Susan Cook. 1990.

66. Early History of The Site Proposed For The Elm Tree Heights Project, St. Helena, Ca. For Seacliff Financial Inc. 1990.

65. An Historical Review of The Laurent/Markham Winery, St. Helena, California. For The Markham Winery, 1989.

64. George Yount and The Establishment of Viticulture in Napa Valley, California. A Collection of Historical Materials Documenting The First Planting of Grapes and Winemaking By Yount in Napa Valley. 1989.

63. Stag's Leap Wine Cellars Site History-Parker Hill. For Stag's Leap Wine Cellars. 1989.

62. Martha's Vineyard of Napa Valley. A Historical Overview. For Tom and Martha May. 1989.

61. Vine Cliff of Napa Valley, California. For Charles and Nell Sweeney. 1989.

60. Wine and Viticulture History in The Lakeville District, Petaluma, Sonoma County, Ca. For Sangiacomo & Sons. 1989.

59. Vineyard Designations on Wine and Champagne Labels in California and The United States. For Domaine Mumm. 1988.

58. Winemaking and Viticulture in Mendocino County With Particular Emphasis on The Parducci Winery of Ukiah. For Brown, Forman & Co. 1988.

57. Marketing California Wine in Glass: The Wine Label and Marketing Slogans, Beaulieu Vineyard's 'Private Reserve'. For Beaulieu Vineyard. 1988.

56. St. Michael's Vineyard. A Brief History From The California Gold Rush to More Recent Times. For St. Michael's Vineyard. 1989.

55. Domaine Carneros. A Brief History of The Site. For Domaine Carneros. 1988.

54. The Ewer & Atkinson Winery. Edward St. Suprey. Preliminary Report on Research into The Name St. Suprey. For St. Suprey Winery. 1988-1989.

53. Theodore Gier of The Napa Redwoods and Oakland, California. A Biography. For Hess Collection Wines. 1987.

52. Stag's Leap District Viticultural Appellation. An Update on The History Relating to Yountville Crossroads Inclusion. For Stag's Leap Appellation Committee. 1987.

51. Mountain Or Hillside Grapes Versus Valley Floor Grapes in The Napa Valley. For Hess Collection Wines. 1987.

50. Wild Horse Valley's Viticultural History. Napa Valley/ County, California. For Heron Lake Vineyard. 1986.

49. A Wine and Viticulture History of The 'Mt. Veeder-Napa Redwoods' in Napa County, California. For Hess Vineyards. 1986.

48. Talcoa. A Brief History of The Ranch, Vineyards and Winery in The Carneros Region of The Napa Valley. For Rancho Huichica Vineyards. 1985.

47. Chateau Chevalier of Napa Valley. A History. For Chateau Chevalier Winery. 1985.

46. The Zinfandel Grape in Sonoma County's 'Dry Creek Valley'. For Preston Vineyards. 1985.

45. A Brief Historical Overview on The Meaning of The Phrase 'Stag's Leap' and Its Geographic Boundaries. For Stag's Leap Wine Cellars. 1984.

44. A Brief Glimpse into The History of Wildwood Winery & Vineyards, Glen Ellen, California. 1984.

43. A History of Champagne in California and The United States. With Particular Emphasis on How The Word "Champagne" Has Been Used By Journalists and Writers; and The Understanding of Its Definition By The American Wine Consumer. For F. Korbel & Bros. 1984.

42. The Stag's Leap Resort and Winery. For Carl Doumani. 1984.

41. Report For Warren Winiarski, Stag's Leap Wine Cellars Napa, Ca. on The Quality of Wine Produced in California Prior to Prohibition, and The Types of Grapes Used in The Making of That Wine. 1984.

40. Pierre Pellier and The Founding of The Pellier/Mirassou Family Wine Making Tradition, Dating to 1854. For Mirassou Vineyards. 1983.

39. The Life and Times of Almond Raleigh Morrow, 1862-1951. First President of The Wine institute. For The Lamont Winery, 1982.

38. Historical Background to The Proposed "Sobre Vista Vine Yards" Viticultural Appellation, Sonoma County, California. For Myron Freiberg. 1982.

37. An Historical Overview of The Geographic Relationship of Alexander Valley, Sonoma County, to The town of Cloverdale, Sonoma County, California. 1982.

36. Napa Valley's Oldest Winemaking Family—The Raymonds. For The Raymond Winery. 1982.

35. The Production and Marketing of "Chablis" Wines in California and, incidentally, in The United States, Circa 1880s to The 1940s. For The Wine Institute. 1982.

34. An Examination of Historical Records and Related Documents With Regard to The Claim By The Thomas Winery, 8916 Foot Hill Boulevard, Cucamonga, California, to Being The First Commercial Winery in California. 1982.

33. "Northern Sonoma"-Historical Background on Winemaking and Viticulture in The Region As Well As Its Geographic Boundaries. For The E & J Gallo Winery. 1982.

32. A Chronology of The Life of Adrian Georges Chauche and The Mont Rouge Winery, Livermore Ca. For Kraft Foods, 1981.

31. The Viticulture and Winemaking History of Knight's Valley, Sonoma County, California. For The Beringer Winery and Appellation Committee. 1981.

30. A Brief Viticulture and Winemaking History of The Sonoma Chalk Hill District. For The Chalk Hill Appellation Committee. 1981.

29. The Domeniconi/Pine Ridge Winery, Napa, California: A Brief Review of Its History. For Pine Ridge Winery. 1981.

28. A Brief History of Grape Growing and Winemaking in The Carneros Region of Napa Valley, California. For The Beaulieu Winery. 1980.

27. The Korbel Winery of Sonoma County, California. An Examination of Historic Records Relating to The Establishment of The First Winery and The First Production of Brandy on The Site. For The Korbel Winery. 1980.

26. The Temecula Valley of Riverside County, California. An Historical Overview With Emphasis on Its Viticulture and Winemaking History. For The Temecula Appellation Committee. 1980.

25. The Vineyards and Wine of H.W. Crabb, Oakville, California, and His "To-Kalon" Label. For The Robert Mondavi Winery, 1980.

24. A Review of The Historical Uses of The Terms "Napa Valley" and "Napa County". For The Napa Appellation Committee and Butte's Gas & Oil Co. 1979.

23. Grapes and Wine in California's Alexander Valley: A History. Alexander Valley Appellation Committee. 1979.

22. Inglewood—The Jaeger/Alton L. Williams Home, St. Helena, California. For The Jaeger Family. 1979.

21. The Stag's Leap Winery of Alexander Valley, California: A Brief History. 1979.

20. A Brief History of The Stone Building Now Occupied By The Complete Winemaker, St. Helena, California. For The Complete Winemaker. 1979.

19. The Wine and Grape Heritage of Dry Creek Valley, Sonoma County, California. For The E & J Gallo Winery. 1979.

18. The Far Niente Winery, Oakville, California and Its Founder, John Benson. For The Far Niente Winery. 1978.

17. Research and Preparation of Applications For Hanns Kornell Champagne Cellars (Larkmead Winery), St. Helena, California. For Listing in The National Registry of Historic Places. For The Hanns Kornell Winery. 1978.

16. The San Martin Winery, San Martin, California. For The San Martin Winery. 1977.

15. The Alicante Bouschet Grape and Alicante Bouschet Wine in California and The United States, 1883-1975. For The Angelo Papagni Winery. 1976.

14. Historical Research of The Conradi Winery, Spring Mountain Road, St. Helena, California. For Robert Keenan Winery, 1976.

13. Agriculture and Winemaking in California's Calaveras County, California: A Brief History. For Calaveras County, 1976.

12. A Search of All Historical Documents Relating to The Geographic Definition of "North Coast". For The North Coast Grape Growers Association. 1976.

11. A Chronology and History of The Eschol-Trefethen Vineyards and Winery, Napa Valley, California. For The Trefethen Winery. 1975.

10. Villa Mt. Eden Vineyards, Oakville, California. For Charles and Ann McWilliams. 1975.

9. Freemark Abbey Winery of Tychson Hill, St. Helena, California. For The Freemark Abbey Winery and Charles Carpy. 1975.

8. The Charles H. Brockhoff Winery, West Zinfandel Lane, St. Helena, California. 1975.

7. The Beaulieu Winery, Rutherford, California. A Brief Historical Study, 1890-1950. For Beaulieu Vineyards. 1974.

6. Souverain Winery Site, Geyserville, California. A Brief History. For Pillsbury Flour Mills. 1973.

5. The Geyser Peak Winery: A Chronological Sequential History, 1880-1972. For Schlitz Brewing Co. 1973.

4. The Inglenook Winery: A Listing in Chronological Sequence of Significant Events in Its Early History. For United Vintners. 1973.

3. Gustave Niebaum: A Character Study. For United Vintners. 1973.

2. The Simi Winery: A Narrative History, 1873-1970. For Russell Green. 1972.

1. The Montecillo Vineyards of Glen Ellen: A Brief History. 1971.

CHAPTER NOTES

NOTES — CHAPTER ONE

1. Elizabeth Cyrus Wright, "Early Upper Napa Valley," Napa County Historical Society, Series No. 1, December, 1978.

2. *Historical and Descriptive Sketch Book of Napa, Sonoma, Lake, and Mendocino.* See pages 156-157.

3. A. H. Grossman, letter to the *Napa Register*, August 2, 1889. ". . . Let us go back to '72. In that season I leased the Huicha [sic] vineyard of W.H. Winters for a term of six years. It was then the largest vineyard in Napa county."

4. *History of Howard and Cooper Counties, Missouri*, 1883, pp. 152-156.

5. Robert Kirsch and William S. Murphy, *West of the West*. (New York: E.P. Dutton & Co., 1967), p. 194.

6. Charles Brown manuscript, D53, Bancroft Library, University of California, Berkeley, p 8.

7. This reference was first published in the *California Farmer*, San Francisco, Ca. on October 19, 1855.

8. This manuscript was published years later by the California Historical Society, San Francisco as *The Chronicles of George C. Yount, California Pioneer of 1826*. That date is likely in error as Yount did not reach Sonoma, Ca. until 1833 which would have given him six years to roam the state. He never mentioned such a possibility. References in the manuscript by the editor to viticulture often seem ambiguous, it not being clear when Yount was being quoted or the editor was making use of conjecture.

9. *St. Helena Star*, March 18, 1875: "Mr. John York—one of the respected citizens and pioneers who settled way back in 1845, and planted the first vineyard in the county . . . informs us that his grapes have never failed to produce a crop during all that time."

10. The testimony was given in Land Case Number 32, the United States versus George Yount and involved disputes over the boundary of his first land grant. This document is at the Bancroft Library, University of California, Berkeley.

11. *Official Report of the California State Agricultural Society's Third Annual Fair*, 1856. p. 11.

12. Agoston Haraszthy has been widely credited with first proposing that grape vines did not need irrigation in California. Obviously, Thompson would have been following this farming practice with grapes as well as fruit trees. Haraszthy did not arrive in Sonoma until 1857. The Hungarian would have purchased grape varieties from Thompson that were not in his own collection.

13. "William A. Trubody and the Overland Pioneers of 1847." *California Historical Society Quarterly*, June, 1937,

14. *History of Solano and Napa Counties*, Vol. I, p. 341.

15. *Sketch Book*, p. 203.

16. *Farmer*, August 10, 1860, p. 1.

17. *Independent Calistogian*, Calistoga, Ca., January 23, 1878.

18. *Farmer*, July 1, 1859.

19. *Star*, December 19, 1890.

20. *Farmer*, November 4, 1859.

NOTES — CHAPTER TWO

1. *California Farmer*, August 3, 1860, see "Napa and Napa Valley."

2. (New Haven, Conn.: Yale University Press, 1931).

3. August 10, 1860.

4. *Ibid.* There are two stories in the *Star* written by Crane. For this quotation see "Viticulture: Looking Back Some Thirty Years." His other story, "Pioneer Days," also contains some viticulture history.

5. July 29, 1864.

6. *Alta California*, March 11, 1866.

7. *Star*, December 19, 1890.

8. *Farmer*, May 15, 1866.

9. *Star*, December 19, 1890.

10. *Farmer*, June 22, 1860.

11. In a special article on "Railroading" for the *Star* of December 19, 1890, Gordon Backus—who claimed to know most of the details of the building of the railroad—added this observation: "Had there been no railroad through Napa Valley where would be the fine wine cellars of Beringer Bros., Weinberger, Krug, Laurent, Lyman, Sciaroni, Lewelling, Wheelers, and last, but not least, the magnifi-

cent cellar of W. B. Bourn. . . and others, all in Napa Valley and looking to railroads to give them rapid transit to the markets of the nation, yes to the markets of the world, for the finest wines produced on earth."

12. As quoted in the *History of Napa and Lake Counties, California,* page 328. Copies of the Register for this date do not exist.

13. Until the mid-1870s, all vine statistics in California were "number of grape vines planted." From 1880 on, this was changed to "acres" of grape vines. Attempting to arrive at a general figure for vines planted per acre, however, is exceedingly difficult. *Southern Vineyard,* Los Angeles, of Oct. 2, 1858 claimed: "The average yield of vines may be placed at ten pounds per vine, and a thousand vines per acre." The *Atlantic Monthly* of May 1864 states: "In Los Angeles County most of the vineyards have 1,000 to the acre. In Sonoma the number varies from 680 to 1,000." The *Sacramento Daily Union* of Feb. 18, 1865 stated: "In Los Angeles County the distance is six feet each way, or one thousand vines to the acre. In Sonoma, the distance in the vineyards set out before 1865 is eight feet or six hundred eighty vines to the acre." Seven hundred vines to the acre for Napa Valley seems a good average.

14. *Historical and Descriptive Sketch Book,* pages 56-57.

NOTES — CHAPTER THREE

1. *History of Napa and Lake Counties,* 1881. Page 470.

2. *Report of the State Board of Equalization, For 1870-71.* (published in 1872), pp. 22-23.

3. As reprinted in the *California Farmer,* October 25, 1866.

4. W.W. Lyman, "The Lyman Family", *Napa County Historical Society Gleanings,* April 1980.

5. *Napa Reporter,* October 11, 1873, "Itinerant Field-Notes."

6. Ibid., April 19, 1873.

7. Ibid., September 27, 1873.

8. *History of Napa and Lake Counties,* 1881. p. 204.

9. December 16, 1875.

10. For construction of Pope Valley Road see the *Napa Reporter* of October 11, 1873. Lewelling's fire story is in the *Star* of July 29, 1875. See the *Star* also for Thompson story, January 5, 1877.

11. *Star,* November 15, 1878.

12. Ibid., February 4, 1875.

13. *Napa Reporter,* February 22, 1873.

14. *Star,* October 16, 1874.

15. Ibid., October 14, 1875.

16. Bancroft Scraps, Volume 19, Part II. See letter signed "R. W. Montgomery."
17. *Star*, October 29, 1874.
18. Ibid., April 15, 1876.
19. Ibid., See issues of November 16, 23, 30 and December 7, 14, 1877.
20. As reprinted in the *Star*, March 1, 1873.
21. Ibid., September 19, 1879.

NOTES — CHAPTER FOUR

1. *For The Years, 1882-3 and 1883-4.* (Sacramento: State Printer), 1884. p.42.
2. *Star*, August 25, 1882.
3. Ibid., as reprinted on January 31, 1879.
4. Ibid., as reprinted on December 19, 1879.
5. *Healdsburg Enterprise*, January 26, 1882.
6. Ibid., same date.
7. As reprinted in the *Star*, April 2, 1880.
8. *First Annual Report of the Board of State Viticultural Commissioners* (Sacramento: 1881). p 9-10.
9. *Star*, October 25, 1878.
10. Ibid., August 21, 1884.
11. Several writers on early Napa Valley history erroneously claim Watson ran a health resort. Early descriptive pieces on Inglenook were written in such a manner as to convey the concept that paying guests were accepted at the ranch.
12. *Star*, July 1, 1881: "The cellar rebuilt on its new site with the addition of a crushing room, covers a space of 55 x 120 ft."
13. Ibid., August 12, 1881.
14. Ibid., October 27, 1882.
15. *Report of the Sixth Annual Viticultural Convention, San Francisco, March 7,8,9,10, 1888.* (Sacramento: 1888.) p.86.
16. Napa Register, October 4, 1889.
17. *The Life of Henry Wadsworth Longfellow.* Edited by Samuel Longfellow, 1891. Vol. I, p.187.
18. *San Francisco Merchant*, April 11, 1884.
19. As reprinted in the *Star*, April 29, 1881.
20. *Annual Report For the Year 1887.* p.44.
21. *Star*, June 8, 1885.
22. The Laurent winery survives down to the present time, renamed the Markham Winery. Remodeled and enlarged by Bruce Markham and recent Japanese owners, the facility has survived a myriad of owners and troubled times. Laurent died in October, 1890.

23. *Star,* August 12, 1881.

24. *Annual Report of the Board of State Viticultural Commissioners, For 1887.* (Sacramento: 1888.) p.45.

25. Reprinted in *Resources of California,* San Francisco, April 1883.

26. *Star,* March 9, 1888.

27. *Second Annual Report of the Chief Executive Officer,* Board of State Viticultural Commissioners, (Sacramento: 1884). p.127.

NOTES — CHAPTER FIVE

1. D. Leigh Colvin, *Prohibition in the United States,* 1926. p.75.

2. *Healdsburg Tribune,* February 28, 1891. Excerpted from the *Annual Report of the Board of State Viticultural Commissioners* — no date cited.

3. As reprinted in the *Napa Register,* May 31, 1890.

4. May 31, 1891.

5. *History of Fresno County.* pp.831-832.

6. Memoir of Jack Becker, "Rennie Brothers Winery," sent to the author, February 1985. Becker is a grandson of William Rennie.

7. Ira B. Cross, *Financing An Empire. History of Banking In California.* (Chicago: S. J. Clarke, Co., 1927) pp. 616-624.

8. *Napa Register,* January 24, 1893.

9. See "Report of H.W. Crabb", *Annual Report of the Board of State Viticultural Commissioners,* 1893-94. (Sacramento: 1894.) p 28.

10. *Star,* September 30, 1887 and September 6, 1889; *Independent Calistogan,* August 14, 1889.

11. *Star,* January 24, 1894.

12. See "California Wines at the Columbian Exposition," N.A. in Charles Wetmore, *Treatise on Wine Production,* Board of State Viticultural Commissioners. (Sacramento: 1894). p. 43.

13. *Report of the Board of State Viticultural Commissioners for 1893-94.* (Sacramento: 1894). pp 6-12.

14. As reproduced and translated to English in the *Pacific Wines and Spirit Review,* San Francisco, December 9, 1895.

15. Ibid., April 8, 1892.

16. *Healdsburg Tribune,* April 23, 1896.

17. *Star,* May 19, 1882.

18. Arthur P. Hayne, Ph.D. *Resistant Vines* (Sacramento: University of California, College of Agriculture, 1897). For the Lenoir see especially pages 34-35.

19. *Report of the Board of State Viticultural Commissioners For 1893-94.* (Sacramento: 1894). p.23.

20. *Star,* February 1, 1901; also February 16, 1900, January 26, 1900 and April 27, 1900.

21. See March 25, 1895 and probably later issues. For reprints of several of the articles in one issue see the *Register* March 29, 1895.
22. Undated and unattributed newspaper clipping in the "Napa County Scrapbook," California History Room, State Library, Sacramento. The opening remark that "Napa County" lies 40 miles north and east of San Francisco and 70 miles southwest of Sacramento leads one to believe it was a Sacramento newspaper.

NOTES — CHAPTER SIX

1. From a taped interview with Ponti, by the author, at his Rutherford home, November 13, 1973. Ponti died in February 1975.
2. Harrison should long ago have been honored for his early contribution to Napa Valley architecture and building. A small fraction of his buildings include all or part of the Sunny St. Helena winery, the Jackse Winery, Keller Market, buildings at Inglenook, the Martinelli Olive Oil Factory, and dozens of others scattered widely in Napa Valley.
3. Taped interview with Forni at his home in St. Helena, by the author, on February 13, 1975.
4. For quoted material see issue of January 31, 1904. The Italian Swiss Colony story is told in the issue of August 31, 1905. Cecil Munsey's book *The Illustrated Guide to Collecting Bottles*, published in 1970, gives the history of Owens and his bottle machine.
5. *Pacific Wine and Spirit Review*, May 31, 1910.
6. Ibid., May 31, 1903, "The Manufacture of Wine in California."
7. Taped interview with Schmidt at St. Helena, Ca, by the author, April 4, 1978.
8. Taped interviews at his home in St. Helena, Ca., by the author, December 16, 1980 and November 4, 1987.
9. *Star*, September 6, 1912.

NOTES — CHAPTER SEVEN

1. *Sonoma Index Tribune*, Sonoma, California June 28, 1919.
2. "Paradoxes of Prohibition," December 1920.
3. *California Grape Grower*, San Francisco, Ca. January 1933.
4. *Star*, October 3, 1919 and November 7, 1919.
5. *Grape Grower*, January 1933. See final paragraph of the story which lists 694 bonded wineries in 1922.
6. All of the correspondence of the Commissioner for the 1920s has been preserved. Photocopies are also available at the Napa County Library, Napa, Ca.
7. Ernest Wente interviews, University of California, Berkeley, Ca., Oral History Series, by Ruth Teiser. Pages 21-22.

8. Obituary of Eugene Romer. *Daily Evening Encinal.* Alameda, Ca. July 19, 1895.
9. "Economic Status of the Grape Industry," published in 1924 by the University of California Experiment Station.
10. *Star,* April 11, 1924 and September 18, 1925.
11. Taped interview conducted at his home in Napa, Ca. by the author, July 30, 1980.
12. Personal interview on several occasions by the author at Healdsburg, Ca. during the 1970s and 1980s. Vercelli has phenomenal historical recall. See also Oral History interviews, Sonoma County Wine Library, Healdsburg.
13. Taped oral history interview at his home in Mira Loma, Ca. by the author, August 28, 1992.
14. Taped oral history interview at his home in Napa, Ca. by the author, May 23, 1980 and February 7, 1984.

NOTES — CHAPTER EIGHT

1. See "Selling wine out of a barrel," *Wine Review,* October 1934.
2. "Of Interest to Growers." *Star,* May 4, 1934.
3. Taped interview with Forni, St. Helena, Ca. Feb. 13, 1974, by the author. (Forni is deceased).
4. "The Great Wine Boom." May 1941. No author.
5. Taped interview with Ponti, St. Helena, Ca. November 17, 1973, by the author. (Ponti is deceased).
6. Letters to the Editor, January 1956.
7. Taped interview with Abruzzini, Napa, Ca. May 23, 1980, by the author. (Abruzzini is deceased).
8. Leon Adams, *Wines Of America,* second edition, 1978, p.308.
9. Justin Meyer, "The History of the Christian Brothers Wineries in California," unpublished mss. 1966.
10. Taped interview with Brother Timothy, Napa, Ca. September 8, 1980, by the author.
11. Taped interview with Stralla, St. Helena, Ca. June 27, 1977, by the author. (Stralla is deceased).
12. Telephone interview with Louis P. Martini, November 18, 1993, by the author.
13. Taped interview with Robert Mondavi, Oakville, Ca. February 21, 1984 and telephone conversation November 18, 1993, by the author.
14. Ibid.
15. *Wines &Vines,* September 1949.
16. See remarks of Robert Mondavi, "Probe of Wine Awards Suggested by Chairman," Star, October 19, 1951.

17. "Wines and Otherwise," *Wines &Vines*, May 1957, p. 13.

18. "Special Wine Types Make Good, Too." *Wines &Vines*, September 1957. page 24.

NOTES — CHAPTER NINE

1. Minutes, Board of Directors, Napa Valley Cooperative Winery, June 1949.

2. "Imported Wine a Real Threat," *Wines & Vines*, April 1955.

3. "Wine Prospects for 1953," *Wines & Vines*, February 1953.

4. See especially "The 7 Fat Years of Table Wine Sales In California," *Wines & Vines*, October 1953.

5. Minutes, Annual Membership Meeting, April 21, 1967.

6. "Napa Valley Cooperative Winery Marks Silver Anniversary," *St. Helena Star*, August 20, 1959.

7. "What the U.S. Public Thinks About Wine," *Wines & Vines*, October 1955.

8. "Spending the Wine Advertising Dollar," by Frank Bruguierre, November 1957.

9. Telephone conversation with the author, December 1993.

10. "How the Grape Grower Fares," September 1956.

11. Taped oral history interview, March 19, 1986, by the author.

12. Personal interview with Nemeth, at the Pannonia winery, Napa, Ca., August 30, 1981, by the author.

13. "Rapid Increase in Winery Visitors Noted by Speaker," *St. Helena Star*. July 16, 1965.

14. All figures used are from the Statistical Issues of *Wines & Vines*, for the years 1967-1970.

15. "Martha's Vineyard of Napa Valley: A Historical Overview." April 1989. Private research study for the Mays, by the author — page 69.

16. Ibid.

17. Taped oral history, August 1, 1984 by the author.

18. *St. Helena Star*, September 26, 1968. See photograph and non-captioned story on page one.

19. "Combating Frost with Wind dates to 1945 in Calif." "Heintz On History" column, *Wines & Vines*, May 1984. Spraying water on vines is part of the column.

20. Baldwin died July 10, 1984 at the age of 84.

21. "Lunch with the Brotherhood," by Tom Eurch, San Francisco *Examiner*, October 13, 1974. Magazine section.

NOTES — CHAPTER TEN

1. *Wines & Vines*, November 1972 and September 1973. In the latter issue see "World's Largest Bank Sees 650 Million Gallon Market . . ."

2. Taped oral history, May 2, 1989, by the author.

3. *Star*, April 5, 1979. Figures provided were for the year 1978.

4. For an excellent summary of the Mondavi family dispute, see *New West* magazine, November 8, 1976.

5. *Wines & Vines*, April 1976. See "The Experts reveal the latest data in effective Mechanical Harvesting."

6. March 1970. "Grapes are Busting Out All Over."

7. Taped oral history, August 1, 1984, by the author.

8. April 4, 1974. See photograph of an architectural rendering of proposed structure and outline.

9. As reported in the *San Francisco Examiner*, May 13, 1984. See "Diet natural drinks keep soda sales bubbling."

10. *Ladies Home Journal*, "Wine & Women," study published in 1977, page 5.

11. *Wines & Vines*, January 1980. "White Continues to March."

12. *Sonoma Index Tribune*, Sonoma, Ca. July 22, 1981. "Grafting figures show white wine dominance."

13. Taped oral history, February 1, 1984, by the author.

14. Taped oral history, August 7, 1986, by the author.

15. Taped oral history, December 15, 1983, by the author.

16. See issue of October 23, 1980, page 10.

17. *Wines & Vines*, July 1979. See "The ring master of wine."

18. As reported in his column published in the *Orlando Sentinel* (Florida), June 30, 1983.

19. San Francisco *Examiner*, July 10, 1982.

20. Taped oral history, August 8, 1983, by the author.

21. "A gamble paid off" in Lonsford's column "Wine World," January 27, 1983.

NOTES — CHAPTER ELEVEN

1. Remarks of the author before the BATF panel in Napa, California.

2. "Napa Winery Sold to Japan Beer Company." *Santa Rosa Press Democrat*, June 24 1987.

3. *Star*, "County Ag Production Soars $10 Million in '80." April 2, 1981.

4. *Santa Rosa Press Democrat*, January 4, 1988.

5. Taped oral history, March 20, 1984 by the author.

6. *Napa Reporter*, "Napa Wines," December 6, 1878.

7. See "Condition of Grape Culture in California." p.55l.

8. Taped oral history, May 17, 1985, by the author.

9. Telephone interview by the author, November 12, 1976.

10. Telephone interview by the author, October 10, 1995.

11. First aired September 18, 1995.
12. "Food and Wine: Together At Last," March 23, 1983.
13. "Main Street" column, January 27, 1983.
14. Telephone conversation with Gould, by the author, October 7, 1995.
15. From a telephone conversation with the author, November 12, 1976.
16. From a telephone conversation with Allegra, October 12, 1995.
17. *Star*, "Investment Alters Direction of Wine Train," April 2, 1987.
18. Ibid.: "Mobile Units May Supply Housing," January 31, 1991.
19. Telephone interview with Harris at his St. Helena real estate office, November 17, 1995, by the author.
20. *San Francisco Chronicle*, "Napa Valley Gets Another Appellation," January 27, 1989.
21. Taped oral history with Skupny, November 2, 1995 by the author.
22. Telephone interview with Peter Mondavi, Sr., November 11, 1995, by the author.
23. Telephone interview by the author, November 28, 1995.
24. Taped oral history with Battat, May 25, 1983, by the author.
25. Taped oral history March 10, 1986 by the author and telephone conversation of November 29, 1995.
26. Michael Castelma, "The Grape Debate," *San Francisco Focus* February 1995, quoting Dr. Wells Shoemaker.
27. San Francisco Examiner, October 6, 1988. "Mondavi Rallies Support For Wine."
28. "Premium wine sales up in Napa," *St. Helena Star*, March 21, 1991

NOTES — CHAPTER TWELVE

1. Taped oral history interviews with Beckstoffer in St. Helena, from July, 1993 to February, 1996, by the author.
2. Telephone interview with Ryman, April 7, 1998, by the author.
3. Taped oral history with Bernard and Belle Rhodes, St. Helena, Ca. March 22, 1988, by the author.
4. Telephone interviews with Thomas, June 15, 1985, March 2, 1998.

ACKNOWLEDGEMENTS

Libraries are the life-blood of the historian. This book could not have been written without the help of many, many staff members at public, state and university libraries.

I am most indebted to the St. Helena Public Library, in which I have almost lived for months at a time. Clayla Davis, head librarian, goes back to the beginning of my work, as do Julie and others. At the Napa City & County Library I have thumbed through the index to old Napa newspapers (only complete to 1900) hundreds of times. Research staff have helped, including microfilm librarians, and most of all Tom Trice, an historian disguised as a head librarian. Many professionals in the field wear more than one hat.

At the Shields Library, University of California, Davis, Axel Borg also walks the thin line between librarian and historian. I have never met anyone so willing to serve the library patron with such enthusiasm. John Skarstad, head of Special Collections for Shields, has always accorded me the recognition and assistance usually reserved for department heads.

Two other libraries deserve recognition and superlatives for their help. First is the History Room of the San Francisco Public Library. There Gladys Hansen first introduced me to the *Pacific Wine & Spirit Review*, a major source for wine and viticulture research for all of California. Ms. Hansen, now retired, has founded and supervises the Museum of the City of San Francisco, presently housed at the Cannery. History has always been her first love.

No library west of the Rocky Mountains can match the archives in the Bancroft Library, University of California, Berkeley. Hubert Howe Bancroft started collecting historical documents and information during the 1850s, and the library is a gold mine for all that has made California, from wine and viticulture to the Chinese.

At the library of the San Francisco Wine Institute Joan Ingalls once ruled like a Roman emperor; one had to search for her soft side. She is long deceased, and much missed. Pat McCalvey, who filled in for far too short a time and then moved on, was of great help to me. She too, is missed.

In the wine industry, the list of those who gave me assistance is far too long to record here. Robert Mondavi was the first to suggest I tackle a book-length study of Napa's history. He heard me expounding for ninety minutes at the 1980 BATF hearings on a Napa Valley viticultural appellation, and politely never mentioned I ran overtime by an hour.

Brother Timothy (Diener) of the Christian Brothers should never have given up teaching to make wine, but it is too late to correct that mistake. The Napa wine industry would be far different without him. He once taught chemistry to high school students, but would have switched to history in time, I suspect. He recalls historical facts with great facility, and has given me invaluable assistance.

The Raymonds have been especially helpful in providing information from their vast experience as vintners. Roy, Sr., has survived six decades in the wine industry without losing his marvelous sense of humor. Roy, Jr., has never, I think, quite understood me as a historian who asks far too many personal questions during an interview.

Two people who are now gone, and sorely missed, are Charles Carpy and Hanns Kornell. Both were generous with their time and their enthusiasm for the book. Others who deserve special thanks are John and Janet Trefethen, Mario Perelli-Minetti, the late Louis Martini, Jr., Francis Mahoney (he holds a B.A. in history), Tom May, and Larry Chalacombe. Jess Doud is also deceased, but I honor his spirit, which hovers still over this work.

Vera (Hansen) Lewelling, well into her 90s, talked to me at length about the history of her family and the valley. She generously granted permission to use many photos from the Lewelling collection.

Lynne Ingraham corrected and typed much of this manuscript. Nan Perrott has used her editing pencil on many chapters.

Many others have helped over the long gestation of the manuscript: Joan Chadd, Lew and Pat Zuelow, Daphne Bossie, Roland and Hazel Todd, who first told me about Leopold Justi; Tim Tesconi, the most sensitive wine writer at the Santa Rosa Press Democrat. Special thanks go to a patient soul, Diane Ballard, Director of the Napa County Historical Society.

No one provided more inspiration, encouragement, or assistance than my long-time friend, Robert E. Berner, to whom this book is dedicated.

— William F. Heintz

INDEX

THE CI

2018

BIG OAT N

Ranch
2204
CK MOUNT

Island
AKED HILL

Duncan

SC

21

722

65

09

53

97